WHITMAN COLLEGE LIBRARY

D0400104

TAKING SIDES

**Clashing Views
on Controversial
Economic Issues**
fourth edition

*Where there is much desire to
learn, there of necessity will be much
arguing . .*

John Milton

WHITMAN COLLEGE LIBRARY

TAKING SIDES

Clashing Views on Controversial Economic Issues

fourth edition

Edited, Selected and with Introductions by

Thomas R. Swartz

and

Frank J. Bonello

The University of Notre Dame

Withdrawn by

Whitman College Library

The Dushkin Publishing Group, Inc.

HC
106.7
.T34
1988

This book is dedicated to the thousands of students who have persevered in the "Bonello/Swartz-B.S." introductory economics course sequence at the University of Notre Dame. It is also dedicated to our children and T.R.'s one grandchild. In order of their birthdates, they are:

Mary Elizabeth, Karen Ann, Laurel Ann, Jennifer Lynne, John Anthony, Anne Marie, Koren Elizabeth, Rebecca Jourdan, David Joseph, William Alexander, and Stephen Thomas.

Copyright © 1988 by the Dushkin Publishing Group, Inc. Guilford, Connecticut 06437. All rights reserved. No part of this book may be reproduced, stored, or otherwise transmitted by any means— mechanical, electronic, or otherwise— without written permission from the publisher.

Library of Congress Catalog Card Number: 87-072958
Manufactured in the United States of America
Fourth Edition, First Printing

ISBN: 0-87967-740-6

The Dushkin Publishing Group, Inc.
Sluice Dock, Guilford, CT 06437

PENROSE MEMORIAL LIBRARY
RECEIVED

JUN 15 1990

ACQUISITIONS DEP'T
JUN 18 1990

PREFACE

Each member of our society is affected by the economic policies adopted by our government. Whether or not we understand the intricacies of economic theories, we must deal with their impact.

In a democracy such as ours, one way to deal with the effects of economic policy is to vote for or against political candidates on the basis of their economic convictions. In order to do this wisely, it is necessary to understand both the economic issues facing us and the conflicting opinions concerning these issues. That is the purpose of this volume. Presented here are twenty of the most critical and divisive economic issues. The outcome of the debates over these issues will have an impact on everyone living in America today. The taxes you pay, the safety of a blood transfusion, the level of government protection you can expect, all of these are, in part, determined by economists operating on the basis of certain assumptions and certain convictions. After you have studied the issues in this volume, you will have a greater understanding of the nature of economics itself. You will also learn to associate the headlines and news stories you read with several distinct schools of economic thought.

As you read this book and find yourself in agreement or disagreement with the opinions presented, turn to the "Contributors" pages at the back. There, you will discover the identities of the people who make the decisions and pronouncements that so vitally concern your life. Make a mental note of these people. You can be sure that, as time passes, you will be hearing more from them.

The twenty issues that have been selected for inclusion in the fourth edition of *Taking Sides: Clashing Views on Controversial Economic Issues*, are arranged under four headings: Microeconomic Issues, Macroeconomic Issues, International Issues, and Problems for the Future. You may choose to read these issues in sequence; you may prefer to read the macroeconomic issues before you read the microeconomic issues; or you might decide to read first those issues you find most interesting. Although we have clustered these issues by topic and ordered them in a sequence that is often found in a standard introductory text, the individual topics can stand alone.

Of course, another decision we had to make concerned which issues to include in this volume. We have received many helpful comments and suggestions from our friends and readers across the country and in Canada. Their suggestions have markedly enhanced the quality of this edition of *Taking Sides*. We hope that as you read this book you too will be reminded of an essay that could be included in a future edition. If this is the case, please drop us a note. We very much appreciate your interest and help.

PLUMROSE MEMORIAL LIBRARY
RECEIVED
MAY 1 1991
ACQUISITIONS DEPT

ACKNOWLEDGEMENTS

Those who have shared their good thoughts with us were: Parker Cashdollar; Benedict Clements; John R. Chism; Therese Decanio; Eric Elder; John Grady; John Hansen; Charles P. Hayes; Jong-Chol Hau; Bentzil M. Kasper; Andrew Larkin; Lois Ann McElroy Lindell; Glen Mitchell; Alexis G. Lebedeff; Allan B. Mandelstamm; K. Mehtabdin; Margaret D. Moore; Robert Pennington; Patrick Rooney; Thomas G. Rose; Richard Trieff; and Kenneth Turner. Our editorial advisor at the Dushkin Publishing Group, who cleared away many obstacles, loaned us support and encouragement, and helped us meet our deadlines, was John Holland. Our typists, Frank J. Bonello and Deanna Graybosch, almost never complained about TR's tortured handwriting. Our graduate assistant Curtis Brock was always willing to drop whatever he was doing to collect an article or two from the Hesburgh Library. To these folks, we owe a huge debt and many, many thanks.

TRS/FJB
Notre Dame, Indiana

CONTENTS IN BRIEF

CONTENTS

PART 1: Microeconomic Issues

Free market economist Milton Friedman contends that the sole
responsibility of business is to increase its profits. Philosopher Robert
Almeder maintains that if capitalism is to survive, it must act in socially
responsible ways that go beyond profit making.

Representative Dorgan of North Dakota fears that public policy has
become too concerned with the interests of the large corporate farms
while ignoring the small family farm that has "made agriculture one of
the few American industries still competitive in international markets."
Columnist Chapman argues for "rugged individualism." He asserts that:
"If Americans still believe in the virtue of hardy rural self-reliance, they
should tell Washington to get out of the way and let farmers practice it."

Economist Eckert maintains that the problem with the blood banking
industry is that "increased regulation" has led to "a basically
noncompetitive environment that is inferior to a competitively organized
blood market." Physician and Professor of Laboratory Medicine Bove

argues that "directed donor programs" might "jeopardize the national blood supply."

Social critic Hackett argues that comparable worth would put an end to the "laws of supply and demand or other economic principles that determine wage rates for different kinds of work." Labor economist Needleman contends that pay differentials between men and women cannot be traced to differentials in "human capital." She concludes that these differentials result from discriminatory practices and attitudes.

Political science professor Houseman asserts that the economic rewards reaped by Wall Street takeover artists come at the expense of workers, stockholders, and the general public. Business economists Paulus and Gay argue that the corporate restructuring of the 1980s is a direct result of the need to increase productivity in the face of declining U.S. competitiveness.

Weidenbaum asserts that government decision makers should face the same economic constraints as business executives do in the private sector. They must insist that the benefit of their actions at least match the cost of their actions. The editors of *Dollars and Sense* contend that although benefit-cost analysis seems to have a "certain simple logic," it is neither simple nor objective. Rather, they believe benefit-cost analysis and the related cost- effectiveness approach are fatally flawed by an inherent social bias.

Professors Bluestone and Harrison assert that large modern corporations (particularly conglomerates) systematically milk profits from healthy firms, mismanage them, fail to maintain them, and then shut them down on the grounds that they are inefficient. Professor McKenzie argues that in a healthy market economy it is natural and necessary for some firms to move and others to close in order to achieve the benefits of economic efficiency.

Supporters of H.R. 4300 maintain that there is a "growing conflict between work and family" that can be corrected by guaranteeing workers the "right to unpaid family leave." The dissenting members of the House Committee on Education and Labor argue that H.R. 4300 may be "well-intentioned," but it is also "rigid and inflexible."

The editors of *The Nation's Business* insist that support for the minimum wage is based on eight myths that ignore the fact that if the Kennedy-Hawkins bill passes, it "hurts the very employees it is intended to help." Economist Ghilarducci maintains that both "advocates and detractors of the minimum wage" have ignored the impact it has had on the economic well-being of "women workers."

PART 2: Macroeconomic Issues

Former Treasury Secretary Simon argues that government has gone too far in its efforts to provide "cradle-to-grave security." According to Simon, wealth can only be created through the free operation of markets, and it is imperative that productivity and the growth of productivity be given the highest economic priority. Harvard economist Galbraith believes that the services provided by government contribute as much to the well-being of society as those provided by the private sector. Although taxes may reduce the freedom of those who are taxed, the freedom of those who benefit from the tax-financed programs is enhanced.

Economist Heller argues that history demonstrates that an activist government can improve macroeconomic performance. Heller believes that a return to activist government with proper alignment and execution of monetary and fiscal policies would solve problems in poverty and productivity. Journalist Levinson believes that the economic environment has changed. The internationalization of the U.S. economy means that "even the greatest of economic powers can no longer control its own destiny."

Economist Aaron believes that the Tax Reform Act of 1986 represents "a major tax overhaul that deserves to be honored as reform." Although the new tax legislation can be criticized for certain things, Aaron argues that it has made the tax system "more conducive to economic efficiency and growth, fairer, and simpler." Reporter Gutmann sees a number of problems with the Tax Reform Act, and believes it is "a clear step backward for the progressive idea of taxation."

Researcher Murray believes that the welfare reforms of the 1960s and the changes in the ways government treated the poor caused low income youth to "become decoupled from the mechanism whereby poor people in this country historically have worked their way out of poverty." College professor Coe and researcher Duncan argue that "typical welfare spells are brief, interspersed with work, do not break up families, and are not passed on from parent to child."

Economist Eisner believes that to correctly measure the impact of the deficit on the economy, the budget figures must be adjusted for changes in output or employment and inflation. His analysis also suggests that an effort to achieve a conventionally measured balanced budget would cause a severe recession. Professor Paul Wonnacott, an economist at the University of Maryland, also discusses the need to adjust the budget deficit for the level of unemployment. But he rejects the idea of further adjustments for inflation, and he concludes that it may not be completely necessary to eliminate the current deficit completely.

Economist Roberts believes that the stock market crash was caused by the tight monetary policy of the Federal Reserve System. Glassman argues that the crash represented a return to more realistic, more reasonable stock prices because in October 1987 the market was overvalued.

PART 3: International Issues

Columnist Kuttner writes that "comparative advantage" is determined by exploitative wage rates and government action; it is not determined by free markets. Social critic Kinsley replies that we do not decrease American living standards when we import the products made by cheap foreign labor. He claims protectionism today, just as it did in the eighteenth century, weakens our economy and only "helps to put off the day of reckoning."

Business journalist Hector argues that the danger of an international financial calamity "now appears remote." Economist Watkins suggests that a "rather simple benefit-cost analysis" indicates that "default may be the most viable and profitable option" for the debtor nations.

Management experts Beaty and Harari argue that whether or not disinvestment will hurt black workers must be examined in light of the belief of many blacks that "investment hasn't helped them in the first place." Helen Suzman, a long- time member of the Progressive Federal Party in the South African Parliament, argues that economic sanctions will ruin the South African economy for all.

PART 4: Problems for the Future

Katharine L. Bradbury, an economist formerly with the Federal Reserve Bank of Boston, believes that the middle class is shrinking; that is, there was a decline in the percentage of families with middle class incomes between 1973 and 1984. Frank Levy, an economist at the University of Maryland, sees substantial stability in the distribution of income over time.

McUsic, a former researcher at the Federal Reserve Bank of Boston, examines the behavior of output, employment, and productivity in U.S. manufacturing and finds that manufacturing has maintained its relative share in U.S. total production. Perna, an economist with General Electric, is pessimistic about recent changes in the structure of the economy and identifies several symptoms of ill health in manufacturing.

INTRODUCTION

Economics and Economists: The Basis for Controversy

Thomas R. Swartz
Frank J. Bonello

"I think that Capitalism, wisely managed, can probably be more efficient for attaining economic ends than any alternative system yet in sight, but that in itself it is in many ways extremely objectionable."

Lord John Maynard Keynes, *The End of Laissez-Faire* (1926)

Although more than sixty years have passed since Lord Keynes penned these lines, many economists still struggle with the basic dilemma he outlined. The paradox rests in the fact that a free-market system is extremely efficient. It is purported to produce more at a lower cost than any other economic system. But in the process of producing this wide array of low-cost goods and services, problems arise. These problems—most notably a lack of economic equity and economic stability—cause problems for some economists. Other economists choose to ignore or minimize these issues. These problems form the foundation of this book.

If the problems raised and analyzed in this book were merely the product of intellectual gymnastics undertaken by "egg-headed" economists, then we could sit back and enjoy these confrontations as theoretical exercises. Unfortunately, we are not afforded that luxury. The essays contained in this book touch each and every one of us in tangible ways. They are real-world issues. Some focus upon the current state of the United States economy and examine the underlying causes, effects, and cures for inflation, unemployment, and recession. Another set of issues deals with "microeconomic" topics. We refer to these issues as "micro" problems not because they are small problems, but because they deal with small economic units such as households, firms, or individual industries. A third set of issues concerns international aspects of economic activity. This area has grown in significance as the volume of international transactions has grown and as society has come to realize the importance of international interdependence. The final set of issues touch on our future directly, and force us to consider whether or not we should consider fundamental changes in our economic policy.

For each of the twenty issues considered in this book we have isolated those areas that currently generate the most controversy among economists.

In a few cases, this controversy represents a confrontation between extreme positions. Here, the views of the "free market economist" are contrasted with the views of the "radical reformist economist." In other cases, the conflicts are not as extreme. Rather they represent conflicts between one extreme and economists of more moderate persuasions. Finally, we could not ignore the conflicts that occur among economists who, on other issues, generally agree. Economists, even economists who identify strongly with a given philosophical perspective, rarely agree on all issues. Thus, these otherwise like-thinking economists sometimes differ on specific topics.

The underlying reason for this apparent conflict and disagreement among economists can be explained, at least in part, in terms of Lord Keynes' 1926 remark. How various economists will react to the strengths and weaknesses found in an economic system will depend upon how they view the importance of efficiency, equity and stability. These are central terms, and we will define them in detail in the following pages. For now the important point is that some economists may view efficiency as overriding. In other cases, the same economists may be willing to sacrifice the efficiency generated by the market in order to ensure increased economic equity and/or increased economic stability. Determining when efficiency should be given a high priority and when efficiency should give way to other considerations occupies a large portion of the professional economist's time.

Given this discussion of conflict, controversy, and diversity, it might appear that economists rarely, if ever, agree on any economic issue. We would be most misleading if we left the reader with this impression. Economists rarely challenge the internal logic of the theoretical models that have been developed and articulated by their colleagues. Rather, they will challenge either the validity of the assumptions used in these models or the value of the ends these models seek to achieve. For example, it is most difficult to discredit the internal logic of the microeconomic models employed by the "free market economist." These models are elegant and their logical development is most persuasive. However, these models are challenged. The challenges typically focus upon such issues as the assumption of functioning, competitive, markets and the desirability of perpetuating the existing distribution of income. In this case, those who support and those who challenge the operation of the market agree on a large number of issues. But they disagree most assuredly on a few issues which have dramatic implications.

This same phenomenon of agreeing more often than disagreeing is also true in the area of economic policy. In this area, where the public is most acutely aware of differences among economists, these differences are not generally over the kinds of changes that will be brought about by a particular policy. Again, the differences more typically concern the timing of the change, the specific characteristics of the policy and the size of the resulting effect or effects.

As an example, consider the tax reform debate which occurred during the middle 1980s. Most economists of both liberal and conservative persuasions agreed that tax reform was needed to make the system fairer, less complex, and less of a distorting influence on private, economic decision making. The necessity of tax reform was so apparent that a call for tax reform was included in the 1984 political platforms of both the Democratic and Republican parties. The former stated:

> Our country must move to a simpler, more equitable, and more progressive tax system. Our tax code can let the market put our country's savings to the best use. There must be a fair balance between corporate and personal tax increases. Wealthier taxpayers will have to shoulder a greater share of new tax burdens. Economic distortions must be eliminated.

The Republican platform was no less explicit:

> The Republican party pledges to continue our efforts to lower tax rates, change and modernize the tax system, and eliminate the incentive-destroying effects of graduated tax rates. We therefore support tax reform that will lead to a fair and simple tax system and believe a modified flat tax—with specific exemptions for such items as mortgage interest, is a most promising approach.

These statements not only document the agreement on the need for tax reform, they also reflect the practical differences regarding the specific character of the tax reform. For example the Democratic position supported a more progressive tax system where a greater tax burden would be placed on the wealthy while the Republicans wanted to move toward a flat rate tax system, that is, a proportional rather than a progressive tax system. Moreover, the general setting for tax reform was very different: the changes proposed by the Democrats were intended to increase the amount of taxes collected by the Federal government while the Republican proposals were intended to leave the total tax collection unchanged or revenue-neutral.

As the tax reform debate first took shape in Congress during 1985, further differences in the Democratic and Republican approaches were revealed. The plan presented by the Reagan administration included the following features: a highest personal marginal tax rate of 35 percent, mortgage interest deductibility limited to principal residence, some taxation of employer-provided health insurance, no deductibility of state and local taxes, and a maximum corporate tax rate of 33 percent. The legislation which emerged from the Democratically-controlled House Ways and Means Committee offered in contrast the following revisions: a highest personal marginal tax rate of 38 percent, mortgage interest employer-provided health insurance, full deductibility of state and local taxes, and a maximum corporate tax rate of 36 percent.

The legislation that was finally produced by these two houses of Congress represents a compromise between the equity concerns of the Democrats who supported the taxation of corporations and high income individuals and the more free market-oriented Republicans, whose concern for economic efficiency resulted in their support of tax provisions that encourage work, savings, and investment. Even after this legislation was enacted into law, the debate continues. As the debate in Issue 12 indicates, it is unclear whether or not the Tax Reform Act of 1986 is an "Impossible Dream Come True."

ECONOMISTS: WHAT DO THEY REPRESENT?

Newspaper, magazine and T.V. commentators all use handy labels to describe certain members of the economics profession. What do the headlines mean when they refer to the "Chicago School," the "Keynesians," the "Antitrusters," or the "Radical Economists"? What do these individuals stand for? Since we too use our own labels throughout this book, we feel obliged to identify the principal groups or camps in our profession. Let us warn you that this can be a most misleading venture. Some economists, perhaps most economists, defy classification. They float from one camp to another selecting a gem of wisdom here and another there. Many are practical men and women who believe that no one camp has all the answers to all the economic problems confronting society. As a consequence, they may be ardent supporters of a given policy recommendation of one philosophic group but vocal critics of other recommendations emanating from the same philosophic group.

Recognizing this limitation, four major groups of economists can be identified. These groups are differentiated on the basis of several criteria: how they view efficiency relative to equity and stability; what significance they attach to imperfectly competitive market structures; and how they view the evolution of an economic society. Before describing the views of the four groups on these criteria, it is essential to understand the meaning of certain terms to be used in this description.

Efficiency, equity and stability represent goals for an economic system. Efficiency reflects the fact that the economy produces those goods and services which people want and that it does so without wasting scarce resources. Equity in an economic sense has several dimensions. It means that income and wealth are distributed according to an accepted principle of fairness; that those who are unable to care for themselves receive adequate care; and that mainstream economic activity is open to all persons. Stability is viewed as the absence of sharp ups and downs in business activity, in prices, and in unemployment. In other words, stability is marked by steady increases in output, little inflation, and low unemployment.

When the term market structures is used, it refers to the number of buyers and sellers in the market and the amount of control they can exercise over price. At one extreme is a perfectly competitive market where there are so many buyers and sellers that no one has any ability to influence market price. One seller or buyer obviously could have great control over price. This extreme market structure, which we call pure monopoly, and other market structures which result in some control over price are grouped under the broad label of imperfectly competitive markets. That is, imperfect competition is a situation where the number of market participants is limited and as a consequence the participants have the ability to influence price. With these terms in mind, we can begin to examine the various schools of economic thought.

Free Market Economists

One of the most visible groups of economists and perhaps the easiest group to identify and classify is the "free market economists." These economists believe that the market, operating freely without interferences from government or labor unions, will generate the greatest amount of *well being* for the greatest number of people.

Economic efficiency is one of the priorities for free-market economists. In their well developed models, "consumer sovereignty"—consumer demand for goods and services—guides the system by directly influencing market prices. The distribution of economic resources caused by these market prices not only results in the production of an array of goods and services which are demanded by consumers, but this production is undertaken in the most cost-effective fashion. The free market economists claim that at any point, some individuals must earn incomes which are substantially greater than other individuals. They contend that these higher incomes are a reward for greater efficiency or productivity and that this reward-induced efficiency will result in rapid economic growth which will benefit all persons in the society. They might also admit that a system driven by these freely operating markets will be subject to occasional bouts of instability (slow growth, inflation, and unemployment). However, they maintain that government action to eliminate or reduce this periodic instability will only make matters worse. Consequently, government, according to the free market economist, should play a minor role in the economic affairs of society.

Although the models of free market economists are dependent upon functioning, competitive markets, the lack of these competitive markets in the real world does not seriously jeopardize their position. First, they assert that the imperfect competition found in the real world allows a firm to produce at an efficient level and these savings in turn provide for even greater efficiency since costs per unit of output are lower. Second, they suggest that the benefits associated with the free operation of markets are so great compared to government intervention that even a "second best solution" of imperfectly competitive markets still yields benefits far in excess of government intervention.

Lastly, the free market economists clearly view the market as the highest form of economic evolution. The efficiency of the system, the simplicity of the system, the power of the system, and above all, the personal freedoms inherent in the system demonstrate its superiority.

These advocates of the free market have been given various labels over time. The oldest and most persistent label is "classical economists." This is because the classical economists of the eighteenth century, particularly Adam Smith, were the first to point out the virtues of the market. Smith captured the essence of the system with the following words:

"Every individual endeavors to employ his capital so that its produce may be of greatest value. He generally neither intends to promote the public interest nor knows how much he is promoting it. He intends only his own security, only his own gain. And he is in this led by an invisible hand to promote an end which was no part of his intention. By pursuing his own interest he frequently promotes that of society more effectively than when he really intends to promote it."

Adam Smith, *The Wealth of Nations* (1776)

Since free market economists, and those who echo their views, resist most forms of government intervention, they are also sometimes referred to as "conservatives" or "libertarians." These labels are as much political labels as they are economic characterizations. It must be recalled that the classical economists of the eighteenth century not only embraced the political philosophy of laissez-faire (roughly translated to: leave it—the economy—alone), but developed a set of economic theories which were totally consistent with this political theory. These "political-economists" were, as a result, called libertarians because they espoused political and economic policies which maximized personal freedoms or liberties. The nineteenth-century libertarians are not to be confused with twentieth-century liberals. Modern-day liberals, as we shall explain shortly in more detail, are often willing to sacrifice some freedoms in the marketplace in order to ensure the attainment of other objectives.

Still other labels which are sometimes attached to the free-market economists are "monetarists," "Chicago School Economists" or "Friedmanites." Here the reference is to the modern-day practitioners of free market economics. Most notable among this group is the Nobel laureate, Milton Friedman, formerly of the University of Chicago. He and others argue that the government's attempts to promote economic stability through the manipulation of the money supply actually causes more instability than would have occurred if the government had not intervened. As a consequence, this group of scholars advocates that the money supply should be allowed to grow at a reasonable, steady rate.

More recently, a new group of free market economists has been formed, the so-called "supply-siders." These economists, led by Arthur Laffer, also believe strongly in the market. What makes them unique is the specific proposals they offer to reduce government intervention in the economy: They contend reductions in marginal tax rates will stimulate private activity.

Before turning our attention to the other major camps of economists, we should note that the free market economists have been very successful in influencing the development of economics. Indeed, most introductory economic textbooks present major portions of the basic theoretical concepts of the free market economist. It is because of this influence in many areas of both microeconomics and macroeconomics over long periods of time, that so many labels are used to describe them, so much is written about them and so much is written by these conservative economists. In the twenty issues which are considered in this book, the free market position is represented in a substantial number.

Liberal Economists

Probably the single largest group of economists in the U.S. in one way or another can be classified as "liberal economists." Liberal in this instance refers to their willingness to intervene in the free operation of the market. These economists share with the free market economists a great respect for the market. However, the liberal economist does not believe that the explicit and implicit costs of a freely operating market should or can be ignored. Rather, the liberal maintains that the costs of an uncontrolled marketplace are often borne by those in society who are least capable of bearing them: the poor, the elderly, the infirm. Additionally, liberal economists maintain that the freely operating market sometimes results in economic instability and the resultant bouts of inflation, unemployment and slow growth. Thus, although liberal economists believe that economic efficiency is highly desirable, they find the attainment of economic efficiency at any cost to be unacceptable and perhaps even "extremely objectionable."

Consider for a moment the differences between free market economists and liberal economists at the microeconomic level. Liberal economists take exception to the free market on two grounds. First, these economists find a basic problem with fairness in the marketplace. Since the market is driven by the forces of consumer spending, there are those who through no fault of their own (they may be aged, young, infirm, physically or mentally handicapped) may not have the wherewithal to participate in the economic system. Others, however, perhaps because they are extremely lucky or because they have inherited wealth, may have not only the ability to participate in the system, but they may have the ability to direct the course of that system. Second, the unfettered marketplace does not and cannot handle spill-over effects or what are known as "externalities." These are the third party effects which may occur as a result of an economic act. Will a firm willingly compensate its neighbors for the pollutants it pours into the nearby lake? Will a truck driver willingly drive at 55 MPH and in the process reduce the highway accident rate? Liberal economists think not. These economists are therefore willing to have the government intervene in these and other, similar cases.

The liberal economists' role in macroeconomics is more readily apparent to the layman. Ever since the failure of free market economics during the Great Depression of the 1930s, Keynesianism (still another label for liberal economics) has become widely known. Lord John Maynard Keynes' 1935 book entitled *The General Theory of Employment, Interest and Money* laid the basic groundwork for this school of thought. Keynes argued that the history of freely operating market economies was marked by periods of recurring recessions, sometimes very deep recessions which we call depressions. He maintained that government intervention through its fiscal policy—government tax and spending power—could eliminate, or at least soften these sharp reductions in economic activity and as a result move the economy along a more stable growth path. Thus for the Keynesians, or liberal economists, one of the "extremely objectionable" aspects of a free market economy is its inherent instability. Their call for active government participation is in sharp contrast to the policies of the free market economists who argue that economic stability (growth, employment, and prices) can be achieved only if government intervenes less and not more.

Liberal economists are also far more concerned about the existence of imperfections in the marketplace than are their free market counterparts. They reject the notion that imperfect competition is an acceptable substitute for competitive markets. These economists may agree that the imperfectly competitive firms can achieve some savings because of their large size and efficiency, but they assert that since there is little or no competition the firms are not forced to pass these cost savings on to consumers. Thus liberal economists, who in some circles are labeled "antitrusters," are willing to intervene in the market in two ways. In some cases they are prepared to allow some monopolies, such as public utilities, to exist, but they contend that these monopolies must be regulated by government. In other cases they maintain that there is no justification for monopolies and they are prepared to invoke the powers of antitrust legislation to break up existing monopolies and/or prevent the formation of new monopolies.

Unlike the free market economist, the liberal economist does not believe that the free marketplace is the highest form of economic evolution. By definition, the liberal economist asserts that the highest form of economic evolution is a "mixed economy"—an economy where market forces are tempered by government intervention. These economists do not advocate extensive government planning and/or government ownership of productive resources. But, they are not always willing to allow the market to operate on its own. They maintain that the immense power of the marketplace can be controlled with government intervention and the benefits generated by the unfettered market can be equitably distributed throughout society.

We can conclude this section by making a hazardous guess. It would appear that during the 1940s, 1950s, 1960s and up to the middle 1970s, liberal economics dominated economic policy in the U.S. In the late 1970s, there was a reemergence of the free market economics, which for nearly forty years had played an important but clearly secondary role. In the early 1980s, free market economics has come to dominate public policy decisions, but policymakers employing these classical models will encounter some stubborn economic problems. This will cause the pendulum to swing once again. The resting point of the pendulum may be liberal economics but it might also swing past this point and stop in the domain of "institutional economics" or "radical reformist economics." These two schools of thought are the subject of the next sections.

Institutional Economists

One of the most difficult groups of economists to classify and, as a consequence, one of the most misunderstood groups of economists is the "institutionalists." The difficulty in understanding and classifying this school of economists stems from the fact that institutional economics has no single body of theories. Institutional economists are vocal critics of traditional economics—the economics espoused by free market economists and liberal economists. They maintain that the models which are constructed by these economists may explain how economic actors would behave *if* these actors behaved in a rational, self-interested manner and *if* they lived in a competitive world. However, they assert that consumers, business firms, and other economic actors do not always act in a rational, self-interested fashion. They also see the world in which we live as a dual-economy world. One part of that world is competitive. Another part of that world is dominated by a few firms which have the power to set prices. The institutional economists, as a consequence, find traditional economics to be an eloquent theory that does not conform to reality. Unfortunately, to date, institutional economists have not developed their own set of integrated economic propositions or laws which they can offer as a substitute for traditional economics.

This does not mean however, that the institutionalists have nothing to offer. In their attempts to make economics conform to the reality it claims to explain and predict, institutional economists have shed light on many diverse topics. For example, some members of this school of thought have concentrated their efforts on the structure of corporations, particularly the multinational corporations, as economic institutions. These economists, sometimes referred to as structuralists, examine the economic planning these large economic units undertake; the impact they have on the system; their influence on inflation, unemployment, income distribution and efficiency; and the role they play in international affairs. Other institutional economists take a broader perspective. Since they generally believe that large corporate entities engage in massive economic planning that affects the whole of society, some institutional economists analyze alternative forms of regional and national economic planning which can be undertaken by the government. The basic point is that institutional economists work in many, seemingly unrelated, areas. Since they have no integrated theory to tie all these pieces together, and since many of their ideas such as utility regulation, antitrust action, price controls, etc., have been accepted as public policy, it is at times difficult to keep in mind that the early work of Thorstein Veblen on financial capitalism, the more recent work of John Kenneth Galbraith on industrial structure, and many economists in between are all part of the institutional school of economics.

On the basis of our first criterion, institutional economists differ dramatically from free market economists and liberal economists. By rejecting the assumptions of rationality and self-interest, they maintain that whatever you set as your highest priority—be it efficiency, equity, or stabilization—you cannot achieve it by using the abstract models of the market economists. Indeed, their analysis indicates that the market as it exists in its concentrated form today leads to inefficiency, inequity and inherent instability.

The second and third criteria further distinguish the institutional economists from the other schools of economics. For the institutionalist, economics is in a constant state of evolution. (The importance of evolution for the institutional economists is best underscored by noting that this school is also referred to as evolutionary economics.) At one time, perhaps when Adam Smith and his fellow classical economists were formulating their basic models, the economy could be legitimately characterized as competitive. At that moment, free market economics reflected reality and therefore could explain that reality. At this time, functional competition does not exist and a new body of theorems and concepts must be developed to explain this reality. At some future date, still another set of economic institutions will exist and still another body of theorems and concepts will be needed. Consequently, the institutional economists does indeed attach a great importance to the existence of imperfect competition and to the process of economic evolution. The institutionalist knows that new theories must be developed to explain today's reality of imperfect competition, and they know that the economy is always in a constant state of evolution. What they don't know with certainty is which direction future evolution will take our current reality.

To confuse the issue further, there is yet another group within the structuralist-institutionalist camp. These economists call themselves the post-Keynesians. They are post-Keynesians because they believe that they are closer to the spirit of Keynes than is the interpretation of Keynes which is used to support the liberal economists' position. As some authors have suggested, the key aspect of Keynes' work as far as the post-Keynesians are concerned is his assertion that "expectations of the future are not necessarily certain." On a more practical level, post-Keynesians believe, among other things, that the productivity of the economic system is not significantly affected by changes in income distribution, that the system can still be efficient without competitive markets, that conventional fiscal policies cannot control inflation and, that "income policies" are the means to an effective and equitable answer to the inflationary dilemma. (This listing is drawn from Alfred S. Eichner's "Introduction" in *A Guide to Post-Keynesian Economics*, White Plains: M.E. Sharpe, Inc., 1978.)

Radical Reformist Economists
As we move further and further away from the economics of the free market, we encounter the "radical reformist economists" or the "left." These econo-

mists, who actually spring from several theoretical foundations, share a belief that the market and the capitalist system, no matter how well disciplined, is fatally flawed and doomed to eventual failure. Out of the ashes of this system which is guided by the "invisible hand" of self-interest will rise the "visible hand" of public interest. That is, the fundamental institutions of private ownership will slowly fade and be replaced by government ownership of productive resources.

This does not mean that all private ownership will cease to exist at some distinct moment. Rather, many radical reformists maintain that it is the ownership of the one thousand largest firms which cause the basic problems for the "capitalist economy." It is the operation of these highly concentrated economic entities for the benefit of a few which cause the basic problems and it is the private ownership of these one thousand firms which must eventually fade away. As a result, not all property must be owned collectively. Only the most radical of the left would go that far.

As was the case with our other three broad clusters of economists, there is much diversity within this fourth cluster of economists. One group of economists within this cluster contains the radical, political economists who often focus upon microeconomic issues. They are concerned with issues such as the abuses which may result from "administered prices"—prices which can be administered or set by a firm because of the firm's monopoly influence in the marketplace. Another identifiable subgroup is the "Marxists." Their lineage can be traced to the nineteenth-century philosopher-economist Karl Marx. Ironically, Marx himself shares his economic roots with the free market economists. Before writing his most impressive work, the three volumes of *Das Kapital*, Marx studied the work of the classical economists and incorporated a basic tenent of those works—David Ricardo's "labor theory of value"—into his own work. But unlike free market economics, which Marx prophesied would fall of its own weight, Marx laid the foundation for "socialism." Socialism, where some form of public ownership of the means of production is substituted for private ownership, is far more prevalent throughout the world than is capitalism. Thus, we in North America cannot afford to ignore this group of economists.

Note that socialism may take many forms. It varies from the democratic socialism of the United Kingdom to the Eastern European socialism—communism—of the Soviet Union. The one common characteristic is public ownership of the means of production. However, the extent of this public ownership varies dramatically from one socialistic country to another.

Although it may be difficult to classify the different subgroups of radical reformist economists, we can differentiate them from the other broad classifications of economists on the basis of our three criteria. In terms of the first criterion—the relative importance of economic efficiency, equity and stabilization—they are clearly set apart from their non-radical counterparts. Not only do they set a much higher value on equity and stability when compared to the free market economists, (a posture they share with the liberal and institutional economists) but they have developed a set of economic models that attempts to ensure the attainment of equity and stability. The radical reformist economists assert that not only is the economic efficiency which is supposed to exist in a market economy an illusion, but the market system is fundamentally flawed. These flaws, which result in unacceptable inequities and recurring bouts of economic instability, will eventually lead to the market's demise.

The radicals are concerned by the existence of imperfect competition. For them the current reality is an immense concentration of economic power which is a far cry from Adam Smith's world of competitive markets. Today, in their view, the market economy operates to benefit a few at the expense of the masses. Firms with monopoly power control the economy. They administer prices. They are the invisible hand that guides the economy to their benefit.

So strong is their aversion to the market economy that they predict its demise as we know it. Indeed, if we look to the Marxist camp, they see capitalism as one step, a necessary step, in the evolution of economic systems. Capitalism is needed to raise the economy out of the chaos of a feudal society. But after capital has been accumulated and a modern economy is developed, the basic inequities and instabilities will bring the market economy to its knees and socialism will emerge. Socialism itself is not the end of the evolutionary process. Socialism will eventually give way to communism—where government is non-existent and everyone will work "according to their ability" and receive "according to their need."

Of course, not all radical reformist economists are Marxist. However, most radicals do share a desire for some form of socialism. Unlike their Marxist colleagues, most do not see socialism as evolving automatically, and they certainly do not see communism emerging at the end of an evolutionary process. Rather these economists see a need to explicitly encourage the development of some form of socialism for North America. The socialism which results is then considered to be the likely end of the evolutionary process.

Before we turn to the next section, we must warn you again to interpret these labels with extreme care. Our categories are not hard and fast. There is much "grayness" around the edges and little that is "black and white" in these classifications. This does not mean, however, that there is no value to these classifications. It is important to understand the philosophical background of the individual authors. This background does indeed color or shade their work. This is best demonstrated by examining several of the issues included in this volume.

However, before discussing a few of the issues, it is useful to repeat several of the themes developed in the preceding section. First, there is much disagreement among economists and others on economic problems. There is, however, rhyme and reason to this disagreement. In large measure the disagreement stems from various ideologies or basic philosophies which these individuals may espouse. Indeed, the differences which exist between economists and groups of economists can be most sharply defined in terms of their respective views of efficiency, equity, and stability; on the relative merits of imperfect competition; and on the place of the current economy in the evolutionary process peculiar to economic systems.

Second, the identification of causes, effects, and cures for economic problems must be undertaken at the practical level. At this level, sharp distinctions tend to disappear, and actions may be recommended by certain individuals which seem inconsistent with their ideology. Here the economist must sacrifice "ideological purity" for practical solutions. The science of economics must deal with real-world problems or it loses its meaning for most people.

THE ISSUES

It is not difficult to identify major problems in the American economy. Each month the news media discuss in detail the newly released statistics which reveal the success of failure of policies designed to reduce inflation and unemployment. As we noted, for example, the 1984 political platforms were very concerned with economic issues. In addition to the issue of tax cuts, the Democratic and Republic platforms outline general principles as well as specific actions that should be undertaken to spur spur productivity, to stem the rising tide of automobile imports and to make the American economy dynamic and vital. Each day it seems that some businessman, some labor leader, some consumer advocate, or some public official releases a new proposal that will remedy pollution, improve the quality and the safety of products or the workplace, restore health to the social security system, or halt and reverse the decay of our cities. Thus the difficulty in developing this book was not in identifying real and important economic problems or in locating alternative views on those problems. Rather, the difficulty was one of selecting only twenty issues from what, at times, appears to be an endless list of both problems and views on those problems.

We have resolved this difficulty by attempting to provide a broad coverage of the conflicts which society faces. We have provided this generality in three different ways. First, the twenty issues represent six macroeconomic, nine microeconomic, three international and two issues dealing with the future. Second, within these sets of issues, the range of topics is broad. For example, within the macroeconomic set there are issues which represent basic disagreements among economists on specific policy topics, such as the desirability of reforming the current federal income tax system, as well as disagreements that can be characterized as basic philosophical conflicts such as the appropriate size of government. The third dimension concerns the ideologies of the views that are presented. The list of authors includes well-regarded academic economists, politicians, businessmen, and labor leaders. These individuals represent the far right, the far left, and many positions in between. Although ideology is sometimes tempered by practical considerations, the basic ideological positions remain apparent.

A summary of several of the issues may serve to indicate the extent of this generality. This discussion will also demonstrate the interplay that exists between basic philosophy and practical considerations in arriving at a real-world solution or position on an economic problem.

One of the macroeconomic issues is: "Is the welfare system creating poverty?" Conservatives generally believe that we have indeed gone too far with our anti-poverty programs, contending that we have made them so attractive that people may choose not to work and instead will stay at home and receive benefits available under several different welfare and income security programs. In taking this position, the conservative or free market economist stresses individual self-interest and the need to provide appropriate work incentives. They believe that if we as a society provide an incentive not to work, individuals acting in their own self-interest will choose not to work. Thus, they argue, we must keep the benefits of anti-poverty programs low and/or impose rigid eligibility requirements so that those who are able to work are not able to "live off" the rest of hard-working and "honest" society. Liberals, on the other hand, believe that the individual is not such a shrewd calculator of the costs and benefits of working. They believe that people would rather work even if they could be somewhat better off by not working. This is the case, they contend, because individuals increase their self-esteem in taking care of themselves and their families. Moreover, liberals believe that if society is to make a mistake, the error should be in favor of equity and not efficiency. That is, it would be worse for society to set benefits too low or eligibility requirements too high and thus deny benefits to someone who is needy than to allow some people who are not needy to receive benefits. In the two readings on this issue, these positions are outlined.

Of course, institutionalists and radical reformers have taken positions on this issue. The institutionalists would probably side with the liberals but argue that it might be more appropriate to attack poverty through institutional change rather than through the current maze of anti-poverty programs. While institutional changes are being made (such as improving the educational system and increasing labor mobility), it would be better to be too generous rather than not generous enough, they say. To the radical reformer, the whole question is just another example of the inherent contradictions of a market economy. And in a class society, poverty programs are a means by which the dominant class can maintain its position. Radical reformers might even join conservatives in an effort to eliminate poverty programs. However, for the radical reformer, the motivation for opposing these programs is not greater efficiency, but rather an effort to polarize the class struggle and bring ever-closer the day of revolution.

"Should the federal government deregulate American business?" is one of the nine microeconomic issues. Again we can associate a position on this issue with each of the four basic economic philosophies. Clearly conservatives would strongly oppose government regulation. In support of their position they would cite the self-regulating nature of a free market capitalist system. No rational individual would buy products of inferior quality or products which are unsafe if alternatives were available at competitive prices. No rational individual would work for a firm that maintained an unsafe job site unless that individual found that job to be to his or her economic advantage. On the question of pollution or other so-called externalities, regulation, the conservatives might suggest, should be undertaken, but only if the benefits of regulation clearly are greater than the costs of the regulation.

Liberals of course, are much more tolerant, indeed supportive, of government regulation. In part, this follows from their emphasis on equity, but also because they may have a different measurement of both the costs and the benefits of regulations. Liberals generally estimate the costs lower and the benefits higher than their conservative colleagues. The institutionalists would also support the notion of regulation. Their support of regulation follows from their view that the structures and institutions of free market capitalism have changed in such a way that safe and high quality products and safe job sites are no longer assured. In the absence of perfect competition, regulation of industry is in order. It is necessary, to prevent abuses by both buyers and sellers.

The radical reformists believe that most current regulation, to the extent that it exists, benefits the power structure; that regulation by definition serves the regulated. They attack the basic notion of cost-benefit analysis as a method of determining the appropriate amount of regulation. After all, they ask, how can one measure the worth of the benefits of saving a single life by making a job site safer?

In selections addressing this issue, the emphasis is on the usefulness of cost-benefit analysis as a technique for determining the proper level of government regulation. One selection suggests that the use of cost-benefit analysis implies that government regulation is excessive. The other selection attacks the very heart of the cost-benefit procedure, laying bare all the implicit assumptions which such procedures make. In this sense the selections can be viewed as an argument between the conservative position and the radical reformist position.

We should mention an apparent paradox with respect to regulation policy. The above discussion implies that liberals should be more supportive of regulation than conservatives. However, deregulation or decontrol was a basic policy stance of the Carter administration. The Democratic Congress passed and the Democratic executive branch signed into law, legislation which deregulated the airline industry, the trucking industry, and financial intermediaries. Again, practical considerations rather than basic philosophies often determine specific policy actions. Reality and philosophical considerations make strange bedfellows.

One of the three international issues concerns the policies of the white-dominated government of the Republic of South Africa: "Is the Pain and Suffering Associated with Disinvestment and Sanctions Worth It for Black South African Workers?" This issue represents a clash between two liberals. On the one side of this debate is Helen Suzman, a member of the Progressive Federal Party in South Africa who has over a long period been a vocal critic of the white South African Policy. She argues that the good intentions of those whom support the imposition of economic sanctions and disinvestment threaten the economic welfare of those who the sanctions are intended to help. The opposing view is captured in the interviews of Beaty and Harari who surveyed many black workers in this racially torn country. Their interviews suggest that the cost of sanctions may be a reasonable price to pay since "investment hasn't helped them in the first place."

It is important to note that both essays in this issue assume that markets work. Indeed, they assume that markets have yielded huge economic rewards for some in the economy. Both essays also recognize the injustices that result from the white monopoly power that characterizes South Africa. In essence, they only differ on how and when economic power should be wrested away from the white monopolists.

This debate could be joined by conservatives, institutionalists and radical reformists. Conservatives would take their traditional position to the right of Ms. Suzman. They would maintain that the market is proving its value by generating incomes in South Africa which are well above the incomes of neighboring countries. They would go on to argue that the only way to improve the well-being of the black majority would be to improve the well-being of the economy at large. That is, as John F. Kennedy asserted, "a rising tide raising all boats." In this case the rising tide would raise the economic boat of the black worker. Finally, they would agree with Helen Suzman's assertion that interfering with the market would only hurt those whom the liberal community hopes to protect.

The institutionalists, as usual, would position themselves between the liberals and the radical reformists. They would argue that the colonial-type institutions that dominated the southern tip of Africa for the past 150 years must give way to the political reality of a black majority. In short, the white community can no longer ignore and manipulate 73 percent of the population. it must provide them with the economic rights that a modern day society provides all members of the community.

Finally, radicals would take their position on the far left by asserting that the crisis in South Africa reflected the corruption that is an inherent part of a market economy. They would remind us that 27 percent of the population controls the majority population. Those who hold that power will exercise it for their own benefits. Indeed, those who maintain the monopoly stranglehold on the black community will continue to brutalize that community until the only option that remains is revolution.

SUMMARY

It is clear that there is no shortage of economic problems. These problems demand solutions. At the same time there is no shortage of proposed solutions. In fact, the problem is often one of oversupply. The twenty issues included in this volume will acquaint you, or more accurately, reacquaint you, with some of these problems. And, of course, there are at least two proposed solutions for each of the problems. Here we hope to provide new insights regarding the alternatives available and the differences and similarities of these alternative remedies.

If this introduction has served its purposes, you will be able to identify common elements in the proposed solutions to the different problems. For example, you will be able to identify the reliance on the forces of the market advocated by free market economists as the remedy for several economic ills. This introduction should also help you understand why there are at least two proposed solutions for every economic problem; each group of economists tends to interpret a problem from its own philosophical position and to advance a solution which is grounded in that same philosophical framework.

Our intention, of course, is not to connect persons to one philosophic position or another. We hope instead to help discussion and promote understanding. To do this, people must see not only a proposed solution, they must also be aware of the roots of that solution. With greater understanding, meaningful progress in addressing economic problems can be achieved.

PART 1

MICROECONOMIC ISSUES

Our lives are profoundly affected by economic decisions made at the microeconomic level, and all the issues debated here are central to microeconomics.

MA Dept. of Commerce and Development, Div. of Tourism

Are Profits the Only Business of Business?

_____

Should We Try to Save the Family Farm?

_____

Should We Create More Competition in the Blood-Banking Industry?

_____

Is "Comparable Worth" Worthless?

_____

Are There Too Many Hostile Takeovers?

_____

Should the Federal Government Deregulate American Business?

_____

Do Firms Exploit Workers and Local Communities by Closing Profitable Plants?

_____

Should Congress Guarantee U.S. Workers the Right to Parental Leave?

_____

Is It Time to Abolish the Minimum Wage?

ISSUE 1

Are Profits the Only Business of Business?

YES: Milton Friedman, from "The Social Responsibility of Business Is to Increase Its Profits," *New York Times Magazine* (September 13, 1970)

NO: Robert Almeder, from "The Ethics of Profits: Reflections on Corporate Responsibility," *Business and Society* (Winter, 1980)

ISSUE SUMMARY

YES: Free market economist Milton Friedman contends that the sole responsibility of business is to increase its profits.
NO: Philosopher Almeder maintains that if capitalism is to survive, it must act in socially responsible ways that go beyond profit making.

Every economic society—whether it is a traditional society in Central Africa, a centrally planned Eastern European society or the wealthy capitalist society of North America—must address the basic economic problem of resource allocation. These societies must determine *what* goods and services they can and will produce, *how* these goods and services will be produced, and *for whom* these goods and services will be produced.

The *what, how,* and *for whom* questions must be answered because of the problem of scarcity. Even if a given society were indescribably rich, it would still confront the problem of scarcity—in this case, "relative scarcity." It might have all the resources it needs to produce all the goods and services it would ever want, but it couldn't produce all these things simultaneously. Thus, it must set priorities and produce first those goods and services with the highest priority and postpone the production of those goods and services with lower priorities. If time is of the essence, *how* should these goods and services be produced? And since this society can't produce all it wants instantly, *for whom* should the first bundle of goods and services be produced?

Few, if any, economic societies are indescribably rich. On the other hand, there are many examples of economic societies that face grinding deprivation daily. In these societies and in all the societies which fall between poverty and great affluence, the *what, how,* and *for whom* questions are immediately apparent. Somehow these questions must be answered.

In some societies, such as the Amish communities of North America, the answers to these questions are found in tradition. Sons and daughters follow in their parents' footsteps. Younger generations produce *what* older generations produced before them. The methods of production—the horsedrawn plow, the hand-held scythe, the use of natural fertilizers—remain unchanged; thus, the *how* question is answered in the same way that the *for whom* question is answered—by following historic patterns. In other societies—for example, self-sustaining religious communities—there is a different pattern of responses to these questions. In these communities, the "elder" of the community determines *what* will be produced, *how* it will be produced, and *for whom* it will be produced. If there is a well-defined hierarchical system, it is similar to one of the command economies of Eastern Europe.

Although elements of tradition and command are found in the industrialized societies of Western Europe, North America, and Japan, the basic answers to the three questions of resource allocation in these countries are determined by profit. In these economic societies, *what* will be produced is determined by what will yield the greatest profit. Consumers, in their search for maximum satisfaction, will bid for those goods and services that they want most. This consumer action drives the price of these goods and services up, and, in turn, these higher prices increase producers' profits. The higher profits attract new firms into the industry and encourage existing firms to increase their output. Thus, profits are the mechanism that ensures consumers get what they want. Similarly, the profit-seeking behavior of business firms determines *how* the goods and services that consumers want will be produced. Since firms attempt to maximize their profits, they select those means of production that are economically most efficient. Lastly, the *for whom* question is also linked to profits. Wherever there is a shortage of goods and services, profits will be high. In the producers' attempts to increase their output they must attract factors of production (land, labor, and capital) away from other economic activities. This bidding increases factor prices or factor incomes and ensures that these factors will be able to buy goods and services in the open marketplace.

Both Almeder and Friedman recognize the merits of a profit-driven economic system, and they do not quarrel over the importance of profits. But they do disagree over whether or not business firms have obligations beyond making profits. Almeder contends that businesses must act according to higher moral principles, to prevent the damage done in the name of profits. Friedman holds that the *only* responsibility of business is to make profits. He argues that anyone who maintains otherwise is "preaching pure and unadulterated socialism."

3

YES

Milton Friedman

THE SOCIAL RESPONSIBILITY OF BUSINESS IS TO INCREASE ITS PROFITS

When I hear businessmen speak eloquently about the "social responsibilities of business in a free-enterprise system," I am reminded of the wonderful line about the Frenchman who discovered at the age of 70 that he had been speaking prose all his life. The businessmen believe that they are defending free enterprise when they declaim that business is not concerned "merely" with profit but also with promoting desirable "social ends; that business has a social conscience" and takes seriously its responsibilities for providing employment, eliminating discrimination, avoiding pollution and whatever else may be the catchwords of the contemporary crop of reformers. In fact they are—or would be if they or anyone else took them seriously—preaching pure and unadulterated socialism. Businessmen who talk this way are unwitting puppets of the intellectual forces that have been undermining the basis of a free society these past decades.

The discussions of the "social responsibilities of business" are notable for their analytical looseness and lack of rigor. What does it mean to say that "business" has responsibilities? Only people can have responsibilities. A corporation is an artificial person and in this sense may have artificial responsibilities, but "business" as a whole cannot be said to have responsibilities, even in this vague sense. The first step toward clarity in examining the doctrine of the social responsibility of business is to ask precisely what it implies for whom.

Presumably, the individuals who are to be responsible are businessmen, which means individual proprietors or corporate executives. Most of the discussion of social responsibility is directed at corporations, so in what follows I shall mostly neglect the individual proprietor and speak of corporate executives.

In a free-enterprise, private-property system, a corporate executive is an employee of the owners of the business. He has direct responsibility to his employers. That responsibility is to conduct the business in accordance with

From *New York Times Magazine*, September 13, 1970. Copyright © 1970 by The New York Times. Reprinted by permission.

their desires, which generally will be to make as much money as possible while conforming to the basic rules of the society, both those embodied in law and those embodied in ethical custom. Of course, in some cases his employers may have a different objective. A group of persons might establish a corporation for an eleemosynary purpose—for example, a hospital or a school. The manager of such a corporation will not have money profit as his objective but the rendering of certain services.

In either case, the key point is that, in his capacity as a corporate executive, the manager is the agent of the individuals who own the corporation or establish the eleemosynary institution, and his primary responsibility is to them.

Needless to say, this does not mean that it is easy to judge how well he is performing his task. But at least the criterion of performance is straightforward, and the persons among whom a voluntary contractual arrangement exists are clearly defined.

Of course, the corporate executive is also a person in his own right. As a person, he may have many other responsibilities that he recognizes or assumes voluntarily—to his family, his conscience, his feelings of charity, his church, his clubs, his city, his country. He may feel impelled by these responsibilities to devote part of his income to causes he regards as worthy, to refuse to work for particular corporations, even to leave his job, for example, to join his country's armed forces. If we wish, we may refer to some of these responsibilities as "social responsibilities." But in these respects he is acting as a principal, not an agent; he is spending his own money or time or energy, not the money of his employers or the time or energy he has contracted to devote to their purposes. If these are "social responsibilities," they are the social responsibilities of individuals, not of business.

What does it mean to say that the corporate executive has a "social responsibility" in his capacity as businessman? If this statement is not pure rhetoric, it must mean that he is to act in some way that is not in the interest of his employers. For example, that he is to refrain from increasing the price of the product in order to contribute to the social objective of preventing inflation, even though a price increase would be in the best interests of the corporation. Or that he is to make expenditures on reducing pollution beyond the amount that is in the best interests of the corporation or that is required by law in order to contribute to the social objective of improving the environment. Or that, at the expense of corporate profits, he is to hire "hardcore" unemployed instead of better-qualified available workmen to contribute to the social objective of reducing poverty.

In each of these cases, the corporate executive would be spending someone else's money for a general social interest. Insofar as his actions in accord with his "social responsibility" reduce returns to stockholders, he is spending their money. Insofar as his actions raise the price to customers, he is spending the customers' money. Insofar as his actions lower the wages of some employes, he is spending their money.

The stockholders or the customers or the employes could separately spend their own money on the particular action if they wished to do so. The executive is exercising a distinct "social responsibility," rather than serving as an agent of the stockholders or the customers or the employes, only if he spends the money in a different way than they would have spent it.

But if he does this, he is in effect imposing taxes, on the one hand, and deciding how the tax proceeds shall be spent, on the other.

This process raises political questions on two levels: principle and consequences. On the level of political principle, the imposition of taxes and the expenditure of tax proceeds are governmental functions. We have established elaborate constitutional, parliamentary and judicial provisions to control these functions, to assure that taxes are imposed so far as possible in accordance with the preferences and desires of the public—after all, "taxation without representation" was one of the battle cries of the American Revolution. We have a system of checks and balances to separate the legislative function of imposing taxes and enacting expenditures from the executive function of collecting taxes and administering expenditure programs and from the judicial function of mediating disputes and interpreting the law.

Here the businessman—self-selected or appointed directly or indirectly by stockholders—is to be simultaneously legislator, executive and jurist. He is to decide whom to tax by how much and for what purpose, and he is to spend the proceeds—all this guided only by general exhortations from on high to restrain inflation, improve the environment, fight poverty and so on and on.

The whole justification for permitting the corporate executive to be selected by the stockholders is that the executive is an agent serving the interests of his principal. This justification disappears when the corporate executive imposes taxes and spends the proceeds for "social" purposes. He becomes in effect a public employee, a civil servant, even though he remains in name an employee of a private enterprise. On grounds of political principle, it is intolerable that such civil servants—insofar as their actions in the name of social responsibility are real and not just window-dressing—should be selected as they are now. If they are to be civil servants, then they must be selected through a political process. If they are to impose taxes and make expenditures to foster "social" objectives, then political machinery must be set up to guide the assessment of taxes and to determine through a political process the objectives to be served.

This is the basic reason why the doctrine of "social responsibility" involves the acceptance of the socialist view that political mechanisms, not market mechanisms, are the appropriate way to determine the allocation of scarce resources to alternative uses.

On the grounds of consequences, can the corporate executive in fact discharge his alleged "social responsibilities"? On the one hand, suppose he could get away with spending the stockholders' or customers' or employes' money. How is he to know how to spend it? He is told that he must contribute to fighting inflation. How is he to know what action of his will contribute to that end? He is presumably an expert in running his company—in producing a product or selling it or financing it. But nothing about his selection makes him an expert on inflation. Will his holding down the price of his product reduce inflationary pressure? Or, by leaving more spending power in the hands of his customers, simply divert it elsewhere? Or, by forcing him to produce less because of the lower price, will it simply contribute to shortages? Even if he could answer these questions, how much cost is he justified in imposing on his stockholders, customers and employes for this social purpose? What is the appropriate share and what is the appropriate share of others?

And, whether he wants to or not, can he get away with spending his stockholders', customers' or employes' money? Will not the stockholders fire him? (Either the present ones or those who take over when his actions in the name of social responsibility have reduced the corporation's profits and the price of its stock.) His customers and his employes can desert him for other producers and employers less scrupulous in exercising their social responsibilities.

This facet of "social responsibility" doctrine is brought into sharp relief when the doctrine is used to justify wage restraint by trade unions. The conflict of interest is naked and clear when union officials are asked to subordinate the interest of their members to some more general social purpose. If the union officials try to enforce wage restraint, the consequence is likely to be wildcat strikes, rank-and-file revolts and the emergence of strong competitors for their jobs. We thus have the ironic phenomenon that union leaders—at least in the U.S.—have objected to Government interference with the market far more consistently and courageously than have business leaders.

The difficulty of exercising "social responsibility" illustrates, of course, the great virtue of private competitive enterprise—it forces people to be responsible for their own actions and makes it difficult for them to "exploit" other people for either selfish or unselfish purposes. They can do good—but only at their own expense.

Many a reader who has followed the argument this far may be tempted to remonstrate that it is all well and good to speak of government's having the re-sponsibility to impose taxes and determine expenditures for such "social" purposes as controlling pollution or training the hard-core unemployed, but that the problems are too urgent to wait on the slow course of political processes, that the exercise of social responsibility by businessmen is a quicker and surer way to solve pressing current problems.

Aside from the question of fact—I share Adam Smith's skepticism about the benefits that can be expected from "those who affected to trade for the public good"—this argument must be rejected on grounds of principle. What it amounts to is an assertion that those who favor the taxes and expenditures in question have failed to persuade a majority of their fellow citizens to be of like mind and that they are seeking to attain by undemocratic procedures what they cannot attain by democratic procedures. In a free society, it is hard for "good" people to do "good," but that is a small price to pay for making it hard for "evil" people to do "evil," especially since one man's good is another's evil.

I have, for simplicity, concentrated on the special case of the corporate executive, except only for the brief digression on trade unions. But precisely the same argument applies to the newer phenomenon of calling upon stockholders to require corporations to exercise social responsibility (the recent G.M. crusade, for example). In most of these cases, what is in effect involved is some stockholders trying to get other stockholders (or customers or employes) to contribute against their will to "social" causes favored by the activists. Insofar as they succeed, they are again imposing taxes and spending the proceeds.

The situation of the individual proprietor is somewhat different. If he acts to reduce the returns of his enterprise in order to exercise his "social responsibility," he is spending his own money, not someone else's. If he wishes to spend his money on such purposes, that is his right, and I cannot see that there is any objection to his doing so. In the process, he, too, may impose costs on employes and customers. However, because he is far less likely than a large corporation or union to have monopolistic power, any such side effects will tend to be minor.

Of course, in practice the doctrine of social responsibility is frequently a cloak for actions that are justified on other grounds rather than a reason for those actions.

To illustrate, it may well be in the long-run interest of a corporation that is a major employer in a small community to devote resources to providing amenities to that community or to improving its government. That may make it easier to attract desirable employes, it may reduce the wage bill or lessen losses from pilferage and sabotage or have other worthwhile effects. Or it may be that, given the laws about the deductibility of corporate charitable contributions, the stockholders can contribute more to charities they favor by having the corporation make the gift than by doing it themselves, since they can in that way contribute an amount that would otherwise have been paid as corporate taxes.

In each of these—and many similar—cases, there is a strong temptation to rationalize these actions as an exercise of "social responsibility." In the present climate of opinion, with its widespread aversion to "capitalism," "profits," the "soulless corporation" and so on, this is one way for a corporation to generate goodwill as a by-product of expenditures that are entirely justified in its own self-interest.

It would be inconsistent of me to call on corporate executives to refrain from this hypocritical window-dressing because it harms the foundations of a free society. That would be to call on them to exercise a "social responsibility"! If our institutions, and the attitudes of the public make it in their self-interest to cloak their actions in this way, I cannot summon much indignation to denounce them. At the same time, I can express admiration for those individual proprietors or owners of closely held corporations or stockholders of more broadly held corporations who disdain such tactics as approaching fraud.

Whether blameworthy or not, the use of the cloak of social responsibility, and the nonsense spoken in its name by influential and prestigious businessmen, does clearly harm the foundations of a free society. I have been impressed time and again by the schizophrenic character of many businessmen. They are capable of being extremely far-sighted and clear-headed in matters that are internal to their businesses. They are incredibly short-sighted and muddle-headed in matters that are outside their businesses but affect the possible survival of business in general. This short-sightedness is strikingly exemplified in the calls from many businessmen for wage and price guidelines or controls or incomes policies. There is nothing that could do more in a brief period to destroy a market system and replace it by a centrally controlled system than effective governmental control of prices and wages.

The short-sightedness is also exemplified in speeches by businessmen on social responsibility. This may gain them kudos in the short run. But it helps to strengthen the already too prevalent view that the pursuit of profits is wicked and immoral and must be curbed and controlled by external forces. Once this view is adopted, the external forces that curb the market will not be the social consciences, however highly developed, of the pontificating executives; it will be the iron fist of Government bureaucrats. Here, as with price and wage controls, businessmen seem to me to reveal a suicidal impulse.

The political principle that underlies the market mechanism is unanimity. In an ideal free market resting on private property, no individual can coerce any other, all cooperation is voluntary, all parties to such cooperation benefit or they need not participate. There are no "social" values, no "social" responsibilities in any sense other than the shared values and responsibilities of individuals. Society is a collection of individuals and of the various groups they voluntarily form.

The political principle that underlies the political mechanism is conformity. The individual must serve a more general social interest—whether that be determined by a church or a dictator or a majority. The individual may have a vote and a say in what is to be done, but if he is overruled, he must conform. It is appropriate for some to require others to contribute to a general social purpose whether they wish to or not.

Unfortunately, unanimity is not always feasible. There are some respects in which conformity appears unavoidable, so I do not see how one can avoid the use of the political mechanism altogether.

But the doctrine of "social responsibility" taken seriously would extend the scope of the political mechanism to every human activity. It does not differ in philosophy from the most explicitly collectivist doctrine. It differs only by professing to believe that collectivist ends can be attained without collectivist means. That is why, in my book "Capitalism and Freedom," I have called it a "fundamentally subversive doctrine" in a free society, and have said that in such a society, "there is one and only one social responsibility of business—to use its resources and engage in activities designed to increase its profits so long as it stays within the rules of the game, which is to say, engages in open and free competition without deception or fraud."

NO

Robert Almeder

THE ETHICS OF PROFIT: REFLECTIONS ON CORPORATE RESPONSIBILITY

I. INTRODUCTION

International Telephone and Telegraph Corporation is alleged to have contributed large sums of money to 'destabilize' the duly elected government of Chile; General Motors Corporation and Firestone Tire and Rubber Corporation are both alleged to have knowingly and willingly marketed products which, owing to defective design, had been reliably predicted to kill a certain percentage of users. Finally, it is frequently said that numerous advertising companies happily accept and earnestly solicit accounts to advertise cigarettes, knowing full well that as a direct result of their advertising activities a certain number of people will die considerably prematurely and painfully. We need not concern ourselves with whether or not these charges are true; for our concern here is with what might count as a justification for such corporate behavior when it occurs. What is interesting is that sometimes, although not very frequently, corporate executives will admit to such behavior informally and then proceed proximately to justify that behavior in the name of their responsibility to the shareholders or owners to make as much profit as is legally possible. Thereafter, less proximately and more generally, they will proceed to urge the more general utilitarian point that the increase in profit engendered by such corporate behavior begets such an unquestionable overall good for society that the behavior in question is morally acceptable if not quite praiseworthy. More specifically, the justification in question can, and usually does, take two forms.

The first and most common form of justification consists in urging that, as long as one's corporate behavior is not illegal, the behavior will be morally acceptable because the sole purpose for being in business is to make a profit; and the rules of the marketplace are somewhat different from those in other places and must be followed if one is to satisfy the responsibility to the shareholder. Moreover, proponents of this view hasten to add that, as Adam

From *Business and Society*, Vols. 19-2 and 20-1. Reprinted by permission of the author.

Smith has claimed, the greatest good for society is achieved not by corporations seeking to act morally, or with a sense of social responsibility in their pursuit of profit, but rather by each corporation seeking to maximize its own profit, unregulated in that endeavor except by the laws of supply and demand along with whatever other laws are inherent in the competition process. Smith's view, that there is an invisible hand, as it were, directing an economy governed solely by the profit motive to the greatest good for society, is still the dominant motivation and justification for those who would have an economy unregulated by any moral concern which would, or could, tend to decrease profits in order to attain some alleged social or moral good. Milton Friedman, for example, has frequently asserted that the sole moral responsibility of business is to make as much profit as is legally possible. By that he means to suggest that attempts to regulate or restrain the pursuit of profit to effect what some people believe to be socially desirable ends are in fact *subversive* of the common good, since the greatest good for the greatest number is achieved by an economy maximally competitive and unregulated by moral rules in its pursuit of profit. So, under this view, the greatest good for society is achieved by corporations acting legally but with no regard for what may be morally desirable. This begets the paradox that, *in business*, it is only by acting without regard for morality that the greatest good for society can be achieved. This is a fairly conscious commitment to the view that while one's personal life may well need to be governed by moral considerations, it is a necessity that, in the pursuit of profit, one's corporate behavior be unregulated by any moral concern other than that of making as much money as is legally possible; for, curiously enough, it is only in this way that society achieves the greatest good. So viewed, it is not difficult to see how a corporate executive could consistently adopt rigorous standards of morality in his or her personal life and yet feel quite comfortable in abandoning those standards in the pursuit of corporate profit. Mr. Carr, for example, likens the conduct of business to playing poker. As Carr would have it, moral busybodies, who insist on corporations behaving morally, might just as well censure a good bluffer in poker for being deceitful. Society, lacking a perspective such as Friedman's and Carr's, is only too willing to view such behavior as strongly hypocritical and fostered by an unwholesome avarice.

A second way of justifying, or defending, corporate practices which may appear quite morally questionable is to argue that even if corporations were to take seriously the idea of limiting profits because of a desire to be moral or more responsible to social needs, they then would be involved in the unwholesome business of selecting and implementing moral values which may not be shared by a large number of people. Besides, there is the overwhelming question of whether or not there can be any non-questionable moral values or non-controversial list of social priorities for corporations to adopt. After all, if ethical relativism is true, or if ethical nihilism is true (and philosophers can be counted upon to argue for both positions), then it would be fairly silly of corporations to limit profits for what may be quite a dubious reason, namely, being moral, when there are no clear grounds for doing so. In short, business corporations could argue (as Friedman has done) that corporate actions in behalf of society's interest would require of corporations an ability to clearly determine and rank in non-controversial ways the major needs of society, and it does not appear that this can be successfully done.

Perhaps another, and easier, way of formulating this second argument is to hold that, since philosophers generally fail to agree on what are the proper moral rules (if any) as well as on whether or not we should be moral, it would be imprudent to sacrifice a clear profit for a dubious or controversial moral gain. That would appear to be an abandonment of a clear responsibility for one that is unclear or questionable.

If there are any other basic modes of justification for the sort of corporate behavior noted at the outset, I cannot imagine what they might be. So, let us examine these two modes of justification. In doing this, I hope to show that neither argument is sound and, moreover, that corporate behavior of the sort in question is clearly immoral. In the end, we can reflect upon what effective means can be taken to prevent such behavior and what is philosophically implied by corporate willingness to act in such ways.

II.

Essentially, the first argument is that the greatest good for the greatest number will be, and can only be, achieved by corporations acting legally, but unregulated by any moral concern, in the pursuit of profit. As noted above, the evidence for this argument rests on a fairly classical and unquestioning acceptance of Adam Smith's view that society achieves a greater good when each person is allowed to pursue his/her own selfish ends than when each person's pursuit of his own selfish ends is regulated in some way or other by moral rules or concern. I know of no evidence ever offered by Smith for this latter claim although it seems clear that those who adopt it generally do so out of respect for the perceived good that has emerged for various modern societies as a direct result of the free enterprise system and its ability to raise the overall standard of living of all those under it. At any rate, there is nothing inevitable about the greatest good occurring under an unregulated economy. Indeed, we have good inductive evidence from the age of the Robber Barons that unless the profit motive is regulated in various ways (by statute or otherwise) great social evil can occur because of the natural tendency of the system to place ever increasing sums of money in ever decreasing numbers of hands. And if all this is so, then so much the worse for all philosophical attempts to justify what would appear to be morally questionable corporate behavior on the grounds that corporate behavior, unregulated by moral concern, is productive of the greatest good for the greatest number. Moreover, a rule-utilitarian would not be very hard-pressed to show the many unsavory implications to society as a whole if it were to take seriously a rule to the effect that, provided only that one acts legally, it is morally permissable to do whatever one wants to do to achieve a profit. Some of those implications we shall discuss below before drawing a conclusion.

The second argument cited above asserts that even if we were to grant, for the sake of argument, that corporations have social responsibilities beyond that of making as much money as legally possible for the shareholders, there would be no non-controversial way for corporations to discover just what these responsibilities are in the order of their importance. Since even philosophers can be expected to disagree on what one's moral responsibilities are, if any, it would seem irresponsible to limit profits to satisfy dubious moral responsibilities. But there are a few things wrong with this line of reasoning.

For one thing, it unduly exaggerates our potential for moral disagreement. Admittedly, there might well be important disagreements among corporations (just as there could be among philosophers) as to a priority ranking of major social needs; but that does not mean that most of us could not, or would not, agree that certain things ought not be done in the name of profit even when there is no law prohibiting such acts. There will always be a few who would do anything for profit; but that is hardly a good argument in favor of their having the moral right to do so. Rather, it is a good argument that they refuse to be moral. In sum, it is hard to see how this second argument favoring corporate moral nihilism is any better than the general argument for ethical nihilism based on the variability of ethical judgments or practices. Apart from the fact that it tacitly presupposes that morality is a matter of what we all in fact would, or should, agree to, the argument is maximally counterintuitive (as I shall show) by way of suggesting that we cannot generally agree that corporations have certain clear social responsibilities to avoid certain practices. Accordingly, I would now like to argue that a certain kind of corporate behavior is quite immoral (although it may not be illegal) and that all corporations willing to act in this way do a disservice to humanity and themselves.

The basic point I wish to make is that, Friedman notwithstanding, it is not difficult to show that there are some things that corporations ought not do in the pursuit of profit; even if there were no laws against such acts. But it is quite difficult to convince corporations, like persons, that they ought to be moral. I would like to probe the source of this difficulty in fairly general terms, concluding with a recommendation.

III.

Without entering into the reasons for the belief, I assume we all believe that it is wrong to kill an innocent human being for the sole reason that doing so would be financially more rewarding for the killer than if he were to earn his livelihood in some other way. Nor, I assume, would our moral feelings in this matter change depending upon the amount of money involved. Killing an innocent baby for fifteen million dollars would not seem to be any less objectionable than killing it for twenty cents. It is possible, however, that some self-professing utilitarian might be tempted to argue that the killing of an innocent baby for fifteen million dollars would not be objectionable if the money were to be given to the poor; for under these circumstances, greater good would be achieved by the killing of the innocent baby. But, I submit, if anybody were to argue this, his argument would be quite deficient because he will not have established what he needs to establish in order to make the argument sound. What is needed is a clearly convincing argument that raising the standard of living of an indefinite number of poor people by the killing of an innocent person is a greater good for all those affected by the act than if the standard of living were not raised by the killing of an innocent person. This is necessary because part of what we mean by having a basic right to life is that a person's life cannot be taken from him or her without a good reason. And if our utilitarian cannot convincingly justify his claim that a greater good is served by killing an innocent person to raise the standard of living for a large number of poor people, then it is hard to see how he can have the valid reason he needs to deprive an innocent person of his or her life. Now, it seems clear that there will be anything but unanimity in the moral community on the question of whether there is a greater good achieved in raising the standard of living by killing an innocent baby than in leaving the standard of living alone and not killing an innocent baby. Moreover, even if everybody were to agree that the greater good is achieved by the killing of the innocent baby, how could that be shown to be true? How does one compare the moral value of raising the standard of living by the taking of that life? Indeed, the more one thinks about it, the harder it is to see just what would count as objective evidence for the claim that the greater good is achieved by the killing of an innocent baby. Accordingly, I can see nothing that would serve to justify the utilitarian who might be tempted to argue that if the sum is large enough, and if the sum were to be used for raising the standard of living for an indefinite number of poor people, then it would be morally acceptable to kill an innocent person for money.

These reflections should not be taken to imply, however, that no utilitarian argument could justify the killing of an innocent person for money. After all, if the sum were large enough to save the lives of a large number of people who

would surely die if the innocent baby were not killed, then I think one would as a rule be justified in killing the innocent baby for the sum in question. But this is obviously quite different from any attempt to justify the killing of an innocent person in order to raise the standard of living for an indefinite number of poor people. It makes sense to kill one innocent person in order to save, say, twenty innocent persons; but it makes no sense at all to kill one innocent person to raise the standard of living of an indefinite number of people. And this is because in the latter case, but not in the former, a comparison is sought as between things that are incomparable.

Assuming all this, it is remarkable and somewhat perplexing that certain corporations should seek to defend practices that are in fact instances of killing innocent persons for profit. Take, for example, the corporate practice of dumping known carcinogens into rivers. On Friedman's view, we should not regulate or prevent such companies from dumping their effluents into the environment. Rather we should, if we like, tax the company after the effluents are in the water and then have the tax money used to clear up the environment. For Friedman, and others, the fact that so many people will die as a result of this practice seems to be just part of the cost of doing business and making a profit. If there is any difference between such corporate practices and murdering innocent human beings for money, it is hard to see what it is. There are a host of other corporate activities which amount to deliberate killing of innocent persons for money. Such practices number among them: contributing funds to 'destabilize' a foreign government, advertising cigarettes, knowingly marketing children's clothing containing a known cancer-causing agent, and refusing to recall (for fear of financial loss) goods known to be defective enough to directly maim or kill a certain percentage of their users. On this latter item, we are all familiar, for example, with convincingly documented charges that certain prominent automobile and tire manufacturers have knowingly marketed equipment with defects which increased the likelihood of death of the users. Yet, they have refused to recall these products because the cost of recalling or repairing them would have a greater adverse impact on profit than if the products were not recalled and the company paid the projected number of suits predicted to be filed successfully. Of course, if the projected cost of the suits were to outweigh the cost of recall or repair, then the product would be recalled and repaired, but not otherwise. In cases of this sort the companies involved may admit to having certain marketing problems or design problems, and they may even admit to having made a mistake; but they do not view themselves as immoral or as murderers for keeping their product in the marketplace when they know people are dying because of it—people who would not die if the defect were corrected.

In all of this, the point is not whether in fact these practices have occurred in the past, or occur even now; for there can be no doubt that such practices have occurred and do occur. Rather, the point is that when companies as a matter of policy act in such ways, they must either not know what they do is murder (i.e., unjustifiable killing of innocent persons), or knowing that it is murder, seek to justify it in terms of profit. My argument is that it is difficult to see how any corporate manager could fail to see that

these policies amount to murder for money, although there may be no civil statutes against such corporate behavior. If so, then where such policies exist, we can only assume that they are designed and implemented by corporate managers who either see nothing wrong with murder for money (which is implausible) or recognize that what they do is wrong, but simply refuse to act morally because it is financially rewarding to act immorally.

Of course, it is possible that some corporate executives do not recognize such acts as murder. They may, after all, view murder as a legal concept involving one person or persons deliberately killing another person or persons and prosecutable only under existing civil statute. If so, it is somewhat understandable how corporate executives might fail, at least psychologically, to see such corporate policies as murder rather than as, say, calculated risks. Still, for all that, the logic of the situation seems clear enough.

IV. CONCLUSION

In addition to the fact that the only two plausible arguments favoring the Friedman doctrine are unsatisfactory, a strong case can be made for the claim that corporations *do* have a clear and noncontroversial moral responsibility not to design or implement, for reasons of profit, policies which they know, or have good reason to believe, will kill or otherwise seriously injure innocent persons affected by those policies. And we have said nothing about wage discrimination, sexism, discrimination in hiring, price fixing, price gouging, questionable but not unlawful competition, or other similar practices some will think businesses should avoid by virtue of responsibility to society. My main concern has been to show that since we all agree that murder for money is generally wrong, and since there is no discernible difference between that and certain corporate policies which are not in fact illegal, then these corporate practices are clearly immoral (that is, they ought not to be done) and incapable of being morally justified by appeal to the Friedman doctrine since that doctrine does not admit of adequate evidential support. In itself, it is sad that this argument needs to be made and, if it weren't for what appears to be a fairly strong commitment within the business community to the Friedman doctrine in the name of the unquestionable success of the free enterprise system, the argument would not need to be stated. Moreover, the fact that such practices do exist because they are designed and implemented by corporate managers who, for all intents and purposes, appear to be upright members of the moral community, only heightens the need for effective social deterrence. Naturally, any company willing to put human lives into the profit and loss column is not likely to respond to moral censure. This, I submit, implies that perhaps the most effective way to deal with the problem consists in structuring legislation such that principle corporate managers who knowingly concur in practices of the sort listed above can effectively be tried, at their own expense, for murder, rather than censured and fined a sum to be paid out of corporate profits. This may seem somewhat extreme or unrealistic. However, it seems more unrealistic to think that aggressively competitive corporations will respond to what is morally necessary if failure to do so could be very or even minimally profitable. In short, unless fairly strong and appropriate steps are taken to prevent such practices, society will continue to reinforce a mode of behavior which is destructive because it is maximally disrespectful of human life. It is also reinforcing a value system which so emphasizes monetary gain as a standard of human success that murder for profit would be a corporate policy if the penalty for being caught at it were not too dear.

In the long run, of course, corporate and individual willingness to do what is clearly immoral for the sake of monetary gain is a patent commitment to a certain view about the nature of human happiness and success, a view which will need to be placed in the balance with Aristotle's reasoned argument and reflections to the effect that money and all that it brings is a means to an end, and not the sort of end in itself that will justify acting immorally to attain it. What that beautiful end is and why being moral allows us to achieve it, may well be the most rewarding and profitable subject a human being can think about. Properly understood and placed in perspective, Aristotle's view on the nature and attainment of human happiness could go a long way toward alleviating the temptation to kill for money.

In the meantime, any ardent supporter of the capitalistic system will naturally want to see the system thrive and flourish; and this it cannot do if it invites and demands government regulation in the name of the public interest. A strong ideological commitment to what I have here described as the Friedman doctrine is counterproductive and not in anyone's long-range interest, since it is most likely to beget more and more regulatory laws. The only way to avoid such encroaching regulation is to find ways to move the business community into the long-term view of what is in its interest, and effect ways of determining and responding to social needs before society moves to regulate business to that end. This, of course, is to ask business to regulate its own modes of competition in ways that may seem very difficult. Indeed, if what I have been suggesting is correct, the only kind of capitalism that is likely to survive indefinitely is a humane one; and a humane one is one that is at least as socially responsible as society needs. By the same token, contrary to what is sometimes felt in the business community, the Friedman doctrine, ardently adopted for the dubious reasons generally given, will most likely undermine capitalism and motivate an economic socialism by assuring an erosive regulatory climate in a society that expects the business community to be socially responsible in ways that go beyond just making legal profits.

In sum, being socially responsible in ways that go beyond legal profit-making is by no means a dubious luxury for the capitalist in today's world. It is a necessity if capitalism is to survive at all; and, presumably, we shall all profit exceedingly with the survival of a vibrant capitalism. If anything, then, rigid adherence to the Friedman doctrine is not only philosophically unjustified, and unjustifiable, it is also unprofitable in the long run, and therefore, downright subversive of the common good in the long run. Unfortunately, taking the long run view is difficult for everyone; and that, of course, is for the obvious reason that for each of us, tomorrow may not come. But living for today only, does not seem to make much sense either if that deprives us of any reasonable and happy tomorrow. Living for the future may not be the healthiest thing to do; but do it we must,

if we have good reason to think that we will have a future. The trick is to provide for the future without living in it, and that just requires being moral.

EPILOGUE

After this article was written, an Indiana superior court judge refused to dismiss a homicide indictment against the Ford Motor Company. The company was indicted on charges of reckless homicide stemming from a 1978 accident involving a 1973 Pinto in which three girls died when the car burst into flames after being slammed in the rear. This is the first case in which Ford, or any other automobile manufacturer, has been charged with a criminal offense.

The indictment went forward because the state of Indiana adopted in 1977 a criminal code provision permitting corporations to be charged with criminal acts. At the moment, twenty-two other states allow as much.

The judge, in refusing to set aside the indictment, agreed with the prosecutor's argument that the charge was based not on the Pinto's design fault, but rather on the fact that Ford had permitted the car "to remain on Indiana highways knowing full well its defects."

This is an interesting example of social regulation which could have been avoided if corporate managers had not followed so ardently the Friedman doctrine. If society continues to regulate the business community, the emerging socialism (and all that it implies) can only be viewed as a direct effect of the business community's refusal to act morally because of its unquestioning adoption of the Friedman doctrine.

POSTSCRIPT

Are Profits the Only Business of Business?

Economist Friedman dismisses the pleas of those who argue for socially responsible business action on the grounds that these individuals do not understand the role of the corporate executive in modern society. Friedman points out that these executives are responsible to the corporate owners, who expect these executives to do everything in their power to earn the owners a maximum return on their investment. If the corporate executive takes an action that he or she feels is "socially responsible" and this reduces the owners' return on their investment, he or she has spent the owners' money; this, Friedman maintains, violates the very foundation of our political-economic system: individual freedom. He believes that no individual should be deprived of his or her property without his or her permission, that if the corporate executives wish to take socially responsible actions, they should use their own money; they shouldn't prevent the owners from spending their money on whatever social actions they might wish to support.

In philosopher Almeder's response to Friedman he argues that some corporate behavior is immoral and that defense of this immoral behavior imposes great costs on society. More precisely, Almeder likens corporate acts such as advertising cigarettes, marketing automobiles that cannot sustain moderate rear-end collisions, and contributing funds to destabilize foreign

governments to unjustifiably murdering innocent children for profit. He goes on to argue that although these acts are not illegal and may improve profits for business firms, society must not condone this behavior. Instead, he believes that, through federal and state legislation, society must continue to impose regulations upon businesses until businesses begin to regulate themselves.

Perhaps no one topic is more fundamental to microeconomics than the issue of profits. Many articles have been written in defense of profits such as Milton and Rose Friedman's *Free to Choose: A Personal Statement* (Harcourt, Brace and Jovanovich, 1980), Ben Rogge's *Can Capitalism Survive?* (Liberty Fund, 1979) and Frank H. Knight's classical book *Risk, Uncertainty, and Profits* (Kelley Press, 1921). In recent years a number of new books that are highly critical of the Friedman-Rogge-Knight position have appeared on the market, including James Robertson's *Profit or People? The New Social Role of Money* (Merrimack Book Service, 1978), Sam Aaronovitch's *Political Economy of Capitalism* (Beekman Publishers, 1977) and Sherman Howard's *Radical Political Economy: Capitalism and Socialism from a Marxist Humanist Perspective* (Basic Books, 1972).

ISSUE 2

Should We Try To Save the Family Farm?

YES: Byron Dorgan, from "America's Real Farm Problem: It Can Be Solved," *The Washington Monthly* (April 1983)

NO: Stephen Chapman, from "The Farmer on the Dole," *Harper's Magazine* (October 1982)

ISSUE SUMMARY

YES: Representative Dorgan of North Dakota fears that public policy has become too concerned with the interests of the large corporate farms while ignoring the small family farm that has "made agriculture one of the few American industries still competitive in international markets."
NO: Columnist Chapman argues for "rugged individualism." He asserts that: "If Americans still believe in the virtue of hardy rural self-reliance, they should tell Washington to get out of the way and let farmers practice it."

The one sector of the United States economy which closely mirrors a textbook's view of the world is agriculture. This industry is populated with a large number of farms—approximately 2.3 to 2.4 million—most of which are too small to influence market prices. These farms produce commodities that are, more often than not, homogeneous. (That is, Farmer A's red winter wheat is identical to Farmer B's red winter wheat.) Compared to many industries, there is relatively free entry into and exit from the agricultural industry, as demonstrated by the recent rash of bankruptcies and bank foreclosures.

Because this is a highly competitive sector of the economy, it is particularly susceptible to wide swings in profitability. When times are good, profits are very good, but, when times are bad, they are very bad. This vulnerability can be traced to two factors, which are ultimately related to the nature of competitive markets: First, if market prices fall, the small producers, who are already operating on a tight budget because of debt obligations, respond out of desperation by increasing supply. They do not bring less to the market; they bring more. Their acts of desperation drive market prices down further. Second, although the majority of farmers have little or no control over the price at which they sell their products, the goods and services they must buy from the non-agricultural community often come from firms that do have monopoly power. (The petro-chemical industry, the farm implement industry, and the money markets are hardly "competitive" in a textbook sense.)

In this contest of market power, farmers must lose, and lose they have. Over time, the profits the farmers receive for their output are much lower than the prices they must pay for their inputs. The net result is that the farmers' relative income falls.

This phenomenon is exaggerated during periods of recessions. Indeed, during the depression of the 1930s, the disparity between farm income and non-farm income became so great that the United Stated inaugurated its first farm price support program: the Agricultural Adjustment Act of 1933. This legislation, based on the notion of *parity* (the notion that the value of farm output be maintained relative to the value of non-farm output), became the mainstay of United States agricultural policy in the 1930s, 1940s, and 1950s. In short, this policy was designed to protect the small family farm by reducing the supply of agricultural commodities that found their way to the marketplace. This reduced supply, increased agricultural prices, and, in turn, increased incomes in the agricultural community.

During the 1960s and 1970s, agricultural policy was refocused. The opening of world markets and the presence of poor harvests in many parts of the world meant that the demand of United States-produced food and fiber were at all-time high levels. As a result, there was much less need to publicly support agricultural prices. Public policy shifted toward improving the operation of agricultural markets and reducing the cost of producing agricultural products.

The 1980s witnessed yet another shock to the farming community. Farmers were buffeted about by a number of events that were largely out of their control. First, the economy was gripped by "stagflation." The prices of inputs (non-agricultural products) that farmers had to buy skyrocketed, while at the same time the domestic demand for agricultural products slackened. Second, the monetary authority dramatically raised interest rates. In the agricultural sector—which is dependent upon loans to pay for its seed, fertilizer, and equipment—this represented a major financial blow. Third, the bubble burst on agricultural land speculations. In the face of a very deep recession, land prices leveled off and began to fall. Since farmers are land-intensive, the value of their major asset seemed to disappear before their eyes. Lastly, world demand for United States-produced food and fiber fell sharply. This was the result of a world recession, bumper crops throughout the world, and United States grain embargoes, which were imposed for political purposes. The net result was falling agricultural prices and incomes.

Farm price support programs automatically came to the rescue of the ailing farm community. Indeed, for fiscal year 1983, United States farm programs were expected to cost taxpayers $21 billion or seventy-five percent more than the previous year. But even in the face of these huge dollar expenditures, farmers—particularly small farmers—were facing bankruptcy proceedings at a rate unmatched since the depression of the 1930s.

Congressman Dorgan is shaken by the prospect of losing the family farm. He argues that the "invisible hand" of the market can "end up shooting farmers in the foot." Free market advocate Chapman replies that if we want to preserve the "cherished American tradition" that is embodied in the notion of a family farm, we should "tell Washington to get out of the way" so farmers can do their jobs.

21

YES

Byron Dorgan

AMERICA'S REAL FARM PROBLEM:
IT CAN BE SOLVED

Recent scenes from America's farm belt seem like a grainy film clip from the thirties. Young families putting their home and farm machinery on the auction block. Men, choked with emotion, breaking down in tears as they describe their plight. Angry farmers organizing, getting madder and madder.

It's not as bad as the thirties yet; no governor has called out the National Guard to stop the foreclosures, the way North Dakota's William "Wild Bill" Langer did in 1933. But the pain is running deep. Losing a farm is not like have a new Chevrolet or a color TV repossessed. In many cases, what's lost is land that's been in the family for generations—and a way of life that for many is the only one they've ever known or wanted.

It's not that other victims of the recession deserve less sympathy. But there's an important difference between the plight of the farmer and that of other producers. What's happening in the farm belt is a far cry from what's happening in Pittsburgh and Detroit. Nobody is berating our farmers for falling behind the foreign competition and losing their edge, like the auto and steel industries. Nobody is shoving books on Japanese management into their faces. To the contrary, American farmers are our all-star economic performers. When other countries want to find out how to improve agriculture, they don't send their delegations to Tokyo. They send them to Iowa and Kansas and the Dakotas.

And the farmers' reward? Most North Dakota wheat farmers are getting $4 for a bushel of wheat that costs them $5.50 to grow. Farmers are making less in real income today than they did in 1934. Creditors are foreclosing in record numbers; the Farmers Home Administration alone reports that at least 4,000 of its borrowers were forced out of business in 1982.

From "America's Real Farm Problem: It Can Be Solved," by Byron Dorgan, *The Washington Monthly*, April 1983. Copyright © 1983 by The Washington Monthly Co., 1711 Connecticut Avenue, NW, Washington, DC 20009. (202) 462-0128.

RURAL MYTHS

Agriculture is a $140 billion-a-year industry, our nation's largest, far bigger than steel, automobiles, or any other manufacturing enterprise. Farming and food-related businesses generate one out of five jobs in private industry and account for 20 percent of our GNP. Sooner or later the problems on the farm catch up with the rest of us, as the laid-off employees of International Harvester already know too well. Students of the Depression will also recall that it was long *before* the 1929 crash—while the market was still revving up—that farm income began falling. The troubles on the farm were a large part of the weight that ultimately dragged the entire economy down into the Depression.

If you read the editorial columns of *The Wall Street Journal*, you know that some people have a simple explanation for the farmers' plight. Too much production is the problem, they say, and if government would only stop subsidizing overproduction by keeping prices artificially high, the free market would work its will and weed out the inefficient producers. What's more, many conservatives and liberals alike believe farmers are only getting their just deserts, having grown fat and happy on government price supports and double-digit inflation. You've seen the caricatures on "60 Minutes"—farmers driving big Cadillacs, spending their winters in Boca Raton—and still complaining that the government doesn't pay them enough *not* to grow certain crops.

Those aren't the farmers I know. But with less than four percent of all Americans now living on farms, it's little surprise people have so many misconceptions about our farm program. Start with the "overproduction" argument. There are children and older people in this country who still don't have enough to eat, and roughly 450 million people in the world who go hungry most of the time. That people talk about "overproduction" rather than "underdistribution" is rather telling in itself. But more to the present point: almost from the time the early settlers planted their first row, American farmers have been growing more food than the nation could consume. The tendency toward producing surpluses is a perennial problem. It hardly explains the extraordinary difficulties our farmers now face.

As for the "60 Minutes" caricatures, they are just that—caricatures. Last year (1982) the federal government paid farmers $1.5 billion in direct subsidies (it loaned another $11.4 billion that farmers must repay). Money from these federal programs came to about two percent of total receipts in 1982 for the average farmer, whose farm netted just $8,000. Add in what he and his family earned away from the farm, and his household still made less than a GS-11 civil servant and about half as much as a young lawyer on Wall Street. That's for working from morning to night and doing what many Americans no longer do—produce something the rest of us need.

But this is no blanket apology for the nation's farm policies—far from it. There are some farmers who get more than they deserve from the government, and nobody gets madder about that than the vast majority of farmers who bear no resemblance to them. Egregious abuses do exist, and it's time that representatives from the farm states (of which I'm one) begin to eliminate them. If we ignore such problems or dismiss them as inevitable, they will continue to act as lightning rods for attacks on all farm programs. Representatives of farm states must clean their own house for if they don't, I'm afraid, someone else will do it—hurting farmer and non-farmer alike.

The nation needs a federal farm program; to think otherwise in today's highly competitive international economy is self-defeating and naive. But we need the *right* kind of farm program, one that not only meets the test of fairness, but that promises to keep American agriculture second to none.

Unfortunately, that's not the kind of farm program we now have. Approaches that were fine in the thirties are no longer doing the job. In fact, what began as survival programs for family farmers are becoming the domain of extra-large producers who often elbow aside the very family farmers for whom these programs were originally intended. Congress must bear much of the blame for this. We continue to target most farm assistance not according to the circumstances of the individual farmer but largely according to the volume of the commodity he grows. While these federal programs have all been done in the name of the family farmer, the interests of the various commodity groups have not always been identical to those of the nation's family farmers.

This is not to criticize these groups, for everyone is entitled to his say. But it is to suggest that we in Congress have talked too much about programs for feed grains and wheat and corn and assorted "market prices" and "loan rates"—and not enough about the kind of agriculture that's best for the country. And we've done more than waste money in the process. For if our agricultural policy continues largely unchanged, I'm concerned the criticisms that now so trag-ically apply to the nation's automakers—that they became too big, too inflexible, and too inefficient to compete—may one day be appropriate for America's agriculture.

FARM ECONOMICS

To understand the failings of existing farm programs, it's important to understand the roots of the current farm crisis. At the heart of the problem is money—how much there is and how much it costs to borrow.

A farmer is a debtor almost by definition. In my own state, it's not unusual for a wheat farmer with 1,000 acres to owe several hundred thousand dollars for land and machinery. In addition to making payments on these loans, it's common for such a farmer to borrow about $40,000 each spring to cover fertilizer, diesel fuel, seed, and other operating expenses. The months before the harvest will be anxious ones as the farmer contemplates all the things that could bring financial hardship: bad weather, crop disease, insects, falling commodity prices. If he has a good year, the farmer can repay his loans and retain some profit; in a bad one, he can lose his whole farm.

Money thus becomes one of the farmer's biggest expenses. Most consumers can find some refuge from high interest rates by postponing large purchases like houses or cars. Farmers have no choice. In 1979, for example, farmers paid $12 billion in interest costs while earning $32 billion; last year they paid $22 billion in interest costs, while earning only $20 billion. In a business in which profit margins are small, $4,000 more in interest can mean the difference between profit and loss. Since 1975, 100,000 family farms have disappeared, and while interest rates have fallen recently, they still imperil the nation's farmers.

This is why the most basic part of our nation's farm policy is its money and credit policy—which is set by Paul Volcker and the Federal Reserve Board. The Federal Reserve Board's responsibility for nearly ruining our economy is well-known. What's often overlooked is how the board's policies have taken an especially devastating toll on farmers. While high interest rates have increased farm expenses, they've also undermined the export market farmers have traditionally relied on. High interest rates, by stalling our economic engines, have been a drag on the entire world's economy. Developing and third-world nations have been particularly hard hit; struggling just to meet interest payments on their loans from multinational banks, they have had little cash left over to buy our farm products.

Even those countries that could still afford our farm products abandoned us for other producers. Our interest rates were so high they attracted multinational bankers, corporations, and others who speculate on currencies of different countries. These speculators were willing to pay more for dollars in terms of pesos, yen, or marks because those rates guaranteed them such a substantial return.

The news commentators called the result a "strong dollar," which gave us a rush of pride. But what did this strong dollar really mean to the farmer? It meant people in other countries found themselves suddenly poorer when they went to buy something made or grown in America. In 1981, for example, West Germans paid 21 percent more for American soybeans, even though our farmers were getting 11 percent *less* for those very same soybeans than they had the previous year. Overall, our "strong dollar" has been jacking up the price of American farm exports by a full 25 percent, biting our potential foreign customer with a 25 percent surcharge the moment they start thinking of buying American. No wonder these exports have dropped for the first time in 12 years. This isn't a strong dollar, it's a big banker's dollar—and with a central bank like the Federal Reserve Board, who needs soil erosion, grasshoppers, or drought?

To be fair, interest rates aren't solely responsible for undercutting our farmers' export markets. President Carter's grain embargo did more than close the Russian market; it also drove away other foreign customers who wondered how dependable we were. Reagan has lifted the embargo, but to little avail, since he still refuses to sign a long-term grain contract with the Soviet Union. Meanwhile, our foreign competitors have quickly stepped into the breach, supporting their farmers with generous subsidies that make ours look miserly by comparison. Last September, for example, wheat from the U.S. and the Common Market countries was selling for almost the same price on the international market. But while the U.S. farmer was getting about $3.40 a bushel, his Common Market counterpart received $5.37.

Both the Federal Reserve Board's market-skewing policies and the hefty subsidies that foreign agriculture receives illustrate an important point. Those who say America should go back to a "free market" in agriculture are asking our farmers to go back to something that no longer exists. In today's world there's no free market in agriculture, just as there is none in steel, automobiles, or other major industries.

We learned during the Depression that agriculture, by its very nature, requires a moderating hand to smooth out the violent cycles that otherwise could destroy even the best farmers. No other producers have to confront the sudden price shifts with which farmers regularly contend. Automakers, for example, don't have to worry that prices for their product may drop 50 percent, as wheat prices did from 1974 to 1977. This is why even that bastion of free-market orthodoxy, the Heritage Foundation, concedes the need for a government role in agriculture.

HOME-GROWN DEPRESSION

For the nation's first 150 years, there was no farm program as such. The Department of Agriculture wasn't created until 1862, and when President Lincoln proposed it to Congress he could applaud the nation's farmers as a "great interest so independent in its nature as to not have demanded and extorted more from government." For the next 70 years the department limited itself largely to statistics and research. Farmers received little in the way of subsidies; like all other consumers, they helped subsidize manufacturers through the tariffs they paid on imported goods.

Contrary to popular belief, the Depression hit our farms long before the Okies started their desperate treks across the dust bowl in their sputtering Models T's. During World War I Europe bought our food like it was going out of style. Prices rose to record heights; farmers expanded their operations and borrowed heavily to do so.

Then the war ended. Export markets quickly dried up as European countries started to rebuild their own agriculture. American farmers watched helplessly as prices plummeted, leaving many with huge debts to repay and no income with which to pay them. A rash of foreclosures followed, rehearsing a cycle that bears an eerie similarity to the current one. By 1932 farm income was less than one-third of what it had been in 1919. During this period, more than 1.5 million Americans left the farm. (The exodus was reversed during the Depression, when many returned to the farm in order to survive.)

Then, as now, the conventional economists and their camp followers in Congress and the press found little alarming in this hardship. The "invisible hand," they said, would force farmers to produce less until prices returned to normal levels. The "weak" and the "inefficient" might be cut down in the process, but that was the way the free market was supposed to work. It didn't.

Unfortunately, someone forgot to tell the nation's farmers about the economic etiquette that professors and journalists expected of them. As prices continued to fall, the farmers didn't produce less—they produced more. It's not hard to understand why. Farmers have certain set costs—such as debt—whether or not the plant a single seed. When prices dropped, many tried to produce more to make up the difference. Besides, to farm is to hope. The market may be terrible one year, but who knows what will happen next? Will there be drought in Europe? Blight in Russia? When you have to decide how much to plant in the spring, you have little idea what the market will really be in the fall. The worse things look, the more you pin your hopes on a sudden surge in prices. So you plant.

Those who put all the blame on government for today's excess production and low prices are long on theory and short on history. We produced "too much" throughout the twenties, when there was no farm program to speak of. And it wasn't the weak and the inefficient who tumbled then. It was just about everybody.

BLIND GENEROSITY

The New Dealers recognized that when it comes to agriculture, the invisible hand can end up shooting farmers in the foot. Their solution was straightforward—and effective. Remedies like the Agricultural Adjustment Act were begun to prop up the prices of certain commodities so that the farmers who grew them could count on at least a minimal return. The main approach was to link government assistance to the farmers' agreement to cut production, thus forcing prices to rise according to the laws of supply and demand.

These relief programs were not geared to the circumstances of individual farmers. They were aimed at regulating the supply and price of certain commodities. Still, the commodity approach amounted to a relief program for the family farm because there just weren't many other kinds of farms around. In 1932 one of four Americans lived on a farm, and for that reason the commodity programs were a major part of the whole New Deal relief effort.

Over the last half century, this commodity approach has remained relatively unchanged, while American agriculture has changed radically. The number of farms today is one-third what it was during the Depression, and just seven percent of these control over half the farmland and account for over half the sales. Yet while farming has become

more concentrated, the government still dispenses federal aid with a blindfold on, treating a multi-thousand-acre agrifactory giant as if it were a bedraggled Okie with a handcrank tractor and a cow. As a result, 29 percent of all federal farm benefits to the top one percent of our farmers.

The government distributes this largess in a variety of ways. Some programs amount to government - guaranteed prices. For a few crops—tobacco and peanuts, for example—the government sanctions an allotment system by which the marketing of these is strictly controlled. The government also provides crop insurance, disaster relief, and subsidized loans for such things as purchasing more farmland and meeting operating expenses.

The traditional mainstay of the farm program is the "commodity loan." Each year the government establishes a loan rate for major crops, including wheat, corn, barley, sorghum, and soybeans. The rate for wheat, for example, was $3.55 per bushel in 1982. Early in the year, a farmer must decide whether he is going to sign up for the program; if he does, he may have to agree to cut back his production to help keep surpluses down. If the eventual market price goes above the loan-rate level, the farmer simply repays the loan, takes back his wheat, and sells it on the open market. But if the market price is below the loan rate, the farmer may take the money and leave the wheat with the government. In addition to the commodity loan, there is a "deficiency payment" that supposedly helps bridge the gap between what the farmer earns in the market and what his crop costs to produce.

It's important to understand two things about this price-support program.

First, a guaranteed price is not a guaranteed profit. The loan rates and deficiency payments do not necessarily return the farmer's cost of production, and in recent years they haven't. In 1982, for example, the target price for wheat was more than a dollar less than the farmer's cost of production.

More important, the way these programs work, the more you have, the more the government gives you. A wheat farmer with 250 acres producing 30 bushels per acre gets a support loan of $26,625. A farmer with 2,500 acres of similarly productive land gets approximately ten times that much. The deficiency payments work in pretty much the same way.

For deficiency payments there is a nominal $50,000 cap that in practice does not have much effect. For support loans, there is no limitation at all. Thus, while smaller farmers get a little help, the largest farms walk off with a bundle. In a recent editorial attacking all farm subsidies, The Wall Street Journal fumed about a midwestern wheat grower who received $68,760 last year from the government yet "rides around his 4,000-acre farm on a huge four-wheel-drive tractor with air conditioning and a radio."

I'll bet the editorial writers of The Wall Street Journal have air conditioning, radios, and a whole lot more in their offices; still, they do have a point. As Don Paarlburg, a conservative agricultural economist who toiled in the last three Republican administrations, has put it, the result of the present federal farm program is that "average farm income is increased by adding more dollars to those already well-off and adding little or nothing to those at the low end of the income scale."

This bias toward bigness runs through most of the federal government's farm program. One of the best illustrations is the Farmers Home Administration, a case study of how a federal program that began to help only those in need became a safety net for just about everybody else.

The FmHA was created in the depths of the Depression as a lender of last resort for small and beginning farmers who had a reasonable chance to survive. For most of its life, the agency did serve family farmers struggling to get their operation on its feet and unable to obtain credit elsewhere. But in the 1970s, Congress tacked on something called the Economic Emergency Loan program. To qualify for this new program you didn't have to be small, needy, or even a family farmer. You just had to be in economic trouble. Soon the "economic-emergency" loans were pushing aside the kinds of loans the FmHA was originally intended to provide. By 1980 FmHA was lending *four times* as much in such "emergency" assistance as it was in the so-called "limited-resource" loans for needy farmers who were now receiving less than ten percent of the agency's total. Ninety percent of these emergency loans went to bigger, more established farms, many of which were unlikely candidates for public philanthropy. One politician and judge with a net worth of $435,000 and a nonfarm income of $70,000 a year received $266,000 in such low-interest "emergency" loans.

After "60 Minutes" exposed a $17 million emergency loan to a California agrifactory, an embarrassed Congress imposed a $400,000 limit on the program. Though this was an improvement, the still-generous limit enables the larger farms to eat up the bulk of FmHA's loan resources.

Showing nicely its concept of the "truly needy," the Reagan administration tried to abolish completely the limited-resource loan program that was targeted to the smaller farmers the agency was established to help in the first place. Congress wouldn't let it, so the Reaganites discovered the value of bureaucracy and gave it the redtape treatment. Nationwide, the FmHA in 1982 managed to lend only about half the money Congress had approved for these loans—this during the worst year for farmers in half a century.

In fairness, the administration has also stopped making economic-emergency loans. But that misses the point. Those loans should be made, but only to family farmers who need them. The FMHA's recent crackdown on delinquent borrowers, moreover, has fallen most heavily upon the smaller farmers. It's cruel irony: having lavished so much money on the largest farmers, at least some of whom could have gotten credit elsewhere, the government now has too little left for smaller farmers who have nowhere else to turn. Not surprisingly, many are going under.

Meanwhile, the Reagan administration has introduced a Payment-In-Kind program that gives farmers government surplus commodities they in turn can sell, if they agree to take acreage out of production. PIK is thus a variation on traditional New Deal programs. But while the PIK program offers many beleaguered farmers some genuine help, it also embodies the same most-for-the-biggest approach.

AGRICULTURAL BLOAT

Of course, some will argue there's nothing wrong with a farm policy that encourages bigger and bigger farms. This will only make them more efficient, so the argument goes, and past gains in agricultural productivity will continue indefinitely as farms get bigger.

To such people, a concern for the family-size farm seems a mushy and misplaced Jeffersonian nostalgia. In fact, it is anything but. Family farming is practical economics. Anyone who's looked recently at our automobile and steel industries knows that economies of scale stop beyond a certain point. When Thomas Peters and Robert Waterman examined successful American businesses for their book *In Search of Excellence*, what were the qualities they found? Small work units. Lean staffs. A minimum of management bureaucracy. Managers who get their hands into what they manage. Enterprises that stick to their knitting instead of using their assets to flit from one business to another.

It sounds like a profile of the American family farm. It's also a description of what we *lose* when we allow factory-in-the-field agglomerations to gobble up individual family farmers.

There's growing evidence to suggest that in agriculture, as in other endeavors, the old "bigger is better" saying is a myth. A decade ago the Department of Agriculture was telling Congress the optimum size for a California vegetable farm was 400 acres, though 73 percent of the state's vegetables were already produced on farms much larger than that. A 1979 USDA study found that the average U.S. farm reaches 90 percent of maximum efficiency at just 314 acres; to attain 100 percent efficiency, the average size has to quadruple to 1,157 acres. Beyond that, farms don't get any better—they just get bigger. They may even become more bureaucratic and less efficient.

Consider, for example, the matter of debt. The very largest farms are twice as debt-prone as smaller family farms. This is of little consequence when times are flush. But when trouble hits, as it has with Mr. Volcker's interest-rate policies, it's like sending a fleet of large sailing ships heading into a gale with twice the sail they normally carry.

Just as a rope of many strands is more flexible and resilient than a single strand, a diverse agriculture of many relatively small units can adjust and change. Unlike the very largest operations, family farmers don't have so much capital tied up in what they did yesterday to keep them from doing what needs to be done tomorrow. Small farmers don't have to push paper through tedious chains of command. If they see a way of doing something better, they can do it right away. This kind of flexibility is important if sudden shifts in market conditions warrant different crops or production techniques.

There's also the question of rural communities. I grew up in Regent, North Dakota, a farming community of 400 people. Family farms were and are the economic bloodstream of that town. When such farms are eaten up by larger ones, towns like Regent wither, and the government finds itself with a tax-consuming social problem instead of a healthy and tax-providing community.

In short, there is a link between the *way* we have farmed—in traditional family-size units—and the extraordinary productivity of our agriculture as a whole. Yet our farm policies are pushing us towards a top-heavy agriculture that threatens to mimic the same problems we are facing in other areas of our economy. The high interest rates of the last two years have made the problem even worse: whether family farmers go bankrupt or simply decide to sell out, the trend toward concentration is hastened.

Even worse, this trend feeds on itself. The alteration of the FmHA is instructive. Having helped create large farms, the government felt compelled to keep them from failing. When a small family farmer bites the dust there may be a few condolences but nobody worries much. When a multi-thousand-acre agrifactory totters, its bankers and creditors get the jitters over the millions of dollars at stake. It's a prairie twist on the maxim familiar to international bankers: "Make a small loan and you create a debtor. Make a big loan and you create a partner."

Are we encouraging farms so big that we can't afford to let them fail? I fear we are and I think it's an ominous prescription for slowly but inevitably undermining the very things that have made agriculture one of the few American industries still competitive in international markets. Despite high interest rates, agriculture still contributed more than $40 billion in export sales last year, helping defray the costs of our unhappy dependence on imported oil and automobiles.

HELP FOR THE FAMILY FARMER

What does all this mean for our farm policies? Mr. Paarlburg recommends that we eliminate the current "tilt in favor of big farms" in our federal programs, and at least keep the playing field level. I agree with that, but would go a step further. For the reasons I've discussed, I think we should retarget the current programs toward family-size unites. For example, we should put a cap on the commodity price-support loans to eliminate the exorbitant amounts going to the very largest farmers, thus freeing up more for those who need it more. In 1981, for example, I proposed capping these loans at $150,000, which would have affected less than ten percent of all farmers but would have enabled us to increase the support price by about 35 cents per bushel for the rest. (This new level, incidentally, would have still been below production costs.) Farmers could become as large as they wanted—the federal government just wouldn't pay them for doing so.

We should alter the FMHA loan program in similar fashion, restoring this agency to its original purpose of providing economic opportunity to beginning and smaller farmers. In the present crisis, the money saved should be used to extend loan deferrals to family farmers who have fallen behind on their FmHA loans because of economic circumstances beyond their control. At the same time, we should alter other federal policies, such as tax laws that invite lawyers and doctors to invest in farms as tax shelters, driving up land prices to the detriment of the beginning farmer.

Of course, it would not be fair to pull the plug suddenly on these larger farm operations. Many are essentially family farmers who overextended themselves during the 1970s, with a good deal of encouragement (including subsidized loans) from the government. Some of these farms may need emergency loans;

the question is the direction in which our farm program goes from here.

These are the broad outlines of a farm program that I think would dispense agricultural benefits more fairly while promoting the right kind of agriculture. But the high interest rates of the last two years should serve as a stark reminder that the best farm program in the world will not do a great deal when a Federal Reserve Board accountable to no one can unleash an interest-rate tornado that levels the economic landscape. The best thing the government can do for the nation's farmer is not to subsidize him, but to promote the kind of monetary policies that make credit available at a fair price. . . .

More than a century ago, President Abraham Lincoln warned us that "the money power of this country will endeavor to prolong its reign until all wealth is aggregated in a few hands and the Republic is destroyed." While its policies have moderated somewhat in recent months, the board has taken us in precisely this direction. Money and credit should serve production, not the other way around. Regaining control over them is of utmost importance not only to the family farmer, but to all independent businessmen as well—not to mention the rest of us.

NO

Stephen Chapman

THE FARMER ON THE DOLE

The family farmer is a durable feature of American folklore. From its beginning America was regarded by Europeans as a pastoral Eden, shielded from the corrosive influences of city and commerce. American soil was cultivated, not by serfs and peasants as in the Old World, but by self-supporting landowners, thought to be the soul of a healthy democracy. In 1797 the *Encyclopaedia Britannica* stated that "in no part of the world are the people happier . . . or more independent than the farmers of New England." Thomas Jefferson frequently cited the blessings of America's agricultural character. "Those who labour in the earth are the chosen people of God, if ever he had a chosen people, whose breasts he has made his peculiar deposit for substantial and genuine virtue," he wrote in *Notes on the State of Virginia*. "Corruption of morals in the mass of cultivators is a phaenomenon of which no age nor nation has furnished an example."

This vision of a nation of small farmers has always been largely mythical. Jefferson urged his fellow Americans, "Let us never wish to see our citizens occupied at a workbench, or twirling a distaff," lost in the "mobs of great cities." When he wrote those lines, one in three of his countrymen already lived away from the farm. Many of the rest were on slaveholding farms and plantations in the South, not exactly compatible with Jefferson's ideal.

Today, only 2.8 percent of the American population lives on farms, and fewer than half of these citizens depend on farming as their principal source of income. If independent family farmers are indeed the bedrock of the republic, that foundation has long since been eroded. But the idealization of the family farm persists, along with the impulse to preserve it at whatever cost. These sentiments know none of the usual ideological or partisan boundaries.

Democrat Jim Hightower, a self-styled populist . . . quotes approvingly this characteristically apocalyptic complaint from the National Farmers Organization: "The farmhouse lights are going out all over America. And every time a light goes out, this country is losing something. It is losing the

From *Harper's* magazine, October 1982. Copyright © 1982 by *Harper's*. All rights reserved. Reprinted from the October 1982 issue by special permission.

precious skills of a family farm system. And it is losing free men." Over on the other side of the political spectrum, conservative senator Robert Dole strikes a similar pose. "Family farms represent the very essence of what this country is about," he says. "They are the backbone of America." Like Hightower, Dole is worried about the decline of the family farm. "The farms are getting fewer, and the time has come for Congress to act," he argues.

Such emotionally charged pleas tend to strike a responsive chord in Congress, which, in fact, has been acting to protect the family farm for half a century. The array of programs ostensibly designed to preserve the nation's stock of sturdy yeomen has made agriculture the most heavily subsidized sector of our economy. The expense of these programs has grown even as the importance of farms in the economy has inexorably declined— from nearly a tenth of the nation's income in 1933, when most of the existing farm programs were initiated, to 2.6 percent in 1980. Last year the government spent over $11 billion on various forms of farm assistance—virtually all of them justified by pitchforkfuls of "save the family farm" rhetoric.

Even critics of the government's farm policies usually accept the goal of family-farm preservation, tending only to question whether the programs really help the beleaguered family farmer rather than his larger corporate competitors, or arguing simply that the expense has become excessive in a tight-budget era. These concerns are well founded, but they ignore the more basic question: why, exactly, does the tiny fraction of our population that chooses to practice family farming deserve all this solicitude in the first place?

So potent is the traditional image of the family farmer, and so unacquainted are most Americans with the real thing, that his actual characteristics are often ignored. For one thing, farm families are not worse off than their fellow citizens. Fifty years ago, the per capita income of farm dwellers was only 33 percent of the figure for nonfarmers; but since 1971 the recorded income of farm dwellers has amounted to 97 percent of that for nonfarmers, with the average farm family taking home $23,822 in 1980.

But the official figures undoubtedly underestimate the financial health of family farmers, given their ability, as self-employers, to underestimate their income when reporting it to the authorities (not to mention the favorable tax treatment those authorities accord what income farmers do report). Also, statistics on farm income typically include the nearly two million farmers—often retirees or disenchanted urbanites—who farm more as a hobby than anything else. The average income of commercial farmers (those who actually do it for a living) is an impressive $34,000. And the typical farmer (even counting the hobbyists) has even greater wealth than income, largely because he owns, on average, 400 acres of land. That and other assets bring his family's net worth to about $300,000, approximately twice the average for other American households.

In short, today's family farmer is typically not a desperate homesteader, but a sophisticated, relatively prosperous businessman. His success—which is simply the success of American agriculture— should not be resented, but it hardly makes him an obvious candidate for massive government assistance.

Why do we hear so much, then, about the family farmer's decline? The most striking illustration of his plight, supposedly, is the continuing decrease in the number of farms and farmers. At the turn of the century, thirty million Americans lived on 5.7 million farms. By 1979, only 6.2 million people lived on 2.3 million farms. Projecting this trend far enough, it is easy to predict that soon there will be no farmers and no farms. This makes as much sense as assuming that because American fertility rates have declined steadily since the nation was founded, eventually no one will reproduce at all.

The decline of the farming sector is both perfectly natural and wholly beneficial. It reflects two welcome phenomena: the increasing productivity of American farms and the rising living standards of all Americans. Seventy years ago, 106 man-hours of labor and seven acres of land were needed to produce 100 bushels of wheat; today it takes only nine man-hours and three acres. Technological improvements in machinery, fertilizer, pesticides, and seed have made the difference. Hence fewer farmers cultivating roughly the same amount of land as in 1910 can feed a much larger number of people.

Then there is the effect of the growing affluence of the nation as a whole. In a modern economy, the demand for food grows only about as fast as the population—a reflection of the fact that nearly everyone is adequately fed. The demand for other goods and services grows much faster, meaning that more and more people have to work to provide everything from television sets to medical care, while fewer and fewer have to grow food. It says something about the usual picture of farmers being driven off the land by factors beyond their control that the migration accelerates during times of prosperity, not during slumps. (During the Great Depression, the direction of the migration was actually reversed.) A shrinking agricultural population, far from being a sign of decay, is almost invariably a by-product of material progress. The only economies in which farming is stable are the poorest and most primitive, where most people farm because otherwise they wouldn't eat.

By itself, the, the decline in the number of farms, or farmers, is no reason to worry. Some alarmists, however, blame it on the rise of big corporate farms—agribusiness, as the phenomenon is ominously labeled. Trued, farms have gotten bigger, as has nearly every other type of economic enterprise. They have done so in order to take advantage of the economies of scale offered by modern production techniques. Even so, the average farm has increased only 16 percent in size since 1969. There are still 2.4 million farms. In fact, only 8 percent of all U.S. farmland is farmed by corporations, set up mainly to avoid taxes. When you count only nonfamily corporations, the figure dips to one percent. So much for the fear that agriculture is being concentrated in a few corporate hands.

The number of federal programs directed at saving American farmers from extinction will come as a surprise to anyone familiar with the myth of the independent yeoman. Most farmers have their prices guaranteed by the federal price support program, which applies to wheat, corn, barley, oats, rye, sorghum, sugar, peanuts, soybeans, wool, rice, cotton, tobacco, and dairy products—just about everything, in fact. If the market price falls below the level set by the government, the Department of Agriculture in effect buys the farmers' crop. For many crops, it also provides an additional subsidy—"deficiency payments," which pay the farmer the difference between the market (or support) price and a higher "target price." This year, (1982) the support price for wheat is $3.55 a bushel. The target price is $4.05 a bushel. If the market price were $3.30 a bushel, the farmer could sell his crop to the government for $3.55, and then collect an additional fifty cents for each bushel. Most price subsidy programs also require farmers to "set aside" (that is, not plant) part of their land, in an attempt to hold prices up by restricting production.*

It is widely but mistakenly assumed that Washington has gotten tough with farmers since Ronald Reagan took office. Last year Congress *increased* the support price for nearly every farm commodity covered by USDA programs, and provided for additional increases in subsequent years. The wheat price rose from $3.20 to $3.55 a bushel, corn from $2.40 to $2.55, peanuts from $455 to $550 a ton. Congress also enacted a new system of price supports for sugar, supplementing the existing protectionist tariffs on sugar imports. Reagan did propose abolishing "deficiency payments," but these too were kept, and most of the "target prices" were raised. Even the price support program for tobacco—the least defensible subsidy of all—was left alone.

*President Reagan's version of a "set aside" program is the PIK program introduced in 1983. PIK refers to Payment in Kind. This price support program offers farmers surplus agricultural products which are currently in storage. Farmers are given these surplus stocks if they agree to withhold land from production. It is anticipated that this program will have a double barreled impact on farm prices: surplus or past supplies are reduced and future supplies are reduced. This should result in a rapid increase in the price of agricultural products and of course an increase in the prices paid by consumers.—eds.

The 1982 budget, the vehicle for so many well-publicized Reaganesque spending cuts, actually raised the Agriculture Department's spending by 45 percent. Reagan's 1983 budget would reduce it by almost that much, but less because of newfound austerity than because his advisers expect higher market prices to reduce the direct cost of various commodity programs. That expectation will almost certainly be proved wrong. And Congress is likely to overrule the administration and provide extra dollars to farmers, who, like everyone else, are suffering the effects of the recession.

Aside from the basic programs designed to guarantee farmers comfortably high prices, the government performs dozens of smaller special favors. The USDA offers numerous loans to farmers—operating loans to buy seed, fertilizer, and machinery; real-estate loans to finance purchases of land; homeownership loans to help low- and moderate-income farmers buy houses; loans to help farmers recover from natural disasters, like droughts; loans to finance soil and water conservation projects; even loans to rural communities to pay for sewers. Most of these loans are made at subsidized interest rates. Farmers can also get direct payments (in addition to low-interest loans) to help them cope with disasters. They can buy crop insurance from the government, again at prices subsidized by the taxpayer. The Rural Electrification Administration, a relic of the Great Depression, still runs a $5 billion subsidized loan program. Farmers in most of the West get water from federal water projects at absurdly low rates. So the government spends billions making arid land fertile and then pays farmers to leave it idle.

Finally, the tax codes have often provided particularly rich soil for cultivating farmers. To avoid imposing administrative burdens on farmers, the tax law permits them to use the cash method of accounting. This allows the quick deduction of capital expenses, while much farm income—from the sale of cattle, for example—gets taxed as a long-term capital gain, at 40 percent of the normal rates. True, farmers once had to worry that the very land that made them wealthy might also subject them to high federal estate taxes when the property passed to the next generation—but their representatives in Washington have helped assuage these fears. Congress has decreed that the value of farmland, for estate tax purposes, may be computed according to a special "use value" formula, rather than by its ordinary market value. This formula cuts the value of a farm estate by more than half, on average. The law also lets farm heirs postpone payment of this reduced tax for up to five years, and then pay in ten installments, on which interest accrues at the luxurious rate of 4 percent.

The purpose of these provisions was to prevent family farmers from having to sell their land to pay taxes. But in 1980 Congress (spurred by farm-belt senators) repealed provisions in the income tax law that would have taxed farmers who *do* sell their inherited land on the full increase in its value since its purchase. (Now they need only pay taxes on any increase in value since the land was inherited.) Finally, in 1981—under pressure from farmers who persisted in complaining about their onerous tax burdens—Congress virtually eliminated the estate tax by creating a flat $600,000 exemption (effective in 1985).

This welter of subsidies and privileges constitutes not a safety net for farmers but a cocoon. Unfortunately, like recipients of most federal benefits (Social Security beneficiaries, veterans, students with guaranteed loans), farmers have come to regard them as something they're entitled to. When commodity prices fall below prosperous levels, farmers pour into Washington to demand action; in 1979 one militant group, the American Agricultural Movement, set fire to a tractor in front of the Agriculture Department in protest. AAM also organized an unsuccessful "farm strike" in 1978 in an effort to extract higher prices for their crops. The reaction to the recession of 1981–82 has been equally predictable, as farm defenders in Congress have introduced a "farm crisis" bill that would increase crop subsidies still further, while restricting production in order to force prices up.

Ironically, the most serious threat to the family farm may come from the measures designed to preserve it. For example, tax treatment of farms has become so favorable that high-bracket nonfarm taxpayers—doctors, dentists, lawyers, and the like—now purchase farmland as a tax shelter. Farmers who own their own acreage are tempted to sell it to such absentee landlords—hardly grounds for pitying the farmers who cash in, but still a threat to the owner-operated farm as an institution. Equally important, the absentee tax shelters frequently bid up the price of land so high that aspiring young farmers are unable to acquire it.

. . . [T]he bigger and wealthier the farmer, and the more distant from the traditional image of the family farmer, the more help he gets from the government. Thirty percent of all government payments go to the 11 percent of farmers with the largest farms, measured in annual sales. This is an especially well-off bunch, with an average household income of nearly $46,894 in 1980 (a bad year, by the way), more than double the median family income in the U.S.

The incentives built into these price support programs aggravate the very problem they are supposed to alleviate. Market prices are lower than farmers would like, mainly because of chronic overproduction. Low prices inform farmers that they are producing too much of a given commodity and encourage them to stop. The artificially high prices established by the Agriculture Department send exactly the opposite signal, stimulating farmers to do more of what got them into trouble in the first place. The government tries to address this contradiction by limiting the amount of land each farmer can plant with a particular crop.* But land is only one factor in the production equation. Each individual farmer can circumvent the acreage restrictions by cultivating the remaining acres more intensively. So when the government reduces the allowable cultivated land by 20 percent, it can normally expect to reduce total output by only half that much. Of course, the techniques of intensive cultivation that this system rewards—primarily the use of more machinery, water, pesticides, and fertilizer—are the very techniques in which larger farms are likely to enjoy an advantage over smaller farms.

Who pays to achieve these questionable goals? Price supports, the centerpiece of the farm programs, exact costs in two ways. Taxpayers have to bear the expense of whatever farm produce the Agriculture Department has to purchase when prices fall below the price support level. (In the last fiscal year, these purchases, along with "deficiency pay-

*This is expressly the intent of PIK—eds.

ments," cost more than $7 billion.) But that isn't the end of it. The whole point of the program is to "support" market prices—to keep them artificially high—so as to minimize or even eliminate direct government expenses. So consumers pay higher prices in the grocery store for everything from bread to milk to peanut butter. Unfortunately, not all consumers suffer equally. The higher prices act as a regressive tax—placing the heaviest burden on the poor and the lightest on the rich. This is because the lower your income, the greater the share of it you have to spend on necessities like food. It is not an exaggeration to say that, under the price support system, slum children in Harlem go without milk so that dairy farmers in Wisconsin may prosper.

Even if family farms were in danger of extinction, and even if federal farm programs served to preserve them, why should we? We don't try to preserve the family grocery store, the family pharmacy, or the family clothing store, and for good reason. In many industries and businesses, bigger has turned out to be better—better in the sense of providing more and better goods and services at a lower cost to consumers. In a relatively free market, large firms will drive out small ones only when their size allows greater efficiency. Such increases in efficiency are desirable because they raise living standards. If family farms were too inefficient to compete with huge corporate farms (which all evidence suggests they aren't), they would soon disappear in the absence of special aid. That might be unpleasant for family farmers. But it would increase the country's productivity, which tends to make everyone better off.

The usual rationale for aid to family farmers is that it preserves a cherished

American tradition of self-sufficiency—a supposed contrast to the gray conformity of life in the corporate sector. But the farm programs preserve the tradition's form without its content. Whatever the hardship and rigors of rural life, farmers are no longer rugged individualists, responsible to no one but themselves. They have become welfare addicts, protected and assisted at every turn by a network of programs paid for by their fellow citizens. In exchange, most farmers allow Washington to dictate much of what they do. They have abandoned independence for security. Today's family farms are to Jefferson's vision what government consultants are to Horatio Alger. If Americans still believe in the virtue of hardy rural self-reliance, they should tell Washington to get out of the way and let farmers practice it.

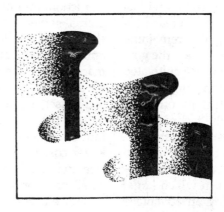

POSTSCRIPT

Should We Try to Save the Family Farm?

Although the dollar costs of federal farm programs have reached an all-time record, Congressman Dorgan is concerned that too many of these dollars are being diverted from the family farm and ending up in the pockets of large corporate interests. He maintains that if this pattern persists, farms may become too much like our nation's automakers or steelmakers: they may become "too big, too inflexible, and too inefficient to compete" in the world marketplace. Thus, Dorgan argues that to keep our competitive advantage in agriculture, we must preserve the institution that has given us the competitive advantage; we must nurture and protect our family farmers.

Chapman responds that the "decline in the number of farms, or farmers, is no reason for worry," maintaining this is a natural course of events. He argues that farmers and other economic enterprises have gotten bigger so that they can take advantage of "the economies of scale offered by modern production techniques." He goes on to assert that "even if family farms were in danger of extinction"—a proposition he soundly rejects—"why should we try to preserve them?" He contends that in an economy that is driven by markets, inefficient farms, whether they are small family farms or large corporate farms, will be driven from the marketplace. According to Chapman, "that might be unpleasant" for those who go broke, but it "tends to make everybody better off."

Whether you believe the growing presence of corporate agribusiness is a sign of economic growth and vitality or whether you see this as a sign of future economic problems depends upon how you view the presence of imperfectly competitive firms in the marketplace.

The library is filled with books and articles that discuss United States farm policy. Partly, this large amount of literature reflects the importance that we, as a society, have placed upon the values embodied in a rural life style. But, in part, the attention we have paid to agriculture reflects the importance that this sector has played and continues to play in our general economy. For an introduction into agricultural economics and United States agriculture policy, see the following three essays that appeared in the *Monthly Review*, which is published by the Federal Reserve Bank of Kansas City: C.E. Harshbarger and R.D. Rees, "The New Farm Program—What Does It Mean" (January 1974); M.R. Duncan, B.W. Bickel, and E.H. Miller, Jr., "International Trade and American Agriculture" (March 1976); and M.R. Duncan and C.E. Harshbarger, "A Primer on Agricultural Policy" (September/October 1977). Two additional articles addressing the unique problems of agriculture in the early 1980s are: Mary Strange, "Feeding the Farm Credit Crisis," *Food Monitor* (January/February 1983) and Harold F. Breimyer, "Agriculture: Return of the Thirties?" *Challenge* (July/August 1982).

ISSUE 3

Should We Deregulate the Blood Banking Industry?

YES: Ross D. Eckert, from "Aids and the Blood Bankers," *Regulation* (September–October 1986)

NO: Joseph R. Bove, M.D., "Directed Donations," *Legal Issues in Transfusion Medicine (American Association of Blood Banks 1986)*

ISSUE SUMMARY

YES: Economist Eckert maintains that the problem with the blood banking industry is that "increased regulation" has led to "a basically noncompetitive environment" that is "inferior to a competitively organized blood market."

NO: Physician and Professor of Laboratory Medicine Bove argues that "directed donor programs" might "jeopardize the national blood supply" and in the process establish a system where "people who have a higher intelligence, who are better connected in society, who have more friends and relatives and contacts" are more likely to get "better blood" than those who are less fortunate.

Slowly, but ever so surely, America is coming to learn of the menace of Acquired Immune Deficiency Syndrome (AIDS). No longer can we ignore the fact that more than 22,000 Americans have succumbed to this horrid disease. No longer can we ignore the fact that 17,000 others have been diagnosed with AIDS; 300,000 are living with AIDS-Related Complex (ARC)—the precondition for the disease; and probably more than one million people in America have, in one way or another, been exposed to the deadly AIDS virus. No longer can we say: "This is not my problem because I am not homosexual or bisexual, and I am not a drug abuser."

The fact of the matter is that if the nation's blood supply is contaminated, we all run the risk of contracting AIDS. For none of us know when we, or a loved one, might be in need of that precious fluid that sustains life. And since none of us know whether or not we will be one of the 3.5 million Americans who are likely to be transfused this year, none of us knows whether or not we will be forced to lie awake at night worrying about the quality of the blood we were given.

But need we worry if we, or a loved one, have received blood from our national blood system? The answer to that question is not immediately obvious, and it is at the heart of Issue 3. In order to understand this debate, a brief history of our blood bank system is useful.

The ability to collect, store, and deliver blood to a recipient has only been possible in this century. Previously, blood had to be transfused directly from one individual to another. By World War I, with the introduction of chemicals to prevent clotting and the availability of refrigeration, blood could be stored for as long as two weeks. Modern day techniques have extended the shelf life of blood to 42 days and, if properly frozen, the Federal Drug Administration (the federal agency responsible for insuring a safe blood supply) allows it to be stored for up to three years.

The delivery system for blood took on its modern day characteristics during World War II. The American Red Cross responded to the military's need for blood by opening 35 regional blood donation centers. At the end of the war years, the Red Cross found that they were not the only agency interested in serving the blood needs of the military and civilian medical community. Hospitals and community centers began to collect blood. Indeed, more that 2,400 of these centers are now under the umbrella of either the American Association of Blood Banks (AABB) or the Council of Community Blood Centers (CCBC). These centers and hospital blood banks collect about 50 percent of the 12 million one-pint units that are annually donated. The remaining 50 percent is collected by the American Red Cross, whose blood bank system has grown to 57 regional centers.

The majority of the blood collected passes through not-for-profit organizations and is generally donated. This latter characteristic is a rather new development. In the 1960s about one-third of the total blood supply was purchased from donors. This practice of purchasing blood fell out of favor. By 1971 purchased blood was down to 11 percent and currently it represents only 2 percent of the total supply. Even "directed donations"—where a unit of blood is earmarked for a particular individual or group—increasingly fell from favor until the recent concern over AIDS.

Twenty-five years ago blood that was purchased in the marketplace was viewed with wary concern. Today many now plead for a system where blood is bought and sold. We should not be confused by this apparent inconsistency. Those who rejected the notion of paying cash for blood in the 1960s and 1970s had every right to this position. Blood banks that offered to pay for their deposits attracted the poor and the sick and provided them with a cash incentive to lie about their health. The effects of this market-driven system was obvious to anyone who cared to examine the evidence: the U.S. system of two-thirds volunteer, one-third commercial blood caused four times as many cases of hepatitis than the British system which was fully voluntary.

The question now is whether or not a modified market system for blood will better protect us from AIDS than the "potluck blood" that is available through our volunteer donor system. Economist Eckert reminds us that "it took AIDS . . . spread by noncash blood . . . for some to reconsider the conventional wisdom." Dr. Bove rejects this notion. He argues that "the extremely low incidence of AIDS from transfusion . . . makes it doubtful that any program of directed donations can lower the overall incidence significantly." Should we let the market work its magic or should we depend upon a voluntary system that is driven by altruistic motives?

YES

Ross D. Eckert

AIDS AND THE BLOOD BANKERS

Since December 1982, when it became clear that Acquired Immune Deficiency Syndrome (AIDS) could be transmitted by blood transfusion, the
blood bankers and their federal regulators have been unwaveringly optimistic that the spread of this lethal new disease by transfusion could be
controlled. In June of 1983, Edward Carr, the president of the American
Association of Blood Banks (AABB) said "there is little or no danger to the
general public." Then-Secretary of Health and Human Services Margaret
Heckler announced that "there should be no fear among the public that they
may develop AIDS through . . . blood transfusions."

Two-and-a-half years and over 250 cases of transfusion AIDS later, Secretary Heckler described a new blood test for the antibody to the AIDS virus
(HTLV-III) as "the answer to the prayers of thousands of Americans facing
surgery or otherwise requiring blood." The Centers for Disease Control
(CDC), after analyzing the initial results of the test's efficacy, proclaimed it
"just fantastic" and "a tremendous accomplishment," concluding that "people should not be concerned about accepting blood," and that "we have
pretty much solved the transfusion-associated AIDS cases." According to the
CDC, any new cases of transfusion AIDS would be those caused by infection
before the antibody test became available.

From the start, the public has been skeptical. Within months after AIDS
was linked to blood transfusions, patients began forming "blood clubs" and
recruiting personal donors. In September 1985, a few months after the CDC's
claims about the efficacy of the antibody test were publicized, a *Washington
Post-ABC News* poll found that 67 percent of those surveyed remained fearful
of getting AIDS via transfusion. In a January 1986 poll commissioned by the
AABB, only 21 percent to those surveyed said they would trust information
on the subject of AIDS from government officials and blood bankers.

Officials and blood bankers have tended to dismiss the public's concerns
as unwarranted hysteria. But public concern about blood safety has been
rational. AIDS is one of the few uniformly fatal diseases. It can incubate for
up to seven years and be communicated before an individual is aware of

From "AIDS and the Blood Bankers," by Ross D. Eckert, *Regulation*, September/October
1986. Copyright © 1986 American Enterprise Institute. Reprinted by permission.

having contracted it. And transfusion AIDS is growing both absolutely and relatively. While there was a total of 40 cases of transfusion AIDS documented prior to January 1984, there were 62 new cases reported in 1984 and 192 new cases reported in 1985. As of June 1986, transfusion AIDS cases totaled 396. This is a lower bound, however, as many blood recipients with documented exposure to the virus have not yet developed all the symptoms necessary to meet the CDC's definition, and some cases simply are not reported. Between 1984 and 1985, the ratio of reported AIDS cases attributable to transfusion to the total number of AIDS victims rose from 1 percent to almost 2 percent.

Transfusion AIDS is a potential risk for everyone. Over three million Americans receive blood transfusions each year, and 95 percent of the population will have been transfused by age 72. While the antibody test is a major advance, its true effectiveness is still uncertain. In a tragic turn of events, the CDC announced in June that two individuals had developed AIDS from blood deemed safe to use. The blood had been collected and tested so soon after the donor was infected by AIDS that the test failed to detect antibodies to the virus.

AIDS is a tiny fraction of all transfusion disease. Hepatitis is estimated to strike about 10 percent of all transfusion recipients—roughly 1,000 per day—of whom a few die of hepatitis and perhaps 100 eventually develop cirrhosis. But the urgent public concern over the spread of AIDS has focused new attention on the safety of our blood supply, attention that is well placed because our blood is not as safe as it should be. Current federal policy encourages local monopolies or cartels in the supply of blood and dis-

courages price competition in the blood banker's acquisition of blood. Blood banks in almost every state are exempt from strict tort liability for collecting and distributing contaminated blood. These policies leave the blood bankers with seriously inadequate safety incentives. FDA regulation is a potential substitute for market competition and private liability, but in practice it is dominated by the interests of the blood bankers themselves. The result is that rates of transfusion AIDS and hepatitis are unnecessarily high. A different public policy would bring them down at low cost.

THE EVOLUTION OF THE BLOOD CARTELS

Most blood banks in the United States operate as nonprofit monopolies or cartels. Some big-city hospitals collect a little blood from staff or families of patients, but they avoid soliciting donors openly in head-to-head competition with the blood bank in their region.

The American National Red Cross emerged from World War II with 35 regional centers where blood was collected for our armed forces. To sustain the size and enthusiasm of its volunteers during peacetime, the Red Cross began in 1948 to collect blood for civilian use. This effort had the support of the government, the American Medical Association, and public opinion.

At the time, hospitals collected blood in many communities. Blood was collected under the direction of hospital pathologists and distributed at prices based on fee-for-service, with charges levied for blood not replaced by patients. Hospitals were threatened by the Red Cross, which aimed to provide free of charge 100 percent of the blood supply of every community served. As stated in 1972, the Red Cross supports "a voluntary, nationwide, nonprofit blood service with uniform standards of operation—medical, technical, and administrative." In 1947, the AABB was formed by hospitals and other non-profit blood collectors to oppose the Red Cross in some areas and preempt it in others.

For 30 years the Red Cross and the AABB contested some local markets and were rivals for national influence, but neither could establish a single nationwide system. Despite these rivalries both groups were committed to nonprofit status and to the collection of blood from volunteers without cash payment. They opposed competition from commercial blood banks, which by 1971 bought about 9 percent of the nation's blood from cash donors. Their opposition was strengthened by studies during the 1960s linking cash blood to higher rates of post-transfusion hepatitis. The idea that derelicts and poor people who sold their blood to commercial blood banks might lie about their health to get a few dollars, but that volunteer donors would not, was accepted by many physicians and health officials. It is worth noting, however, that from the standpoint of the blood banks, a policy of volunteers-only amounts to setting a uniform maximum price—zero—on a key factor of production; this eliminates price competition in a manner analogous to setting a minimum price on the output of rival suppliers.

In 1973, the Department of Health, Education and Welfare (HEW) declared a National Blood Policy intended "to encourage, foster, and support efforts designed to bring into being an all-voluntary blood donor system and to eliminate commercialism in the acquisition of whole blood and blood components for transfusion purposes." In 1978, the FDA required separate labeling of cash and noncash blood, which put hospitals and physicians using cash blood at greater liability risk and hastened the conversion to noncash blood. In California, it became a misdemeanor to use cash blood unless the attending physician certified that compatible noncash blood was unavailable.

HEW also sought to encourage the development of noncompetitive regional blood banks committed to noncash blood. Believing this would reduce donor recruitment costs, it created the American Blood Commission (ABC) to cartelize regions where more than one nonprofit blood bank was entrenched. The ABC is a federation of blood banks, consumer and civic groups, and medical research charities, supported by member dues and federal and corporate grants. It promotes "regional associations" of local blood banks and hospitals to collaborate on donor solicitation and blood allocation. The ABC cannot restrict entry but tries to discourage it by mediating disputes over geographic markets (boundaries between regions become a problem if regions with many donors grow relative to regions with many patients) and similar issues. These efforts were assisted by HEW's implicit threat of direct federal action. By 1984 the ABC had "regionalized" almost half the nation's blood supply, and expected to cover three-quarters by 1992.

The National Blood Policy is not a law or regulation, only a statement of goals. Cash blood is not illegal, only officially stigmatized. The FDA has not used its licensing authority over blood banks to establish rigid barriers to entry or marketing orders, as other agencies have sometimes done. Nevertheless, the direction of federal policy has been clear and its effects have been pronounced. Competition has been discouraged and cash blood has all but disappeared. By the late 1970s almost all commercial firms had switched from supplying cash blood to hospitals for direct transfusion to buying plasma for manufacture into various products for clinical or laboratory use. The cash plasma and blood products market remains exempt from the provisions of the National Blood Policy that stigmatize cash blood, and commercial firms dominate this market.

Until recently, hospitals that wanted better blood than that supplied by their regional blood banks have had few alternatives. Either they recruited and screened donors themselves or bought it from outside sources—which risked incurring the displeasure of their regional blood monopolies or cartels, and could be considered only by large hospitals in "weak" regions. In addition, the idea that cash blood is of lower quality became entrenched among physicians and nonprofit blood bankers even though hepatitis from noncash blood remained high. It took AIDS, a far worse disease spread by noncash blood from the established nonprofit blood banks, for some to reconsider the conventional wisdom.

THE INCENTIVES
OF BLOOD BANKERS

Blood is not free. The nonprofit blood banks collect blood from volunteer donors without cash compensation, but they generally sell blood to hospitals and blood products to commercial manufacturers for a price. Hospitals pay "cost recovery fees" to cover donor recruitment, testing and preparation, and storage and delivery, which are in turn shifted to patients. Fees vary markedly among blood banks due to differences in costs, cost-allocation rules, and demand. Manufacturers pay for blood plasma either directly from cash donors or from blood banks as a by-product of noncash donations. This plasma is used to manufacture coagulants, albumin, gamma globulin, and many other products. The Red Cross contracts with a blood bank and several manufacturers to produce pooled products from donated plasma, which are sold at the market price and carry the Red Cross label.

Having foresworn paying for blood, the blood bankers must beg for it, which is a difficult way to do business. Many donors respond to altruistic appeals, but not as many as the bankers would like. Under a regime such as this, blood bankers naturally want to reject as few donors as possible.

Blood banks are staffed with laboratory technologists, donor-center personnel, and physicians to handle the expected volume of donations. Donations decline during summer vacations and at Christmas, but a permanent drop in inventories is a blood banker's greatest fear. A marked and prolonged drop in donations or the amount fit for transfusion would raise the prospects of staff layoffs, smaller organizations, and blood shortages. Such a development could lead hospitals to shop for new suppliers or form blood banks themselves. Evidently, the fewer donors disqualified, and the fewer units of blood that do not meet testing standards, the less likely it is that this fear will come true.

For most goods and services, consumers can switch producers to indicate dissatisfaction with price or quality. But patients who want to shop for blood that is safer than what their regional monopoly or cartel provides potluck may have to switch regions as well as physicians or hospitals. This is out of the question for emergencies and too costly for many illnesses. The incentive for blood bankers to offer the quality consumers want is thus weak.

Another reason blood bankers' safety incentives are weak is that they are exempt in almost every state from strict liability in tort for transfusion diseases. In those states, blood banks are liable for death or disease caused by transfusion only if plaintiffs can prove they were negligent—blood transfusion is exempt from strict liability (where only causation need be proved) by statute or common law, usually by declaring that blood is a "service" rather than a "product." Because courts usually determine negligence by asking if a defendant's practices conformed to the "custom of the trade," blood banks and manufacturers of blood products can usually escape liability by showing that they conformed to FDA licensing regulations and followed the prevailing blood testing and donor screening half-measures which are described below.

Most exemptions date to the 1960s before the first blood test for hepatitis was discovered. They were justified on the grounds that blood banks (nonprofit and for-profit) should not be liable for transmitting a germ that could not be detected. This justification, doubtful in the 1960s, is thoroughly obsolete today. It lives on, and has even been extended to cover transfusion AIDS, due to political pressures from the blood bankers and the misapprehension by judges and legislators that exemption is necessary to maintain an adequate supply of blood.

The blood banks do take precautions, some of them quite elaborate, to prevent transfusion injuries that are immediately lethal and hence inexpensively traceable. For example, one horrible transfusion outcome, rarer than AIDS or hepatitis, is an acute hemolytic reaction—death by transfusing blood that is not compatible with the patient's blood. Death is rapid and the cause is clear; careful and costly procedures are standard. But in the case of transfusion injuries that are delayed and therefore less certain, the blood banks do not take many of the precautions they would take in a competitive market under appropriate liability standards, and which the FDA could require them to take.

FDA TRANSFUSION STANDARDS

The FDA sets minimum standards for screening potential donors for risk of AIDS and for testing blood for contamination. For advice on how to set these standards, the FDA generally relies on the blood bankers. As a result, when trade-offs must be made between the health interests of blood consumers and the convenience and privacy interests of blood donors, the latter often prevail. . . .

. . . [T]he three blood-collecting organizations argued that tighter screening was unjustified because "the cause of AIDS is unknown and . . . evidence for its transmission by blood is inconclusive" and "still unproven." The FDA was more candid in explaining that it set weaker standards for noncash donors at nonprofit blood banks than for cash donors at for-profit plasma banks and that the standards "were carefully developed with the major organizations responsible for blood supply and . . . [were] intended to limit the adverse impact on blood availability."

Introduction of the AIDS antibody blood test in the spring of 1985 provided evidence that some donors either had not understood from reading the self-screening pamphlet that they belonged in one of the high-risk groups or did not appreciate the importance of belonging to one of these groups. In one study, the Red Cross reported that out of a small group of 41 "regular blood donors" who were found to have positive antibody tests, 36 were homosexual or bisexual males, female sexual partners of drug abusers, persons heterosexually active with prostitutes in Africa and recipients of transfusions in the previous six to 30 months.

These findings led the CDC to acknowledge that "there are people who have been donating blood and who have not considered themselves at risk for AIDS and who were a potential source of transmitting this disease." Accordingly, in September 1985, the FDA extended its definition of high-risk donors to include "any male who has had sex with another male" even once—a decision which would have been timely about 32 months earlier. Such a time lag has tragic consequences. The giant blood bank serving the New York metropolitan area announced in July that it was trying to identify 700 people who might have been infected by the AIDS virus before the antibody test was implemented. These were people who received blood between 1977 and 1985 from donors who were not screened out by prevailing measures but have since tested positive to the antibody test.

If undetected, screening lapses have the capacity to infect many persons. Most patients are transfused not with whole blood but with one of several extracted components. Any particular donor pint may be used, therefore, to treat several patients. The plasma components, which are pooled from several thousand donors, make batch products used to transfuse many people.

The new blood test is a big step forward but no substitute for vigorous donor screening. The test detects antibodies to the HTLV-III virus, not the virus itself. Because the antibody response takes time (as many as six months in some individuals) a person infected by HTLV-III can donate blood before enough antibodies develop for the test to register positive—as illustrated by the two individuals the CDC recently announced had contracted AIDS from infectious blood that had not registered positive on the antibody test.

A study published in *Lancet* in December 1984, coauthored by the American discoverers of HTLV-III, found that in a group of 96 healthy, symptom-free, high-risk individuals, four had the virus but no antibody. If the antibody test now used in blood banks misses four infective persons for each one hundred it finds, I estimate with conservative assumptions that 80 new AIDS cases could occur each year. This estimate is uncertain because: the true efficacy of the antibody test remains uncertain; people exposed to AIDS are developing the disease at an uncertain rate; and AIDS is spreading in the heterosexual population (including many individuals who would not be identified as high risks by donor screening) at an uncertain rate.

Clearly the AIDS antibody test has not "pretty much solved" the AIDS transfusion problems the CDC initially concluded. The American Red Cross, in an unusual and little noticed departure from its practice of coordination with the other major blood-banking organizations, recently voiced concern about the antibody test. Testifying before a Senate appropriations subcommittee on September 26, 1985, a vice president of the Red Cross stated that measuring an antibody response "has both theoretical and practical defects" and that we need tests that directly identify infective blood. He is right, but what can be done in the meantime? The important questions are whether superior, cost-effective screening and testing procedures are currently available and, if so, whether the blood bankers can be induced to use them.

WHAT CAN BE DONE?

Four urgently needed measures would enhance the quality of the blood supply at relatively low cost. They could be introduced either by increased direct safety regulation by the FDA, or by less regulation and a change in the market and legal environments in which the blood banks operate. I will first describe what the FDA could and should do immediately, then explain why I believe nonregulatory changes would accomplish the same results.

•**Donor Registries.** Presently, blood banks attempt to maximize the number of donors through media solicitations and by mobile donor centers sent to businesses and shopping malls. The average donor gives only about 1.5 times a year; in a normal year about 8 million Americans donate 12 million pints of blood. Blood banks try to solicit repeat donors by telephone, but this is usually insufficient. In some urban areas 25 percent of the pool consists of first-time donors. Such pools are too large, recruited too randomly, and turn over too quickly to contain the spread of disease.

Safer blood requires more frequent donations from low-risk persons, even if this means fewer donors. To achieve this end, the FDA should require all licensed blood banks to maintain registries of permissible donors including only individuals who: (1) are known to be in good health; (2) have not been transfused since at least 1977; (3) agree to an extensive and confidential medical history, including questions not currently asked about venereal diseases and multiple sex partners; and (4) agree to have their blood tested not only for syphilis, which is now routine, but also for surrogate markers which indicate possible exposure to infections transmissible by blood.

Registries may cost more than random solicitation, but they have been successful at reducing disease. In the 1970s, registries of cash and noncash donors at the Mayo Clinic in Rochester, Minn., had rates of hepatitis B virus markers well below those of the nonprofit blood bank in the same region. (The registries are still in use today, although Mayo now collects mainly noncash blood.) The position of the nonprofit blood banks, that registries can work in rural Minnesota but not in big cities, has never been put to the test. It is also inconsistent with the procedures commonly followed to prevent acute hemolytic reactions—maintaining a rare-donor registry of persons asked to donate only when called. If rare-donor registries are cost-effective, then standard registries, offering the prospect of avoiding far more transfusion infection and death, are likely to be cost-effective as well.

•**Cash Blood.** Getting enough low-risk, registered donors may require compensating donors for their time and expenses. Commercial blood banks once were popular. They kept bigger inventories, were open on weekends, and gave hospitals faster service than nonprofits. They were in downtown areas where the big hospitals and inexpensive donors were.

Unfortunately, paid blood still suffers undeservedly from the reputation it got in the 1960s. Critics alleged that skid row donors would lie about their health to get five dollars even if this put patients at risk. It is true that many cash donors were unhealthy, so the quality of much cash blood in this era was poor, and some of it was awful. But partly this was due to the concentration of blood banks in inner cities and partly it was due to the nature of hepatitis—many hepatitis carriers never have jaundice or other overt symptoms that would make them aware they have the disease (this was before the blood test was developed to screen for hepatitis).

What at first was not recognized, and later discounted, was that cash blood collected through registries like the Mayo Clinic's was superior to some noncash blood. A 1976 study of hepatitis rates among various groups of cash and non-cash donors by the General Accounting Office—the most through published study of its kind—showed that the key determinants of blood quality were the donors' characteristics and the blood bank's location, not whether blood was sold or donated. Closing off the supply of cash blood has not ended post-transfusion hepatitis, and transfusion AIDS has spread almost entirely by noncash blood.

I do not propose buying blood from those who are down-and-out or in poor health as in the 1960s. It should be bought selectively from healthy low-risk people who may not be altruists, whose employers do not pay wages while they donate, and whose time is relatively valuable. Cash could be used, among other things, to attract more women donors. AIDS overwhelmingly occurs among men. Hepatitis predominantly occurs among men. But only about a third of all donors are women. Some pathologists have acknowledged that women donors are now safer as a rule (the exception is nurses and hospital workers, who have a higher incidence of hepatitis exposure). Male donors outnumber females in part because women are often underweight or have inadequate blood iron. In addition, to minimize cost per donation, the blood bankers send mobile donor units mainly to employers where men predominate. They do not offer travel or child care services for women who work at home or consider taking less than full pints from women who can safely give smaller amounts.

An FDA requirement that blood banks adopt donor registries would oblige the nonprofits to consider the use of cash incentives. At the same time, the FDA should encourage more careful donor solicitation by repealing its labeling regulation and withdrawing its policy pronouncements against cash blood.

•**State-of-the-art Blood Testing.** Too little blood testing is undertaken at present, particularly for hepatitis. Post-transfusion hepatitis, which strikes many more people than AIDS, is caused by at least three viruses, of which only the marker for the hepatitis B virus has been identified and can be detected by blood tests. Hepatitis B is the most severe form, but accounts for only about 10 percent of all transfusion hepatitis cases. Non-A non-B hepatitis accounts for the rest.

Roughly half of hepatitis victims have either no symptoms or symptoms so mild that the disease can be identified only by a blood test. Many hepatitis victims also become "symptomless carriers" of the disease via transfusion or household contacts. Carriers of non-A, non-B hepatitis viruses are widespread in our society, although the full magnitude of the problem is unknown.

Although non-A, non-B hepatitis viruses cannot be detected in blood, surrogate tests to spot mild hepatitis in symptomless transfusion recipients can be used to identify blood donors who do not realize they have been infected. Papers published in 1981 in the *Journal of the American Medical Association* and the *New England Journal of Medicine* showed that one surrogate test (for abnormal liver enzymes) could eliminate between 29 percent and 40 percent of non-A, non-B hepatitis cases, and half of the worst cases. Another study published in *JAMA*, in 1984, showed that this test was cost-effective, considering the cost of replacing discarded blood, but ignoring lost wages. A National Institutes of Health study published in *Annals of Internal Medicine* in 1986 showed that a second surrogate test (for the hepatitis core antibody) would cut non-A, non-B disease by 43 percent, and that both tests were justified since each detected infection in different donor populations. Each study involved noncash blood almost exclusively. The FDA should require both tests of all nonprofit blood banks and for-profit plasma collectors. . . .

•**Designated Donations.** Many believe it has always been normal practice for blood banks to provide patients with designated blood donated by family and friends, but this is not so. Traditionally, all donations went into the regional inventory, from which potluck shipments were made to hospitals. Only recently have hospitals begun to permit patients to receive blood designated for their use by self-recruited donors. Most blood banks still refuse to permit designated donations, even if patients are willing to pay the cost.

The three major blood-collecting organizations claim there is no proof that designated donations are safer than potluck blood. This is true: The practice is still too recent and limited to provide conclusive evidence one way or the other. But it stands to reason that designated donors, because of their personal ties to patients, would provide an important degree of accurate self-screening on top of the current screening and testing procedures and the additional ones advocated here. And if patients are willing to pay the extra costs of customized blood, it is difficult to understand why it should not be provided.

The blood bankers also claim that donors who give for friends will donate less often for strangers, reducing inventories and leaving patients who cannot find donors out of luck. The evidence is against them here; hospitals allowing designations find that inventories grow because blood not used by the intended patients is available for strangers. The FDA should require blood banks to provide designations to patients willing to pay the costs.

MARKET COMPETITION WITH STRICT LIABILITY

The regime described above, involving increased regulation in a basically noncompetitive environment, is inferior to a competitively organized blood market operating under strict liability. The first step in achieving this end is for the federal government to revise its current policies that discourage competition. The FDA's labeling requirement for cash blood should be rescinded and the National Blood Policy should be revised to favor competition over cartelization. Public financing of the American Blood Commission should be withdrawn and careful scrutiny should be given to the commission's regionalization arrangements and other industry behavior for possible cases of noncompetitive conduct. For example, on September 9, 1985, the executive director of the Red Cross Regional Blood Services for Los Angeles and Orange Counties cautioned hospitals about buying even some blood from lower-priced "outside sources." He quoted a remark by the AABB president that "a coordinated, cooperative blood-collection system is essential to maintain the public trust, rather than a competitive system fraught with frustration and suspicion." These appear to be invitations to avoid competition.

In addition, blood banks should be held strictly liable for damages caused by contaminated transfusions. Negligence liability is inappropriate for blood banking and results in too few safety precautions, as the economist Reuben Kessel argued in an authoritative 1974 article. In the language of tort law, contaminated blood is a "manufacturing defect" (where only manufacturers can take additional precautions to reduce injuries) rather than a "design defect," (where both manufacturers and consumers can take precautions). The professional consensus among leading tort scholars, including Richard Epstein, William Landes, Richard Posner, and Steven Shavell, is that strict liability is the correct standard for manufacturing defects, because manufacturers are in a much better position than consumers to minimize such defects. If blood bankers are held strictly liable for damages caused by contaminated transfusions, they will take all cost-justified precautions to reduce those damages—including, I am confident, the relatively low-cost, high-benefit screening and testing measures I have advocated. Those receiving blood are in a relatively poor position to distinguish defective from safe blood or to adjust their use of blood according to their understanding of the risks involved. . . .

Fears that blood bankers or manufacturers will withdraw from production if they were held strictly liable for injuries caused by transfusion are baseless. A point often overlooked in the product liability debates is that consumers pay the costs of defective product—in the form of product price or injury costs—regardless of whether liability is strict or negligence. Under strict liability, state-of-the-art blood testing and donor screening would increase the costs of blood banking and manufacturing, but these costs would be far more than offset by lower costs of transfusion diseases and death.

My prediction is that in this more competitive setting, all blood bankers would be induced to use registries, and their current, implicit agreement to pay no more than a zero price for blood would break down. Blood would be bought only from low-risk people with good health records, and increasingly from women. In addition, competition would likely lead blood collectors to adopt the two surrogate tests for hepatitis and in some urban areas, the T-cell surrogate test as well.

But market competition and private liability are more than indirect means of accomplishing what the FDA could accomplish directly. In a market environment blood bankers would be guided more by consumer demand and less by the institutionally cautious forces of the FDA and official medical research, and would be less able to control industry practices according to their own views and interests. This would foster a greater diversity of approaches to improving the blood supply, and probably result in innovations neither the FDA nor a private student of the industry such as myself would come up with. The supply responses to the next threat to the blood supply would surely be swifter than in the case of AIDS. Indeed, there is already evidence that the blood market, regimented as it currently is, is responding to the AIDS threat more quickly than the regulators.

WHAT IS BEING DONE

There have been many new developments bearing on the quality of the blood supply in recent months, largely as a result of AIDS. In general, the government is responding grudgingly and in some cases perversely, while the market is responding in ways that are, under the circumstances, helpful and encouraging. . . .

Market Responses. The most promising development in blood banking is the recent resurgence of competition in supply. Hospitals, increasingly subject to fixed-fee rather than cost-plus reimbursement for their services, are seeking business and cutting expenses. Price is now more important, and new blood suppliers are beginning to cut price. Loyalties to regional blood banks are weakening because of the widely held view that they have not done all they could to prevent transfusion AIDS.

In Tucson, Ariz., last year, United Blood Services, a nonprofit blood service that contracts with 835 hospitals in 18 states, undercut by 40 percent the prices that the Red Cross charged to the University of Arizona Hospital. The hospital's expected annual savings were $250,000. In other cities, United Blood Services has forced the Red Cross to cut prices to keep its business. The Red Cross blood center in Salt Lake City closed after losing business to a large hospital that collected blood for itself and other hospitals. Mergers are under discussion in several regions. A new nonprofit blood bank has recently been formed in the San Diego area. And competition has led to new practices in the San Francisco Bay area without new entry. Media attention over Stanford's use of surrogate testing allowed Stanford to attract patients from surrounding communities; blood banks in nearby San Francisco and San Jose then adopted surrogate testing as a defensive measure.

The blood bankers' failure to provide services consumers want has led to innovations that are reducing the demand for potluck blood. More hospitals are offering designated and autologous donation, where patients pre-deposit their own blood for planned surgeries. A new specialty for-profit center in Los Angeles offers transfusion materials from donors designated by patients or from its registry of select, repeat, cash donors. Registry donors are asked to sign affidavits that they are not in high-risk groups, and agree to screening and testing in excess of typical blood-bank standards. This development may suggest that registries will emerge even where transfusion liability is limited, as in California—not to reduce suppliers' liability exposure, but as a market signal of higher-quality blood.

Finally, firms in Miami and New York have begun to store blood for an upcoming surgery or freeze it for three years for either the donor's use or a designation. They operate on a 7-day, 24-hour basis and say they will ship anywhere. An Arizona firm is franchising personal blood-storage operations in hospitals. Patients or friends donate whole blood, the red cells are frozen for transfusion, and the hospital owns the various by-products.

The developments may do more to improve the operations of the established nonprofit blood banks than anything the FDA is likely to contemplate. Although the FDA has yet to act on its advisory committee's recommendations for the two additional hepatitis tests, this past spring the Red Cross announced it would require one of them at some future date, and shortly afterwards the AABB said it would require both of them before the end of this year. More AABB members are also beginning to accommodate demands for designated blood. And most gratifying is the recent complaint of an official of the American Blood Commission that "there is substantial evidence that competition is beginning to erode the effectiveness of some regional associations."

AIDS surfaced in 1977 but was not scientifically described until 1981, not officially recognized as a threat to the blood supply until 1983, not isolated in this country until 1984, and not countered with a surrogate blood test until 1985. Eight years is not a very long time in medical research or in government rulemaking, but it is an eon in the marketplace. The AIDS epidemic might just be dislodging the sclerosis in our blood supply system so that it will be better prepared to respond to the next health threat.

NO

Joseph R. Bove, M.D.

DIRECTED DONATIONS

Directed donation refers to a procedure whereby a recipient, or a parent or a guardian, is allowed to select the donors for the transfusion that the patient will later receive. The procedure, which was for all practical purposes unknown until the recent AIDS epidemic, raised concerns in the minds of some individuals about the safety of our blood supply. We did have occasional requests, particularly from groups who wanted only to receive blood from one radical group or another, but these were easily put aside and easily ignored.

When it became clear, however, that AIDS could be transmitted by transfusions of blood, plasma, hemophiliac factor concentrates or other blood components and derivatives, anxious recipients throughout the country began to request, and in some cases even to demand, that they be allowed to select the donors whose blood they would later receive. These requests were prompted by a justified concern about transfusion-associated AIDS and by a belief that patient-selected donors would be safer than the donors available from the existing system.

Blood banking organizations responded by issuing statements supporting the status quo and suggested that directed donation programs would not be in the best interest of most patients who depend on the nation's blood banks. The issue has been put in somewhat sharper focus by a recent article in the *Journal of the American Medical Association*, which suggested that "Directed donations should be encouraged and requests from patients for such accommodations should be met."

As with all issues raised by the AIDS epidemic, there is no easy solution, but physicians and lawyers should understand the issues involved and should understand the reasons, at least, why blood banking organizations appear to be unresponsive to patient concerns. You've heard a lot about the national blood supply. . . . Let me say, again, lest you missed it, that just about all of our blood in this country is obtained from volunteers. Nobody really knows, but the percentage of commercial blood, plasma, or platelets in the system is probably under one or two percent. For all practical purposes, there is no commercial blood in the system.

From "Directed Donations," by Dr. Joseph A. Bove in *Legal Issues in Transfusion Medicine: Managing Risk in a Changing Environment*, edited by Gilbert M. Clark, American Association of Blood Banks. Copyright © American Association of Blood Banks. Reprinted by permission.

You've also heard this morning a little about transfusion-associated AIDS. Let me remind you that the number of cases of transfusion-associated AIDS is small. From 1977 (and that's the year that people seem to be going back to) until 1985—that's about eight years—we have transfused somewhere in the neighborhood of 24 million different people with about 80 million units of blood or blood products and have, as one of the most recent reports, about 200 cases of transfusion-associated AIDS. Now, I don't want to try to do arithmetic to give you an incidence rate, but I assure you that the incidence of transfusion-associated AIDS is low. And today it's even lower than those numbers suggest because we have taken steps to eliminate high risk donors from the donor pool. We are now testing all donor units for the presence of an indicator of the HTLV-III virus, which nearly everyone believes is the etiologic agent of AIDS. These steps promise to reduce even further the already low incidence of transfusion-associated AIDS. The current risk of acquiring transfusion-associated AIDS is unknown, but it must be extremely low.

Could directed donations reduce this risk? Concern about the disease has prompted patients to think that they can pick a safer donor than the one provided by the system. Evidence to support or to refute this hypothesis is not available. The extremely low incidence of AIDS from transfusion and its further reduction by the two steps already taken make it doubtful that any program of directed donations can lower the overall incidence significantly. Furthermore, because the incidence is so low, it will be impossible to do any kind of an appropriate scientific study. Neither the blood collecting agencies, who contend that directed do-

nations will not lower the risk, nor the patients or physicians, who think that it will, have reached their conclusions on the basis of scientific evidence, nor will there be any for further conclusions. Given the already low incidence, a further reduction, especially a reduction that could be measured and quantified and proven statistically, is highly unlikely. Directed donation programs cannot be justified scientifically—not with the evidence at hand and not with any evidence that we're likely to get. In individual cases it is possible that a donation from one individual—let's say, a cloistered nun—might be safer than a donation from the system. But for all practical purposes, there is no reason to think that directed donation programs can reduce the overall incidence of transfusion-associated AIDS.

Now, let me make an important point; one that you must carry away from this meeting. This is the matter of directed donations versus directed donation *programs*. The major pressure for directed donation has come from individuals who desire to select one or two donors for a particular patient in a particular circumstance. The major objection from the blood collecting organizations has been based, on the other hand, on concerns about widespread implementation of directed donor programs. They feel that directed donor programs, if widely implemented, might jeopardize the national blood supply. While some, or even most, objections to direct donations seem to be poor, weak or unfounded when considered as an individual case in one patient and one donor, they become far more meaningful when considered as part of the bigger picture of the nation's blood supply.

I think it's safe to say that there is

agreement on all sides that, should directed donations be allowed at all, they must be allowed for everyone. One cannot approve directed donations in cases where the request is made with what has been termed a "high energy level" behind the request, and withhold it from others whose request is less aggressive. Furthermore, it is proper that a blood bank's decision to allow directed donations for anybody must be made in such a way that everybody who is possibly affected by this decision will be well aware of the change in the blood bank's policy. Practices such as allowing a directed donation after much patient pressure, of keeping the procedure's availability relatively secret, or of granting only selected requests, are unacceptable. The concept that we will or should make just one exception is neither appropriate nor tenable. One cannot discuss or plan for a directed donation or two. One must approach the problem as an area- or system-wide problem. Thus, objections which may seem weak for just one case must be considered with a more global view. The issue is not a directed donation, but rather directed donation programs. The first is *ipso facto* the second.

What are the arguments in favor of directed donation? One is that patient-selected donors are safer. That underlies the entire belief by some patients and physicians that they should pick their own donors. I don't want to go into this anymore than I have, except to say that patients who have a belief, unsubstantiated by fact, that their friends or relatives are not members of a high risk group, and are almost surely free from disease may be deceiving themselves. There is no evidence to support the concept, and no way to test it scientifically. But it does remain the essence of all requests for directed donations.

What are the reasons that the blood banking organizations have come out against directed donation programs? Well, in no particular order—and I don't want anybody to think that I'm putting these in an order of importance—we think that there is a possibility that directed donor programs, rather than lowering the risk of transfusion-associated AIDS may increase it. For example, one of the important things related to transfusion safety is the reliability of the donor history. We depend on the donor to tell us the truth when we ask, "Have you been out of the country? Have you had disease? How are you feeling? Are you taking medications? Are you a member of a high risk group?" Now, it's clear that if a donor is pressured by a family member to donate blood, or if the donor is pressured internally by a desire to do something good for someone, that donor may be less honest with the history than he or she would be otherwise. Furthermore, it's conceivable that certain individuals, who are members of high risk groups, or have been shooting drugs, may be unwilling or unable to tell the family that they can't go down the blood bank and give. They can't say, "Ma, I'd like to do that but I've been shooting juice over at the college." We are concerned that the pressures applied by requests for directed donation may cause some donors to be less honest and candid during the donor interview than they should be and in that way increase, rather than reduce, the risk of transfusion-associated AIDS.

We're concerned about the administrative confusion that widespread programs of directed donation could lead to. Remember that we have to get the right unit of blood into the right patient at the right time, and one of the major causes of transfusion-related fatalities is administrative error—getting the wrong blood into the wrong person. I'm embarrassed to stand up in front of you and say that in 1985, with all the technology we have, with computers and everything else, we can't get the right unit of blood into the right patient. But the truth of the matter is, we don't always do it, and that's how we kill people. If in addition to all the things we have to keep straight now, we also had to keep straight a number of units for Mrs. Jones on this shelf or for Mr. Williams on that one and these are coming and going, the administrative confusion of adding that extra dimension to an already tough system would, in the opinion of many, lead to unsurmountable and, perhaps, dangerous problems.

Furthermore, the administrative complexity has no end point. There is one blood bank that has had a request for a complete private storehouse of cryoprecipitate (a material used to treat hemophilia) to be obtained only from a particular church member, to be kept in a separate freezer, and to be used only for one person with hemophilia. The church wanted a whole separate supply of cryo for this patient. We can store blood, as you know, for 3 years, and it's not irrational to think that if the hysteria continues or increases, people will begin to want not only to have directed donations for their pending surgery but would just like to have a little private blood bank stored up for themselves in their own freezer. You laugh, but think back 5 years, and think if any of you thought you would see the kinds of reactions we're having today from the AIDS epidemic.

There are scheduling problems if we go into programs of directed donation. Right now a patient is operated on when it is medically convenient for the patient and the surgeon. If, however, we were dealing with another dimension to this—the directed donations—and a patient who had stored up from friends, relatives or colleagues eight units of blood and was supposed to have surgery tomorrow and came down with a cold, the patient would say, "I've got to be operated on tomorrow because if I don't get operated on tomorrow, the blood's going to outdate." The doctor would say, "I really would rather wait a week. You know, you're coughing and sneezing and I don't like to operate under those conditions." There's another dimension thrown into this whole equation of when to operate on the patient. Right now, the patient is operated on when it's best for the patient and we, the blood bank suppliers, have blood ready. If the patient has stored up a number of private units and they're all going to outdate, there's a new and unnecessary dimension thrown into this.

We have no way to know, if we were to do programs of directed donation, how to select directed donors. I know one blood bank that says we do directed donations only from a parent to a child or, at the very most, from another individual living in the same household, for the child. That has a smidgeon of medical reliability to it, but not much. If one makes a decision that I'm a good donor, a better donor, for my wife, why am I not a better donor for my neighbor's wife? How can you say that somebody who doesn't have relatives, can't go out and get somebody else's relatives? If somebody else's relatives are good for him, why are they not good for this other person? In truth, once you start, there is no way to put restrictions on who may donate for whom.

If you can't put restrictions on directed donations, then the next step is that groups will establish their own blood banks. This already happened, I am told, in a well-to-do community where a particular country club wanted to establish a private blood bank. You laugh, but it happened. The country club opened negotiations with the local blood center to see if they couldn't have a private supply; country club members giving only to country club members. In a Houston newspaper, there was an advertisement saying that an organization was going to set up a quasi-commercial blood bank and, for money, would freeze your blood for you and then make the hospital give you your blood back. What's to prevent an enterprising college student setting up a little business, saying, "For 25 bucks, I'll send you a tested, female donor, who is much purer than the system supplies." Once you get started, there is no way to put restrictions on it and we are on the road back to commercial blood, which we don't think is good.

There are other arguments. We're concerned abut the disruption of the blood supply. Anybody who is connected with blood banking knows that always, no matter what else we are doing, we are always struggling to keep the blood supply adequate. The number of donors is often just adequate to meet the need, and we're concerned that, if individuals get started on programs of directed donation, this blood supply, which is always adequate to treat emergency victims—people with hemorrhage, people who get in trouble during pregnancy, automobile accidents—may get to the point where we don't have enough blood in the pipeline. We're concerned that widespread programs of directed donation may lead to blood shortages. Not one directed donor unit certainly, but I've already said I don't believe you can talk about just one unit.

Furthermore, I'd like to ask those of you out there, "If we had a directed donation program—and one of the places that's done it has had as much as 20 percent of the blood supply on the shelf at any one time categorized for somebody else—who owns the blood?" If you have an O-negative lady who's hit by a car, and you happen to have five units of O-negative blood in the bank and 15 or more O-negative units that are sitting on shelf #2 with individual's names and that lady needs, probably, 13 units of blood, who owns those 15 units on shelf #2 that have been given and directed for specific people? Do you let a patient die or get the wrong blood when you've got the right blood and you don't give it to him or her because it's got somebody's name on it? Who owns the blood? We're concerned about these things and concerned that directed donation programs might, in some way, backfire and lead to shortages which, for the larger population, will be deleterious.

I don't want to spend a lot of time talking about cost. Dr. Schmidt threw some numbers out, but I haven't got any numbers. The requests that I have had for directed donation have almost always been, "Hey, Doc, if it's going to cost any money, I'll pay it out of my own pocket." Now, that, of course, is not acceptable. We haven't heard that any third party groups would be willing to pick up these increased costs—and there certainly will be increased cost—nor is it appropriate or proper or acceptable that only those who can pay out of their own pockets should have this particular facet of medical care. If the country embarks on widespread programs of directed donation, there will be a tremendous increase in the cost, and I think we have to figure out who's going to pay for it, should we do it. . . .

Let me go on to another issue. There are some ethical issues about directed donation programs that need to be thought about. If we mount programs of directed donation, if we allow people to select their own donors, it will mean, inevitably, that there will be two kinds of blood in the blood bank—the standard blood and the blood that is, perhaps, or thought to be, better blood. It will mean that there will be two kinds of recipients—recipients who get the regular blood and recipients who get the supposedly better blood. Now, for better or for worse, I don't think most of us really want to segregate the national blood banking system that way because, inevitably, if that happens, the better blood will go to the people who have a higher intelligence, who are better connected in society, who have more friends and relatives and contacts. The supposedly less safe blood will go to the people who are in the minority groups, the disadvantaged, the elderly, and the people who just don't have connections to the social structure. I, for one, don't want to see blood banking work that way (and I'm not sure most people do, if they have a choice) on a system-wide basis.

I do think that we, in blood banking, have a responsibility to alleviate the anxiety of patients; to do everything we can to see that when people get transfused, it isn't an occasion for extra tension or anxiety. I think, perhaps, that the press, and our own publicity, needs to be more aggressive about how good the blood supply is without going beyond it. There are a whole host of risks and it isn't perfectly safe. But I, for one, do not believe that widespread programs of directed donation have anything to offer patients, physicians or the system. I remain opposed to them and am concerned about the very great pressures that we in blood banking are beginning to feel from patients, from lawyers and from doctors to change what, I think, is a good system.

POSTSCRIPT

Should We Deregulate the Blood Banking Industry?

This debate boils down to what system is safer: the current system that depends almost exclusively on blood that is voluntarily and freely contributed to the national blood supply or a modified system where some individuals either put their own blood aside for future use or obtain the blood they need—perhaps by buying it—from a pool of donors who are "low-risk persons." It is unlikely that both systems can exist side by side.

Bove argues that typically the amount of "blood in the pipeline" is "just adequate to meet the need." But if we siphon off some of this blood and put it aside for some who may never use it or for others who are members of some elite group, there may not be enough left "to treat emergency victims." He asks us if we really want a system where we would allow "a patient to die" because the blood that is on hand has someone else's name on it or is being sold to the highest bidder. This is particularly vexing for Dr. Bove who believes that the current system is fundamentally sound. He admits that there are special circumstances where a donation for a particular individual might be safer than "potluck blood"—he uses the example of a "cloistered nun"; but Bove maintains that "for all practical purposes, there is no reason to think that a direct donation program can reduce the overall incidence of transfusion-associated AIDS."

Eckert's view is in sharp contrast to Bove's position. Eckert finds ample reason to be worried about the "blood bankers and their federal regulators." He believes that the "public concern about blood safety has been rational" and because of this he argues for a series of major reforms within this

industry. As it should be expected, this free market economist pleads with us to harness the power of the price system in our attempts to reign in the run-away effects of the AIDS epidemic. He asks for "donor registries," "cash blood," " state-of-the-art blood testing," and "designated donations." He goes on to argue that market competition and strict liability is far superior to the current "non-competitive environment," which involves "increased regulation."

We invite and encourage you to read beyond these two essays. Modern medicine to date has proved powerless in its attempts to stop the ever-widening circle of devastation that is caused by AIDS. Would testing for AIDS slow down its spread? Mathelde Krim in the November/December 1987 issue of *The Humanist* and Alan Otten in the June 16, 1987 issue of the *Wall Street Journal* say no. (Gerald F. Seib in the same issue of the *Wall Street Journal* argues the other side.) Should we turn to a system of "autologous blood"—where we put aside our own blood for our own use? The TRB column of the December 1, 1986 issue of *The New Republic* finds this to be one more example of Reagan's legacy: a "narrowing of the sense of community." Do we really understand the complexities of the blood banking system in the U.S. after reading the two essays in Issue 3? If not, perhaps you can gain some additional insights by reading Andrea Rock's essay, "Inside the Billion-Dollar Business of Blood," which appeared in the March 1986 issue of *Money* magazine.

ISSUE 4

Is "Comparable Worth" Worthless?

YES: Clifford Hackett, from "Woman, Work and the Question of 'Comparable Worth': Better from a Distance," *Commonweal* (May 31, 1985)

NO: Ruth Needleman, from "Pay Equity: Freeing the Market from Discrimination" (January 1986)

ISSUE SUMMARY

YES: Social critic Hackett argues that comparable worth would put an end to the "laws of supply and demand or other economic principles that determine wage rates for different kinds of work."
NO: Labor economist Needleman contends that pay differentials between men and women cannot be traced to differentials in "human capital." She concludes that these differentials must result from discriminatory practices and attitudes.

The term "comparable worth" may be relatively new, but the problem it addresses is quite old: women are and have been paid less than men. Today the pay differential means that the average woman earns about 64 cents for every dollar earned by a man.

This is not a problem that has been ignored by public policy. As early as 1917, the federal government created the War Labor Board in part to handle charges of sex discrimination in the war industries. In the face of these charges, the Board ordered that the wages of women should equal the wages paid to men when the service rendered was equal. During World War II the War Labor Board again attempted to establish the basic concept of equal pay for equal work. This time the Board was less successful. A few corporations, notably Westinghouse and General Electric, persisted in setting different wages for men and women doing equal work.

Although women continued to lobby for federal legislation that would guarantee equal pay for equal work throughout the decades of 1940 and 1950, this right was not established by Congress until 1963 when the Equal Pay Act was passed. The following year Congress took yet another step toward closing the wage gap by enacting Title VII of the Civil Rights Act which broadly prohibited employment discrimination based upon race, color, national origin, religion, or sex. The net result of these two major legislative initiatives was to establish clearly the right of women to "equal pay for substantially equal work."

Yet more than twenty years after these laws were passed, large wage differentials between men and women still exist. The laws have eliminated most of the blatant discrimination where women and men doing the same jobs are paid different wage rates; but, the law did little to eliminate the alleged discrimination that exists because the vast majority of women hold jobs that are low-paying and traditionally considered to be female jobs.

Proponents of comparable worth argue that on the basis of objective criteria—job skill requirements, job responsibilities, education, training, and experience levels needed—many low-paying women's jobs are as demanding as some high-paying male-dominated jobs. These proponents go on to argue that the only way to correct these wage differences which reflect institutional sex discrimination is to objectively judge each job classification and correct any sex-biased differences that are uncovered. .

In 1981, the Supreme Court issued a decision in the *Washington County v. Gunther* case which appears to make it possible to bring these cases to the courts. Additionally, thirty-three states have introduced or are attempting to introduce comparable worth legislation, while six states have implemented explicit forms of comparable worth programs for their public employees. Lastly, a number of trade unions are bringing this issue to the bargaining table.

This groundswell in support of comparable worth has alarmed many free market economists. They insist, as Clifford Hackett insists, that "comparable worth destroys the link between work and its marketplace evaluation." Proponents of comparable worth, on the other hand, argue that the market reflects "discriminatory attitudes and practices" and these prejudices led to wage rates which are substantially lower in women-dominated occupations than they are in male-dominated occupations.

YES

Clifford Hackett

BETTER FROM A DISTANCE

Should women be paid for jobs on the basis of what men earn in entirely different jobs? The answer would seem to be yes following the federal equal-pay-for-equal-work law of 1963 which laid the ground for improved work opportunities for women. Yet the idea, called comparable worth, is finding it difficult to emerge, as some had predicted it would, as the "issue of the 80s" for women.

The appeal of comparable worth is considerable—especially from a distance. It seems to address a basic economic injustice: men earn more than women whether the measure is annual income, average hourly wages, starting salaries, or concentration in top-paying jobs. This differential also exists within jobs and professions, and persists even as women are moving into new job fields and upward in career tracks. Clearly, comparable worth defenders say, these discrepancies are unfair, perhaps illegal, and should be ended by law.

There is another broad appeal to justice related to the issue: the seeming inability of the free market economy to provide reasonable pay scales crossing vocational lines. Some of us are appalled by plumbers who get $40 for a house call; others are repelled by lawyers who earn $200 an hour. Johnny Carson and NFL football players prompt many to say, "No one can be worth that much!" An unstated comparison in our minds pits these "over-paid" exemplars against those of us who perform the hum-drum jobs which keep the economy going or who (and these are mostly women) undertake the most humane, compassionate, and bedeviling jobs in all societies: nursing, child care, and primary education—all low-paying labors. Is this pay disparity fair? Clearly not.

But the closer one looks at comparable worth, the more doubtful its real value appears. Instead of helping move women into new jobs as the equal-pay law did, comparable worth seems to give up that fight. It pleads for higher pay for women on two quite different, but equally dubious, bases: first, it argues that jobs women actually perform are undervalued and should be upgraded by law; second, it maintains that women's abilities, education,

From *Commonweal*, May 31, 1985. Copyright © 1985 by the Commonweal Foundation.

and experience are undervalued and they should get more money no matter *what* jobs they do.

Whatever happened to the premise of equal pay for women, that if women earned the same as men in a particular job category they would more surely compete for those jobs? For many reasons, women still do not always seek the same jobs men do. Comparable worth advocates conclude society must reevaluate the work women do choose. But this revaluing without regard to the job market is at the heart of the comparable worth dispute, the cause of dismay among almost everyone except those who think women would gain from a radical remaking of the economy.

Comparable worth entails assigning numbers to every important aspect of every paying job. Some incredible mechanism of government would then insure that everyone with the same numbers would get the same pay. Who assigns the numbers and weighs job skills against education, experience versus risks, and so on? A committee of personnel experts! But doesn't the open market already perform its own kind of valuation when people put their skills out for examination and competition? Yes, but unfairness results because women's work or women themselves are undervalued.

Let's be clear about what comparable worth is and isn't. It is not about the fact that football players and movie stars earn too much money, but that women make less money than men. Comparable worth is not concerned with the kinds of jobs women do, only how much they earn. Finally, comparable worth is not about job opportunity, job mobility, or job advancement, but about whether the open marketplace for jobs, with its flaws, should be abolished.

What is wrong with this new approach? First, it ignores the source of the problem: the labor pool has an oversupply of women who are available for too limited a number of entry-level jobs. Second, even admitting that economic life is not always fair, who is wise enough to evaluate continuously the varying worths which society applies to jobs? Who will decide, for instance, the worth of four years studying elementary education at a first-class university compared to four years studying engineering at a community college? Who will weigh the relative worth of a super-salesman who actually spends much of his time preparing for a few million-dollar sales a month and a senior secretary whose long hours and mental strain are usually endured under someone else's direct control?

The answer of comparable worth advocates is that these factors be judged by a committee of personnel experts who regularly analyze job content and make comparisons of skills and experience in large firms and within government. Yet such experts as Norman D. Willis, head of a personnel advisory firm which the state of Washington employed in one of the most famous comparable-worth cases, says he recoils at the possibility that his classifications, or anyone else's, should become law.

Even if large numbers of employers were persuaded to apply comparable worth, the concept could not be limited to women alone. It would have to apply to men's jobs as well. Would not church workers and writers, to take just two obvious examples of underpaid professions, have claims on higher pay based on the comparable worth of their education, skills, and contributions to society? It's not hard to see why private employers cannot take seriously the idea of actually setting pay by comparable-worth rules.

Private employers pay the lowest possible wages needed to stay in competition. As long as the competition remains relatively open, workers benefit by maintaining the mobility and skills to move into better paying or more interesting jobs. The two are not always the same, but moving up usually means more demanding work. It may include not only greater skills but longer or irregular hours, and sometimes higher risks. Firefighters are paid for risking their lives in a pattern which alternates boredom with real danger. Most workers do not desire such a life, and those who do are thus able to demand higher wages and earlier retirements. Often the demands consist of entrance hurdles, like bar exams, advanced degrees and other qualifiers. Comparable worth proponents are sometimes accused of "credentialism" for seeking more pay for those women, like nurses and librarians, who also face educational hurdles for qualifications. But the pay which women, as well as men, receive is based not only on the credentials but also on market competition. If women want higher wages, they soon learn to avoid jobs with many qualified competitors, whether men or women. Why should employers pay librarians as much as electricians when the supply of the former will produce ample numbers at little more than the minimum white collar wage, while electricians are almost always scarce and, therefore, expensive?

Facing great hostility in the private sector, comparable worth has moved with some success into closed markets like state and local government where worker and union pressures combine with trendy political constituencies. Minnesota, a progressive state by most stan-dards, recently passed laws requiring a study of job characteristics of all government jobs, state and local, and set aside money to start applying the program. In San Jose, California, a similar plan was initiated with $1.5 million for pay equity adjustments. What is wrong, then, with these plans, especially if they have public support?

The long-term problem is that comparable worth destroys the link between work and its marketplace evaluation. In the private sector, this linkage is vital to keep a company competitive. In government, paying secretaries without regard to their cost in the local job market destroys confidence in government's ability to match the efficiency of business. Eventually, elected officials will have to account for the pay of their secretaries and their plumbers. If the secretary earns premium pay in order to match the plumber's wage, private sector workers who pay the taxes will object. It is not possible, over the longer term, to have pockets of comparable worth in an otherwise competitive economy without problems.

Take the case of San Jose. It conducted a jobs study as the result of a strike over comparable worth. The study concluded that both librarians and electricians were worth $3,000 a month. In the local, competitive economy, however, librarians could be hired for much less while electricians in the area were paid more. The city must now pay electricians more than the study said they were "worth," while librarians are being paid above-market salaries. With victories like that, comparable worth will eventually fall of its own weight.

Behind all the arguments and the tactics of the comparable worth debate is the strong conviction that discrimination against women is a major factor in the labor market. But a careful look at female employment proves inconclusive on this point. Labor economists start by identifying known differentials on jobs and pay by sex, race, age, and occupational group. They weigh factors like intermittent and part-time work, interruptions for pregnancies, and other causes for lower pay for women. But because of the complexities in the job market there are always too many "other" or "unknown" factors of such analyses to explain the residual differential of lower pay for women. Yet, this inconclusive method of reductional analysis is at present the only "proof" of discrimination against women.

A recent article in a U.S. Labor Department journal by Janice Shack-Marquez, a federal economist, says, "Most of the studies of the pay disparity between men and women have been motivated by a desire to quantify the effects of discrimination in the labor market on women's earnings." Labor market discrimination, she notes, may be only one answer, of undetermined importance, in assessing women's lower pay. The pay difference, she says, is much smaller when narrowly-defined white collar jobs are compared for men and women than in broader studies. Ms. Shack-Marquez says "not enough is known" about individual earnings "to be confident that all the labor market variables in which men and women differ have been isolated."

No such caution animates the comparable worth advocates. Editors of a recent book *Comparable Worth and Wage Discrimination* (Temple University Press, $39.95, 311 pp.) note that the authors, mostly women, represent a "broad spectrum" of views on the issue. Yet they agree that salary disparities between male- and female-dominated jobs "are based in large part on discrimination."

For the women's movement itself, comparable worth seems a very depressing course to take. To back the principle that women must be paid more because they are women implies a pessimism about the chances of full integration of women in the job market. If women can compete, this argument goes, they will; otherwise, they want to doctor the system so that the work they do gets more pay through government or judicial fiat.

Comparable worth advocates answer this argument in several ways, none fully cogent. First, they say, this competition of women in a men's job market will be enhanced if women in lower-paying jobs get the same pay as comparable men. Employers would then choose workers by merit, not gender. Second, the predominance of women in some low-paying jobs—retail clerking, secretarial and clerical work, child care and domestic work—has patterned so many women for so long that many are now too old to be retrained. Third, pay equity advocates say, these jobs are undervalued simply because women hold them. Why should women, who like to nurse or teach school, change jobs just to earn as much as men with comparable skills, education, and experience? Society is, in fact, subtly undervaluing jobs only because women perform them. And that, advocates say, is discrimination.

Correcting this discrimination will not bankrupt the country, proponents of comparable worth say, pointing to several cases where the system has been applied to government and private organizations. But these instances provide thin gruel to nourish the cause. While the only large-scale case, involving the state of Washington, is still in the courts, state taxpayers may have to pay over $1 billion if the suit prevails. The Washington state legislature's study of state jobs, which used the Willis scale, concluded that women's work was underpaid. Yet the governor's request for funds to implement the study was rejected in a budget crisis. The federal judge who heard the case decided that the state acted in bad faith by commissioning a study whose findings of pay discrimination were then not implemented. The state is certain to appeal the decision to the Supreme Court.

Even if the Washington state decision is sustained and the state government gets a huge bill for back wages, the case's impact on comparable worth remains unclear. Failure to pay, not the principles of comparable worth, are at issue here. Federal courts have, in several other cases, specifically excluded comparable worth from decisions about pay differences between men and women.

In a major decision in 1977 (*Christensen v. Iowa*), the Supreme Court cited the attempt to use the Civil Rights Act of 1964 as a basis for comparable worth. It rejected this approach saying: "We find nothing in the text and history of Title VII (of the Act) suggesting that Congress intended to abrogate the laws of supply and demand or other economic principles that determine wage rates for different kinds of work." Even in the 1981 *Gunther* case, cited most often by women as holding the door open for comparable worth actions, the Supreme Court said that the women prison guards' claim of lower pay because they were women "is not based on the controversial concept of 'comparable worth.' "

In order to make progress and to avoid another stalemate like the ERA, comparable worth advocates will have to either change the law or convince judges that existing laws require comparable worth interpretations. Neither the mood of the present Supreme Court, nor the explicit scorn of the Reagan administration is promising in this regard.

Over a dozen states have passed laws which refer to comparable worth, pay equity, or similar goals in their civil service systems, but most of these laws are too new or too vague to have established comparable worth up to now. Minnesota's 1982–83 laws on the subject were backed with an initial appropriation of $27 million to adjust state salaries. Until further studies are done, no one knows what the total cost to the state and its local governments, also covered, will be.

Comparable worth is like the parable of the golden egg. If its advocates insist on using political pressures to pay women in government more than wages in the private sector, cities and states will eventually react to increased costs by contracting much of "women's work" to the private sector.

In conclusion, if comparable worth seems such a mistaken solution for misconceived problems, here are several principles with which to insure that maximum benefits accrue to women in their search for true pay and job equity:

Not every difference between men and women in the job market comes from malevolent causes. Even if we reach the most perfect system of job access and pay for women, there may still be important differences in both the jobs they hold and what they earn. The values that women share may always be different from those of men. Anticipation of motherhood, its arrival, and its consequences will always affect women in the job market. Women's values, and the jobs they embody, are important for society and for the women who perform them, even when the pay is not high.

Economic rewards are not the only measure of job value for women or men. Many male-dominated jobs also pay less than others with lower investments of skills, education, and experience. The churches, the universities, art, and the government often pay less than business and industry. But pay, for these lesser-paid workers, is fortunately not the only consideration in their jobs.

Choosing motherhood may not be fully compatible with other career choices. This is such an old truth that it may *have* to be completely forgotten so we can learn it again. Yet many women know this before motherhood or shortly after. This fact of maternal life is not, in itself, unfair or a matter for the courts to handle. But motherhood should not bar the maximum participation a woman wants in the job marketplace. A genuine problem, worth some of the attention given to comparable worth, is how mothers of all ages can gain and hold such participation without sacrificing, jeopardizing, or postponing motherhood.

Comparable worth may have some benefits as an ideal if it leads toward better job integration. Even if most plumbers will always be men and most day-care workers women, society benefits when rigid job segregation by sex is softened. First, most women do not want to be shunted away, by gender, from certain jobs even if they choose other work. Second, men and women complement each other in social values, temperaments, and sensitivities. This relation may help and almost certainly does not hinder any workplace, even if not all jobs are interchangeable.

Women should consider more selective and specific approaches to better pay and job integration. In Colorado, nurses sought better wages through comparable worth action but lost in court. When they went on strike, however, they won. Job actions—whether in a single job, in one business or industry at a time, or nation-wide—will probably command more attention and get more results in the long term than the murky concepts of comparable worth.

There will be no revolution in the workplace no matter what the strategy. There have been important changes this century in women's wages which have risen faster than men's since 1900, according to a recent Rand Corporation study. The sixty cents a woman earns today, on average, to a man's dollar, will rise to seventy-four cents by the end of the next decade. But the competing interests of blacks, Hispanics, and others who want to change the job market according to their legitimate grievances will prevent a clear field for women. Black women, for example, have now closed the wage gap with white women. Black men, however, hold many of the male-dominated blue collar jobs which comparable worth proponents cite as examples of unfairly high pay. Further, the private sector has so far largely ignored the comparable worth approach as a frothy concoction of no import. If state or court actions move toward serious implementation of the concept, a fierce reaction to the perceived threat against the free market will come. This assault against comparable worth could make the ERA debacle look mild by comparison. To avoid this course, more measured, more confident, and more reasonable goals are needed for women.

One unspoken premise of the comparable worth fight is resentment against the male domination of the political, social, and economic life of our society. However, the appropriate response to this male dominance is a realistic demand for fairness to women in the job market, not a casually conceived and marginally tenable idea like comparable worth.

NO

Ruth Needleman

PAY EQUITY: FREEING THE MARKET FROM DISCRIMINATION

Why are women paid only 64 cents on the average for every dollar paid to men? Is this wage difference the inevitable result of a "free market" system at work? Or, on the contrary, have discriminatory attitudes and practices influenced wage-setting as they have influenced employment opportunities in general for minorities and women?

The controversy surrounding this question has centered on the issue of pay equity or comparable worth. These two interchangeable terms refer to the policy of equal pay for comparable work; a policy that holds that a job should be compensated based on objective criteria like skill, education, training, responsibility and work conditions and not on the race or sex of those who traditionally perform the job. The goal of pay equity is to eliminate sex and race-based wage discrimination from the labor market.

Consider this example of sex-based wage discrimination: The Department of Labor compiles a *Dictionary of Occupational Titles* (DOT) which includes ratings for each job category. Ratings are used in establishing wage scales. Dog pound attendants and zoo keepers, according to the DOT, are rated more highly than nursery school teachers and day care workers. Research undertaken to identify how the DOT ranked job-related skills found that the Department had not even counted skills associated with taking care of children. In contrast, skills associated with caring for animals had received high point scores. Why? Because the Department of Labor decided that knowing how to care for children is not a job-related skill, since it involves qualities intrinsic to being a woman.[1]

AT&T provides a second example. The company carried out a job evaluation study of all positions, including managerial. In assessing skills and attributing points, the company ranked "customer contact" extremely high for its managerial staff, but failed to count "customer contact" when it evaluated its telephone operators. As a result, the study ranked the operator's job low in points and recommended an equally low wage. Criticized for

From "Pay Equity: Freeing the Market from Discrimination," by Ruth Needleman. Copyright © 1986 by Ruth Needleman. Reprinted by permission of the author.

setting up two separate standards, one for a male-dominated profession and another for a female-dominated one, AT&T acquiesced and upgraded the job ranking and wages for its operators.[2]

Contrary to what opponents claim, pay equity does not demand that traditionally women's jobs be paid the same as men's regardless of the work performed and skills required. What pay equity addresses is the discrimination that has resulted from continued and pervasive sex segregation in the labor market. Despite civil rights legislation and the development of affirmative action programs, women have not made significant inroads into the male-dominated sectors of the job market. An overwhelming majority of women—nearly 80%—still work in jobs traditionally considered female; 55% are employed in two occupational groups alone, clerical and service. The Equal Pay Act of 1963 is designed only to eliminate discrimination in pay where women and men are employed to do the same or similar work. But most women perform different work, though often comparable in terms of requirements, responsibilities and tasks.

The fact is women's work has been systematically undervalued and wages *artificially* depressed. Why else would a nurse, with a college degree, responsible for human life, working weekends and rotating shifts, be paid only 75% of the salary, say, of a vocational education teacher, a job rated as equivalent by a Minnesota job evaluation study?[3] Less than 3% of all employed women earn over $50,000 a year, but more than 50% earn between $3,000 and $15,000 annually.[4] Pay scales for jobs held predominantly by women are across-the-board 20–30% lower than pay scales for male occupations.

WHAT ACCOUNTS FOR THE WAGE GAP?

Pay equity cannot and is not meant to eliminate all wage differentials. There are many legitimate factors involved in determining wage scales which have contributed to the earnings gap between women and men. Unionization is one of them. Membership in a labor organization generally insures a worker wages 30% above the industry average. Not as many women as men are unionized—although two-thirds of all new union members in the last decade are women—and those occupations traditionally dominated by women are among the least unionized. Nevertheless, since only 18% of the U.S. workforce is unionized, this particular factor has had only minimal impact on average earnings.

Human Capital Variables

Unquestionably, factors like education and training affect one's ability to earn money. Critics of pay equity, however, tend to attribute the wage gap almost entirely to human capital variables. Were it not for the differences in labor force attachment, education and skill levels, the argument goes, women's earnings would not lag behind men's. What's more, some opponents would add, women have chosen to enter the lower-paying jobs as part of a trade-off for other advantages like shorter hours, easier work and employment more "suitable" to a woman. It is worth examining each of these points to determine which factors actually contribute to the wage gap and which ones reflect gender-based myths and stereotypes.

Labor Force Attachment: For decades employers have viewed women as temporary workers, taking a job until marriage and then remaining at home throughout their child-rearing years. A Westinghouse manual on wages pointed to this pattern of female work behavior as the reason for the company's own lower and separate wage scales for women:

> The gradient of the women's wage curve is not the same for women as for men because of the more transient character of the service of the former, the relative shortness of their activity in industry, the differences in environment required, and extra services that must be provided, overtime limitations, extra help needed for the occasional heavy work, and the general sociological factors not requiring discussion herein.[5]

Although arguments such as these still have their adherents, they lack substance. Developments over the past two decades have radically altered women's labor force participation. In the last ten years alone, more than 11 million women have entered the job market. Women of child-bearing age and mothers in particular have sought jobs outside the home in greater numbers than ever before. Forty percent of all new women workers since 1970 are mothers, and 58% of women with children under 18 work. As a result, women's average worklife is increasing dramatically. As recently as 1950, a 26-year gap separated the average worklife of a woman from that of a man. By 1960, however, the difference had closed to 21 years; by 1970, to 17, and by 1977 there was only a ten year difference. For women entering the labor market today, their worklife expectancy is almost identical to men's.[6]

Are women more inclined than men to switch jobs? Statistics indicate that workers in low-paying and dead-end jobs are more likely to have higher turnover rates, but that this behavior is related to work status and not gender. Nonetheless, men in such jobs have demonstrated higher turnover rates than women, especially during their first years in the labor market.[7]

Education: Among the human capital arguments most commonly used to account for wage differentials are those related to educational levels and previous work experience. According to an editorial in one Indiana newspaper: "women with credentials and experience comparable to their male counterparts make at least as much on the average."[8] Nothing could be further from the truth. The Bureau of Labor Statistics estimates that the median income of a woman with postgraduate college experience is less than the median for a male with a high school diploma. More than half of all women college graduates earn *less* than a male high school dropout with eight years or less of education.[9] Even in cases where experience is also comparable, for example in entry-level jobs, the disparity is striking. A recent study of Harvard graduates sets the average salaries for male graduates of the School of Public Health at $37,800 a year and for women at $21,300.[10]

Former Secretary of Labor and economist Ray Marshall maintains that "less than half of the gross earnings differentials can be accounted for by such human capital factors as education, training, experience and skill requirements."[11] Average occupational earnings tend to vary inversely with the percentage of women among job-holders regardless of human capital factors.

The Free Market Argument

Discounting discrimination as a factor, pay equity opponents resort to a combination of "free market" theory and gender-based stereotypes to explain away the remaining wage gap. For example, the chairman of the University of Chicago's Economics Department recently argued that women selected jobs in areas like health care since they "appealed to women with homemaking responsibilities because they are less strenuous and provide more flexible hours than factory work."[12] In reality, this statement has very limited validity. Hospital work generally has worse hours and schedules than most factories. Weekend work and rotating shift schedules are extremely common. The work, moreover, is not only physically but emotionally strenuous, without much in the way of monetary compensation or other benefits.

Critics of pay equity are concerned, above all, with what they perceive as a threat to the free market system. They are wrong, in the first place, in assuming that a free market economy still exists. Second, it is equally incorrect to assume that the impersonal forces of supply and demand actually determine wage levels. Since the emergence of trusts and monopolies toward the end of the nineteenth century, accompanied by an increase in government regulation, a very *modified* market economy has replaced laissez-faire economics. Corporate price and wage-fixing and control over product markets occur routinely in the global marketplace. One example of wage-fixing surfaced during court hearings on a comparable worth suit in Denver: nurses introduced evidence proving that hospital administrators citywide had been meeting each year to decide wage rates.

Supply and Demand: The role of supply and demand in setting pay scales deserves more comment. Women receive lower wages in traditionally female jobs, according to the free market proponents, due to an oversupply of qualified workers. If a plumber, for example, receives more than a librarian, it is because the market places greater value on scarce resources, i.e., the plumber. But, if this were really the case, what then would account for the low wages of nurses and teachers, even during years of critical shortages? When the supply of nurses dipped far below the demand, hospital management did not boost salaries to attract additional job-seekers. Instead they worked through the media and educational institutions to lure more people into nursing careers, while, at the same time, relying on the government's help to encourage thousands of foreign-born nurses, particularly Filipinas, to accept jobs in the U.S. at even lower than market rates.

A similar manipulation of supply occurred during the 1950s, when industrial expansion absorbed large numbers of minority workers who had been farm laborers. Agribusiness did not allow wages to rise to draw these workers back into the fields; they pressured the government to negotiate a farm-labor program (*Bracero* Program) with Mexico to open the borders to immigrants during the harvest. Average wage levels declined as a result of the program. In both examples, sex and race discrimination interfered with how supply and demand set wages; pay equity, in contrast, would "free" the market from that kind of intervention.

Government Intervention

Equally central to the free market argument is the resistance to outside or government intervention. Employers have always opposed government reforms affecting labor markets. Despite protests, though, restrictions on child labor, as well as fair labor standards, minimum wage and civil rights legislation have been passed to prevent employer abuses. With pay equity, many critics fear that "some incredible mechanism of government" will be established to dictate wage rates to private employers. More than other arguments, this one involves the gravest distortion of fact. No pay equity suit or advocate has called for government action in wage-setting in the private sector; nor has anyone suggested that wage rates should or could be established according to national standards.

Job Evaluation

One of the most common procedures for determining wage scales in the private and public sector is job evaluation and work measurement. Because employers value jobs differently, because jobs and requirements vary from one employer or industry to the next, no absolute standard would be feasible. Job evaluations are generally carried out by individual employers, involving two dimensions: 1.) an internal one looking at the relative value of jobs within a single firm; and 2.) an external one looking at the value of a job with respect to prevailing labor market rates. According to the National Research Council of the National Academy of Science:

> Paying jobs according to their worth requires only that whatever characteristics of jobs are regarded as worthy of compensation by an employer should be equally regarded irrespective of the sex, race or ethnicity of job incumbents.[13]

In cases where a job evaluation study has led to a pay equity settlement, it was the employer who commissioned the study. Perhaps the most famous case occurred in Washington State, where job evaluation studies were undertaken by the government. The results indicated that female-dominated occupations were paid on the average 20–35% less than male-dominated occupations regardless of their evaluated worth. An LPN, for example, was rated equivalent to a campus policeman in terms of total points, based on skills, education, responsibility and work conditions. The jobs themselves were not compared. But an LPN earns only $739 a month, 69% of a campus policeman's salary. The gap, according to the study, was not due to any productivity-related job content or to supply and demand factors in the market. The gap resulted from sex-based wage discrimination.[14]

Legal Status

. . . As early as 1981, in *County of Washington v. Gunther*, the Supreme Court found that intentional sex-based wage discrimination was illegal under Title VII of the 1964 Civil Rights Act, and that similar cases could be brought under Title VII, since they did not meet the strict eligibility requirements of the Equal Pay Act. Those who argue that pay equity suits have no legal basis are relying on a distorted definition of pay equity/comparable worth, built on the idea of general across-the-board job comparisons rather than on concrete job evaluation studies. While it is true that federal court justices have refused to do job comparisons, because they lack both the authority and the expertise, they have consistently accepted employer job evaluation studies. In fact, they have ruled that a discrepancy between the evaluated worth of a job and its actual pay level constitutes evidence of intentional discrimination.

One further objection to comparable worth involves the cost; some employer groups are estimating a price tag of $2 to $150 billion. Their assumption, however, is that all pay equity settlements would be made at one time. But, as has occurred with all social reforms, pay equity adjustments are being implemented gradually over many years. The Minnesota legislature, for example, appropriated 1.25% of its annual personnel budget for the *first phase* of a settlement. A formula for future allocations has been jointly negotiated by labor and management. Many of the current settlements have, in fact, been voluntarily agreed to through collective bargaining.

IS PAY EQUITY ONLY A WOMEN'S ISSUE?

Although sex and race-based wage discrimination involves occupations historically dominated by women or minorities, all current employees in such jobs are affected. Not only have men benefitted from pay equity settlements, but the number of male beneficiaries is increasing as men are forced to seek work in traditionally female job areas. Over the past decade, with the decline in blue-collar manufacturing jobs, even more men are becoming telephone operators, nurses and public school teachers. For them, pay equity is no less a priority.

Pay equity is also a family issue. Faced with a deteriorating standard of living, many families could not have made ends meet without the addition of a woman's wage. Over 55% of married women are in the labor force. Yet 50% of all two-wage earner families have incomes *under* $25,000 a year. Families headed by women are in much greater financial trouble. Department of Labor figures place one-third of all these families below the poverty line; 80% of female-headed families earn under $15,000.[15] Any measure to reverse the effects of sex-based wage discrimination will have a long-term positive effect on the family.

Is equal pay for comparable work a viable policy? Not only is pay equity viable and an important vehicle for reducing discrimination in the job market, but it is currently being implemented. Thirty-three states have pay equity legislation passed or pending, and existing pay equity settlements are beginning to exert pressure on wage structures in surrounding labor markets. Pay equity is an idea whose time is already here.

NOTES

1. Witt, Mary and Patricia K. Naherny. *Women's Work: Up From 878—Report on the DOT Research Project*. Madison: Women's Educational Resources, University of Wisconsin-Extension, 1975.

2. Steinberg, Ronnie J. " 'A Want of Harmony': Perspectives on Wage Discrimination and Comparable Worth," in *Comparable Worth and Wage Discrimination*, ed. Helen Remick. Philadelphia: Temple University Press, 1984, p. 22.

3. Grune, Joy Ann and Nancy Reder, "Pay Equity: An Innovative Public Policy Approach to Eliminating Sex-based Wage Discrimination," in *Public Personnel Management*, 12, 4 (1983), p. 398.

4. U.S. Department of Labor, *Time of Change: 1983 Handbook on Women Workers*. Bulletin 298. Washington, D.C., pp. 51-57.

5. Steinberg, p. 8.

6. Smith, Shirley J. "New Worklife Estimates Reflect Changing Profile of Labor Force," in *Monthly Labor Review*, 105, 3 (March 1982), pp. 15, 17 & 18.

7. Kanter, Rosabeth Moss. "The Impact of Hierarchical Structures in the Work Behavior of Women and Men," in *Women and Work* ed. Rachel Kahn-Hut, Arlene K. Daniels and Richard Col-

vard. New York: Oxford University Press, 1982, pp. 234–35.

8. "Dangerous Policy Is on the Horizon," *The Times.* Hammond, Indiana (May 29, 1985).

9. *Time of Change,* p. 98.

10. Marshall, Ray. *Women & Work in the 1980's.* Washington, D.C.: Women's Research and Education Institute of the Congressional Caucus for Women's Issues, 1983, p. 16.

11. ibid.

12. Becker, Gary S. "How the Market Acted Affirmatively for Women." *Business Week* (May 13, 1985), p. 16.

13. Milkovich, George T. "The Emerging Debate" in *Comparable Worth: Issues and Alternatives* ed. E. Robert Levernash. Washington, D.C.: Equal Employment Advisory Council, 1980, p. 70.

14. Steinberg, p. 17.

15. Levitan, Sar A. and Richard S. Belous. "Working Wives and Mothers: What Happens to Family Life?" *Monthly Labor Review,* 104, 9 (September 1981), p. 29 and *Time of Change,* p. 19.

POSTSCRIPT

Is "Comparable Worth" Worthless?

Free market supporter Clifford Hackett submits that comparable worth laws and regulations represent a direct attack upon the free market. He reasons that wages are low in some occupations because there is an excess supply of labor in those areas. If we were to artificially increase wage rates in these occupations, the problem would only be worsened. Even more women would gravitate to those occupations that are already overpopulated. This can only result in more downward pressure on the wage rate. Finally he is amazed that anyone would seriously think that "some incredible mechanism of government" could assign wage rates more efficiently and equitably than the time-tested and honored market mechanism.

Labor economist Ruth Needleman challenges the assertion that pay differentials between men and women are the result of differentials in human capital—skill, education and training levels. Although the free market is supposed to capture these differentials, the market simply fails when it comes to assigning appropriate wage rates in traditional women's occupations. Her survey of the empirical evidence in this field suggests that "earnings tend to vary inversely with the percentage of women among job holders regardless of human capital factors." Thus for Needleman there are a number of myths and misconceptions surrounding the causes of the wage gap: (1) human capital differences can't explain this gap; (2) women's worklife is now nearly as long as men's; (3) the market is really not free to set wage rates; (4) low wages in some occupations is not traceable to an oversupply of labor; and, (5) government intervention will not distort the free market.

During the past five years, much has been written about the advisability and inadvisability of comparable worth. An excellent introduction to this topic by an advocate of comparable worth is in Helen Reinick, ed., *Comparable Worth and Wage Discrimination* (Philadelphia: Temple University Press, 1984). The opposition's arguments are well argued in E. Robert Levernash, ed., *Comparable Worth: Issues and Alternatives* (Washington, D.C., Equal Employment Advisory Council, 1980). An extremely readable and informative set of Congressional hearings is found in U.S. Congress, Hearings before the Subcommittees on Human Resources, Civil Service, Compensation and Employee Benefits, Committee on Post Office and Civil Service, *Pay Equity: Equal Pay for Work of Comparable Worth*, 97th Congress, 2nd session, 1982.

ISSUE 5

Are There Too Many Hostile Takeovers?

YES: Gerald L. Houseman, from "The Merger Game Starts with Deception," *Challenge* (September-October 1986)

NO: John D. Paulus and Paul S. Gay, from "U.S. Mergers Are Helping Productivity," *Challenge* (May-June 1987)

ISSUE SUMMARY

YES: Political science professor Houseman asserts that the economic rewards that are reaped by Wall Street takeover artists come at the expense of workers, stockholders, and the general public.
NO: Business economists Paulus and Gay argue that the corporate restructuring of the 1980s is a direct result of the need to increase productivity in the face of declining U.S. competitiveness.

The wave of mergers and acquisitions in the 1980s has sent many of us back to our textbooks in search of some guidance. What laws and court decisions control acquisitions and mergers? What is the difference between the current merger movement and the mergers and acquisitions that took place before the 1980s? And finally, do friendly mergers and acquisitions have the same economic consequences as unfriendly, or hostile, takeovers?

The answers to these questions are found in part in our economic history. Mergers and acquisitions have appeared in four waves. Just before the turn of this century the first great merger movement dominated the economy. The Whiskey Trust, the Sugar Trust, the Cotton-Oil Trust, the Standard Oil Trust were attempts to pull together small and larger firms into new business organizations that could act collectively to reduce supply and increase price. Since Congress concluded that these new business organizations could inflict abuses upon society, which were in direct conflict with the tenets of a free market economy, Congress passed our first antitrust legislation, the Sherman Act of 1890.

But this act did not slow the approach of the second wave of mergers and acquisitions that appeared shortly after World War I. This wave had many of the same characteristics as the first wave. Business combinations were generally in the form of horizontal mergers (mergers of firms at the same stage of production within one industry, such as merging two steel manufacturers). At the same time, however, two new forms of mergers and acquisitions began to appear: vertical mergers (mergers of firms at different stages of production within one industry, such as merging a firm that manufactures shoes with another firm that is a retail chain) and conglomerate mergers (mergers between a firm in one industry and a firm in a totally different industry, such as the merger of an oil company with a department store chain). In the face of this second wave of mergers and acquisitions, Congress attempted to strengthen the Sherman Act by passing the Clayton Antitrust Act of 1914.

The third wave of mergers and acquisitions took place from 1948 to 1979. The Federal Trade Commission (FTC)—the federal agency that is responsible for assuring competitive markets in the U.S.—estimates that of the more than 2,000 large mergers in manufacturing and mining that occurred in this period, three-fourths of these mergers and acquisitions were conglomerate mergers.

Lastly, and of immediate importance for this issue, is the forth wave of mostly hostile takeovers that have occurred in the 1980s. In these cases, the acquiring firm is able to complete the merger without the aid and cooperation of the acquired firm. This is usually accomplished by quietly buying a controlling quantity of the acquired firm's publicly held stock. Since the threat of a hostile takeover constitutes a direct challenge to the management of the acquired firm, management is forced into evasive action. In extreme cases, this results in the payment of greenmail—buying back the stock from the corporate raider at inflated prices. Thus corporate raiders such as Rupert Murdock, the Bass Brothers, T. Boone Pickens, and Ivan Boesky have made huge speculative gains by merely *starting* to acquire the stock of an unsuspecting firm.

In self-defense, firms have pushed their state legislatures for laws that would protect them from unfriendly advances. Currently, twenty-one states restrict unfriendly takeovers and more states are likely to follow now that the Supreme Court has upheld in the Arvin Case (1987) the right of states to regulate takeovers. On April 21, 1987, in a 6 to 3 vote, justices from both the conservative and the liberal sides of the Court joined retiring Justice Lewis Powell in his majority opinion that state action in this area was not a burdensome infringement on interstate commerce.

The success in state legislatures has encouraged others to push for federal legislation that would protect firms in all fifty states from hostile takeovers. Even if this does not occur, some professionals, for example Gerald L. Houseman, maintain that much " . . . could be accomplished without enacting any new laws." He argues that the present state of affairs demands that we utilize the antitrust tools that we already have at hand. Paulus and Gay would be horrified by the prospect of renewed antitrust action. They maintain that the "corporate restructuring" that has occurred in the 1980s represents our " . . . best hope for resolving our current trade problems" and for keeping " . . . inflation remarkably quiescent for the foreseeable future."

YES

Gerald L. Houseman

THE MERGER GAME
STARTS WITH DECEPTION

You've got perhaps ten men guiding the future of corporate America.
—Ivan Boesky, well-known merger investment specialist*

Mergers, acquisitions, and hostile take-overs are hot stuff. There are now some 3,000 a year taking place compared to 1,500 in 1980. The dollars involved were less than $20 billion a year in 1974, more than $40 billion a year in 1980, and approximately $173 billion in 1985. A more than fourfold increase in five years' time indicates that a major restructuring of corporations is now going on—and the end is nowhere in sight. Ivan Boesky, one of the best-known take-over artists, [in 1986] decided to increase his leveraging account from $200 million to $1 billion, and anyone [could have bought] into this deal for a cool million. With this money, he [would have stood] as a threat to many boards of directors and managements, and he [would have undoubtedly wreaked] havoc on workers threatened with unemployment; stockholders who want to stay with the corporate entity as is; the general public as it is increasingly faced with monopolistic or oligopolistic business practices; and the economy, which is already afloat in the junk bonds which threaten its growth and vitality. There are also taxation questions raised by such activity, and there is little question that the capital resources used up in such games has a deleterious effect upon research and development. There are at least indirect effects upon such global concerns as international trade and Third World development. And most importantly, the entrepreneurial myths in American capitalism tend to be exploded when the various tax incentives found in our laws and the much-trumpeted abilities to create product innovations and new jobs are lost in these money-shuffling and debt-creating machinations.

This combination process begins with deception. The Williams Act of 1968 requires disclosure of ownership of significant blocks of securities. If a take-

*Eds: This article was written and published shortly before Ivan Boesky was indicted on numerous counts of insider trading.

From "The Merger Game Starts with Deception," by Gerald L. Houseman, *Challenge*, September/October 1986. Copyright © 1986. Reprinted with permission of M.E. Sharpe, Inc., publishers, Armonk, NY 10504.

over artist such as Carl Icahn or Victor Posner acquires as much as 5 percent interest in a company, this must be disclosed. When this information is provided to the Securities and Exchange Commission, it must be accompanied by an explanation. This explanation—sometimes reported on in the press—is invariably a statement that the acquirer has bought into the company for investment purposes only. Few knowledgeable observers believe this, particularly when the "investor" is a well-known take-over artist.

THE "INSIDER" ISSUE

Before such an item ever appears in the financial press, however, informed investors will have bought into the stock; for despite the rules against "insider" trading or disclosure, the tips will be out on Wall Street. This is shown by the almost invariable uptick in the price which occurs *before* the take-over artist's announcement is made. When the stock really begins to take off as a result of the buy-out expectations and the premium price that is anticipated, these "insiders" will take their profits. The biggest "insider" of all, of course, is the investor who has reported his 5 percent or greater interest; he or she can be expected to profit merely from buying into the company and staking out an interest. Since the stock goes up on this information in nearly all circumstances, the acquirer can determine his or her own profit in a way that is analogous to shooting fish in a barrel.

At this very outset of the takeover or merger process, then, there are ethical and legal questions to grapple with: whether deception has occurred; whether "insider" money-making is involved caused by the announcement; and whether the self-directed "insider" has an advantage in raising the price of securities merely by indicating an interest in them.

ANTITRUST VIOLATIONS AND NONENFORCEMENT

A second set of problems presented almost immediately by buy-out activity is found in antitrust considerations. In particular, this is the case in proposals for mergers or takeovers which are "horizontal"; that is, those which involve the combining of former competitors. There is still a major problem, however, when a "vertical" union is proposed—one in which the firms involved are not direct competitors. These arrangements can often be just as bad for the economy and for the general public as the "horizontal" deals. Centralization seems to produce no particular efficiencies; indeed, the economic evidence appears to be the contrary. (It is interesting to reflect upon the Reagan administration's attitudes about bureaucracy that seem to support an unlikely thesis that while government, in the nondefense sector, gains efficiency as it grows smaller, corporations gain efficiency as they grow larger.) In order to determine whether monopolistic or oligopolistic conditions are threatened by a proposed merger, the present administration has devised an "HHI Index" (named for its creators, Herfindahl and Hirschman) which, though it is a lax and watered-down guide to measuring monopoly or oligopoly, has the virtue of relying upon a simple formula. Unfortunately, the formula is observed in the breach as much as in application, so that, by and large, the administration has all but abandoned antitrust enforcement.

QUALMS GENERATED
BY BUY-OUT ACTIVITY

Receipt of the offer of purchase causes no particular worries in the board room or in top management if the offer is "friendly"; that is, if it is presumed that the buy-out forces do not plan to replace them. Employees, of course, may lose out even in a friendly merger. And it should be borne in mind that even a friendly merger is often an unproductive use of capital. The recent General Electric acquisition of RCA Corporation, for example, was regarded by many Wall Street observers as an uninspired use of $12 billion; and this was a cash deal, the kind which presumably does the least harm to the economy.

Unfriendly offers, which are assumed by the target company's leadership to mean the likely end of their careers with the firm, may be unanticipated and can cause a great deal of consternation. Will the firm continue to exist in some recognizable form or another? In the case of many companies, the answer clearly has been negative. What about existing labor contracts? And what will happen to middle management? Book company managements have been known to be replaced by broadcast people when the latter took over the book firm; it was explained that, after all, broadcast people, like book people, are in communications.

Experience shows that the very top-level people in a firm have nothing worse to fear than a "golden parachute" arrangement of pay and other conditions of severance which will make them rich even if they are no longer powerful.

All kinds of factors can obtain, of course, in a buy-out deal. It may be in the best interests of the top leaders of a firm, and even of its stockholders and employees, to acquiesce; or it may be best to fight. Sometimes it is possible to win by losing—by paying the take-over artist to leave the company alone.

GREENMAIL

Many offers to take over a company (so-called "tender offers") are made with little or no thought of actually taking it over. The objective in these cases is to threaten the board and management but, after a variety of financial and legal skirmishes, to withdraw—if the company will pay off with "greenmail." Greenmail, technically speaking, is the premium over market value paid by a company to the raider for its own stock in order to obtain withdrawal from a proxy fight (the fight for control of the firm). Let us assume a market value of $40 per share. The stock goes to $52 on the news of the take-over attempt. (Again, the reader is reminded that there is already a great short-term gain on the investment which has occurred only because the take-over artist decided to make it happen.) After considerable public and private maneuvering, let us assume that the take-over investor is prevailed upon (more likely, advised by the legal and financial staff at his disposal) to sell his interest in the company and to give up the thought of taking it over. When this occurs, a contract is drawn up which guarantees that the raider will not try to do this again for a set number of years. In exchange for this agreement, he sells his stock back to the company for a price of, say, $62. (The terms of the agreement outlined in this example are quite typical.) The take-over artist, or "broker," which is his usual title, has been well rewarded for notifying the SEC about buying into the company "for investment purposes" and for carrying out a war of nerves against the firm.

Most hostile take-over attempts result in greenmail; in other words, they are "unsuccessful" and, it is often alleged, are meant to be. The take-over investor would actually have to run the company if he won control, and that is not usually the object of this game. Greenmail amounts can be substantial. Some recent examples are $100 million paid to Sir James Goldsmith by St. Regis Paper; $163.3 million paid to Carl Icahn by Chesebrough-Ponds; $180 million given to Rupert Murdoch by Warner Communications; $325 million paid to Saul Steinberg by Walt Disney Productions; $471.7 million awarded to the famous (or infamous) T. Boone Pickens by Phillips Petroleum; and $178 million turned over to the Bass brothers by Texaco.

Greenmail payments can substantially weaken a corporation. In the Disney case, for example, the floating of a large amount of debt was necessary to pay off Steinberg and the company's debt-to-equity ratio was severely affected. This ratio is presently at near-record levels for all of corporate America, and much of the reason is found in these kinds of activities. Some companies sell off assets while others turn to the high-interest instruments known as "junk bonds." Whatever financial strategy is decided upon, the corporation can only come off badly from a take-over battle.

The game for the greenmailer, which is uninhibited by the law, goes on. There are thousands of available targets. Some companies have erected defenses against take-overs, but they are not impenetrable. One of the most pernicious of these defenses is the "poison pill," or the ac-

quisition of debt (often in "junk bonds" form) in order to make the target firm less attractive. Needless to say, companies that involve themselves in this kind of activity weaken their capital structure and may also hurt the economy generally because of the increased floating of questionable instruments of indebtedness.

LEVERAGED BUY-OUTS

Most mergers, acquisitions, and hostile take-overs are leveraged buy-outs if they succeed. A leveraged buy-out is an acquisition of a company which leaves the acquired operating entity with a greater than traditional debt-to-equity ratio. There are varieties of leveraged buy-outs, to be sure. They can be aimed at asset acquisition or stock acquisition or both. They can be aimed at a division or part of a company such as those found in a conglomerate. And they can be fostered by arrangements involving secured or unsecured financing. The tendency today, in our increasingly loose and ungovernable financial markets, is toward the latter. "Junk bonds" are expected to do their magic.

A host of arrangements are available for a leveraged buy-out, but one particular form deserves special comment. This one, which is increasingly in vogue, involves only a small number of investors, bankers, and company officials who manage to take a company out of the stock market altogether. It "goes private." This has happened recently in the case of Beatrice, R. H. Macy, and other companies, some of them extremely large, with assets in the billion-dollar range. The primary actors in such a deal are the managements of public companies. These individuals may start out with relatively few shares. In the course of the buy-out, however, they acquire all of the company (with the help of a few select outside investors and a huge amount of debt, much or most of it in the form of "junk bonds"). Some of these deals leave the company with debt-to-assets ratios as high as 80 percent. Often there is conflict of interest set up by this arrangement, because the management, rather than representing the interests of the stockholders as imposed by their fiduciary relationship and responsibilities, may well be imperiling the company's financial stability. The argument that a discontented stockholder can always sell her or his shares begs the question of the long-term interests of the firm and the economy in general. The process of "going private" is, naturally, the ultimate defense against take-overs or, in the words of one merger lawyer, "the ultimate lock-up."

"JUNK BONDS"

"Junk bonds" have been overwhelmingly important engines of the merger, acquisition, and take-over activity of recent years. The brokerage industry prefers the term "high-yield" bonds, but "junk bonds" is the most descriptive of these admittedly shaky debt instruments.

These bonds have been around most of this century, but they have had no great importance in securities markets until about 1980. They are indeed high-yield, which reflects their stature in the world of securities and debt instruments. A further reflection is their rating: neither Moody's nor Standard and Poor's, the two bond-ranking services, gives them any rating at all. They are not AAA, AA, B, C or any other bond. They get no rating because they apparently deserve none.

The classic use of junk bonds has been to get a company "over the hump"; that is, to give it perhaps one last chance to become profitable again by allowing it to borrow at high rates of interest. The investors who buy such instruments realize that the purchase is risky.

No great threat was posed to the economy as long as junk bonds represented something like 3 or 4 percent of the debt instruments in the market. But today they comprise nearly 20 percent of the debt instruments floating around, and the reason for this is simple enough. They are the preferred vehicles for mergers, acquisitions, hostile take-overs, and all sorts of leveraged buy-outs. Their value, which is dubious, is premised upon the future sale of assets of the target firm. In other words, junk bonds are nothing, in most instances, except a promise to liquidate some of the assets of a company once a take-over attempt has succeeded.

This brings up an important point. Hostile take-overs and many or most leveraged buy-outs have *asset liquidation*—the selling off of company assets—in mind as the way out of the intensely leveraged debt situation they create. Ted Turner, for example, intended to float vast amounts of junk bonds, as many as he could print, in order to take over CBS. His intention, never unclear, was to sell off such company assets as rich local outlets or this or that division. His effort did not succeed for a variety of reasons, including prudent defenses established by CBS. There is no doubt that a smaller CBS would have been the result of these machinations if they had succeeded.

While it can be seen that unhealthy social, political, and economic effects can flow from the overuse of junk bonds, there is a critical factor today that may be overlooked. In the past, junk bonds were almost all held by banks. Banks are best equipped to invest in these instruments because they have the ability, after all, to be understanding if the bond-floating firm faces new hurdles. Since junk bonds have historically been held by banks, it has always been possible to alleviate some of their bad economic effects.

Now, however, junk bonds are found in every nook and cranny of the investment market. Not only banks, but thrift institutions (who buy many of them), insurance companies, investment funds, and brokerage houses are among the purchasers, and many individual investors are attracted to their high yields as well. This array of institutions and individuals cannot provide the same debt management advantages and help that the banks can. They can hardly be understanding about new problems or unanticipated developments faced by the debtor firm. The junk-bondholders of today, then, are brittle rather than flexible, rigid rather than liquid. If a junk-bond-floating company runs into trouble, there is a good chance that it will go under.

The implications are broad indeed. The next crash, in fact, could be a "junk-bonds crash," and this possibility is recognized even by many of the brokers who underwrite such instruments.

These concerns were unquestionably behind the recent proposal of Federal Reserve Board Chairman Paul Volcker to establish margin requirements on the floating of junk bonds. Until January 1986, it was possible to issue junk bonds on the strength of only 10 percent of their capital value. Volcker proposed that all junk bonds be issued with a margin requirement of 50 percent. The Reagan administration strongly objected, although its reasons were never very clear, for the most part befogged in platitudes about free enterprise. During the period of one month (early December 1985 to early January 1986) in which the Federal Reserve Board took opinions on the proposed rule, a compromise was worked out: a 50 percent margin is required in the event of a hostile take-over attempt; only 10 percent is necessary, however, in order to float these dubious instruments for the sake of a friendly mergers or acquisitions or leveraged buy-outs of most kinds. Since hostile takeovers represented fewer than 20 of the 2,500 mergers of 1985, this compromise was clearly an administration victory.

NOW AND FUTURE

There are some weak arguments presented from time to time in favor of all of this churning and empire-building. T. Boone Pickens and other take-over artists say that they can engage in their activities because their targets have stock that is priced too low, and that this low price reflects mismanagement. A *Business Week* article recently stated that, although we do not see the benefits at the present time, the wave of mergers, acquisitions, and take-overs will yield great—but unspecified—benefits to all of us.

In my view, apologists for this phenomenon are caught in any number of dilemmas when they accept the manic drive behind these power trips of managers and directors, brokers and financiers, proxy fighters and take-over specialists as the exercise of free enterprise. If making their argument to Adam Smith, they would have to do an overarching amount of backing and filling to show how new conditions, or the anomalies of corporate structure, or the record of government intervention—or perhaps our astrological bearings!—have altered our classic understanding of the meaning of market competition.

All kinds of policy prescriptions suggest themselves as recent corporate history is surveyed. Simply removing the tax incentives, such as deductions for interest on debt for merger-acquisition-take-over activity would be a good start. Volcker's original margin requirement for junk bonds—50 percent for all of them, not just those used for hostile takeovers—is a worthwhile proposal. Better disclosure rules in corporate governance and especially in merger-acquisition-take-over activity would help to alert the public, stockholders, and various affected parties. The use of junk bonds should probably be restricted in various ways. Greenmail should probably be against the law, and both civil and criminal sanctions should be enacted. A much clearer statement of the real intentions of investors can be mandated. The stock exchanges should guarantee that firms they list treat all stockholders equally.

A great deal could be accomplished without enacting any new laws or regulations. The re-establishment of regulation, the renewal of antitrust enforcement, and a vigorous policy of requiring adherence to the law could all do a great deal to bring about a measure of social and financial (if not political) responsibility to the corporate world. The tools are already there on the law books. This is not to say that enforcement, or even the laws themselves, were adequate prior to the gross laxity of recent years; but it would be healthy for the American polity to return to a rule of law in matters of corporate organization and restructuring.

NO

John D. Paulus and Robert S. Gay

U.S. MERGERS
ARE HELPING PRODUCTIVITY

The last few weeks of 1986 could well go down as a watershed period in the competitive struggle facing corporate America. General Motors, IBM, and AT&T—all giants without peer in U.S. industry—introduced significant restructuring programs aimed at restoring their preeminence as low-cost producers. This spate of announcements represents the frankest admission yet of America's international competitiveness problem, symbolized so dramatically by the soaring trade deficit.

The flip side of this shortfall, the dependence on foreign capital to finance the grade gap, implies that Americans presently are living beyond their means. Such a trend cannot continue, and thus the United States is finally facing up to the fact that it either will have to accept a lower standard of living or become more competitive by raising worker productivity.

The American competitiveness problem has its roots in the inflation of the 1970s. During that decade, productivity growth slipped badly, as ever-rising product prices protected inefficient production practices. Moreover, many workers represented by strong unions were able to extract wage gains which failed to reflect the slump in output per hour. In some industries—such as steel, autos, and trucking—wage premiums, or the excess of wages in a given industry over the national average, vaulted from the 30–40 percent range at the beginning of the 1970s to over 70 percent by the end of the decade.

The problem became increasingly obvious as import penetration rose substantially in the 1970s, even before the U.S. dollar skyrocketed during the first half of the 1980s. For example, the share of U.S. expenditures on manufactured goods devoted to imports roughly doubled from 1968 to 1981, rising from 4.3 percent to 8.4 percent. For some industries, the increase in penetration during this time frame was truly spectacular: for apparel, imports rose from 4.2 percent to 13.7 percent; for leather and leather products, from 8.9 percent to 24.7 percent; for steel, from 12.2 percent to 21.8 percent; for machine tools, from 14.6 percent to 29.4 percent; and for motor vehicles and parts, from 5.7 percent to 21.7 percent.

From "U.S. Mergers are Helping Productivity," by John D. Paulus and Robert S. Gay, *Challenge*, May/June 1987. Copyright © 1987. Reprinted with permission of M.E. Sharpe, Inc., publishers, Armonk, NY 10504.

The sharp rise in the dollar from 1981 to 1985 worsened the competitive disadvantage of U.S. firms and contributed to the burgeoning trade deficit. Thus, with high costs, increased import penetration, and a strong dollar, corporate America would have to undertake a massive adjustment program to repair the damage done to the nation's competitive position.

COPING THROUGH RESTRUCTURING

The United States has reacted to its competitive inadequacies largely (though not exclusively) by redeploying assets in configurations aimed at enhancing productivity. The popular term for this process is "corporate restructuring," which refers to such practices as closing inefficient plants and modernizing others, shedding businesses that require specialized management skills, granting wage concessions, and paring "fat" from bloated corporate bureaucracies. Even deregulation, as applied to the trucking and airline industries, for example, represents a form of restructuring, which, in turn, intensifies competition since new firms entering the industry operate at costs lower than those existing companies.

Playing an integral role in the overall restructuring are mergers, acquisitions, and leveraged buyouts, which facilitate transfers of ownership, and ultimately, changes in management and work practices. Moreover, the mere threat of such a change in ownership may induce senior managers to reshape their corporations before outside forces enter the picture. At the very least, financial restructuring is a natural by-product, and perhaps an important catalyst, in corporate America's struggle to regain its once preeminent competitive stature.

A precise measure of the extent of corporate restructuring is impossible. But the dollar value of merger and acquisition activity is certainly related to the degree of restructuring in the broader sense. Using this measure, it is possible to gauge the relationship between the amount of restructuring in a given industry and subsequent gains in productivity and cost control. Such analysis can help to answer the question: "What is corporate restructuring doing to the American economy?" Ultimately it also sheds light on the more important question: "Is America helping herself to improve competitiveness?"

HAS IT WORKED?

Merger and acquisition (M&A) activity began to take off in 1981, not by coincidence, a year when the realities of heightened import penetration began to hit home. The next surge began in 1984 and has continued ever since. Over the past six years a fairly stable proportion of M&A activity—between 50 percent and 65 percent—has occurred in manufacturing and mining, sectors that represent the bulk of our goods-producing infrastructure that has become increasingly vulnerable to foreign competition. In 1985, these two sectors accounted for about 25 percent of U.S. output.

What is particularly intriguing is that there has been impressive improvement in productivity in the manufacturing and mining sectors during the time M&A activity has accelerated. From the first quarter of 1980 to the present, productivity in the manufacturing sector has grown at an average annual rate of 3.3 percent, up significantly from an average of only 1.4 percent for the 1973–80 period, and higher even than the 3 percent average growth recorded during 1960–73.

Such a performance in output per hour in the 1980–86 period is especially impressive since production expanded slowly over those years—at an average rate of only 2.3 percent annually. And it is widely conceded that high rates of productivity growth are much easier to achieve during periods of rapid growth when resources are more intensively utilized.

Moreover, during 1980–86, productivity in manufacturing, where restructuring was especially intense, appears to have greatly outperformed that of the rest of the economy where restructuring was less intense. From 1948 to 1980 productivity growth in the industrial sector was about equal to that recorded for the nonfarm economy overall. However, with restructuring intensifying after 1980, the performance of productivity in manufacturing has been far superior to that of the nonfarm economy as a whole.

A LOOK BY INDUSTRY

If restructuring can, in fact, be linked to the solid improvement of productivity in manufacturing, those industries in which asset redeployment has been most intense should also show the largest gains in output per hour. To test this premise, we have developed a restructuring intensity measure (RIM)—the ratio of the share of M&A activity accounted for by each industry relative to the same industry's share of U.S. output.

For example, if an industry accounted for, say, 10 percent of financial restructuring in a given year, but only for 5 percent of GNP, then its RIM would be 2.0. Thus, if the RIM is greater than 1.0—that is, if the RIM is equal to 1.0, restructuring intensity would be average, and if less than 1.0, below average.

financial restructuring is proportionately greater than output for a given industry—that segment of the economy has been intensively restructured. On the other hand, if the RIM is equal to 1.0, restructuring intensity would be average, and if less than 1.0, below average.

Some stunning productivity success stories for industries that have undergone extensive restructuring are revealed in Table 1. Industry groupings that have RIM ratios greater than 1.0 have experienced substantial improvements in productivity growth in the 1980s, compared with the 1970s.

For example, after eking out very little, if any, productivity gains during the 1970s, industries such as metal mining, coal mining, sawmills, hydraulic cement, steel, primary copper, copper rolling, motor vehicles, tires, and railroad transportation have achieved impressive productivity gains of 5 percent or more annually during the 1980s. These dramatic turn-arounds are all the more remarkable because many of these industries have not enjoyed strong increases in output; indeed, virtually all the rise in production is due to higher productivity. Obviously, the firms involved have taken concerted actions to bolster their competitive position.

To be sure, not all industries have participated in the revival of productivity growth. A number of nondurable goods industries have experienced smaller gains this decade than during the 1970s. Indeed, average productivity performance in the nondurable goods sector (2.8 percent annually) has not been as high as that for durable goods (4.4 percent), perhaps because nondurables producers, in general, have not felt an urgency to revamp production techniques in the face of intense foreign com-

Table 1

Productivity Trends and Restructuring in Selected Industries

	Restructuring intensity measure 1980 to 1985	Average annual productivity		
		1973 to 1980	1980 to 1985	Change in trend
Metal mining	16.4			
Iron ore		1.4%	8.1%	6.7%
Copper		1.1	9.9	8.7
Coal mining	2.5	−1.6	6.5	8.1
Total manufacturing	1.6	1.2	3.7	2.5
Lumber and wood products	2.2			
Sawmills and planing mills		0.6	5.4	4.9
Stone, clay, and glass	0.9[1]			
Hydraulic cement		−1.9	8.7	10.6
Primary metals	1.5			
Steel		−0.5	6.1	6.6
Gray iron foundries		−0.6	3.8	4.3
Primary copper, lead, & zinc		1.3	13.0	11.7
Primary aluminum		0.1	3.7	3.6
Copper rolling and drawing		0.1	6.5	6.4
Fabricated metals	1.4			
Automotive stampings		1.0	4.6[2]	3.6
Machinery, except electrical	1.0			
Refrigeration and heating equipment		−1.3	2.1[2]	3.4
Electric and electronic equipment	1.6			
Radio and television sets		4.2	14.4[2]	10.2
Transportation equipment	1.6			
Motor vehicles and parts		0.8	6.2	5.3
Textile mill products	1.2			
Nonwool yarn mills		2.3	5.3	3.0
Rubber and misc. plastic products	0.8[1]			
Tires and inner tubes		1.1	7.3	6.3
Railroad transportation	3.1	1.5	8.6	7.1

[1]These ratios actually understate the extent of financial restructuring in the subindustries (tires and hydraulic cement) where M & A activity was concentrated.
[2]Productivity statistics are available through 1984.
Sources: Bureau of Labor Statistics, U.S. Department of Commerce; Morgan Stanley & Co.

petition. And industries such as mass transit, electric utilities, and some retailers have suffered outright declines in productivity in recent years, and have not undertaken much restructuring either.

Also notably absent from Table 1 are producers of capital equipment and some other high-tech items. The mediocre productivity performance in high-tech industries, despite considerable financial restructuring, is particularly worrisome. Until the early 1980s, the United States had enjoyed substantial trade surpluses in capital goods, reflecting comparative advantages in productive efficiency.

Over the past few years, however, those surpluses have dwindled steadily to the point where we actually were running a trade deficit in capital equipment in the second quarter of 1986. While the overvalued dollar undoubtedly contributed to that decline, lackluster productivity performance of late also has permitted foreign competitors to close the gap in productive efficiency, which has made the task of regaining lost market share more difficult.

WAGE CONCESSIONS

U.S. industry also has made progress in trimming wage costs. As recently as mid-1981, wage increases in manufacturing industries averaged 10 percent. By 1983, however, wage rate adjustments had plummeted on balance to about 3 percent and have remained around that subdued rate ever since. This deceleration in wages was far greater than would have been expected based on historical relationships with macroeconomic conditions alone—mainly unemployment and inflation. Indeed, from 1983 through 1986, wage inflation in manufacturing averaged an estimated one percentage point per year less than normal. A good deal of the abnormally abrupt easing in wages can be attributed to competitive pressures arising from extensive restructuring.

The unusually pronounced slowdown in wage inflation was concentrated in heavily unionized industries and coincided with an unprecedented outbreak of so-called "concessionary" settlements, which froze or even cut base wage rates over the life of multiyear agreements. In each of the past five years, with the sole exception of 1984, more than half of union workers reaching new labor contracts in manufacturing have accepted initial wage reductions or freezes. Likewise, wage "concessions" were pervasive in mining, construction, and the deregulated transportation industries— airlines and trucking.

Almost invariably, wage cuts and freezes have occurred at firms whose competitive positions deteriorated badly during the 1970s, either because wage premiums had risen substantially or because productivity performance had been dreadful. Moreover, by the 1980s, "new" competition from foreign producers or domestic nonunion firms emerged. Burdened with high costs and besieged by aggressive new competitors, many unionized firms were faced with a case of "do or die." In that light, the expense-cutting efforts of the past five years are an encouraging sign that U.S. industry is chipping away current cost disadvantages.

Table 2 gives some sense of how far we have come. In all of the industries listed, management and unions have negotiated concessionary settlements during the 1980s. As a result, wage premiums— as measured by the ratio of wage rates in the industry to the average for all nonfarm workers—have at least stabilized since 1981 and in some case have declined significantly. Nonetheless, as of 1986 all the ratios were still well above those that prevailed in the late 1960s. The combination of continued high premiums and the fact that the new low-cost competitors will not simply "go away" implies that pressures to reduce premiums further will persist for quite some time.

The bottom line is that the restructur-

Table 2

**Ratio of Hourly Earnings in Selected Industries
to Average for Private Nonfarm Production Workers**

Industry	1969	1973	1977	1981	1983	1985	First half 1986
Trucking[1]	1.31	1.59	1.63	1.73	1.63	1.53	1.50
Autos[2]	1.39	1.45	1.57	1.70	1.70	1.73	1.72
Steel[3]	1.35	1.42	1.64	1.81	1.67	1.63	1.67
Rubber[4]	1.38	1.33	1.38	1.53	1.54	1.54	1.56
Mining	1.18	1.20	1.32	1.38	1.41	1.40	1.42
Machinery[5]	1.16	1.21	1.27	1.32	1.28	1.27	1.28
Primary metals	1.25	1.28	1.41	1.49	1.42	1.36	1.37

[1]Straight-time hourly wage rates are specified in Master Freight Agreements.
[2]SIC 3711, motor vehicles and car bodies.
[3]SIC 3312, blast furnaces and steel mills.
[4]SIC 301, tires and inner tubes.
[5]SIC 353, construction.

ing of U.S. industry during the 1980s has helped considerably to keep labor cost pressures at a minimum. As shown in Figure 1, over the past five years labor costs per unit of output in manufacturing literally have been flat. More significantly, the usual pattern of increasing cost pressures over the course of economic expansions has been decisively broken during the current business cycle. As we enter the fifth year of the upturn, unit labor costs in manufacturing still are showing no signs of a pickup.

THE TASK AHEAD

Much remains to be done before America's competitiveness problem disappears. The trade deficit, the most succinct measure of the severity of the difficulty and its principal symptom, is likely to shrink only marginally in 1987. Moreover, as noted earlier, many industries have made little progress as yet in improving productive efficiency.

The United States has three choices in confronting the problem. First, corporate restructuring can continue, raising productivity and lowering costs in the process. This constructive solution could eventually narrow the trade deficit, while

Figure 1

Growth of Unit Labor Costs in Manufacturing
(in percentages)

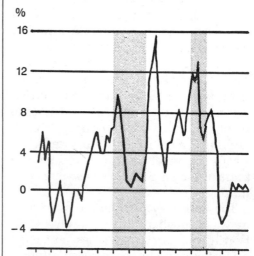

Shaded areas indicate recessionary periods as designated by the National Bureau of Economic Research.

enabling the nation to protect an enhance its high standard of living.

Second, the government could undertake monetary and fiscal-policies designed to lower the foreign exchange value of the dollar significantly. However, this alternative would make the nation poorer, since for a given endowment of human and fixed capital, the lower dollar merely raises the cost of foreign goods and services.

Third, the United States could erect meaningful protectionist barriers, turning this country into the world's premiere high-cost producer. In this event, even fewer foreigners would want to buy our high-priced products and services than currently do. In the end, even without foreign retaliation, which most likely would follow, protectionism would impoverish the nation just as lowering the dollar would.

We believe the United States will continue to restructure its economic base until America again becomes competitive in global markets. This implies further substantial downward pressures on costs and on inflation. In short, continued corporate restructuring represents not only the nation's best hope for resolving our current trade problems, but also will keep inflation remarkably quiescent for the foreseeable future.

POSTSCRIPT

Are There Too Many Hostile Takeovers?

Houseman asserts that the hands-off approach of the free marketeers within the Reagan Administration has provided the takeover artist with an unfair advantage in the stock market. Men such as Ivan Boesky, Carl Icahn and Victor Posner have capitalized on these opportunities and in the process have accumulated millions of dollars of questionable gains. They play with the advantage of insider information. They force firms to pay greenmail, and if a takeover is actually consummated, it is more often than not heavily leveraged and underwritten by junk bonds. The end result of the exploits of these corporate raiders is a loss to the workers, stockholders and the economy at large.

Paulus and Gay are unconcerned about the merger/acquisition wave of the 1980s. Indeed, they see direct and immediate benefits to this movement. These business practitioners see this activity as part of the process of corporate restructuring—a process that closes inefficient plants, modernizes others, sheds business with specialized management skills, bargains wage concessions and pares " 'fat' from bloated corporate bureaucracies." They argue that this is necessary if the U.S. is to remain competitive in the world market and avoid the ravages of inflation.

Recent professional and popular publications contain many articles on the recent wave of hostile takeovers. Charles R. Knoeber's essay entitled "Golden Parachutes, Shark Repellents, and Hostile Tender Offers," which appeared in the March 1986 issue of the *American Economic Review*, presents the best summary currently available for the more technically minded. A number of other quasi-professional journals have also provided us with a number of essays about hostile takeovers, particularly after the Ivan Boesky insider trader scandal made the national headlines. For articles which are generally sympathetic toward mergers and acquisitions see *Dunn's Business Month, Business Week, Forbes,* and *Fortune.* Another perspective is provided by Paul O. Gaddis in the July-August 1987 *Harvard Business Review.* In this essay entitled "Taken Over, Turned Out," Gaddis provides a first hand account of what happens when a company is "taken over."

ISSUE 6

Should The Federal Government Deregulate American Business?

YES: Murray L. Weidenbaum, from "Weidenbaum Analyzes Benefit-Cost Analysis," *Across the Board* (February 1982)

NO: The editors of *Dollars and Sense,* from "The Cotton Industry Passes the Boll," *Dollars and Sense* (May/June 1982)

ISSUE SUMMARY

YES: Weidenbaum asserts that government decision makers should face the same economic constraints as business executives do in the private sector. They must insist that the benefits of their actions at least match the cost of their actions.

NO: The editors of *Dollars and Sense* contend that although benefit-cost analysis seems to have "a certain simple logic," it is neither simple nor objective. Rather, they believe benefit-cost analyses and the related cost-effectiveness approach are fatally flawed by an inherent social bias.

The key issue of the free market economists' attack on government intervention is their campaign to eliminate, or at least reduce substantially, the regulation of private enterprise. These economists contend that this regulation results in higher consumer prices, reduced worker productivity, declining innovation and investment, rising unemployment rates, reversals in our balance of payments position, increases in our federal budget deficit, and just about every other problem that can be faced in our economic system. They are so alarmed about this issue because government intervention—particularly intervention that directly affects the productive process—is in direct violation of the precepts set down by Adam Smith and his fellow classical economists.

This has been a growing problem for the free market economist because Congress markedly increased regulatory activity during the late 1960s and early 1970s. In order to offset this new wave of regulations, a counter-offensive was spearheaded by organizations such as the American Enterprise Institute, of which author Weidenbaum is a former president. Members of this group and other groups such as the Heritage Foundation, the Hoover Foundation, and the Foundation for Economic Education have testified before Congress, initiated their own journals (such as the *Journal of Regulation*), written numerous popular and professional articles, elicited growing financial support from the business community, and established endowed professorships at a number of universities. Above all, they have directly influenced public opinion.

The free market economists' impact has affected more than public opinion. The Democratic Congress that supported and sponsored many of the government regulations, despite the opposition of their conservative counterparts, is the same Congress that began to dismantle these regulations during the Reagan years. Legislation was passed deregulating the airlines, the trucking industry, and the natural gas industry. The Occupational Safety and Health Administration (OSHA), the Equal Employment Opportunity Commission (EEOC), and the Environmental Protection Agency (EPA) have all felt the effects of substantial budget and staff reductions. The tide has apparently turned, and the free market economists can rejoice in their triumphs under the Reagan administration.

Perhaps a bit late, the liberal community recognized the groundswell that was engulfing their programs. They reacted by engaging in their own rhetorical battles. But their emotional appeals to protect government regulation have, until late, been ineffective. The editors of *Dollars and Sense*, a radical magazine, have attempted to take the arguments about government regulation beyond rhetorical exchanges. Their essay represents a frontal attack upon Weidenbaum's benefit-cost analysis.

Thus, in the selections which follow, Weidenbaum outlines the basic arguments that have been used by the free market economists to discredit and limit the extent of government regulation. The editors of *Dollars and Sense* present the liberal community's response to these arguments.

YES

Murray L. Weidenbaum

WEIDENBAUM ANALYZES BENEFIT-COST ANALYSIS

Discussions of government regulation of product hazards, such as toxic substances, frequently conclude that decision-makers would be aided by the results of benefit-cost studies and related economic analyses. This article tries to explain the role of such quantitative analyses in the regulatory process.

The motive for incorporating benefit-cost analysis into public decision-making is to lead to a more efficient allocation of government resources by subjecting the public sector to the same type of quantitative constraints as those in the private sector. In making an investment decision, for example, business executives compare the costs to be incurred with the expected revenues. If the costs exceed the revenues, the investment usually is not considered worthwhile. If revenues exceed costs, further consideration is usually given the proposal, although capital constraints require another determination of the most financially attractive investments.

The government agency decision-maker does not face the same type of economic constraints. If the costs and other disadvantages to society of an agency action exceed the benefits and other advantages, that situation may not have an immediate adverse impact on the agency. However, such an action would have an immediate impact on a private business if one of its executives made an error. Such analytical information rarely exists in the public sector, so that, more often than not, the governmental decision-maker is not aware that he or she is approving a regulation that is economically inefficient. The aim of requiring agencies to perform benefit-cost analysis is to make the government's decision-making process more effective, and to eliminate regulatory actions that, on balance, generate more costs than benefits. This result is not assured by benefit-cost analysis, since political and other important, but subjective, considerations may dominate. This may result in actions that are not economically efficient, but are desired on grounds of equity or income distribution. Yet benefit-cost analysis may provide valuable information for government decision-makers.

From *Across the Board*, February 1982. Copyright © 1982. Reprinted by permission of the Conference Board, Inc.

It may be useful to consider the economic rationale for making benefit-cost analyses of government actions. Economists have long been interested in identifying policies that promote economic welfare, specifically by improving the efficiency with which a society uses its resources.

Benefits are measured in terms of the increased production of goods and services. Costs are computed in terms of the foregone benefits that would have been obtained by using those resources in some other activity. The underlying aim of benefit-cost analysis is to maximize the value of the social income, usually measured by the gross national product (GNP). For many years, certain Federal agencies (such as the Corps of Engineers and the Bureau of Reclamation) have used benefit-cost analysis to evaluate prospective projects.

[Typically,] initial regulatory effort—such as cleaning up the worst effects of pollution in a river—may well generate benefits greater than costs. But the resources required to achieve additional cleanup become disproportionately high, and at some point the added benefits may be substantially less than the added costs. For example, a study of the impact of environmental controls on the fruit and vegetable processing industry revealed that it cost less to eliminate the first 85 percent of the pollution than the next 10 percent. In beet sugar plants, it costs more than $1 a pound to reduce biological oxygen demand (BOD) — a measure of the oxygen required to decompose organic wastes—up to a level where 30 percent of pollution is eliminated. But it costs an additional $20 for a one-pound reduction at the 65 percent control level and an additional $60 for a one-pound reduction when over 95 percent control is achieved.

Another comparison is equally telling. The pulp and paper industry spent $3 billion between 1970 and 1978 complying with Federal clean-water standards, and achieved a 95 percent reduction in pollution. But to reach the new reduction goal proposed by the Environmental Protection Agency (EPA)—98 percent by 1984—would cost $4.8 billion more, a 160 percent increase in costs to achieve a 3 percent improvement in water quality. Thus, it is important to look beyond the relationship of the costs and the benefits of a proposed governmental undertaking to the additional (marginal) benefits and costs resulting from each extension of or addition to the governmental activities.

If regulatory activity goes unchecked, the result could be an excess of costs over benefits. Thus, benefit-cost analyses should be viewed as a tool for identifying the optimum amount of regulation, rather than as a means of debating the pros and cons of regulation in general. To an economist, "overregulation" is not an emotional term; it is merely shorthand for the regulatory activities in which the costs to the public are greater than the benefits. . . .

If a business decision in the private sector places an external burden on its neighbors, such as pollution, the firm does not include such a cost in its accounting, since it does not bear the burden. Public sector decision-makers, however, must, or at least ought to, consider all the effects of such a decision. Because their vantage point is the entire nation, government regulators—unlike their private sector counterparts—should attempt to include all costs and benefits, including those external to the government.

The agencies should do so because most regulatory actions have indirect effects on the economy. For example, requiring safety belts in automobiles has a direct impact on the cost of automobiles and on sales in the safety belt industry. It also influences the severity of auto accidents and has a ripple effect on the suppliers of the safety belt industry and their suppliers, and so on. If a regulatory decision is to be good, these indirect effects, as well as the direct impacts, must be taken into account.

The benefits and costs attributable to regulation are measured by the difference between the benefits and costs that occur in the presence of regulation and those that would prevail in its absence. Although the idea may seem straightforward, its application can be complex. Determining what would occur in the absence of regulation—which establishes a reference point for the calculations—may involve a considerable amount of judgment.

Table 1 shows how the incremental costs (the expenses that would not have been made in the absence of regulation) were computed in one study of water pollution control. Apparently the bulk of the costs would have been undertaken voluntarily.

Sometimes the indirect effects of regulation may be as important as the direct. Consider, for example, the question of mandatory standards to ensure the production of less hazardous consumer products. From time to time, suggestions have been made to require more protection in helmets and other recreational equipment used in playing football. Those using the safety helmets would be expected to receive the benefit of fewer or less severe injuries. However, such a safety standard could impose substantial costs on lower-income youngsters. Perhaps of greater concern, the standards might even contribute to more injuries since the price increases might result in more people playing football without any protective equipment at all. That example illustrates another basic thrust of benefit-cost analysis—to examine the proposed government action not only from the viewpoint of the impact on the business firm but also from the vantage point of the effects on the consumer.

A type of regulatory cost that is large, but difficult to measure, is a grouping that economists refer to as deadweight losses. Regulation often limits the range of permissible prices, practices, or processes. Those legal restrictions may inhibit the most productive use of resources. The loss of the higher output that would result in the absence of the regulatory activity—those deadweight losses—arises from an inefficient combination of factors. For example, the total efficiency of the economy is reduced when regulated transportation rates make it necessary for freight to be moved by rail rather than hauled at a lower cost by truck. That is so because more resources are used to achieve the same objective.

When political judgment suggests that it is not feasible to put a dollar sign on the benefits, a benefit-cost analysis still can be helpful by ranking the cost-effectiveness of alternatives. By using this method, which was originally developed for military programs, estimates are made of the costs of different ways to accomplish an objective. Cost-effectiveness analyses permit policy-makers to identify least-cost solutions. In this more limited approach, the analyst assumes

Table 1

Calculation of Incremental Cost of Regulation

Steps	Example
Company identifies an action taken to comply with a specific regulation.	Installation of wastewater pretreatment system to remove 99 percent of pollutants in compliance with Title 40 of the *Code of Federal Regulations*, Chapter 1, Part 128.
Would action have been taken otherwise?	Pretreatment system without Title 40 would have been designed to remove 95 percent of pollutants.
What was the cost of the action?	$1,200,000 (from fixed-asset ledger data).
How much would the action that would have been taken in the absence of regulation have cost?	$800,000 (the cost of installing a 95-percent system).
What was the incremental cost?	$1,200,000 − $800,000 = $400,000.

that the objective is worth accomplishing. In the regulatory field, this approach may be particularly useful in dealing with programs to reduce personal hazards. Instead of dealing with such an imponderable question as the cost of a human life, the emphasis shifts to identifying regulatory approaches that would maximize the number of lives saved after use of certain resources (such as people or capital), or minimize pain. Rather than a cold, systems approach, such attempts at objective analysis show true compassion for our fellow human beings by making the most effective use of the limited resources available to society.

A regulatory action has an impact not only in the present but also in the future. It is necessary, therefore, to place a lower value on future costs and benefits than on present costs and benefits. The basic notion here is that a given benefit is worth more today than tomorrow, and a given cost is less burdensome if borne tomorrow than today. (This is a restatement of the economic principle that a dollar received today is worth more than a dollar received tomorrow, because today's dollar could be invested and earn a return.) For this reason, future benefits and costs have less weight than today's benefits and costs.

This practice is important in evaluating regulatory actions. If the costs and benefits of two actions appear equal, and most of the benefits of one action occur after five years, while the benefits of the other action occur immediately, then the latter is the preferred alternative. Discounting of the future thus implies that the timing of any proposed action's costs and benefits is an important consideration in its evaluation.

Reliable measures of costs and benefits are not easily achieved or always possible. Should the loss of a forest be measured by the value of the timber eliminated? What of the beauty destroyed? What of the area's value as a wildlife habitat? In view of such questions, it is unlikely that agency decisionmakers will be faced with simple choices.

However, the difficulties in estimating the benefits or costs of regulatory actions need not serve as a deterrent to pursuing the analysis. Merely identifying some of the important and often overlooked impacts may be useful in the decision-making process. Examples on the cost side include the beneficial drugs that are not available because of regulatory obstacles, the freight not carried because empty trucks are not permitted to carry backhauls, and the television stations that are not broadcasting because they were not licensed. On the benefit side, examples include a more productive work force that results from a lower rate of accidents on the job, savings in medical care because of safer products, and a healthier environment that results from compliance with governmental regulations.

At times the imperfections of benefit-cost analysis may seem substantial. Nevertheless, this analysis can add some objectivity to the government's decision-making process. While benefit-cost analysis is capable only of showing the effectiveness of an action, the subsequent decisions of elected officials and their appointees might be envisioned as representing society's evaluations of the equity effects of that action. Economists can provide benefit-cost analyses and studies of the distribution of those benefits and costs, leaving the final decision to society's representatives. Presumably, those individuals are better able to make political decisions on the impacts of the actions they contemplate. Despite its shortcomings, benefit-cost analysis is a neutral concept, giving equal weight to a dollar of benefits and to a dollar of costs.

Not all the criticism of benefit-cost may be valid. The idea of attempting to quantify the effects of regulation outrages some persons. They forget the objectives that economists have in developing such measurements. The goal is not to elimi-

nate all regulation. As economists of all political persuasions have testified before a variety of Congressional committees, it is not a question of being for or against government regulation of business. A substantial degree of intervention in private activities is to be expected in a complex, modern society.

Critics who are offended by the notion of subjecting regulation to a benefit-cost test may unwittingly be exposing the weakness of their position: they must be convinced that some of their pet rules would flunk the test. After all, showing that a regulatory activity generates an excess of benefits is a strong justification for continuing it.

Despite talk of cold, systems approaches, economists are deeply concerned about people as well as dollar signs. The painful knowledge that resources available to safeguard human lives are limited causes economists to become concerned when they see wasteful use of those resources because of regulation.

General Motors, for example, calculates that society spends $700 million a year to reduce carbon monoxide auto emissions to 15 grams per mile, thus prolonging 30,000 lives an average of one year, at a cost of $23,000 for each life. To meet the 1981 standard of 3.4 grams per mile, the company estimates it will cost $100 million in addition, and prolong 20 lives by one year at an estimated cost of $25 million for each life. Human lives are precious, which is why it is so sad to note another use of that money. It has been estimated that the installation of special cardiac-care units in ambulances could prevent 24,000 premature deaths each year, at an average cost of approximately $200 for each year of life. Thus spending the $100 million for the special ambulances conceivably could save 500,000 lives a year.

Part of the problem in setting regulatory policy is that at times the benefits are more visible than the costs—not necessarily greater, but more evident. If the required scrubber for electric utilities results in cleaner air, we see the benefits. The costs are merely part of the higher electric bills we pay. Thus, the cost of regulation takes on the characteristics of a hidden sales tax that is paid by the consumer.

In the final analysis, the political factors in regulatory decision-making cannot be ignored. Many social regulations involve a transfer of economic resources from a large number of people to a small group of beneficiaries. The Occupational Safety and Health Act's coke-oven standard, for example, protects fewer than 30,000 workers, but is paid for by every-

one who buys a product containing steel. So long as regulators avoid concentrating the costs on a small group that could organize political counterpressures, costly regulations can be promulgated easily.

Despite the limitations, there is a useful role for formal economic analyses of regulatory impacts in providing, at least, an ancillary guide to policymakers. As a Federal court stated in striking down [a proposed OSHA regulation]: "Although the agency does not have to conduct an elaborate cost-benefit analysis, . . . it does have to determine whether the benefits expected from the standards bear a reasonable relationship to the costs imposed by the standard." That court's commonsense approach might be the direction to which the public policy debates on regulation could profitably shift.

NO

THE COTTON INDUSTRY PASSES THE BOLL

In 1970 the Department of Labor estimated that about 35,000 cotton workers were permanently disabled and over 100,000 (18% of the industry's workforce) were afflicted by byssinosis, commonly called "brown lung." Only a year earlier, a leading textile trade journal had scoffed, "We are particularly intrigued by the term 'byssinosis,' a thing thought up by venal doctors who attended last year's (International Labor Organization) meeting in Africa where inferior races are bound to be affected by new diseases more superior people defeated years ago."

Those superior people must be the bosses, because byssinosis has been diagnosed in workers of every color since it was first mentioned in medical literature in 1705. Almost three centuries later the manufacturers have finally had to face reality, coping with cotton dust exposure limits mandated by the federal Occupational Health and Safety Administration (OSHA) during the 1970s.

Unfortunately for textile workers, the manufacturers have found a new ally in current OSHA head Thorne Auchter, who is weaving a tangle of complex economic tales to justify severely weakening those cotton dust standards. Blatant racism is no longer used to discredit efforts to fight brown lung, but it has been replaced by a more subtle attempt to do the same thing through technical comparisons of "cost effectiveness."

CUTTING DOWN DUST

Byssinosis, a crippling respiratory disease affecting cotton mill workers, has been recognized in England since 1942 as an occupational illness for which workers deserve compensation. It causes shortness of breath, chest tightness, and coughing upon the employee's return to work on Mondays. Later these symptoms extend to other workdays, and the disease may eventually result in permanent disability or contribute to death.

From "OSHA Hits Brown Lung Rules," *Dollars and Sense*, May/June 1982. Copyright © 1982. Excerpted by permission of the Economic Affairs Bureau, Inc.

The exact cause of the disease is not known, although it is accepted that high cotton dust levels accompany high incidence of the disease. Particularly troubling, it appears, is the dust that comes from "trash" (twigs and the bract that grows at the base of the cotton boll) mixed with the cotton.

Mechanical harvesters, now in common use, yield cotton with a much higher trash content than the old hand-picking method. The cotton is ginned on site, at the fields, to remove the seeds, and is then sold to the mills in huge bales. Unbaling, carding (combining into small strands), weaving, and other processing stages take place at the mills.

One way to reduce the risk of brown lung at all stages would be to improve the ginning process to remove more trash more safely. Ginning, however, is controlled by a different set of owners than milling. It is a seasonal, highly competitive, fluctuating, and low-profit business run by thousands of small operators. Ginners insist that the capital outlays needed for improved equipment would put them out of business.

OSHA proposed weak regulations on ginning in 1977, but the ginners' lobby prevented their adoption. Mill operators claim the high trash content of the cotton they must process is not *their* problem. In short, the ginners and mill owners pass the boll—but neither pays for the damaged health of the workers.

At the mills, however, cotton dust exposure regulations have been in effect since OSHA was created in 1970. The original standard was weak and often unenforced. Political pressure, lawsuits, and direct action by groups like the Brown Lung Association (a group of disabled workers and their supporters) and the Amalgamated Clothing and Textile

Workers Union (ACTWU) resulted in stricter standards in 1976 and again in 1978.

These new standards specified that engineering controls (changes in the workplace, including ventilation and new machinery) had to be the primary long-range solution to the dust problem. Cheaper and less effective measures—such as wearing of respirators and removing workers who show signs of byssinosis—were recommended only as interim methods.

INSTANT POLICY—JUST ADD NUMBERS

The American Textile Manufacturers Institute challenged the 1978 standard on the grounds that OSHA had not justified it on a "cost-benefit" basis, nor proved its economic feasibility. This reasoning had frightening implications for potential regulation of thousands of other hazardous substances and suspected carcinogens. In effect, the companies proposed that a certain number of human lives had to be lost before OSHA could regulate a substance.

Cost-benefit analysis has a certain simple logic: Add up total costs to industry of a regulation and total benefits to workers from the regulation, and then compare. Instant social policy! All you have to do is look out there in the marketplace and see exactly what the regulation will cost, and what the improved health of the workers will be worth.

In fact, there is nothing simple or objective about the method. Any calculation about the size of costs or benefits involves political judgments that will be made differently by different observers. It is precisely because the economic system does not place a high enough value on workers' health (you can't sell it, after all) that regulations are needed in the first place.

On the practical side, how do you decide on a dollar value for a long healthy life, or retirement with dignity? How can you add up the benefits of regulation when the full health impact of brown lung—or asbestos or chemical poisoning—is not yet known? And where do you get reliable figures on the costs to industry?

One way to figure "benefits" to workers is to calculate how much more money a worker who dies or is forced to retire would have made if he or she had worked a normal lifetime. Depending on the prevailing wage, which for cotton mill workers is only 60% of the national average, that could be pretty low. For the 48% of the cotton workforce that is female, and the 20% that is black, expected earnings are particularly low. Does this mean their lives are worth less?

It doesn't take an economic whiz to realize that "benefits," as industry figures them, don't place much value on workers' lives. As a lawyer from the U.S. Chamber of Commerce put it, "Is a human life worth $10? Of course it is. But when you start going up the ladder, you have to start making some judgments, no matter how cold and callous it sounds."

As for costs to industry, the history of vinyl chloride regulation provides a clue to the abuse of cost-benefit techniques. When vinyl chloride standards were debated within OSHA in 1975, plastic manufacturers complained of compliance costs of $90 billion. Not only did that estimate turn out to be 300 times too high, but some manufacturers ended up making money from their efforts at compliance, because the new, safer, equipment also saved labor and materials.

The same may be true for cotton dust compliance. During the 1977 OSHA hearings, the manufacturers insisted that compliance with new standards would cost upwards of $2.3 billion. The figures supporting this estimate were left to the imagination. The companies refuse to release information they had about cost of new equipment that could meet OSHA's standards.

The Textile Workers Union was able to get some of that information from Czechoslovakia, where the more advanced technology is already in use. They also produced copies of requests cotton firms had made to the Treasury Department for rapid depreciation allowances on the old machinery that would have to be replaced. These requests included the industry's estimate of what the new machinery would cost: $450 million over a three-year-period, not $2.3 billion.

The union claimed the true cost would be even lower, because one factor overlooked by the cotton millers (and generally overlooked by manufacturers in any such cost-benefit analysis) was the improved productivity and durability of the new machines.

BACK TO THE DICTIONARY

The manufacturers' challenge to the '78 regulations went all the way to the Supreme Court, which finally didn't buy it. In June 1981, the Court ruled that "Congress has already defined the basic relationship of costs to benefits when it passed the Occupational Safety and Health Act of 1970." That relationship "places the benefit of worker health above all other considerations except the feasibility of achieving that benefit."

That decision sent industry racing back to the dictionary, but by this time they had a new ally—Reagan-appointed OSHA director Thorne Auchter. Less than a year after the Supreme Court decision, the cotton dust standard is again up for grabs, though this time the challenge has come in more subtle garb. Ostensibly because of "new health data," OSHA is now studying the "cost effectiveness of compliance (which) may result in reconsideration of the present standard."

In the new "cost-effectiveness" approach, unlike the cost-benefit analysis, benefits are not weighed against costs. Rather, different methods of complying with a given regulation are compared according to their costs. This makes sense only if the different methods can all reach the same standard, and if they don't compromise the goal of a healthy workplace. That is hardly what's going on, as OSHA's new management attempts to talk itself around the Supreme Court victory the agency's own lawyers won in 1981.

In the cotton dust case, the varying methods under consideration are engineering controls, respirators, and medical surveillance of workers. Only engineering controls—that is actual changes in the machinery used—decrease the dust levels associated with the disease.

Respirators are difficult to work with, and a study by the National Institute of Occupational Safety and Health has found that they are unreliable under real working conditions. Medical surveillance, therefore, has been a favorite of the industry. This involves monitoring of workers' health by the employer, and removal of any worker for whom byssinosis symptoms appear. It can help identify brown lung victims before the disease becomes chronic, but it is not foolproof and often comes too late.

In challenging the 1978 regulations at the time they were proposed, the textile firms argued that medical surveillance would be as effective as engineering controls. In the study that was supposed to back up this claim, however, anyone with a 60% or better breathing capacity was considered "normal" and unaffected by any work-related disease.

What's more, all the data in this study came from company doctors, to whom workers fear admitting brown lung symptoms because the result will be firing or rotation to lower-paying jobs. To top it off, the "study" had no control groups or standard statistical evidence, no clear methodology, no review by other scientists, and no authors willing to answer questions about it!

Yet strangely enough, when these same folks now submit a similar study, Auchter says "new health data" justify reviewing the standard. This time, the manufacturers' association claims that brown lung affects only 0.5% of cotton workers, not 18% as previously thought.

OSHA has not only bought this argument, but is going ahead with the companies' dirty work by commissioning its own "Regulatory Impact Analysis" study, once again relying on the medical and scientific data supplied by the industry. The union charges that four of the five guidelines for this analysis explicitly violate the 1981 Supreme Court decision.

The only way to conduct a meaningful cost-effectiveness study would be to have independent scientists do rigorous long-term studies of the two methods of preventing brown lung — engineering controls and medical surveillance—on two distinct test populations. Instead, it's likely that OSHA will "find" in the existing company health data enough justification to forget about engineering controls altogether, thereby saving millions for the employers.

A victory for the companies on this issue would set a precedent for "reevaluating" other current standards in other industries as well. The potential benefit to industry from avoiding government regulation and investment in a clean workplace is enormous—but the potential cost to workers' health is also.

POSTSCRIPT

Should the Federal Government
Deregulate American Business?

It must be remembered that Weidenbaum does not oppose all government regulation. Rather, he pleads that proposed regulations should pass a simple test: Do the benefits associated with this regulation exceed the extra costs of imposing this regulation? He believes if the benefits do not exceed the costs, the regulation should not be introduced. Weidenbaum goes on to suggest that even when we can't "put a dollar sign on the benefits," we can use the potential benefits to rank the "cost effectiveness" of alternatives. That is, he maintains, the logic of cost-benefit analysis allows us to identify the least costly solutions.

The editors of *Dollars and Sense* challenge the validity of Weidenbaum's simple test. They assert that the application of the benefit-cost rule generally results in an overstatement of the costs and an understatement of the benefits. They also believe that benefit-cost analyses are biased in favor of the more affluent in society and penalize those of lesser means.

How you judge the validity of the above arguments depends in part on how you value the trade-off between equity and economic efficiency.

Recent professional and popular literature contain many articles on government regulation. The impact of the free market economists is apparent in this literature. Nearly all of it is critical of government regulation. Murray L. Weidenbaum has contributed to this growing body of books, pamphlets, and articles. His work with Robert DeFina, *The Cost of Government Regulation of Economic Activity* (American Enterprise Institute, 1978) and his book *The Future of Business Regulation* (Anacorn Press, 1979) are excellent examples of the anti-regulation mood that has swept the country. Pro-regulation articles are now beginning to appear in the literature. For example, Daniel Fusfeld responds to Weidenbaum in a short piece entitled "Some Notes on the Opposition to Regulation," *Journal of Post-Keynesian Economics* (Spring 1980), which details the types of unsafe products that would appear on the market if regulation did not exist, and Mark Green and Norman Waitzman provide a more sophisticated discussion of the social bias associated with benefit-cost analyses in their essay entitled "Cost, Benefit, and Class," *Working Papers* (May/June 1980).

ISSUE 7

Do Firms Exploit Workers and Local Communities By Closing Profitable Plants?

YES: Barry Bluestone and Bennett Harrison, from "Why Corporations Close Profitable Plants," *Working Papers* (May/June 1980)

NO: Richard B. McKenzie, from "Frustrating Business Mobility," *Regulation* (May/June 1980)

ISSUE SUMMARY

YES: Professors Bluestone and Harrison assert that large modern corporations (particularly conglomerates) systematically milk profits from healthy firms, mismanage them, fail to maintain them, and then shut them down on the grounds that they are inefficient.

NO: Professor McKenzie argues that in a healthy market economy it is natural and necessary for some plants to move and others to close in order to achieve the benefits of economic efficiency.

No one denies that economic efficiency in a market economy is achieved by the application of the rule: "survival of the fittest." Inefficient firms are driven out of the marketplace by their efficient competitors. Thus, the ever-present threat of market failure makes each firm strive for the maximum degree of economic efficiency.

The fact that the market weeds out inefficient firms is one of the first lessons in an introductory economics course. It is this mechanism that determines the allocation of resources. That is, when an inefficient firm fails, the supply of factors of production that were previously employed by this inefficient firm are increased. The increase in the supply of factors of production causes factor prices to fall. The lower factor prices make the factors attractive for other, presumably efficient, firms. Thus, resources are "freed" from inefficient firms and "absorbed" by efficient firms.

The current controversy over plant closings does not take exception to this notion of economic justice. Although some economists challenge the underlying assumptions of this allocation mechanism—such as the downward flexibility of wages, the ability to substitute a unit of labor in alternative occupations, or the mobility of labor—the current critics challenge the viability of this mechanism in today's concentrated industrial sector. They are concerned with two basic issues: the impact of large enterprises on local communities and the legitimacy of the allocation process when multiplant firms and multiproduct firms dominate the marketplace.

Critics such as Bluestone and Harrison stress the fact that the firms in today's marketplace are totally different from the firms of Adam Smith's day. If one of the modern-day firms closes its doors, large numbers of individuals are unemployed, and they flood the labor market of that region. Total income in that community falls. This sets off a multiplier effect that reduces business demand and the income of local businesses that provide goods and services to those workers who are now unemployed. Additionally, a plant closing impacts on the local tax base. Not only does the local community lose the property tax assessment of the closed plant (such facilities are rarely sold and renovated for alternative uses), but it loses property tax assessments on workers' homes when the supply of housing increases and home prices fall as workers leave the community. This decline in property tax collections, coupled with falling sales tax and income tax collections, can leave a community financially strapped just when increased demands are placed upon it by its high unemployment rate. Thus, closing a modern-day plant with its 500, one thousand, or five thousand employees is dramatically different than closing Adam Smith's pin factory with its six employees.

The second concern of critics is more fundamental. Multiplant firms and multiproduce conglomerates can work outside the realm of the traditionally conceived marketplace. That is, profits earned in one plant can be siphoned off for the benefit of a totally unrelated activity. This phenomenon forms the crux of this issue.

Professor McKenzie argues that the allocation of funds from one part of an enterprise to another part of the same enterprise is totally consistent with the classical economist's profit maximization rule. Professors Bluestone and Harrison argue that these transfers violate the internal logic of classical economics and that, in the process, these transfers impose immense hardships on the workers these firms employ and on the communities where they are located.

Whether public policy encourages or discourages plant relocations will depend upon the outcome of this debate. Should firms be granted tax concessions for investments in plant and equipment that replicate old plants in another part of the country? Should firms be relieved from retirement program obligations when these production facilities are no longer profitable? Should tax write-offs be allowed for firms that close down a marginally profitable plant? These and other policy questions can be resolved only when the debate between economists such as McKenzie and Bluestone/Harrison is settled.

YES Barry Bluestone and Bennett Harrison

WHY CORPORATIONS CLOSE PROFITABLE PLANTS

Plant closings are becoming a grimly familiar story. The parent conglomerate, usually from a remote home office, announces one day that a well-established local factory is no longer competitive. Typically, the handwriting has been on the wall for years. The machinery is outmoded; the company's more modern factories are using newer equipment—and nothing foreshadows a shutdown like failure to reinvest. The workers have been told to hold down wages, or the plant will have to move; the town had been warned that property taxes must be abated or they will lose the plant altogether. Often these demands have been met.

But the dread day arrives anyway. Hundreds of jobs will be lost; the tax base will be devastated. The town elders wring their hands. Workers with seniority (those with roots in the community) are invited to pull up stakes and take lower wage jobs in company plants out of state.

A last ditch effort by workers to buy the plant fails; they can't raise the necessary capital. Although the factory is obsolete, oddly enough it is worth a king's ransom. Anyway, it must be a real lemon, or why would the company shut it down?

Why indeed?

The editorial pages of the *Wall Street Journal* suggest the reasons for plant relocation are obvious. Don't credit the Sunbelt's climate, says the *Journal*. The real cause of the sunbelt's economic growth is its superior attitude toward business. Labor costs (translation: wages) are lower; tax burdens (translation: public services) are lower. Plants must relocate, therefore, because in the high-cost Northeast and Midwest workers have greedily demanded decent wages, and communities have insisted on adequate school, police, fire, and sanitation services.

And anyway, plant closings, despite their human toll, mean that the system is performing the way it should. Capital mobility is an essential ingredient in our free-market economy. The profit-maximizing entrepreneur must be free to invest capital where it will return the highest possible yield.

From *Working Papers*, Vol. Vii, No. 3, May/June 1980. Reprinted by permission.

Otherwise, we are sanctioning ineffi- ciency: letting the economy as a whole operate below its optimum potential means allowing lower productivity and falling wages. And we surely don't want that.

Again and again, trade unions and state legislatures grappling with plant closings listen to business executives in- sist that plants close because they've ceased to be profitable: "If it could make money, do you really think we would shut it down?"

The contention seems plausible at first but, like so much in textbook economics, it simply fails to describe real life. Large modern corporations—and conglome- rates in particular—will and frequently do close profitable branch plants or pre- viously acquired businesses. They may do so for a variety of reasons that flow from the way conglomerates are orga- nized. Centralized management and control produces pressure to meet corpo- rate growth objectives and minimum an- nual profit targets; it also siphons off subsidiaries' profits to meet other corpo- rate needs. Sometimes management by "remote control" actually creates the un- profitability of the subsidiary that even- tually leads to shutdown—as when the home office is far removed from the pro- duction site or unfamiliar with the indus- try in which a subsidiary competes. Again, the textbook model of competi- tion among entrepreneur-owned and managed businesses utterly fails to ex- plain why plants relocate.

Modern industrial theory says large corporations are under constant pressure to grow, to expand their market share. Stability is often seen as a sign of decline, no matter how well run and steadily productive the plant. In a letter to an executive of the K Mart discount depart- ment chain, Paul McCracken, former head of the President's Council of Eco- nomic Advisors, wrote: "History sug- gests that companies which decide to 'take their ease' are apt to be on the route to decay."

This pressure is reinforced by the cor- poration's need to offer growth stock in order to attract equity capital. Investors in growth stocks make their money from capital gains realized when they sell their stock rather than from steady dividends paid out by the firm. The purchase price of the stock is thus high in relation to the dividends it earns. However, only by growing can a company keep the price- to-earnings ratio high, and continue to attract investors to its stocks. In many situations it is easier for a corporation to boost its price-earnings ratio by acquir- ing efficient and profitable businesses— often in unrelated markets—than by de- veloping new ventures or expanding existing operations. This option was par- ticularly attractive during the mid-1960s and the late 1970s when the stock market tended to undervalue real assets. Then a corporation could acquire those assets at "bargain" prices.

Plants must also meet target rates of return. Many companies that are divi- sions or subsidiaries of parent corpora- tions or conglomerates are now routinely required to meet minimum annual profit targets as a condition for receiving fi- nance or executive "perks" from the home office. Many are ultimately shut down because they cannot achieve what the managers describe as the parent cor- poration's current "hurdle rate."

At Cornell University, studies of con- glomerate destruction of viable busi- nesses have found many cases in which conglomerates abandoned going concerns that did not meet the specified target rates of return. For example,

The Herkimer [New York] plant, producing library furniture, had been acquired by Sperry Rand in 1955. The plant had made a profit every year except one through the next two decades, and yet Sperry Rand decided to close the plant and sell the equipment [in part because it] was not yielding a 22 percent profit on invested capital. That was the standard used by this conglomerate/management in determining an acceptable rate of return on its investments.

Another example is the experience of the Bates Manufacturing Company, a leading Maine textile operation. After several changes of ownership after World War II, all the mills except the one at Lewiston were sold to textile conglomerates. The Lewiston facility, along with a coal and energy business Bates had acquired, was then sold to two New York investors. At the time, Bates offered a steady but low return of 5 to 7 percent. The energy business, however, promised a 15 to 20 percent return. As one longtime manager at Bates put is, "These boys were not textile men, they were money men." And sure enough, they decided to close the textile plant in 1977, in order to put all their money into the energy business.

Again, in the lower Pioneer Valley of central Massachusetts, the Chicopee Manufacturing Company was generating an estimated 12 percent rate of return on its apparel products. The parent firm, Johnson & Johnson (whose principal line is pharmaceuticals), was dissatisfied with anything short of a 16 percent minimum, and announced that Chicopee would be shut down.

As times change, the hurdle rate may rise. In textiles and apparel, for example, Royal Little, the founder of Textron, told a Congressional investigative committee in 1948 that his conglomerate generally insisted that each of its subsidiaries earn 10 percent on total invested capital before taxes or risk being shut down. By the late 1970s, according to its own corporate reports, another clothing conglomerate, Genesco, was imposing a 25 percent hurdle rate on its various companies.

Whatever the target rate in a particular company at a particular time, the existence of the corporate hurdle rate means that in the era of monopoly capital, viable businesses can be closed even though they are making a profit—because it is not enough of a profit. Perhaps the most dramatic example of this phenomenon involved Uniroyal's closing of its eighty-seven-year-old inner tube factory in Indianapolis in 1978. The *Wall Street Journal* reported the story in the following way:

The factory has long been the country's leading producer of inner tubes. Its $7 million to $8 million annual payroll sustains the families of nearly 600 employees.

The company, in a formal statement, cited "high labor costs" and "steadily declining demand." Union and management officials who worked at the plant tell another story. They say that Uniroyal could have kept the plant operating profitably if it wanted to but that under pressure from the securities markets management decided to concentrate its energy on higher-growth chemical lines. Interviews with securities analysts support this theory. Richard Haydon, an analyst at Goldman, Sachs and Co., says: "You have one very large entity looking at a very small entity, but the small entity being very large to those people that work there. I think it's a truism that many companies have grown too big to look at the small market."

One consultant advises his corporate clients that, when the wage bill as a percent of sales rises, or when the rate of return on investment falls below some standard—he proposes the current money market interest rate—it is time to think about shutting down. "If capital does not work for you effectively, it should be invested elsewhere."

The case histories of Bates, Chicopee, and Uniroyal all have happy endings of one kind or another. Jobs at Bates were saved when the mill workers and some of the former managers chose to buy it. They were able to do so through an Employee Stock Ownership Plan arrangement, and in the first year after it was bought Bates earned a 17 percent after-tax profit. (See "Employee Ownership: How Well Is It Working?" by Daniel Zwerdling in *Working Papers* May/June 1979). To keep Chicopee from closing, twenty-one savings banks in the Pioneer Valley created a fund for high-risk business development. This enabled Chicopee's management to buy the company. And Uniroyal factory workers saved their jobs with the help of the presidents of the Indianapolis City Council and the Rubber Workers Union. They persuaded local financiers to put up the capital to purchase the plant from Uniroyal. The profit forecast for the first year of operation predicts that $500,000 will be distributed among the workers, and another $500,000 invested in new machinery. At the moment, all three plants are operating in the black, reconfirming that the corporations had been about to shut down basically profitable enterprises.

Subsidiaries' profits are prey to corporate appropriation. Not only do many parent companies deny their branches and conglomerate subsidiaries the power to establish their own performance criteria, but the profits they *do* earn are generally repatriated to the parent firm, to be reallocated according to the latter's priorities. For example, in one subsidiary of a Fortune 500 corporation, the profits from its local specialty paper products operation are taken by the parent, which returns only enough capital to the mill to meet Environmental Protection Agency and basic maintenance requirements. "In fact, only 5 percent of capital expenditures over the past five years have gone for growth. In that period net assets have declined 26 percent and employment has declined 9 percent . . . "

A healthy subsidiary that generates excess capital is sometimes a "cash-cow." An example of this would be a regional industry that has run out of opportunities for local growth: the New England market for department store sales is thought by industry leaders to be more or less saturated. Therefore, "the local [New England] units of national holding companies and department store chains are made to serve as cash-cows for [stores in other] areas of the country."

The appropriation of a subsidiary's or a branch's surplus by the parent corporation introduces potentially severe structural imbalance into a plant's operations. During years when sales are good, the profits accrue to the parent. When times go bad, the operating company has been stripped of its revenues, and may be forced to go into the local capital markets for a loan. However, lack of control over its own future profit stream makes the servicing of this loan uncertain, and local banks or other leaders will deal with this uncertainty by charging a higher interest rate—and of course the parent firm may not even permit the branch or subsidiary to borrow on its own.

Thus, by becoming the banker to its various constituent plants or companies, the centralized corporation is able to enforce its own growth goals. At best, the subsidiaries are forced to compete directly with one another for access to their own profits. But in fact, conglomerates (and, since 1976, more and more large single-product corporations) have tended to place the capital so obtained into other, often totally unrelated, acquisitions instead of reinvesting in the sector—let alone the specific company—from which the surplus was redistributed.

The managers of K mart, for example, believe that their continuing operations will be throwing off far more cash than the department store business has traditionally been able profitably to absorb. As a result, industry sources estimate that by 1981 fully one-quarter K mart's available cash will have no place to go. One executive told *Fortune* magazine: "Time is running out and we are aware of it. K mart must search out new directions."

Yet at the same time—just to show the chaos and irrationality of the economic era in which we now live—Mobil Oil Corporation used a substantial part of its post-1973 inflated international oil profits not to expand domestic petroleum production, but to purchase Montgomery Ward, an established department store chain!

The diversification in the steel industry that led to the famous shutdown in 1977 of the Campbell plant of the Youngstown Sheet and Tube Company in Ohio began early in the decade. Between 1970 and 1976 the steel industry as a whole paid out 43 percent of after-tax profits in dividends. This rate was above average for all industry, yet the steel industry was simultaneously complaining that required pollution-control expenditures prevented them from upgrading their old plants and equipment. Some Wall Street analysts have seen the high dividend rate as a strategy for holding on to investors while developing a plan for diversifying into new fields. In the late 1970s the industry has done just that—it has shifted capital into cement, petrochemicals, coal, natural gas, nuclear power plant components containers and packaging, and real estate.

According to U.S. Steel's annual reports, for example, the share of that corporation's annual plant and equipment investment going into actual production of steel fell from 69 percent in 1976 to just over half in 1979. For every dollar of old plant and equipment written off, only $1.40 in new investment was undertaken (in fact, the ratio of new capital spending to depreciation in the steel operations fell by 100 percent, from 2.9 to 1.4). But for every dollar of capital depreciation in its nonsteel operations, U.S. Steel spent nearly three dollars in new capital investment. By 1978, 44 percent of U.S. Steel's total worldwide assets were in nonsteel operations.

Youngstown Sheet and Tube Company was not owned by U.S. Steel, but by a New Orleans-based conglomerate, the Lykes Corporation. Lykes purchased it in 1969, when Sheet and Tube was the nation's eighth largest steel-making firm. The acquisition was financed mainly by a major loan package, which Lykes promised to pay off out of Sheet and Tube's very substantial cash flow. During the next eight years, Lykes used Sheet and

Tube's cash to amortize that debt and to expand its nonsteel operations....Before the merger, investment in plant and equipment averaged almost $10 million a year. After the acquisition by Lykes, the average fell to about $3 million per year, and would have had a *zero* trend if not for a few investment projects that were quickly abandoned during the 1975–76 recession. Clearly, Lykes was pursuing a pattern of planned disinvestment in its recent acquisition. This has led most financial analysts to agree that "Lykes must bear responsibility for a good deal of the failure at Youngstown Sheet and Tube." *Business Week* put it in its October 3, 1977, issue: "The conglomerators' steel acquisitions were seen as cash boxes for corporate growth in other areas." In a rather absurd postscript to the closing—which cost 4,100 Ohio workers their jobs—Lykes merged in 1978 with the owners of the Nation's *next* largest steel-maker, the conglomerate Ling-Temco-Vought. The argument used in court by Lykes and LTV to overcome antitrust objections to the merger was that their steel business was "failing," and could only be rescued by achieving financial scale economies through merger! The merger now makes Lykes-LTV the nation's third largest producer of steel. Thus does corporate profit appropriation encourage economic concentration.

This concentration in turn makes it possible for management to impose other costs by "remote control." Centralized control by a home office can impair the profitability of a newly acquired branch or subsidiary, and can even make the business actually unprofitable.

Sometimes the home office requires its new acquisition to carry additional management staff from headquarters, staff the subsidiary did without before and that are probably redundant. For example, in a recent issue of a New England trade magazine, a small manufacturer with 40 percent of the domestic hypodermic needle market was offered for sale by its conglomerate parent. The market analyst notes that "the parent corporation, a Fortune 500 company...has imposed an excess of staff and other requirements which add nonproductive costs to the operation. A *pro forma* [simulated balance sheet] eliminating this overlay of corporate expenses shows a much better picture." Recently freed from its former parent (the Esmark conglomerate), the Peabody tannery in Massachusetts projects a reduction in overhead and administrative support services of almost $500,000 during its first year.

In 1978, the New England Provision Company (NEPCO) of Dorchester, a Boston neighborhood, had its meat-packing operations shut down by the same LTV conglomerate that recently merged with the Lykes Corporation. The firm had been consistently profitable prior to its acquisition by LTV in the late 1960s. One factor turning profits into losses seems to have been LTV's insistence that NEPCO pay a fee to the parent for management services. This practice was also found to be present in the case of the Colonial Press in Clinton, Massachusetts, acquired in 1974 by Sheller-Globe, primarily a maker of auto parts, school buses, and ambulances, and closed three years later, in 1977. Colonial was charged an average of $900,000 a year in corporate overhead charges. Some months it was charged $200,000.

There was little justification for these charges. The Press was being forced to pay the costs of larger corporate activities from which it did not benefit. For example, Sheller-Globe maintained an entire department that was solely responsible for security. Given the conditions in the automotive industry there was some justification for these costs. However, Sheller-Globe's corporate policies meant that the security department applied the same systems to all divisions. The corporation built a link fence around three sides of the Colonial Press plant and hired twenty-two security guards. Upon exiting the plant, employees would often be searched for stolen goods. The level of theft at the Press could not possibly justify the cost of the fences and guards, yet Colonial Press was forced to bear part of these costs.

Sometimes the parent firm forces the subsidiary to purchase from particular distant providers, even if the subsidiary's managers could cut costs by purchasing locally. In the NEPCO case,

the firm was required to buy the meat it processed and packaged from [another LTV subsidiary, Wilson Foods and Sporting Goods] at inflated prices; and an inept marketing company was hired..., the result of a "sweetheart" contract arranged for the benefit of a former LTV executive vice president. . . .

Lykes imposed the same burden on Youngstown Sheet and Tube. According to the Senate hearings, YST ended up paying more for raw materials (coal and iron ore) from Lyke's mines after the merger than it would have paid on the open market. After the merger, YST began purchasing parts and equipment, which had previously been supplied locally, from a Lykes subsidiary at higher rates. This arrangement cost YST $60 million a year.

To tax the subsidiary in order to subsidize the operations of the headquarters (or its friends) is bad enough. But perhaps most serious of all are the cases where home office policy actually creates the unprofitability of the (previously profitable) subsidiary, through clumsy interference with the local managers who know the situation best. William F. Whyte's case study of the Library Bureau, a furniture plant in Herkimer, N.Y., revealed just such a problem.

The plant had always had its own sales force and was not dependent upon Sperry Rand for its market. In fact, being part of the conglomerate imposed serious barriers in marketing. For example, it was a rule of Sperry Rand that the Library Bureau salesmen could not call on any customers served by Sperry Rand. While this left the Library Bureau its main markets with public and educational institution libraries, the rule barred the plant from selling to a large number of industrial and business firms that used library equipment. The [subsidiary] could only enter these markets through Sperry Rand salesmen who were unfamiliar with Library Bureau products and had more important things to sell. The handicaps were similar in the export field. . . . [According to the former] head of sales for Library Bureau . . . "We were not officially barred from exporting, but to sell anything outside of the country, we had to send our proposal to the international division, and it would just die there. We would never hear anything back."

Similarly, after its acquisition of the Colonial Press, Sheller-Globe immediately brought in outside management that, except for the newly installed president, had no experience in the publishing industry. Yet this outside group was given control over the most important decisions. In particular, Sheller-Globe wanted to change Colonial's orientation from sales to manufacturing. It wanted to emphasize producing books more efficiently rather than satisfying more clients. This decision impaired long-standing relations with the publishing companies that were Colonial's clients (these included Reader's Digest and Random House), since Sheller-Globe believed there was not a great deal of difference between "producing a steering wheel and producing a book."

Flexibility to accommodate customer's publication schedules was reduced. Colonial was no longer allowed to offer free warehouse space to publishers. The customer service and order departments were merged, resulting in misplaced orders and deteriorated customer relations. An expensive computerized management information system was installed, which so fouled up operations that "books were lost and there was often general confusion about what materials there were and where they were located." Publishers were no longer given itemized cost estimates, and in general, the management under Sheller-Globe mistreated its customers. As a result of all this, "the publishing industry become alienated and sales declined. . . . Decisions which were appropriate to the automotive industry proved disastrous in the book-printing industry."

This disaster has been somewhat mitigated by the reopening of the Press in 1979, as the Colonial Cooperative Press. With the help of the Massachusetts Community Development Finance Corporation and the Industrial Cooperative Association, the press was sold to the workers as a full-scale cooperative. However, it is a much smaller enterprise and it isn't clear whether or not it will succeed. The Colonial Press had over 1,000 workers. Colonial Cooperative Press has

75. Furthermore, in the two years it took to reorganize the plant, the Press lost many of its customers.

Whether or not it survives, this worker-purchase is another example of an ad hoc solution pulled together by the workers and their community as the conglomerate-owner abandoned them. There is no institution in the U.S. economy to which viable businesses can turn when they are sold out by a parent-corporation. Each plant must find its own solution within its particular local economy. Unlike the Chrysler Corporation they cannot turn to the federal government. But, also unlike the Chrysler Corporation, many of these conglomerate subsidiaries do not *need* to be bailed out, for they were not actually losing money to begin with. What they need is assistance in setting up autonomous, decentralized, locally owned operations.

The conventional wisdom about highly centralized management is that it makes possible a higher degree of efficiency in information and personnel management than ever before. But the evidence suggests that the managers of the giant corporations and conglomerates frequently "overmanage" their subsidiaries, milk them of their profits, subject them to strenuous or impossible performance standards, interfere with local decisions, and are quick to close them down when other, more profitable, opportunities appear. In 1975–76 Gulf and Western almost dumped the Brown Paper Company of Holyoke, Massachusetts, a leading producer of quality papers, and actually did sell off its most profitable product line to a Wisconsin competitor. By 1977 the plant's sales were up again to over $450 million.

Highly centralized organizations like Gulf and Western and Textron have positioned themselves so as to be able to make a profit either from a subsidiary's success or from failure that requires divestiture (since it can be treated as a tax loss and used to offset profits earned in other operations). From the point of view of capital asset management this may be the pinnacle of capitalist institutional creativity. But from the perspective of economic stability for working people and their communities, these clever capitalist giants are a disaster. The much-discussed trade-off between efficiency and equity turns out to mean capital management efficiency, but tremendous inefficiency at the level of actual production, to go along with the inequities imposed on workers and communities.

In short, modern monopoly capitalists will sell off or shut down profitable businesses if they think they can make even more money somewhere else. This strategy is not a recent one, nor have its harmful effects ever been unforeseeable. Here is Emil Rieve, president of the Textile Workers Union of America before a Congressional committee thirty years ago:

> Mr. Little is a capitalist, but in the field of finance rather than the field of production . . .
>
> I say this in the same sense that Hitler and Stalin are in the tradition of Napoleon and Alexander the Great. We have changed our attitude toward financial conquerors, just as we have changed our attitude toward military conquerors. Success is not the only yardstick.
>
> I do not know whether Mr. Little has broken any laws. But if he has not, our laws ought to be changed.

"Mr. Little" is Royal Little, founder of Textron, the Rhode Island conglomerate that first developed many of the strate-

gies now in use. Textron was initially a textile company. This year the Securities and Exchange Commission has charged it with paying over $5 million in bribes to officials in eleven foreign countries in order to "stimulate" sales of its Bell Helicopters. Its chairman at the time was G. William Miller, the current Secretary of the Treasury.

Just as the law in other areas has gradually evolved over the years to recognize that property rights, through dominant, are not absolute, the law must be changed to temper arbitrary plant relocation. Fifty years ago, tenants had no rights arising from their occupancy of a building. Today, the law stipulates that a landlord must keep the building habitable, that he must provide heat and hot water, and that tenants may not be arbitrarily evicted. Some communities have authorized rent control and even rent strikes when the property is not kept in good repair.

Family law has undergone a similar evolution. A wife is no longer her husband's property, and a couple's tangible property is no longer assumed to be the fruits of the husband's labor. Even banking law has been amended to deny banks the right to shut down when the community would be denied essential banking services.

But laws dealing with plant relocation are back in the eighteenth century. Profitability is considered an absolute right, not a relative one; and the right of a plant to relocate in the name of greater profitability is still sacrosanct, even where management's judgment or motive is specious.

As Emil Rieve observed thirty years ago, laws that sanction promiscuous relocations must be changed. A handful of states are considering requiring a year's notice before companies may shut down plants. Legislation is also under discussion to require severance pay, as well as compensation to the community. Companies could be required to pay back all tax abatements; labor contracts could also demand that the parent company not shift the production to other plants; tax write-offs for shutdowns could be prohibited. The proposed legislation to require federal chartering of the largest corporations could also include a range of sanctions against arbitrary relocations.

Far from interfering with industry's "right" to use capital optimally, these sanctions could force parent companies that acquire independent firms to operate them efficiently. As things stand now, conglomerates are being rewarded for running their subsidiaries into the ground—and the employees along with them.

NO

Richard B. McKenzie

FRUSTRATING BUSINESS MOBILITY

Business mobility—the mirror image of the free play of economic forces—is a normal, indeed inevitable, feature of any dynamic and growing economy. Nonetheless, particular moves (plant closings, relocations, and the like) can and do evoke protests by the communities and workers left behind. They see themselves as somehow "wronged." And among the political remedies they seek are restraints on business mobility by government fiat.

Cities are worried about losing employers and tax revenues to the suburbs, the Snowbelt is worried about losing both of those and skilled workers as well to the Sunbelt, and politicians everywhere seem attracted to the notion that economic stability in their areas can be ensured by putting a check on management's freedom to pull up stakes. Two years ago when American Airlines announced its decision to move its headquarters from New York to Dallas, for example, New York Mayor Edward Koch termed it a betrayal, and a taxi union vowed to stop serving the airline's New York terminals. Fortunately for the airline and its passengers, as well as the cabbies, the threat was never made good. And American's headquarters was moved.

In recent years, bills that would seriously restrict business mobility have been introduced in the U.S. Congress and a number of state legislatures.* The scheme is also the centerpiece of Ralph Nader's current campaign to "democratize" corporate America, to make major corporations more responsive to the "general interest." (His vehicle is the Corporate Democracy Act of 1980, H.R. 7010.) If such a measure became federal law, it would substantially increase government intervention in business decision making, alter our national economic system in fundamental ways, and be, on balance, detrimental to the regional and local economies of the country in the bargain.

*At last count eleven, including the northeastern states of Connecticut, Maine, Massachusetts, New Jersey, New York, Pennsylvania, and Rhode Island, plus Illinois, Michigan, Ohio, and Oregon.—eds.

THE "RUNAWAY PLANT PHENOMENON"

The general purpose of the restrictive legislation, which already has been enacted in Maine, is to remedy what has been called the "runaway plant

From *Regulation*, May/June 1980.© 1980, American Enterprise Institute.

phenomenon." Typically, the bills provide for a government agency to investigate business moves and rule on their appropriateness. For example, the National Employment Priorities Act, a 1977 proposal that was reintroduced in the House last August, by Representative William Ford (Democrat, Michigan) and sixty-one co-sponsors, would set up a National Employment Priorities Administration within the U.S. Department of Labor to investigate plant closings, to report its findings on the economic rationale for the decision and on employment losses and other impacts on the affected community, and to recommend ways of preventing or mitigating these harmful effects. (In the 1977 version, the investigation would determine whether "such closing or transfer" was "without [and presumably also "with"] adequate justification.") A bill pending since 1978 in the New Jersey General Assembly would vest similar responsibilities in a state agency called the Division of Business Relocation.

A second typical feature of bills designed to curb business mobility is the levying of penalties on firms that move. The Ohio bill, for instance, would require such firms to dole out to the employees left behind severance pay equal to one week's wage for each year of service and to pay the community an amount equal to 10 percent of the gross annual wages of the affected employees.

Under the Ford bill (H.R. 5040), a business that moved or closed would have to pay the workers left jobless 85 percent of their last two-years' average wage for a period of fifty-two weeks, less any outside income and government assistance. Besides, the firm would have to make a year's normal payments to any employee benefit plan and cover relocation expenses for employees who decided to move to any other company facility within the next three years. Workers over age fifty-four at the time of a move or closing would be entitled to full retirement benefits at age sixty-two instead of sixty-five or seventy. Failure to comply with the act would carry severe penalties—a combination of fines and the denial of tax benefits associated with a move. Finally, the local government would be owed an amount equal to 85 percent of the firm's average tax payments for the last three years. If the firm moved abroad and an "economically viable alternative" existed in the United States, the firm would have to pay "damages" equal to 300 percent of any tax revenue lost to the U.S. Treasury. Any payment required under the act, not met by the firm, and paid by the federal government would become a debt owed by the firm to the federal government.

Third, the kind of legislation under consideration here generally provides for government assistance to the people and entities adversely affected. Under the Ford bill, for instance, the U.S. secretary of labor, with the advice of a relocation advisory council, would be empowered to provide financial and technical assistance to employees who lost their jobs, to the communities affected by plant relocations, and even to businesses themselves—those that might decide *not* to relocate if government assistance were available. Assistance to employees would take the from of training programs, job placement services, job search and relocation expenses, in addition to such existing welfare benefits as food stamps, unemployment compensation, and housing allowances. Federal grants for additional social services and public works projects would go directly to the community. Assistance to businesses would be given as technical advice, loans and loan guarantees, interest subsidies, and the assumption of outstanding debt, but only if the Secretary of Labor were to determine that the aid would "substantially contribute to the economic viability of the establishment." The New Jersey and Ohio proposals provide for similar community and employee aid.

Fourth, under the various bills, firms are required to give advance notice of their plans to move or close—up to two years' notice in the Ohio bill and in the proposed Corporate Democracy Act of 1980. The prenotification requirement in the Ford bill varies with the size of the anticipated loss in jobs: two years for firms expecting the loss to be greater than 500, one year for 100 to 500, and six months for less than 100. The legislation proposed in New Jersey requires only a one-year notice. Exceptions could be made, of course, but generally only if the firms can show that meeting the requirement would be unreasonable.

Fifth, the various bills usually require that businesses offer their employees, to the extent possible, comparable employment and pay at the new location. And finally, each of the bills contains some minimum-size cutoff point. The proposed National Employment Priorities Act, for example, would apply only to firms with more than $250,000 in annual sales. But it should be noted that many McDonald's restaurants do that much business in a year. The bills' reach, typically, is both wide and deep.

DRAWING THE BATTLE LINES

In describing the changing regional structure of the U.S. economy, *Business Week* magazine observed: "The second war between the states will take the form of political and economic maneuver. But the conflict can nonetheless be bitter and divisive because it will be a struggle for income, jobs, people and capital" (May 17, 1976). And so it promises to be. When he introduced the original National Employment Priorities Act in 1977, Representative Ford gave us a preview of the economic rationale of the political battle lines and some flavor of the ensuing debate:

> The legislation is based on the premise that such closings and transfers may cause irreparable harm—both economic and social—to workers, communities, and the Nation....My own congressional district suffered the effects of the runaway plant in 1972 when the Garwood plant in Wayne moved and left 600 unemployed workers behind. . . . [T]he reason these firms are moving away is not economic necessity but economic greed. For instance, the Federal Mogul Company in Detroit signed a contract in 1971 with the United Auto Workers and 6 months later announced it would be moving to Alabama. A spokesman for the company was quoted as saying that they were moving "not because we are not making money in Detroit, but because we can make more money in Alabama."

Two years later, in introducing his significantly revised 1979 bill, Representative Ford stressed that business movements from the Northeast during the last decade had resulted in a million lost jobs in manufacturing and pointed to studies showing the suicide rate among workers displaced from their jobs by plant closings at thirty times the national average. He also noted,

> It is well established that the affected workers suffer a far higher incidence of heart disease and hypertension, dia-

betes, peptic ulcers, gout, and joint swelling than the general population. They also incur serious psychological problems, including extreme depression, insecurity, anxiety, and the loss of self-esteem.

A veritable chamber of horribles!

So it should come as no surprise that the campaign for government restrictions on business mobility adopts the rhetoric of war. Phrases like "second war between the states," "counter-attacks," and "fierce and ruinous state warfare" fill popular accounts of regional shifts. The economic conflict at the heart of attempts to control business relocations is viewed as "us" against "them"— North versus South, the Snowbelt versus the Sunbelt.

Such rhetoric may serve transient political purposes. But it distorts public perception of economic conditions in different parts of the country and hides nonsensical arguments behind the veil of "urgency" as to government action. Thus, it is instructive to examine the major arguments made to support restrictive legislation.

CHANGES IN POPULATION

The contention is made that southward business movements have increased the rates of population growth in the South and Southwest. The corollary is that the North is actually losing people, especially highly educated workers, and that the population shifts that have been occurring are larger than can be accommodated by existing political institutions.

What do the data actually show? First, as is evident in Table 1, the population growth rates of the Northeast and North Central regions have indeed declined significantly since the 1950s, but so have

Table 1

Population Growth Rates, by Region, 1950–1977

Region	1950–1960	1960–1970	1970–1977
Northeast	13.2	9.8	0.4
New England	12.8	12.7	3.3
Middle Atlantic	13.3	8.9	−0.4
North Central	16.1	9.6	2.3
East North Central	19.2	11.2	2.0
West North Central	9.5	6.1	3.4
South	16.4	14.3	11.2
South Atlantic	22.6	18.1	11.8
East South Central	5.0	6.3	8.0
West South Central	16.6	14.0	12.3
West	38.9	24.2	12.7
Mountain	35.1	20.9	21.0
Pacific	40.2	25.2	10.1
U.S. Total	18.5	13.4	6.4

Source: Adapted from Richard B. McKenzie, *Restrictions on Business Mobility* (Washington, D.C.: American Enterprise Institute), Table 1.

the population growth rates of *all* regions, including the South and West. (Only the Middle Atlantic states experienced a net decline in the 1970–1977 period, and that decline was very modest.) Further, and here Table 2 is in point, these changes in population growth rates have been caused as much or more by "natural" factors—changes in family life styles, the costs of rearing children, the widespread use of contraception, and the legality of abortions—as by net outmigration.

Second, aggregate data on population shifts blur the complex picture of who moves and for what reasons. Many of the people who moved south in the 1970s are the same people who moved north in the 1950s and 1960s. Others (for example, retirees) have moved south for reasons wholly unrelated to business location. Still others have moved because of new and expanding industries in the South, not because of relocations from elsewhere. It is also interesting to note that a

Table 2

Average Annual Growth rates in Population by Region and Cause, 1960–1970 and 1970–1976

Region	Population		Natural Increase		Net Migration	
	1970–1976	1960–1970	1970–1976	1960–1970	1970–1976	1960–1970
Northeast	0.1	0.9	0.4	0.9	−0.3	0.1
North Central	0.3	0.9	0.6	1.0	−0.3	−0.1
South	1.5	1.3	0.8	1.2	0.7	0.2
West	1.6	2.2	0.8	1.3	0.8	1.0
U.S. Total	0.9	1.3	0.7	1.1	0.2	0.2

Source: McKenzie, *Restrictions on Business Mobility*, Table 2.

major source of the above average population growth of the South Atlantic states (11.8 percent in the 1970–1977 period) has been the extraordinary growth of a single state, Florida (over 25 percent).

Third, a favorite argument in support of restrictions on business mobility is that the South and West are gaining a disproportionate share of highly educated and highly skilled workers, leaving the North and Midwest with a preponderance of uneducated, unskilled, and thus low-income workers. Now the new wave of outmigration from the North of course includes many highly educated and skilled people; but the proponents of restrictive legislation greatly exaggerate the quite undramatic facts. For instance, in the 1975–1977 period substantially more unemployed male workers moved from the Northeast to the South, (23,000) than from the South to the Northeast (14,000), and virtually the same pattern held for unemployed female workers. (The Northeast also exported more unemployed workers to the West than it imported from the West.)

Other considerations are equally revealing. Far more people below the poverty line migrated from the Northeast to the South (133,000) than vice versa (39,000) in the 1975–1977 period. (Much the same point can be made about the migration of low-income people between the Northeast and West.) In addition, while more people with one or more years of college migrated from the Northeast to the South (151,000) than from the South to the Northeast (102,000), those with *some* college education were a significantly greater proportion of the southern migrants to the North (56.3 percent) than the other way around (40.3 percent). (The same cannot be said about the migration of college-educated people between the Northeast and the West.) In short, it simply is not clear that the South or the West is receiving from the North a disproportionate number of highly trained, high-income people. Some—but no tidal wave.

Finally, most people move within a region, not among regions—and mostly they stay within the same state. Indeed, of the people who moved to a different house in the 1975–1977 period, approximately 60 percent stayed in the same county! Hence, if business relocation rules are seen as a means of restraining migration, and *insofar as migration results from business relocations at all*, these rules will in fact restrain migration *within* regions and states more than *among* regions. And insofar as such rules are designed to retard the economic development of the South and West by restricting the migration of people and jobs, it follows in all likelihood that they also will restrict the economic development of *all* regions, the North along with the rest.

CHANGES IN INCOME

Edward Kelley, in a position paper of the Ohio Public Interests Campaign, claims that business movements are reducing individual incomes and the tax collections of the governments in the North: "As the manufacturing base of the [northern] economy declines, so does the tax base. There are fewer taxable industrial locations and fewer people paying taxes" (*Industrial Exodus: Public Strategies for Control of Runaway Plants*, 1977). Yet in fact individual incomes in the North have been rising over the years. It is also true that individual incomes have been growing faster in the Southeast, Southwest, and West. What is happening, as the accompanying figure clearly shows, is that the relative incomes of the regions are converging. Personal income in the North has decreased relatively (while increasing absolutely), but it still averages 25 percent higher than personal income

in the South. In short, if business movements owe something to the disparity in regional incomes and if regional incomes are converging, it would seem that Representative Ford and Mr. Nader have proposed a solution to a problem that is being solved anyway, and predictably so, by normal market forces. In fact, because of the convergence of regional incomes, business mobility is likely to be less dramatic in the future than it was in the past.

The movement of businesses to the South does not necessarily mean that the North is made worse off, absolutely, or that improvement in living standards there has been retarded. Indeed, the converse may be reasonably argued—namely, that the movement of people and industry south has contributed to an

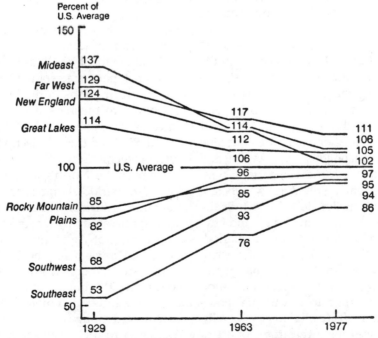

INDEX OF REGIONAL PER CAPITA
DISPOSABLE INCOME

Source: Calculated by Yale Brozen, Department of Economics,
University of Chicago.

improved standard of living in the North. By moving south where production costs are lower, businesses are able—at least in the long run—to provide goods to northern markets at lower prices than if they had stayed in the North. And they can expand production at lower cost. In not too many years, this increases both national income and, because the prices of goods are lower, the purchasing power of *all* workers' incomes, including those in the North.

THE DECLINE IN NORTHERN MANUFACTURING JOBS

The claim that the North has lost a million or so manufacturing jobs in the last ten years suggests an economic problem serious enough to justify severe restrictions on entrepreneurial freedom. In fact, however, the claim misinterprets the actual state of employment opportunities in the North. The narrow focus on *manufacturing* employment hides the very important fact that *total* employment in the North has risen continually and significantly during the last several decades.

As Table 3 shows, manufacturing employment in the Northeast and East North Central regions did indeed decline by about 1 million jobs between 1969 and 1979; but in the same period total nonagricultural employment grew substantially, by 4.5 million jobs, reflecting the strong upward trend in service and government employment during the period. Moreover, since 1975 even manufacturing employment in the North has begun to move up again. If business relocation rules are designed to thwart the movement of manufacturing jobs generally, they may well have the ironic effect of choking off this recent reversal of the

Table 3

Nonagricultural Employment in the Northeast and East North Central Regions, 1965–1979
(in thousands)

Year (monthly average)	Total Employment	Manufacturing Employment
1979 (Dec.)	38,100	10,172
1978	36,331	10,153
1977	35,408	9,886
1976	34,288	9,601
1975	33,376	9,396
1974	34,826	10,423
1973	34,506	10,533
1972	33,358	10,093
1971	32,803	10,027
1970	33,249	10,936
1969	33,358	11,201
1968	32,384	11,055
1967	31,589	11,007
1966	30,867	11,034
1965	29,464	10,472

Note: The Northeast and East North Central regions include Maine, Vermont, New Hampshire, Connecticut, Rhode Island, Massachusetts, New York, Pennsylvania, New Jersey, Ohio, Indiana, Illinois, Michigan, and Wisconsin.
Source: *Statistical Abstract of the United States,* 1965–1977, and *Employment and Earnings,* 1978 and 1979.

long-term downward trend in northern manufacturing jobs.

Finally, it must be stressed that only a very small percentage of the 1 million lost manufacturing jobs in the North can be attributed to business migration in any case. A study by Peter Allaman and David Birch of the Massachusetts Institute of Technology shows that just 1.5 percent of the North's job losses in the 1969–1972 period stemmed from the outmigration of firms, while a recent extension of that study by James Miller of the Department of Agriculture puts the figure at 1.6 percent for the 1969–1975 period. In other words, as Miller concluded, the impact of firm migration on the reallocation of manufacturing employment among regions "was trivial compared to the net effect of starts, closures and stationary firms."

An added inducement to this alleged movement south, it is often argued, is the "wage-attraction" of the South. However, it is more illuminating to assess the impact of "wage-push" in the North. From the wage-attraction perspective, it may appear that low-paid workers in the South are stealing business from and causing economic harm to the North. But the wage-push perspective suggests that wages in the North are higher and on the rise for such classical economic reasons as competition for workers from the developing service sector in the North. In other words, manufacturers are forced to pay higher wages or risk losing their labor force to more rapidly expanding sectors of the economy. Firms that move south are "pushed" south, having been outbid for labor resources in the North. From this perspective, industrial movements to the South are a consequence of gains made by many workers in the North—and the "runaway plant phenomenon" is a positive force in the dynamic and growth economy, South *and* North.

Even if northern manufacturing firms were to be restricted from moving south by legislation, the movement of manufacturing jobs to the South, though impeded, would not be stopped. Firms move because costs of production in the new location are lower—and anticipated profits higher. Restrictions on business mobility would cause new firms to spring up in southern locations and existing southern firms to expand by more than they otherwise would. Because of cost disadvantages, firms in the old northern locations would be induced by natural market forces—*which relocation rules attempt to override*—to contract their operations or to go out of business.

COMPARATIVE COST ADVANTAGES

And this of course is the key, this ill-conceived attempt to improve on "nature" by those who urge regulation to restrict business mobility. Even at the risk of accentuating the obvious, it is helpful to return to a first principle or two. People in different parts of the country trade with one another because differences in their costs of production make it to their mutual advantage to do so. Specialization in trade leads to maximum output from the resources available to the community as a whole. And, because the conditions of production—the availability of resources, technology, consumer preferences for work and for goods—continually change, so do the comparative costs from region to region. What once was relatively advantageous to produce in the North may, for any number of reasons, become less costly to produce in some other region. This constantly shifting calculus of costs can be altered by changes in the relative scarcity of resources, worker education levels, or regional preferences for services. Whatever the reason, the cost of producing any particular good in one region can go up and, as a consequence, the production of that good moves elsewhere—all, to repeat, very "naturally."

Pinning down the precise reasons for changes in regional economic structures is difficult in the best of circumstances. In recent decades, however, the comparative advantages of the North have indeed changed, and for two principal reasons. First, the demand for services in the North has increased rapidly, more so than in other parts of the country; and this in turn has increased the cost of resources, including labor, for all other sectors of the northern economy. Also, environmental legislation has placed more severe restrictions on industrial production in the congested North than in many other parts of the country and has increased the relative costs of manufacturing there. The unavailability of "pollution rights" in the North has caused many firms to look to locations with less present pollution and less stringent immediate pollution-control standards — to the South and West, for example.

Undeniably, these changes in regional production costs, and the economic adjustments that result from them, can and do cause hardship for some. But restricting business mobility is a cure worse than the disease. Such restrictions would force employers to lock labor and other resources into comparatively inefficient uses—resources that could and should be moving into expanding sectors of various regional economies. Thus, governmental rules that impede the movement of manufacturing industry out of the North would not only retard the development of industry in the South (or elsewhere) but, by the same token, would retard the development of the service sector in the North. The overall result would be increased nationwide production costs and reduced national production and income.

THE WORST OF WORLDS

States and communities that are mulling over business mobility restrictions may believe they would be protecting their economies by protecting their industrial bases, but in fact they would be hurting them—and themselves. What company would want to move into an area that had substantial economic penalties for moving out? What entrepreneur would want to start a business in a community or state that had penalties for changing locations? Companies interested in profits will always try to settle in those areas that leave them free to make the basic decisions on when to shift among products, when to close, and when to move. States or communities that do not impose restrictions will obviously have a competitive advantage over those that do—which makes it equally obvious why Representative Ford and others, who want restrictions in their own areas, are seeking through federal legislation to have *all* areas of the country abide by the same rules. And this simply tightens the squeeze on U.S. industry in world markets and provides yet another marginal inducement for U.S. firms to locate their production facilities in foreign countries where such restrictions are not in place.

Indeed, viewed from whatever perspective, restrictions on business mobility constitute an idea whose time one hopes will never come. Predictably, restrictions would tend to reduce the efficiency of resource allocation; reduce national and regional income levels; and reduce the ability of the economy to respond to changes in people's tastes and to changes in technology, in the availability of resources, and in the mix of demand for particular goods and particular services. In short, they represent a bad bargain all around—for the communities and workers affected (in spite of the appearance of near-term relief), for Representative Ford's constituents as much as everyone else, for the U.S. economy generally, for entrepreneur and taxpayer alike.

POSTSCRIPT

Do Firms Exploit Workers and Local Communities By Closing Profitable Plants?

Professors Bluestone and Harrison find that there are several common factors in recent plant closings undertaken by a number of large conglomerates: Excess funds are milked from one enterprise and transferred to a totally unrelated enterprise—often resulting in disinvestment in the "cash cow" and the eventual reduction in its profitability; the parent corporation may assign an unwarranted share of the conglomerate's common costs to one enterprise—thereby reducing its profitability; and management may force the firm to purchase its supplies from other subsidiaries of the conglomerate—even if these supplies are more costly than those from other sources. According to Bluestone and Harrison, the end result is that a potentially profitable plant may be run "into the ground—and their employees along with them."

Professor McKenzie argues that the movement of industry from the Northeast and North Central states to the Sunbelt is a natural economic phenomenon that should be encouraged rather than discouraged. He maintains that plant closings in the North and the movement South and West are caused by differentials in factor costs and that as long as these differentials exist, the migration will continue. Second, McKenzie argues that the labor freed from the industrial plants that are closed in the North can now enter the growing service sector in the North. Prior to the Sunbelt migration, he explains, the North's service sector competed with its industrial sector for labor; this drove the price of labor up and pushed industrial firms out of the North. Third, he believes the North's consumers are benefited by the migration of firms to the South and West. Since production costs are lower, these firms can sell their output at lower prices.

Professor McKenzie's arguments are fully articulated in his recent book *Restriction on Business Mobility: A Study in Political Rhetoric and Economic Reality* (American Enterprise Institute, 1979). An interesting complementary piece to McKenzie that discusses the weaknesses of worker-owner takeovers of closed plants is "Youngstown Sheet and Tube—A Classic Takeover Case," *The Center Magazine* (November/December 1979). Professors Bluestone and Harrison further develop their case in their book, *Capital and Communities: The Causes and Consequences of Private Disinvestment*. Arthur Shostak examines the private costs of displaced workers in his article "The Human Costs of Plant Closings," *Federationist* (August 1980). Lastly, many of the problems articulated by Bluestone and Harrison are contained in the United States Senate, Committee on the Judiciary, *Hearings on Mergers and Industrial Concentration, 95th Congress* (Government Printing Office, 1979).

ISSUE 8

Should Congress Guarantee U.S. Workers the Right to Parental Leave?

YES: "Background and Need for Legislation." Report from the House of Representatives—Committee on Education and Labor, 99th Congress, 2nd Session, *Parental and Medical Leave Act of 1986* (July 21, 1986)

NO: "Separate Dissenting Views on H.R. 4300, The Family and Medical Leave Act of 1986," Report from the House of Representatives—Committee on Education and Labor, 99th Congress, 2nd Session, *Parental and Medical leave Act of 1986* (July 21, 1986)

ISSUE SUMMARY

Yes: The supporters of H.R. 4300 maintain that there is a "growing conflict between work and family" that can be corrected by guaranteeing workers the "right to unpaid family leave."

No: Congressmen Bartlett, Tauke, Armey, Fawell, and Henry, dissenting members of the House Committee on Education and Labor, argue that H.R. 4300 may be "well-intentioned" but it is also "rigid and unflexible," "anti-small business," and the "first attempt by Congress to legislate" national standards for major employee leave and health benefits—a step Congress has avoided in the past.

The American workplace has changed dramatically in recent years as more and more women of all ages have joined the workforce. A few statistics brings this into sharp focus: (1) currently 44 percent of the workforce is female and if current trends prevail, more than 50 percent of the workforce will be female by the end of the century; (2) from the 1950s to the 1980s the percentage of mothers who worked more than tripled, indeed by 1981 mothers with preschool children were more likely to be in the workforce than married women with no children; (3) in the early 1970s, less than 30 percent of married women with a child under the age of two were in the workforce, 15 years later one out of two mothers with children under two years of age worked; and (4) the "Ozzie and Harriet family," in which the husband goes to work and the wife stays home to raise the children, now represents only 7 percent of American households; female-headed households represent 16 percent of all households.

As fewer parents, either by choice or by necessity, stay home to raise their children, the clash between work responsibilities and home responsibilities becomes more apparent. Parents struggle to find ways to accommodate their work schedules to the ever-present and ever-changing demands of their children. Women need medical leave for childbirth. Both men and women need time for early child rearing so that "bonding" can occur. One parent also needs the ability to leave the workplace to care for a seriously ill or injured child. But if there are no parental rights guaranteed in the workplace, a mother or father who attempts to fulfill her or his responsibility may jeopardize her or his job. That is, employers may simply terminate the worker or withhold promotions and/or wage increases in retaliation for absences from the workplace.

Given this real or imagined threat to the economic well-being of a growing number of American families, Congress began to consider the need for some intervention as early as 1968. In that year President Johnson's Advisory Council on the Status of Women suggested that female workers should be safeguarded against the temporary loss of their wages due to pregnancy. Two years later this same Council proposed that pregnancies should be treated in the same manner as any other medical condition. That is, a pregnant women should be entitled to sick leave, disability, and other medical benefits.

Since Congress did not immediately move to enact legislation that would explicitly protect the rights of pregnant workers, attempts were made in the early 1970s to protect the rights of pregnant workers by bringing discrimination cases to the courts under Title VII of the Civil Rights Act of 1964 and the equal protection clause in the U.S. Constitution. These pleas were denied by the Supreme Court and consequently Congress enacted the Pregnancy Discrimination Act of 1978 as an amendment to Title VII. This legislation in large part eliminated the worst abuses that were suffered by pregnant workers. It allowed women to work until childbirth unless medical complications prevented this; it assured women the right to return to their jobs; it provided them with the same benefits given to other temporarily disabled workers, such as paid sick leave, personal leave, disability benefits, hospitalization and medical insurance.

In brief, this legislation was antidiscriminatory in language and intent. It obligated employers to provide the same benefits for workers who were temporarily disabled because of pregnancy as for other temporarily disabled workers. However, if an employer provided no worker with any disability benefits, it was in compliance with the law. In this case, the employer did not "discriminate" against the pregnant worker when the firm did not provide maternity leave.

Although the Pregnancy Discrimination Act has gone a long way toward protecting the rights of millions of working women, it still leaves the rights of many other women and men unprotected. It is in this context that the current congressional initiatives were introduced. The most recent of the congressional initiatives was H.R. 4300, which was introduced on March 4, 1986 by Congressman William Clay (Democrat from Missouri). This legislation was assigned to the Committee on Education and Labor and the Committee on Post Office and Civil Service. The Committee on Post Office and Civil Services by a vote of 18–0 ordered H.R. 4300 to be favorably reported to the full House. Although the Committee on Education and Labor favorably reported H.R. 4300, there were dissenting views. The following excerpts are representative of the debate that surrounded the introduction of H.R. 4300.

YES

BACKGROUND AND NEED
FOR LEGISLATION

The tensions between employment and family life, two of the vital concerns of most Americans, have always existed. Recent economic and social changes have significantly exacerbated the tensions. Private sector practices and government policies have failed to keep pace with and respond to these new realities, imposing a heavy burden on families, employees, employers and society as a whole. This bill provides a sensible response to the growing conflict between work and family by establishing a right to unpaid family leave and temporary medical leave for all workers.

THE NEED FOR FAMILY LEAVE

The United States has experienced what can only be characterized as a demographic revolution with profound consequences for the lives of working men and women and their families. Today, ninety-six percent of fathers work and more than sixty percent of mothers also work. Female participation in the labor force has risen from 19 percent in 1900 to more than 52 percent today; 44 percent of the U.S. labor force is now female. Between 1950 and 1981, the labor force participation rate of mothers tripled. By 1981, a larger percentage of mothers of preschool aged children participated in the labor force than did the percentage of married women with no minor children in 1950 and all women in 1900. The fastest growing segment of this group is comprised of women with children under the age of three. Nearly 50 percent of all mothers with children under one year of age are now working outside of the home. And half of all children in two-parent families have both parents in the workforce.

Equally dramatic is the unprecedented divorce rate of fifty percent and the increase in out-of-wedlock births, which has left millions of women to struggle as heads of households, supporting themselves and their children in an era of high living costs. Women represent the sole parent in 16 percent of all families. At the same time, a majority of women workers remain in female

From "Background and Need for Legislation," in *Parental and Medical Leave Act of 1986,* U.S. House of Representatives.

intensive, relatively low paid jobs and are less likely than men to have adequate job protections and fringe benefits. Each of these phenomena, which affect women of all races, are most pronounced for black and other minority women. Single women heads of households, who work full-time in the labor force, often cannot keep their families above the poverty line.

Another demographic change relevant to the leave needs of all employees involves the growing number of elderly in our society. Currently, more than 2.2 million family members provide unpaid help to ailing relatives. In the case of the elderly, the most common caregiver is a child or spouse. About 38 percent of those caring for elderly relatives are children, and 35 percent are spouses. The average age of persons caring for elderly family members is 57 years.

Similarly, the percentage of adults in the care of their working children or parents due to physical and mental disabilities is growing. There is a trend away from institutionalization, which has been shown to be cost ineffective and often detrimental to the health and well-being of persons with mental and physical disabilities. Though independent living situations are often preferable, deinstitutionalization can result in increased care responsibilities for family members, many of whom are also of necessity wage earners. This trend toward home care is laudable because of the strong benefits it provides to the health and well-being of families; however, it can also add to the tension between work demands and family needs.

The significance of these demographic changes is apparent. Where men and women alike are wage earners, the crucial unpaid caretaking services tradi-tionally performed by wives—care of young children, ill family members, aging parents—has become increasingly difficult for families to fulfill. Yet these functions—physical caretaking and emotional support, are performed best by families. Indeed, in many instances, only families can perform them adequately. Society has long depended on the family to meet these needs and being able to provide such care has supported and strengthened families. Depriving families of their ability to meet such needs seriously undermines the stability of families and the well-being of individuals, with both economic and social costs. Yet today, at a magnitude significantly greater than ever before, American business requires the services of women and men alike. Modern families have made painful sacrifices to adapt to the needs of business and to the demands of wage earning. Business must make some modest accommodations to the needs of working families, in order to preserve the most essential of the traditional functions of the family.

The testimony of individual working people before the Committee demonstrated the difficulties faced by today's working families. Lorraime Poole, an employee of a larger municipality, testified to her heartbreak when she could not accept a long-awaited adoptive baby that had become available to her. Her employer had told her that she would lose her job if she took time off from work to receive the child and the adoption agency would not place the child unless assured that she would take some time off to be with the child. Ms. Poole was left with no choice but decline the placement. Stephen F. Webber, a coal miner and member of the executive board of the United Mine Workers of America, after describing his union's efforts to negotiate for family leaves, stated:

Caring for a seriously ill child presents special problems to working miners. Treatment centers for serious illnesses such as cancer are often located in urban centers, forcing families in rural communities to travel great distances. I think in particular, of one coal miner I know, whose child has cancer, and who must travel nearly 400 miles round trip each month from his rural home to take his child for treatment at a medical center in Morgantown, West Virginia.

His testimony included other compelling examples, including that of a miner whose five-year-old son became comatose after choking on a piece of food and required twenty-four-hour-a-day care, care that the miner, a single parent and sole wage earner, had to provide or arrange. A working mother, Iris Elliot, described to the Committee the difficulties she faced as a full-time worker with a preschool-aged son and a seriously ill infant. Her employer, a national corporation, had no family leave policy. Ms. Elliot was offered a 90-day personal leave, without pay or job protection, but she could not risk losing her position or health benefits as the sole medical insurance carrier for her family. She concluded her testimony by saying "No parent should ever have to be torn between nurturing their seriously ill child and reporting to work like I did."

Experts who testified before the Committee confirmed the importance of family leaves. Dr. T. Berry Braselton, associate professor of pediatrics at Harvard, and Dr. Eleanor S. Szanton, executive director of the National Center for Clinical Infant Programs, provided support for a leave to care for infants, explaining, in the words of Dr. Szanton,

While children require careful nurturing throughout their development, the formation of loving attachments in the earliest months and years of life creates an emotional "root system" for future growth and development. How are these attachments formed? Through the daily feeding, bathing, diapering, comforting and "baby talk" that are all communications of utmost importance in beginning to give the child the sense that life is ordered, expectable and benevolent . . . In short, these factors affect the baby's cognitive, emotional, social and physical development. . . . Once parents and babies do establish a solid attachment to each other, the transition to work and child care is likely to be easier for parents and for the child. Parents who have cared for their infant for several months are likely to understand a good deal about their child's unique personality and the kind of caregiver or setting which will be most appropriate. Babies, for their part, who have already begun the process of learning to love and trust their parents are better able to form—and to use—trusting, warm relationships with other adults.

Meryl Frank, director of the Infant Care Leave Project of the Yale Bush Center in Child Development and Social Policy, reported on the conclusions and recommendations of the Project's Advisory Committee on Infant Care Leave. The Advisory Committee echoed the views of Dr. Brazelton and Dr. Szanton, and concluded that the "infant care leave problem in the United States is of a magnitude and urgency to require immediate national action." The Advisory Committee, whose members include academics and professionals in child development, health and business, recommended a 6 month minimum leave, with partial income replacement for the first 3 months and benefit continuation and job protection for the entire leave period.

The Committee was also provided the recommendations of the Economic Policy Council of the United Nations Association of the United States of America (EPC). During 1984, the EPC, which is comprised of corporate executives, union presidents and academics, studied the economic and demographic trends transforming the family and labor force and issued a report in December of 1985 of its findings, entitled *Work and Family in the United States: A Policy Initiative*. The EPC recommended a 6–8 week job protected maternity leave, with partial income replacement; a 6 month unpaid, but job protected, parental leave; job protected disability leave for all workers; the provision of temporary disability insurance to all workers; and the establishment of a national commission on contemporary work and family patterns.

THE EXTENT OF EXISTING FAMILY AND RELATED MEDICAL LEAVE POLICIES

Many of the various aspects of family and related medical leaves, particularly with regard to pregnancy and parenting, have been extensively studied. However, currently, there is still no comprehensive study of the range of family leaves provided by American businesses. Many employers provide "personal leave" which is often available for family crises such as the serious illness or death of a child or parent. Such leave is almost universally unpaid and highly discretionary. Employees sometimes are able to take their vacation leaves (a benefit that is usually paid) at times of such crises. Only a small percentage of employers have policies providing a leave specifically for purposes of caring for ill family members.

Considerable study and attention has been paid to the aspects of family and medical leave relating to pregnancy, maternity and less frequently, paternity. Such leave has been the subject of litigation since the early 1960's, based upon the Equal Protection Clause of the U.S. Constitution and Title VII of the Civil Rights Act of 1964, as women workers sought equal treatment in the work place. The amendment of Title VII in 1978, by the Pregnancy Discrimination Act (PDA), has especially had a significant impact on the perception of women as wage earners and on the availability and nature of both parental and medical leave. Under the PDA, an employer is prohibited from discriminating on the basis of pregnancy, childbirth and related medical conditions. The PDA further provides that "women affected by pregnancy, childbirth, or related medical conditions shall be treated the same for all employment-related purposes, including receipt of benefits under fringe benefit programs, as other persons not so affected but similar in their ability or inability to work." 42 U.S.C. sec. 2000e-k.

This language requires that employers adhere to two basic principles. First, they must permit physically fit pregnant employees to continue to work just as any other physically fit employee would be permitted to work (traditionally, women were terminated or placed on mandatory unpaid leave early in pregnancy). Second, when they become physically unable to work because of a complication of pregnancy or due to childbirth and the recovery period following childbirth, they are entitled to any sick leave, disability, health insurance or other benefit extended to other employees who, because of a physical condition, are unable to work.

The result has been that employers, to comply with the law, permit pregnant women to work unless or until they are unable to work and then provide whatever compensation or leaves they provide to other employees temporarily unable to work for medical reasons. As a practical matter, this means that many pregnant employees work until they give birth and then are on medical leave (paid if the employer compensates other disabled workers) for the physical recovery period following childbirth (typically 6–8 weeks). Some employers provide an additional unpaid leave period following disability to allow a parent to stay home with a new baby. This additional "parental leave," if given, must, under Title VII, be available to parents of either sex.

In response to litigation and the influence of the PDA, thousands of companies have reevaluated their personnel policies and implemented policies responsive to the needs of their changed workforces. In addition, four of the five states which provide temporary wage replacement under a state disability insurance program (California, New Jersey, New York and Rhode Island) extended their coverage to pregnancy and childbirth related work disabilities. (The fifth state, Hawaii, included such coverage from the inception of its state disability insurance program in 1969.) These long-standing state programs have proven to be both successful and cost-effective wage replacement systems for workers who are unable to perform their jobs due to non-work related illnesses, injuries or other medical reasons.

Several of the recent studies on parental leaves were described to the Committee in hearings held in October 1985 and April 1986. Catalyst, a national non-profit research organization, conducted a survey of the policies of Fortune 1500 companies and issued its *Report on a National Study of Parental Leaves* in 1986. Catalyst reported that 95% of the survey's respondents offered short-term disability leave during a worker's (including a pregnant worker's) period of inability to work; 38.9% with full pay and 57.3% with partial pay. Of this 95%, 90.2% continued full fringe benefits during disability leave. Moreover, 51.8% of the responding companies offered some unpaid leave to women for a parenting leave (as distinct from the disability leave) and guaranteed their right to return; 40% to the same job, nearly 50% to a comparable job. One third of these employers offered four to six months and 7.2% offers over six months of family leave. Only 37% of these companies extended the parental leave right to fathers and often on a different (and less extended) basis than to mothers. Additionally, only 27.5% of the respondents offered benefits to workers who adopt children.

The Catalyst Survey found that approximately 75% of the companies granting both kinds of leaves rerouted the work of employees on leave and a large percentage of the companies hired temporaries to supplement their rerouting strategy or to fully take over the absent employee's work. Significantly, 86.4% of the respondents stated that setting up a leave period and arranging to continue benefits was relatively easy. As part of its report to corporations, Catalyst recommended that companies provide disability leave, with full or partial pay, and unpaid parental leave for up to 3 months, with reinstatement to the same or comparable position after any leave.

The employers who do provide these crucial leaves recognize the significant benefits that flow to employers from doing so. As Ms. Jeanne F. Kardos, director of employee benefits at Southern New England Telephone, explained in her testimony in support of this bill:

There are several factors which caused us to develop our benefit philosophy with regard to maternity and parental care. Along with many leading companies in the country, we recognize that women with children are in the work force to stay. Whether they are single parents or not, they have special needs involving pregnancy and child-rearing at some point after birth or adoption. The special needs of these parents and more than that, the benefits which accrue to them and their children from this early participation in child-rearing, cannot be ignored any more than the widely accepted need for medical or pension benefits.

In addition, one of the most important concerns we share with our employees is an interest in their careers. It is clear that forcing them to choose between the children and their jobs, or to compromise on either, produces at least one loser—maybe two. Adequate disability and parental leave can solve these problems. The employee returns to the company when he or she is prepared to do so, and the company retains an important asset.

Lastly, we want our benefit plans to be recognized as progressive and competitive. We know that it will help in attracting talented individuals and if they are happy with their benefits, they'll want to stay with us.

The Catalyst Survey, because it focused on Fortune 1500 companies, overstates the protections offered to new parents by employers generally. A survey of 1,000 small and medium sized firms, conducted in 1981 by Sheila Kamerman and Alfred Kahn of the Columbia University School of Social Work, provides an important companion to the Catalyst Study. According to Kamerman and Kahn, less than 40% of all working women received paid disability leave for the six to eight week recovery period after childbirth. This figure, which is far lower than the Fortune 1500 figures reported by Catalyst, probably reflects the fact that small and medium size employers are less likely to provide disability benefits to any worker. (These findings may also reflect the earlier survey date of the Columbia Study, which was undertaken much closer in time to the April 1979 effective date of the PDA than was the Catalyst Survey; smaller employers may not yet have adjusted their policies at the time of the first survey.) Eighty-eight percent of the companies provided "maternity" leave, but only 72% formally guaranteed the same or comparable job and retention of seniority. Thirty-three percent of the respondents provided leaves of 2 months or less, 28 percent provided 3 months of leave, 19 percent provided 4–6 months and 8 percent provided over 6 months. Twelve percent granted leave but on a discretionary basis. Only 25 percent of the respondent firms said that they permitted men to take parental leave, and many of those companies did so only for a few days at the time of childbirth.

The Catalyst and Kamerman and Kahn studies, taken together, indicate that employees of large companies are far more likely to be provided with paid disability leave following childbirth than are employees of small and medium sized firms. The small and medium size firms respond to new parent employees by providing unpaid "maternity leaves," a full third of which extend only for the period of the mother's physical inability to work. It is likely that many of those firms providing leave for that period of time also grant unpaid leave to other disabled employees and thus provide the same benefit for both pregnancy and non-pregnancy-related disability. A significant percentage of both Fortune 1500 companies and the small and medium companies studied by Kamerman and Kahn treat fathers seeking parental leave less favorably than mothers, in clear violation of Title VII.

These studies, more fundamentally, indicate the wide variation among employers, large and small, in the provision of parental, as distinguished from disability, leaves, and the inadequacy of many leave policies.

The inadequacy of existing leave policies is perhaps most clearly seen when the family and related medical leave policies of the United States are compared to those of the rest of the world. With the exception of the United States, virtually every industrialized country as well as many Third World countries have national policies which require employers to provide some form of maternity or parental leave. One hundred and thirty-five countries provide maternity benefits, 125 with some wage replacement. These policies are well established, with France, Great Britain and Italy having had laws requiring maternity benefits since before World War I, which are now part of more general paid sick leave laws providing benefits for all workers unable to work for medical reasons. Among the more industrialized countries, the average minimum paid leave is twelve to fourteen weeks with many also providing the right to unpaid, job-protected leaves for at least one year. Leave is provided either through a national paid sick leave system or as part of a national family policy designed to enhance and support families. The long-established practices of these countries stand in marked contrast to the complete lack in this country of a standard minimum policy for family leave. . . .

———————————————————

House of Representatives

SEPARATE DISSENTING VIEWS ON H.R. 4300, THE FAMILY AND MEDICAL LEAVE ACT OF 1986

The Family and Medical leave Act of 1986, H.R. 4300, addresses important issues regarding employee leave-taking to care for the sick and newborn. While well-intentioned, it nevertheless decides what type of leave programs are best for virtually all American employers and employees instead of letting those decisions be worked out on an individual basis. The trend in employee benefits for the past several years has been to establish flexible benefit programs permitting individual employees to choose the benefit package best suited to their needs. H.R. 4300 mandates rigid and inflexible requirements that must be a part of all employer benefit plans, regardless of whether the employees want it or will ever be able to use it.

There is no disagreement that funds available for benefits are limited. H.R. 4300 could place businesses around the country in a position of having to cut back on current benefits in order to pay for those mandated by the legislation. H.R. 4300 is anti-small business. It takes the leave policies of some of the nation's biggest businesses and imposes them on the nation's smallest, without regard to whether they are in a financial position to provide the liberal benefits required.

Further, H.R. 4300 represents the first time that serious consideration has been given to legislating national standards for major employee leave and health benefits. Yet, the Committee on Education and Labor is reporting H.R. 4300 after conducting limited hearings that failed to show that such broad Federal legislation is necessary. It has spent an inadequate amount of time studying this far-reaching proposal which would, upon passage, reshape the current benefit plans of virtually every business in the country.

At first blush, this legislation's flaws are not readily apparent. We urge our colleagues to read the following eight points carefully. In our opinion, H.R. 4300 could work to the detriment of many workers because of a number of reasons, including the reduction of other important benefits.

From "Separate Dissenting Views on H.R. 4300, The Family and Medical Leave Act of 1986," in *Parental and Medical Leave Act of 1986*, U.S. House of Representatives.

1. *H.R. 4300 represents the first time that comprehensive national standards for major employee leave and health benefits have been given serious consideration in Congress.*

H.R. 4300 presents something of a test to us as lawmakers. It poses a significant question—how deeply does Congress want to become involved in employee benefit issues? H.R. 4300 can legitimately be characterized as a Pandora's Box. For example, proponents of the bill have intimated that H.R. 4300, which calls for unpaid leave, will be followed in future years by legislation mandating paid leave. Congress has not yet legislated whether and to what extent health care coverage should be provided, the number of dollars that should be placed in employee pension plans or the amount of life insurance that should be carried for each employee. Mandating the kind of rigid and inflexible leave requirements proposed by H.R. 4300, however, would place Congress in the midst of discussions that, until now, have wisely been left to negotiations between employees and employers.

Having crossed the Rubicon on developing private sector benefit policies with enactment of H.R. 4300, Congress will have great difficulty resisting future demands for more expansive employee benefits.

2. *Requiring businesses to provide one particular benefit, in this case a leave benefit, will force many to cut back on other benefits in order to absorb the cost of those imposed by H.R. 4300.*

The trend in employee benefit programs for the past decade has been away from providing a single benefit program to which all employees must subscribe, and towards serving up benefits "cafeteria style." Recognizing that a business can only allocate a certain dollar amount per employee for benefits, cafeteria plans offer a broad range of choices permitting each employee to select those that meet his or her individual needs.

Previously, two-income families may have carried conventional plans that largely duplicated one another. With cafeteria plans, each wage earner can select a different plan which, when combined, give their family far broader protections that would otherwise be possible. At Procter & Gamble, for example, one of the choices available for employees is buying more vacation time or putting the benefit money away from child care.

The sharp contrast to prevailing practice, H.R. 4300 would legislate against the trend toward flexible benefits. It would require that each employee's benefit "budget" be spent on a benefit that the employee may not need nor want. We would urge our colleagues to ask single employees and married employees with no children whether they want to be legally required to have their benefit dollars used to purchase a parental leave benefit, when they may never be in a position to take advantage of it. Our colleagues may also wish to ask employees who have no dependent parents whether they would have any objection to a law requiring them to carry dependent care coverage. At a time when employees are demanding flexible benefit plans, H.R. 4300 would force less flexibility.

It should also be added that employers are not required to provide health benefits, and that H.R. 4300 only requires that those who currently do so to maintain those benefits while the employee is on leave. Enactment of H.R. 4300, therefore, could force a marginal business to reduce benefit costs by discontinuing them altogether.

3. The Committee of Education and Labor has not given this legislation adequate consideration.

This legislation is being brought to the floor of the House of Representatives on the basis of limited consideration by the Education and Labor Committee. Considering the immense impact that it will have on every form of business in the country, our failure to further explore the impact of this legislation is of great concern.

It would seem that a prerequisite to the Congress accepting a labor law proposed by the House Education and Labor Committee is a comprehensive hearing record containing testimony clearly establishing that institutional abuse or inequity exists requiring a Federal legislative remedy. That has not happened with H.R. 4300.

All members of Congress are painfully aware of how many small businesses have failed recently, and how fragile many business situations—both large and small—are around the country. All of us know of companies in our districts which are barely surviving. It is ironic and telling that the Committee has spent far less time on hearings leading up to this Federally imposed leave policy than a benefits manager would spend designing one for his or her company.

Evidence of the superficial consideration given to the drafting of H.R. 4300 can be found in its numerous flaws. For example, H.R. 4300 confounds the application of Section 504 of the Rehabilitation Act of 1973 which protects persons with disabilities from discrimination in Federally assisted or conducted programs. Despite the fact that H.R. 4300's reemployment guarantees will require increased hiring and discharge of temporary employees, the bill fails to address the distortion that these dis-

charges will create in employer experience ratings in unemployment compensation (UC) programs (experience ratings govern UC taxes; the less terminations, the lower the tax). Further, the legislation requires employers to continue health benefits for leave-taking employees, but does not address H.R. 4300's relationship with similar provisions contained in the COBRA legislation enacted earlier this year. Clearly, legislation as comprehensive as H.R. 4300 should not be rushed forward without its sponsors having first remedied conflicts with other laws.

4. A leave policy drafted in Washington, and applicable to hundreds of thousands of unique employer, employee, business situations around the country could result in a severe economic hardship to a number of businesses, particularly small ones.

In recent days the call from the House floor has been to improve the competitiveness of American industry. The notion of a Federally mandated leave policy stands in direct conflict to our recent deliberations.

One of the principal arguments used in support of this legislation is that other countries, particularly the European industrialized nations, have already enacted some form of parental leave laws. Those same nations, however, are no longer able to generate a significant number of new jobs for their citizens. The combined effect of the liberal European labor laws is such that few companies are willing any more to risk the investment capital in Europe.

Many U.S. businesses are responding to the needs of working parents. A major study of the leave policies of 384 large U.S. corporations prepared by Catalyst, Inc., for example, demonstrated that 95% already provide short-term disability leave and over half give unpaid leave for maternity purposes, the bulk of which lasts three months or longer, with a reinstatement guarantee at the conclusion of the leave period.

Studies such as the one prepared by Catalyst demonstrate that benefit programs are not uniform, but are designed to take into consideration the individual circumstances of each company. No such discretion is available under H.R. 4300's rigid requirements. As explained in more detail in the majority's report, H.R. 4300 takes the employee relations policies of the IMB's of this country and imposes them by law on small typewriter repair companies. It infers that a small office products company in a suburban mall has the same financial and staffing resources as a Fortune 500 corporation doing business world-wide. Small business enterprises employ 49% of the labor force. Last year, 65,000 small business failed. Should it be enacted, H.R. 4300 is likely to contribute to increased failures in future years, in every part of the country.

5. *H.R. 4300 will force a number of marginal businesses to restructure their hiring practices in such a way as to avoid, to the extent possible, hiring women of childbearing age and persons with past histories of serious health conditions and disabilities.*

In order to meet the staffing obligations that would result from H.R. 4300's job guarantee provisions, employers may covertly discriminate in their hiring practices against those who seem likely to utilize the leave benefits. For example, if two equally qualified women were applying for a particular position, and one is of childbearing age while the other is not, H.R. 4300 would encourage the employer to hire the latter person. Similarly, if an individual with a history of serious illness or disability applies for a job, the liberal leave requirements of H.R. 4300 may result in the employer being hesitant to offer the individual a position, knowing that the law permits the individual to take six months leave during each twelve month period.

6. *In a time of limited resources and an explosion of litigation in Federal courts, H.R. 4300 would create a new Federal bureaucracy to enforce the comprehensive requirements of this legislation and a new enforcement scheme involving the Department of Labor.*

A Federally mandated program generates disputes over interpretation of eligibility criteria and the nature of the benefit provided. H.R. 4300, imposed by Congress on an unwilling business community, will result in a rash of disputes. In addition, yet another unwilling partner, the Department of Labor, would be given the responsibility for reviewing all settlements and ensuring enforcement of all decisions. Considering the superficial consideration given the issue and the lack of definition of key terms, passage of H.R. 4300 will yield numerous court cases and administrative disputes.

7. *It is simply inappropriate for the Congress to be mandating parental and medical leave policies for thousands of employers around the country when it is unwilling to accept those policies for itself.*

The Committee would saddle American employers with mandatory leave and benefit requirements, but is unwilling to accept those same requirements for itself. H.R. 4300 would cover nearly all types of American business—private sector employees, Federal government employees, and employees of state, county and local governments. Conspicuously absent from this list are the employees of the United States Congress.

8. H.R. 4300 is not a "no-cost" bill.

The majority report states that the technical changes made during the markup process "further assure the bill will result in long term savings for employers." This statement is highly questionable and defies business practice. One of the fundamental premises of this legislation is that employers should be required to continue the employee's health, disability and life insurance benefits while on leave and then restore the returning employee to the same or similar position at the conclusion of the leave. Employers will be required to hire temporary replacements at full pay and benefits, and then discharge them if another position cannot be found within the company. Because many of these replacement workers can only be promised a temporary position, employers may have to pay premium wage rates to get the quality of help that is needed. In many circumstances, the use of temporary help for long periods of time to replace key regular personnel results in reduced productivity and the remaining employees having to work greater overtime.

In conclusion, we would stress that formulation of employee leave and benefit policies is best left to individual employers and their employees who are in a better position to identify the needs of all concerned. Despite its good intentions, and because of its numerous flaws, H.R. 4300 does not merit support.

Steve Bartlett.
Thomas Tauke.
Richard Armey.
Harris Fawell.
Paul Henry.

POSTSCRIPT

Should Congress Guarantee Workers the Right to Parental Leave?

In this debate, supporters of H.R. 4300 contend that the presence of growing numbers of working mothers in the marketplace creates a conflict between work and family responsibilities. That is, when the head of a single parent family works, or when both parents in a traditional family works, one or both of the parents can be "torn between nurturing their seriously ill child and reporting to work." Similarly, pregnant workers who are employed by firms who do not provide leaves of absence for those who are temporarily disabled are unprotected by the Pregnancy Discrimination Act of 1978. These workers must "choose between the children and their jobs" or they must "compromise" on one or both. This produces at least one loser—maybe two.

The dissenters in this debate argue that H.R. 4300 is inflexible and out of step with the modern day trend of allowing individual workers to choose a benefit package from a menu of alternative fringe benefits. They go on to list eight objections: three political objections and five economic objections. Their economic concerns are: (1) since there is a firm that has a finite budget for fringe benefits, the opportunity costs of this legislation would be to force the firm to "cut back on other benefits"; (2) this legislation would be particularly troublesome for small businesses and it might conflict with attempts to improve the "competitiveness of American industry"; (3) "marginal business" will have an incentive to avoid "hiring women of childbearing age"; (4) "a new federal bureaucracy" will have to be created to "enforce

the comprehensive requirements of this legislation and by definition this will lead to increased costs and inefficiencies"; and (5) firms will have to "pay premium wager rates" and, because they will be forced to "use temporary help for long periods of time," they will experience "reduced productivity."

The debate over this bill did not end in 1986. In the U.S. Senate, Christopher Dodd (Democrat from Connecticut) introduced S. 52278 on April 9, 1986. Senator Dodd's bill, also called the Parental and medical Leave Act of 1986, was referred to the Committee on Labor and Human Resources, In October 1987, this committee began hearing on the S. 52278 bill. A copy of these hearings, including a comprehensive cost study conducted by the General Accounting Office (GAO) should be available in your library. You can also examine the growing body of literature about maternity leave that has appeared in print recently. The most comprehensive review of the proposed legislation appeared in the summer 1987 issue of *Notre Dame Journal of Law, Ethics and Public Policy*. This comprehensive essay by James Carr, "Bringing Up Baby: The Case for a Federal Parental leave Act," discusses the need and feasibility of implementing H.R. 4300. For more background information see Dana E. Friedman's essay in *Across the Board* (March 1987); Nadine Taub's article in *The Nation* (May 31, 1986); David Blakenhorn's opinion in the *New York Times* (April 7, 1987); or the comments found in the *Employee Benefit Plan Review* (June 1986).

ISSUE 9

Is It Time to Abolish the Minimum Wage?

YES: from "Minimum Wage Myths," *The Nation's Business* (June 1987)

NO: Teresa Ghilarducci, from "Women's Jobs and the Minimum Wage," testimony prepared for the Pennsylvania House of Representatives (August 26–27, 1987)

ISSUE SUMMARY

YES: The editors of *Nation's Business* insist that support for the minimum wage is based on eight myths that ignore the fact that if the Kennedy-Hawkins bill passes, it "hurts the very employees it is intended to help." **NO:** Economist Ghilarducci maintains that both "advocates and detractors of the minimum wage" have ignored the impact it has had on the economic well-being of "women workers."

In the midst of the Great Depression, Congress passed the Fair Labor Standards Act (FLSA) of 1938. In one bold stroke, it established a minimum wage rate of $0.25 an hour, it placed controls on the use of child labor, it defined the normal workweek to be 44 hours a week and it mandated that time and a half be paid to anyone working longer than the normal workweek. Fifty years later the debate concerning child labor, the workweek and overtime pay have long subsided, but the debate over the minimum wage rages on.

The immediate and continued concern over the minimum wage component of the FLSA should surprise few. Although $0.25 an hour seems to be a paltry sum compared to today's wage rates, in 1938 it was a princely reward for work. It must be remembered that jobs were hard to come by and unemployment rates at times reached as high as 25 percent of the workforce. When work was found, any wage seemed acceptable to those who roamed the streets with no "safety-net" to protect their families. Indeed, consider the fact that $0.25 an hour was 40.3 percent of the average manufacturing wage rate for 1938, while our current minimum wage rate of $3.35 an hour is only 34.2 percent of the average manufacturing wage rate in 1987.

Little wonder than that the business community in the 1930s was up in arms. They argued that if wages went up, two things would happen and they were both bad. Prices would rise and this would choke off the little demand for goods and services that existed in the marketplace, and the demand for workers would have to fall. The end result would be a return to the depths of the Depression where there was little or no hope of employment for the very people who should benefit from the Fair Labor Standards Act.

In the face of these dire projections, Congress chose to move forward. It was intent upon creating a wage floor that would ensure a standard of living for the working poor which was minimally acceptable to society at large. Over the years this floor has been regularly modified and adjusted. As Table 1 in Ghilarducci's essay indicates, the minimum wage rose from its 1938 level of $0.25 per hour to its current level of $3.35. It is important to note that there have been no increases since the 1981 floor was established. Since no legislation is scheduled for a vote in 1987, this period will represent the longest elapsed time between the establishment of new floors. Prior to this, the 1939–1945 World War II period and the 1968–1974 Vietnam years represented the longest periods without a minimum wage increase. Both of these periods were characterized by rising real wages. Unlike the previous two periods, the current period is one of falling real wages. Indeed, prices have risen by more than 30 percent since the last congressional action in this area.

The erosion of the minimum wage actually can be traced back to 1978. Even though the minimum wage rate was increased in 1979, 1980 and again in 1981, these increases did not keep pace with the rate of inflation. Thus for all practical purposes, the minimum wage has remained unchanged for more than a decade.

This may change in the relatively near future. In early 1987, Senator Edward M. Kennedy (Democrat from Massachusetts) and Representative Augustus Hawkins (Democrat from California) introduced the Minimum Wage Restoration Act of 1987. The Kennedy-Hawkins bill would raise the minimum wage rate to $4.65 per hour in 1990. (This increase would come in increments: $0.50 in 1988 to $3.85, $0.40 in 1989 to $4.25, and an additional $0.40 in 1990 to $4.65). In future years, the floor would be indexed to 50 percent of the average nonsupervisory, private-industry hourly wage rate. If this legislation were passed, this would raise the relative position of the floor in levels that were experienced in the 1950s and 1960s.

The wisdom of the Kennedy-Hawkin's bill is hotly debated in the U.S. Congress, in state legislatures, and in the print and electronic media. It is also debated here as Issue 9. The U.S. Chamber of Commerce's position is well argued by the editors of *The Nation's Business* who maintain that such a bill will not improve the well-being of low-income families. Indeed, they argue that the very people that this bill is intended to help will be very seriously hurt by this legislation. Teresa Ghilarducci, on the other hand, believes that we have all ignored the impact of this legislation on the increasingly large number of women who live in poverty.

YES

MINIMUM WAGE MYTHS

The public will pay for an increase in the federal minimum wage through higher prices and fewer jobs.

That is overwhelmingly the view of an organization of employers from a cross section of American business. And business legislative strategists are trying to convey that view to Congress as part of a campaign to head off a strong drive to raise the wage floor by nearly 40 percent over three years.

The minimum wage is now $3.35 an hour. Legislation pending in Congress would bring it to $4.65 by 1990 and would provide for automatic increases thereafter by setting the wage at 50 percent of the average nonsupervisory, private-industry wage.

At the recent annual meeting of the U.S. Chamber of Commerce, delegates representing grass-roots businesses predicted massive impact on their companies if the wage-increase-and-escalator plan goes through. Three quarters said they would raise prices, cut their existing work forces, defer new hiring or reduce the number of hours that present employees worked.

Others said they would respond to a mandated increase with such steps as cutting profit margins, reducing services or accelerating labor-saving methods. Fifty-five percent of the employers polled said they would have to raise wages of workers who now earn above the minimum to preserve existing differentials.

The principal congressional sponsors of the minimum wage legislation are Sen. Edward M. Kennedy (D-Mass.), chairman of the Senate Committee on Labor and Human Resources, and Rep. Augustus Hawkins (D-Calif.), chairman of the House Committee on Education and Labor. They argue that inflation has drastically eroded the purchasing power of the $3.35 minimum wage since it took effect in 1981 and that many entry-level workers will be condemned to poverty unless that figure is raised substantially.

Leading the opposition are Sen. Orrin Hatch (R-Utah), senior Republican on Kennedy's committee, and Rep. Steve Bartlett (R-Tex.), a member of Hawkins' committee. They spotlight the impact of a wage increase in terms of higher unemployment and higher prices. They argue that a higher wage would actually hurt the very people that proponents say would be helped.

"Minimum Wage Myths," *Nation's Business*, June 1987. Copyright © 1987, U.S. Chamber of Commerce. Reprinted by permission.

At the same time, Hatch and Bartlett say that business people are going to have to become more active in making their views known to Congress if the Kennedy-Hawkins bill is to be stopped.

The congressional push for a substantial increase in the minimum wage is part of an overall campaign by organized labor on several fronts to capitalize on Democratic control of both houses of Congress. The AFL-CIO and other labor organizations played major roles in the 1986 election campaign, where Democrats gained control of the Senate for the first time since President Reagan's first victory in 1980.

While the Democrats retained control of the House throughout the Reagan years, GOP control of the Senate remained a formidable and usually impenetrable obstacle to legislation backed by organized labor and its congressional allies.

Now, says Hatch, "all the labor stuff the unions are trying to put on business is going to be overwhelming." As senior Republican on the Labor Committee, he remains at the head of opposition to labor initiatives he views as detrimental to the economy.

And, in a strong counterattack on the minimum-wage push, Hatch plans to press for a youth minimum wage, which would permit employers to pay younger workers at a rate less than the federal minimum during the summer vacation period. That approach, he says, would encourage employers to hire and train youths they could not afford to hire if required to pay the full minimum.

Meanwhile, the fight over the proposed increase in the current $3.35 wage floor continues. The Minimum Wage Coalition to Save Jobs, the lead (sic) business organization fighting the wage increase, is rallying opposition to the bill because of its potentially adverse impact on the economy. A statement from the coalition says:

"A new minimum wage increase will aversely affect employment opportunities for the low-skilled, especially among our youth. . . . Economic studies show that raising the minimum wage results in massive unemployment and disemployment (which occurs when new jobs are not created because of high labor costs). In other words, the increase hurts the very employees it is intended to help.

"How else can business cope? Raising prices in response to wage increases will only renew the inflation spiral we have finally brought under control. More often, employers are forced to eliminate jobs or reduce employee hours. And the entry-level, low-skilled positions primarily held by young people are the first to go."

Goals of the Washington-based coalition, which represents business and trade associations as well as individual companies, include the closing of "the information gap" on the hidden costs of raising the minimum wage.

"The public does not understand the full economic impact of this increase proposal, which, on the surface, appears well-intentioned," the coalition says.

A key to achieving that understanding, the group adds, is dispelling the myths that surround the wage issue. The coalition makes these comparisons:

Myth: The typical minimum wage earner is a head of a household supporting a family.

Reality: The typical minimum wage employee is young, single, resides at home and works part time.

Myth: Raising the minimum wage is a way to reduce poverty.

Reality: A study by the Congressional Budget Office shows that over 80 percent of minimum wage workers do not fit the profile of the working poor. Seventy percent of minimum wage workers live in a family where at least one other member holds a job.

Myth: Raising the minimum wage has no negative impact on employment.

Reality: The federal Minimum Wage Study Commission reports that each 10 percent of increase in the wage results in a loss of 80,000 to 240,000 jobs for teenagers. In addition, some studies indicate that, although the percentage job loss of teenagers is greater, the absolute number of jobs lost by adults is greater. One study for the commission indicates a 10 percent increase in the minimum wage could wipe out 2.7 million jobs for adults.

Myth: A minimum wage increase is essential to welfare reform.

Reality: Only 16 percent of household heads below the poverty income level work at a full-time job year-round. Raising the required wage payment for low-skilled persons decreases the likelihood of alternative employment opportunities for these people, resulting in more pressure on the welfare system, not less. While tax reform has resulted in removing the disincentives that poor people faced in getting jobs (by eliminating taxes for the working poor), minimum wage increases destroy many entry-level jobs.

Myth: Raising the minimum wage will encourage the low-skilled and unemployed to seek jobs.

Reality: Increasing the minimum wage does not guarantee either a job or a wage increase to the least skilled. The low-skilled are the first to lose their jobs when the minimum wage is raised. Entry-level jobs are not created when labor costs go up. Where are the plentiful gas station attendants and department store clerks of 10 years ago? Their jobs fell victim to the last minimum wage increase.

Myth: Raising the wage floor will affect only those employees currently earning minimum wage.

Reality: An increase in the minimum will "ripple" through the job market and increase wages for skilled and experienced employees earning more than the minimum without corresponding increases in productivity. The Minimum Wage Study Commission reported that wage increases to those already earning more than minimum wage will be more costly to employers than the legislated increase of the minimum wage. The result will be wage-driven inflationary pressure on the economy.

Myth: Businesses can offset higher labor costs through price increases to consumers.

Reality: Some increased labor costs can be offset by higher prices. However, higher prices spark consumer resistance. The result is lessened demand for services, thus fewer workers and firms in service industries. To the extent that higher wages are offset by higher prices, the net result of the minimum wage increase is that employees are back where they started. The only way wages can be increased in real terms is for workers to acquire additional skills through training and education, not for Congress to pass laws that mandate higher wages.

Myth: A rise in the minimum wage has no impact on competitiveness with foreign businesses.

Reality: There are some low-wage manufacturing industries where minimum wage increases will further hurt their abilities to compete. These industries—shoes, textiles, apparel—are already struggling. As these and other industries are forced to raise their basic labor rates, entire wage structures ratchet upward. The effect on international competition is harmful.

Coalition strategists say their initial challenge is to generate as much grassroots support as possible for their plan to show members of Congress the difference between those myths and realities. Their ammunition includes a series of studies and analyses conducted over the past several years.

Some of those studies did not work out as the initiators intended. For example, the Minimum Wage Study Commission cited by the coalition was appointed by President Carter with a mandate to determine, among other things, "the beneficial effects of the minimum wage, including its effect in ameliorating poverty among working citizens."

Commission research, the coalition says, "confirmed the conclusions of all prior empirical evidence—that the minimum wage causes disemployment in teens and has no effect on low-wage incomes." The coalition adds:

"Nevertheless, the commission ignored its own findings and recommended that the level of the minimum wage be raised periodically by indexing it to the average wage paid in the economy and that the coverage of the minimum wage be extended by eliminating from current law various exempt categories of work. These incongruous recommendations are really not surprising in view of the ideological purposes of the commission."

A hard-hitting minority report asserted: "The evidence against the mini-

mum wage is so overwhelming that the only way the commission's majority was able to recommend that it be retained was to ask us not to base any decisions on facts."

Another insight into the issue is provided by the Economic Policy Division of the U.S. Chamber of Commerce, which has documented the inflationary/unemployment impact of a higher minimum wage. Graciela Testa-Ortiz, director of the Chamber's Forecasting Section, comments on the figures: "The evidence is incontrovertible. Nevertheless, the myths persist, and every few years legislators propose yet another increase in the minimum wage. In the process, they congratulate themselves for such a clear expression of their superior morality and compassion. Yet, this exercise in easy ethics only leads to greater hardship for all Americans."

Why, then, does the issue keep recurring? Because, says Testa-Ortiz, "some groups do reap benefits from regulations whose overall impacts on the economy are negative."

She cites various studies showing that the existence of a minimum wage allows a higher union wage structure than would otherwise be possible. Testa-Ortiz further cites a study showing that, as a result of one minimum wage increase, 85 percent of members of labor unions were expected to see higher pay, compared with only 44 percent of nonunion workers.

She comments further: "To young, inexperienced workers, minimum wage jobs are an extension of schooling, since those jobs offer them the training and the work experience to move on to higher paying jobs. The minimum wage deprives the youth of America not only of the opportunity to get a job, but also of needed experience and on-the-job training, while it does nothing to alleviate poverty."

Amid mounting evidence that continuing increases in the minimum wage are hurting those they are supposed to benefit, the basic philosophy of the wage floor is being re-examined.

Richard B. Berman, a Dallas business executive and chairman of the minimum wage coalition, says the concept of a minimum wage has become archaic. The policy of a federally mandated wage level was introduced in 1938, he says, to cover Depression-era conditions that no longer exist.

"A better alternative," Berman says, would be to "let free market forces of supply and demand naturally set the wage floor in a given market, taking into account regional differences in cost of living and unemployment."

NO
Teresa Ghilarducci

WOMEN'S JOBS AND THE MINIMUM WAGE

The following is based on testimony for the Pennsylvania House of Representatives, August 26–27, 1987.

In 1987, working full time in America can make you poor—poorer than collecting welfare. Someone working full time must earn $4.30 per hour to keep a family of 3 out of poverty. Unfortunately, the federal minimum wage requires that employers pay only $3.35 per hour. This means the income for 5 percent of all U.S. workers who earn the minimum wage or less is at the poverty level. Approximately another 5 percent, who earn slightly more than the minimum wage, are not much better off.

One rationale for the minimum-wage law, first established in 1938, was that a minimum wage prevented wages from falling so low that workers could not provide for their own subsistence; the minimum wage was to supply a ballast for our social principles, as well as for the earnings of workers. Since 1938, working full time at the minimum wage yielded a subsistence income (sometimes more) for a family of 3. In 1987, however, the minimum wage is just 78 percent of the poverty wage. This is the lowest percentage of the poverty wage that has existed in the United States since 1950—12 years before the War on Poverty was declared!

The minimum wage does not just establish absolute standards. It also establishes the position of workers relative to one another, in that it influences the size of the gap between the lowest-paid worker in society and the typical manufacturing worker. In 1950, minimum-wage workers earned approximately half of what manufacturing workers earned. In 1987, the minimum wage is 34 percent of the average manufacturing wage. Thus, the wage ratio between the lowest-paid worker and the factory worker went from 1:2 in 1950 to only 1:3 in 1987. The relationship among the minimum wage, the average manufacturing wage, and the poverty wage for selected years from 1938 to 1987 is presented in Table 1.

The minimum wage is due for an increase if it is to achieve its historical purpose. However, a substantial increase in the minimum wage in the late

From "Women's Jobs and the Minimum Wage," by Teresa Ghilarducci *testimony prepared for the Pennsylvania House of Representatives.*

Table 1

The Relationship Among the Minimum Wage, Average Manufacturing Wage, and Poverty Wage, 1938–1987

Year	Minimum Wage	Minumum Wage as a Percentage of Average Manufacturing Wage	Minimum Wage as a Percentage of Poverty Wage
1938	$0.25	40.3%	46.0%
1939	0.30	47.6	46.0
1945	0.40	39.2	57.1
1950	0.75	52.1	79.8
1956	1.00	51.3	94.3
1961	1.15	49.6	98.3
1963	1.25	50.8	104.4
1967	1.40	49.6	107.2
1968	1.60	53.2	117.5
1974	2.00	45.3	103.8
1975	2.10	43.5	100.0
1976	2.30	44.1	103.1
1978	2.65	43.0	103.9
1979	2.90	43.3	102.5
1980	3.10	42.6	96.3
1981	3.35	41.6	95.7
1987	3.35	34.2	78.0

Sources: The Wall Street Journal, September 1987; US Statistical Abstract.
The poverty level in 1967 was adjusted for inflation to obtain the poverty wage for each year.
Full-time work is 2,040 hours per year.

1980s would produce unprecedented effects because the labor market has undergone significant structural changes since 1938. Women have entered the labor market to stay. In a few years, 50 percent of the full-time labor force will be women. Sexism exists as a backdrop to this dramatic change and helps to explain the persistent concentration of women in the lowest-paid occupations and why women are paid less than men are in almost every occupation.

Another factor to be considered in the role of the minimum wage in contemporary society is that an increasing number of working women are becoming heads of households. Thus, the feminization of poverty, the massive entrance of women into the workforce, and the existence of labor-market discrimination against women all suggest a new protective role for the minimum wage. This is the role that the advocates of the minimum wage have failed to emphasize; it may be the most important reason why a minimum-wage increase would enhance social welfare. That is, the minimum wage and female earnings are inextricably linked.

Raising the minimum wage leads the list of labor issues facing the 1987–1988 U.S. Congress. The business community's fierce opposition relies on a 49-year-old case against the minimum wage. The business community's basic argument is that firms should not be forced into bankruptcy because they are required to meet an increase in the minimum wage, as this would diminish the jobs available to the marginal workers. The Chamber of Commerce, small-business organizations, and other employer groups claim this would hurt the people who have the fewest skills and need the work experience the most. A lobbyist for the restaurant industry stated that the minimum wage "is less a business issue than a jobs issue." Moreover, a *ripple effect* is feared: a minimum-wage increase would bump up wages farther along the pay scale and cause price increases and unemployment. These consequences depend on specific economic relationships and on the specific magnitudes of these relationships, which have been debated by economists since the minimum wage was introduced.

WAGES AND EMPLOYMENT

The debate surrounding the minimum wage focuses on the relationship between wages and labor demand. The Minimum Wage Commission in 1981 reported that the effect of the minimum wage on employment is negative, but small. The negligible effect is due to the fact that the demand for labor depends on two factors: the marginal productivity of labor and the overall demand for the product. The commission concluded that if employment demand grows over time, a minimum-wage increase could easily be accompanied by an *increase* in employment, since the negative employment effect might well be smaller than the positive growth effect of the demand for labor. Indeed, if wages do not increase at the same time that the demand for labor increases, then profits grow at the expense of wages.

The importance that small business has attached to defeating a minimum-wage increase is understandable. Since 1981, small businesses have endured a record number of bankruptcies, suffered severe competition from large firms (which in turn have been challenged by international competition), witnessed vanishing support from the Small Business Administration, and watched with alarm the passage of a pro-big-business 1986 tax reform. It is not surprising, therefore, that small businesses vehemently oppose an increase in the minimum wage. The passage of a higher minimum wage would further weaken small businesses' competitive position, while its defeat would give them a victory.

Although small businesses may have good reasons to be interested in defeating a minimum-wage increase, a low minimum wage may not be in their own best interest. It is a collective-action problem: what may be harmful for an individual firm, such as an increase in labor costs, may, in fact, be beneficial for all firms. A higher minimum wage means that firms can retain productive workers without losing their competitive position and will not incur the community's wrath, since they will be seen to be raising wage standards within the community.

In a typical American city experiencing deindustrialization, the major benefit from an increase in the minimum wage is to the growing sectors of trade and services, in which pay is traditionally at or near the minimum level and in which the newest entrants to the labor force are women. The minimum wage would establish a wage floor for these individuals. This would force firms to compete on the basis of efficiency and product quality, rather than on the basis of labor costs. This is especially important in emerging industries and in growing industries.

A survey of the economic studies concerning the minimum wage reveals five generalized conclusions. First, a 10-percent increase in the minimum wage would yield a 1-percent drop in employment, but this drop would likely be accompanied by an increase in schooling among teenagers. Second, the effect on adult employment would be negligible. Third, the ripple effect, the effect of the minimum wage on wages above the minimum, ends at wage rates that are 150 percent of the minimum wage. The ripple effect is smaller when the gap between the minimum wage and the average manufacturing wage is large. Fourth, management productivity and labor productivity would increase. Management would become more efficient in its attempts to make up the increase in costs, and workers would be more committed to the workplace at higher pay levels. Fifth, there is no clear-cut evidence that the cost of a minimum wage would be passed on in the form of increased prices.

Despite the evidence presented in these high-quality studies on the minimum wage, any forecasts based on these studies are subject to serious biases. Conclusions must be based on evidence gathered in a period of time when the majority of minimum-wage workers were not women and permanently in the labor force. This labor-market change will affect significantly the impact of the minimum wage in the next decade. For instance, low-wage workers, most of whom are women (approximately 66 percent), would, theoretically, demand certain products and services if wages were increased. Since the demand for services increases when women work (and women dominate the low-paying jobs in the service, clerical, and sales occupations), we can expect that an increase in the minimum-wage rate would increase the demand for the services produced by minimum-wage workers. This in turn would increase the demand for minimum-wage workers.

THE MINIMUM WAGE AND WORKING WOMEN

In the United States between the years 1970 and 1980, women filled 60 percent of the new jobs created. They also tended to enter the lowest-paying occupations in retail trade, the services, and clerical work. In a city such as South Bend, Indiana, a community that has experienced economic dislocations due to manufacturing-plant shutdowns, the impact of women's entry into the labor force has been profound. Computer simulations for the South Bend Standard Metropolitan Statistical Area (SMSA) revealed that if the minimum wage were raised to $4.65 per hour, women workers' total income would increase by $22 million and overall wage income would increase by $33 million, which would represent only a 5-percent increase in total income within the SMSA.

Several reasons explain why women would receive two-thirds of the benefits arising from an increase in the minimum wage in South Bend (and presumably across the nation). First, the nation has experienced a transition from a manufacturing-dominated economic base to a services-and-trade economic base. Women are entering the labor market at the same time that low-paying industries and occupations are growing and high-paying industries are in decline.

A second reason is that part-time jobs are 6 times more likely to pay minimum wages than full-time jobs, and women are twice as likely to hold part-time jobs than men are (relatively more women than men report involuntary part-time work—they work part time only because full-time work is unavailable). A low minimum wage creates a large gap between the wages of a part-time job and the wages of a full-time job. Firms tend to develop a two-tiered labor force. One tier is comprised of workers who earn high wages, are trained on the job, and have many fringe benefits. The second tier consists of part-time, temporary workers who do not have fringe benefits. A higher minimum wage would reduce the gap between the tiers and may reduce a firm's incentive to substitute part-time jobs for full-time jobs. This would particularly aid women workers.

A frequently cited 1982 study concerning the effects of the minimum wage on adult workers reported that in 1975, relative to men, women received larger pay increases due to a minimum-wage boost in 1974. However, the female layoff rate was much larger in the 1974 recession. Peter Linneman, the author of the study, concluded that this was due to the fact that the 10¢-per-hour minimum-wage increase in 1974 brought the cost of female workers past the point of their marginal productivity. In essence, Linneman presumed that females were less-skilled workers because they earned less than their male counterparts. A subsequent review of the literature dismissed Linneman's study for making stronger-than-warranted inferences about the minimum wage and suggested that women may have been laid off first during the recession for other reasons, such as sex discrimination.

A third reason for why women would benefit more from a minimum-wage increase is that an increase may help reduce poverty rates among children. The relationship between poverty and the minimum wage is not straightforward. Working full time at minimum wage yields less than the poverty-level income for families of 2 or more persons. But most people who make the minimum wage do not live in poor families, although low earners tend to live with other low earners. This fact explains why there is a weak correlation between poverty and the minimum wage but that the probability of being poor is 4 times higher for minimum-wage workers than for other workers. This suggests that the young workers (age 24 years or younger), who constitute 60 percent of those workers who earn less than $4.35 per hour, are supplementing their families' low incomes.

This generalization has one important exception: approximately 35 percent of working women who were heads of households earned less than $159 per week in 1984 (an hourly wage of less than $4.00 per hour). This compares to the fact that fewer than 19 percent of male heads of households earned less than $159 per week. (A related fact to be considered is that male heads of households, unlike female heads of households, often have spouses who provide a second income.)

Finally, women are less likely to be unionized than men; 12 percent of women workers are unionized as compared to 25 percent of working men. This results in women having less bargaining power relative to their employers. In the absence of a union, a minimum-wage law provides an important wage floor.

A minimum-wage increase would restructure the wage distribution at the bottom. Currently, most new jobs created in retail and wholesale trade and in the service sector pay approximately $8,000 per year. One reason why these jobs pay less is because they are nonunion. Nationally, 23 percent of minimum-wage workers are in technical, clerical, and sales occupations, and 52 percent are in service occupations. The fact that these jobs are being created at the same time that adult women are dramatically increasing their labor-force participation means that, in the absence of unionization, a minimum-wage increase would permanently change the wage structure of women's jobs. This could be accomplished without much risk of reducing employment in these expanding occupations and industries. In South Bend, for instance, the service industry provides 26 percent of all jobs but only 23 percent of all income; the retail industry provides 19 percent of all jobs but only 9 percent of total income. Women make up 55 percent of all full-time workers in retail (mostly nonmanagerial jobs) and more than 60 percent in service jobs.

MINIMUM WAGE AND THE LOW-PAID LABOR MARKET

A low-paid labor market can be insulated from other jobs because of the racial, ethnic, and/or gender composition of the workforce, the special features of the industry, and/or certain geographical barriers. If these sources of insulation exist, then some institutional or administered change, whether it be in the form of union activity or in the form of a minimum wage, is needed to shore up wages. In the jargon of economists, this is the process in which monopsonistic exploitation is reduced. Economists posit a formal model for this situation: a segmented labor market. This is a market in which discrimination and other social forces decrease the amount of competition between men and women for all available jobs. This in turn means that competition does not work to achieve an efficient allocation of resources. One piece of evidence that points to a segmented labor market is the distribution of pay by sex and educational level. A college-educated woman earns about the same pay as a male who has dropped out of high school (respectively, $19,885 and $18,575). See Table 2.

Table 2

Average Earnings and Educational Attainment by Sex in 1984

Educational Level	Earnings	
	Women	Men
Some HS	$11,808	$18,575
HS Grad	14,076	22,312
Some College	16,241	24,737
College	19,885	33,086

Source: Barbara Bergmann, *The Economic Emergence of Women* (New York: Basic Books, 1987), p. 67

Economic theory presumes that in competitive markets, wages are set when equally empowered agents haggle and dicker in a free marketplace until all workers receive the highest wage available for their skills. However, the data in Table 2 do not support this view. In noncompetitive markets wages can only be protected from downward pressures by huge increases in demand, by government regulation, or by other measures like collective-bargaining agreements. In the 1930s, when the minimum wage was established, it was high unemployment that kept wages below subsistence levels; in the 1980s, the entry into the workforce of new workers who would accept low wages—women—caused a downward pressure on wages.

In conclusion, the most common argument leveled against a minimum-wage increase is that raising the minimum wage would cause firms to reduce employment. Yet the facts do not support this argument. An advantage of raising the minimum wage at this time is that service and retail industries depend on domestic, geographically based demand (thus, they cannot easily relocate or be replaced by cheap foreign competition). Also, prices in the service and trade sectors are relatively low, and employers enjoy high profits. All of these factors indicate a situation in which employers have the ability to pay higher wages.

It is not likely that hospitals, fast-food restaurants, and department stores will go out of business if they must pay their lowest-paid workers another $1.40 per hour. Even when the percentage increase in wages is large, a large percentage of a small wage is still small; consequently, an increased minimum wage would increase total costs only slightly. Adult employment is not reduced by an increase in the minimum wage, because firms' hiring decisions depend on many factors, including demand for the goods or services and lack of substitutes for the labor inputs. The major factor determining how much firms will pay is what everyone else pays for similar jobs. Therefore, a minimum-wage increase would raise the pay of the lowest earners, increase total industry costs by a small amount, and redistribute income from the economy in general and the employer in particular to the worker. And, as is evident in the 1980s, these workers are mainly women.

Neither advocates for nor detractors of the minimum wage have sufficiently addressed the effect of the minimum wage on women workers. What is new in the minimum-wage debate in the 1980s is that the statutory minimum wage is becoming the major floor beneath women's earnings and, increasingly, it is the standard used by the fastest-growing and most profitable industries in the United States to decide what to pay their employees.

POSTSCRIPT

Is It Time To Abolish the Minimum Wage?

The editors of *The Nation's Business* take a dim view of the Kennedy-Hawkins bill. In short, they argue that the "public will pay" for this legislation in the form of "higher prices and fewer jobs." Their assertions are founded on a number of public and private studies of the minimum wage. Most notably they turn to President Carter's Minimum Wage Study Commission, the Minimum Wage Coalition to Save Jobs, a report issued by a group of business organizations, and analyses conducted by the U.S. Chamber of Commerce. Based on these studies, *The Nation's Business* concludes that support for the minimum wage is grounded on eight fundamental myths that demonstrate that the advocates of the Kennedy-Hawkins bill simply don't understand basic economic principles.

Ghilarducci defends the new minimum wage floor by admitting that the minimum wage may have a negative effect on employment. But she believes this will have a small effect and will be more than offset by the positive value of the new wage floor. In defense of this position, she argues that if over time the demand for the goods and services produced by labor increases, this will in turn increase the demand for labor and "easily" offset a "minimum wage increase." Indeed, under these conditions she speculates that in the absence of a new wage floor, "profits grow at the expense of wages." She goes on to note that the new floor has a benefit that is often overlooked by even its advocates. In particular, she maintains that the Kennedy-Hawkins bill will help redress the wage differential between men and women. In her words, this will provide a "floor beneath women's earnings."

There is much written about the pros and cons of the minimum wage. One excellent review of the history of this legislation and the arguments that have raged back and forth over its legitimacy these last 50 years is found in Howard Wachtel's book, *Labor and the Economy* (Academic Press, 1984). If you care to receive information from the business community, you might write the Minimum Wage Coalition to Save Jobs: P.O. Box 28261, Washington, D.C. 20038. If on the other hand you would care for organized labor's view of this issue, write the AFL-CIO headquarters: 815 Sixteenth St., N.W., Washington, D.C. 20006. Keep abreast of the Congressional Hearing on the Minimum Wage Restoration Act of 1987. You will find this in the Senate as S. 837 and in the House of Representatives as H.R. 1834 in the Government Documents section of your library.

PART 2

MACROECONOMIC ISSUES

Government policy and economics are tightly intertwined. Taxation policy and monetary policy have dramatic impact on the economy as a whole, and the state of the economy can often determine policy goals. Decisions regarding welfare payments or tax rates must be made in the context of broad macroeconomic goals and the debates on these issues are more than theoretical discussions. Each has a significant impact on our economic lives.

Has American Government Become
   Too Big?

Can Monetary and Fiscal Policies Still
   Be Used to Solve Our
   Macroeconomic Problems?

Is Tax Reform an Impossible Dream
   Come True?

Is the Welfare System Causing Poverty?

Can Federal Budget Deficits Be Good
   for the Economy?

Did Monetary Policy Cause the Stock
   Market Crash in 1987?

ISSUE 10

Has American Government Become Too Big?

YES: William Simon, from "The Road to Liberty," *A Time for Truth* (McGraw-Hill, 1978)

NO: John Kenneth Galbraith, from "The Social Consensus and the Conservative Onslaught," *Millenium Journal of International Studies* (Spring 1982)

ISSUE SUMMARY

YES: Former Treasury Secretary Simon argues that government has gone too far in its efforts to provide "cradle-to-grave security." According to Simon, wealth can only be created through the free operation of markets, and it is imperative that productivity and the growth of productivity be given the highest economic priority.

NO: Harvard economist Galbraith believes that the services provided by government contribute as much to the well-being of society as those provided by the private sector. Although taxes may reduce the freedom of those who are taxed, the freedom of those who benefit from the tax-financed programs is enhanced.

Even in a free enterprise, capitalistic, market economy like that of the United States, government has certain legitimate functions to perform. One such function is to provide for national defense. Another is to establish and maintain the code of laws that represents the ground rules for social and business relationships and activities. A third function is to take care of those who, through no fault of their own, are unable to take care of themselves. A fourth is to establish monetary and fiscal policies to promote price stability, employment, and economic growth. Finally, the government must make adjustments if the price a firm charges for its product does not include the costs imposed upon society by the production of that item.

Both liberals and conservatives accept these activities as legitimate governmental functions. The disagreement is over the amount of government action that is necessary and the specific action that should be taken. Conservatives demand that government's role be limited and that, when government must intercede, it should do so in a manner that preserves as much private initiative as possible. Liberals see a need for greater government involvement, with government choosing the quickest and most effective path to its goal.

In their arguments in favor of limited government, conservatives cite the intrinsic value of individual freedom: Individual freedom is an end in itself and is of the utmost importance, they contend. But more than this, individual freedom works to the benefit of the larger society: Society benefits because individual freedom promotes the efficient use of scarce resources. As evidence of this relationship, conservatives point to the great wealth of the United States and the high standard of living enjoyed by the average American, as compared to conditions in countries where government involvement is much more extensive. They also believe that political freedom cannot be maintained without economic freedom. Finally, they seem to view freedom as a fixed entity and contend that any increase in the role of government means an equal reduction in individual freedom and individual incentives.

Liberals do not deny the importance of individual freedom, but they are less willing to accept the notion that economic efficiency is significantly impaired when the government tempers the workings of the market in order to promote equity. They argue that some persons can be taxed with only a minor loss of economic freedom so that the lot of others may be improved. To the question, "Does absolute political freedom demand complete economic freedom for each individual?" liberals respond with a resounding "no!" Indeed, they maintain that restricting the economic freedom of some does not necessarily reduce their political freedom and may, at the same time, enhance the economic freedom of others.

In practice, conservatives give greater emphasis to national defense than do liberals—as witnessed by the continuing battle between the Reagan administration and Democratic members of the Senate and the House. With respect to social welfare programs, the conservative effort is to ensure that only the "truly needy" receive benefits and that the level of these benefits should not reduce individual initiatives or incentives to work. To promote price stability, employment, and growth, conservatives promote slow and steady growth in the money supply, coupled with low rates of taxation and a balance between government taxes and revenues. As for the final function of government, conservatives believe that the difference between private costs and public costs is not as large as the liberals suggest. Accordingly, the need for safety and environmental regulation is less obvious to conservatives than to liberals.

The debate between Simon and Galbraith is not a debate between a conservative and a liberal over some specific issue or program. Rather, it is a debate on philosophic grounds—on the relation between the size of government and the extent of individual freedom, and between individual freedom and economic performance. It is also a debate regarding the appropriate stance one should take regarding the nature of government: Whether individuals should take Simon's position that "state intervention in the private and productive lives of the citizenry must be presumed to be a negative, uncreative, and dangerous act . . . " or whether government programs such as "good education, health care, and law enforcement do not impair liberty or foretell authoritarianism."

YES
William Simon

THE ROAD TO LIBERTY

. . . Normally in life, if one finds oneself in a situation where *all* known courses of action are destructive, one reassesses the premises which led to that situation. The premise to be questioned here is the degree of government intervention itself—the very competence of the state to function as a significant economic ruler. But to question that premise is to hurl oneself intellectually into a free market universe. And that the social democratic leaders will not do. A few may actually understand—as did the brilliant Chancellor Erhard in postwar Germany—that the solution to shortages, recession and unemployment, and an ominous decline in technological innovation is to dispense with most intervention and regulation and allow men to produce competitively in freedom. But they know that if they proposed this, they would be destroyed by the political intellectuals of their countries. . . .

What we need today in America is adherence to a set of broad guiding principles, not a thousand more technocratic adjustments. [I] shall not waste my time or yours with a set of legislative proposals. Instead, I will suggest a few of the most important general principles which I would like to see placed on the public agenda. They are actually the conclusions I have reached in the course of working on this book.

—The overriding principle to be revived in American political life is that which sets individual liberty as the highest political value—that value to which all other values are subordinate and that which, at all times, is to be given the highest "priority" in policy discussions.

—By the same token, there must be a conscious philosophical prejudice against any intervention by the state into our lives, for by definition such intervention abridges liberty. Whatever form it may take, state intervention in the private and productive lives of the citizenry must be presumed to be a negative, uncreative, and dangerous act, to be adopted only when its proponents provide overwhelming and incontrovertible evidence that the benefits to society of such intervention far outweigh the costs.

From "The Road to Liberty," excerpt from *A Time for Truth*, by William Simon (New York: McGraw-Hill Book Company). Copyright © 1978 by William Simon. Reprinted by permission of McGraw-Hill, Inc.

—The principle of "no taxation without representation" must again become a rallying cry of Americans. Only Congress represents American voters, and the process of transferring regulatory powers—which are a hidden power to tax—to unelected, uncontrollable, and unfireable bureaucrats must stop. The American voters, who pay the bills, must be in a position to know what is being economically inflicted on them and in a position to vote men out of office who assault their interests, as *the voters* define those interests. Which means that Congress should not pass bills creating programs that it cannot effectively oversee. The drive to demand scrupulous legislative oversight of our policing agencies, such as the CIA, is valid; it should be extended to *all* agencies of the government which are also, directly or indirectly, exercising police power.

—A critical principle which must be communicated forcefully to the American public is the inexorable interdependence of economic wealth and political liberty. Our citizens must learn that what keeps them prosperous is production and technological innovation. Their wealth emerges, not from government offices or politician's edicts, but only from that portion of the marketplace which is *free*. They must also be taught to understand the relationship among collectivism, centralized planning, and poverty so that every new generation of Americans need not naively receive the Marxist revelations afresh.

—Bureaucracies themselves should be assumed to be noxious, authoritarian parasites on society, with a tendency to augment their own size and power and to cultivate a parasitical clientele in all classes of society. Area after area of American life should be set free from their blind power drive. We commonly hear people call for a rollback of prices, often unaware that they are actually calling for the destruction of marginal businesses and the jobs they furnish. People must be taught to start calling for a rollback of the bureaucracy, where nothing will be lost but strangling regulation and where the gains will always take the form of liberty, productivity, and jobs.

—Productivity and the growth of productivity must be the *first* economic consideration at all times, not the last. That is the source of technological innovation, jobs and wealth. This means that profits needed for investment must be respected as a great social blessing, not as a social evil, and that the envy of the "rich" cannot be allowed to destroy a powerful economic system.

—The concept that "wealth is theft" must be repudiated. It now lurks, implicitly, in most of the political statements we hear. Wealth can indeed be stolen, but only *after* it has been produced, and the difference between stolen wealth and produced wealth is critical. If a man obtains money by fraud or by force, he is simply a criminal to be handled by the police and the courts. But if he has earned his income honorably, by the voluntary exchange of goods and services, he is not a criminal or a second-class citizen and should not be treated as such. A society taught to perceive producers as criminals will end up by destroying its productive processes.

—Conversely, the concept that the absence of money implies some sort of virtue should be repudiated. Poverty may result from honest misfortune, but it also may result from sloth, incompetence, and dishonesty. Again the distinction between deserving and undeserving poor is important. It is a virtue to assist those who are in acute need through no fault of their own, but it is folly to glamorize men simply because they are penniless. The crude linkage between wealth and evil, poverty and virtue is false, stupid, and of value only to demagogues, parasite, and criminals—indeed, the three groups that alone have profited from the linkage.

—Similarly, the view that government is virtuous and producers are evil is a piece of folly, and a nation which allows itself to be tacitly guided by these illusions must lose both its liberty and its wealth. Government has its proper functions, and consequently, there can be both good and bad governments. Producers as well can be honest and dishonest. Our political discourse can be rendered rational only when people are taught to make such discriminations.

—The "ethics" of egalitarianism must be repudiated. Achievers must not be penalized or parasites rewarded if we aspire to a healthy, productive, and ethical society. Able-bodied citizens must work to sustain their lives, and in a healthy economic system they should be enabled and encouraged to save for their old age. Clearly, so long as the government's irrational fiscal policies make this impossible, present commitments to pensions and Social Security must be maintained at all cost, for the bulk of the population has no other recourse. But as soon as is politically feasible—meaning, as soon as *production* becomes the nation's highest economic value—the contributions of able-bodied citizens to their own future pensions should be invested by them in far safer commercial institutions, where the sums can earn high interest without being squandered by politicians and bureaucrats. American citizens must be taught to wrest their life savings from the politicians if they are to know the comfort of genuine security.

—The American citizen must be made aware that today a relatively small group of people is proclaiming its purposes to be the will of the People. That elitist approach to government must be repudiated. There is no such thing as the People; it is a collectivist myth. There are only individual citizens with individual wills and individual purposes. There is only one social system that reflects this sovereignty of the individual: the free market, or capitalist, system, which means the sovereignty of the individual "vote" in the marketplace and the sovereignty of the individual vote in the political realm. That individual sovereignty is being destroyed in this country by our current political trends, and it is scarcely astonishing that individuals now feel "alienated" from their government. They are not just alienated from it; they have virtually been expelled from the governmental process, where only organized mobs prevail.

—The growing cynicism about democracy must be combated by explaining why it has become corrupted. People have been taught that if they can get together big enough gangs, they have the legal power to hijack other citizens' wealth, which means the power to hijack other people's efforts, energies, and lives. No decent society can function when men are given such power. A state does need funds, but a clear cutoff line must be established beyond which no political group or institution can confiscate a citizen's honorably earned property. The notion that one can differentiate between "property rights." and "human rights" is ignoble. One need merely see the appalling condition of "human rights" in nations where there are no "property rights" to understand why. This is just a manifestation of the socialist myth which imagines that one can keep men's minds free while enslaving their bodies.

These are some of the broad conclusions I have reached after four years in office. Essentially they are a set of guiding principles. America is foundering for the lack of principles; it is now guided by the belief that *unprincipled* action—for which the respectable name is "pragmatism"—is somehow superior. Such principles as I have listed do not represent dogma. There is, as I said, nothing arbitrary or dogmatic about the interlocking relationship between political and economic liberty. The history of every nation on earth demonstrates that relationship, and no economist known to me, including the theoreticians of interventionism and totalitarianism, denies this. If liberty is to be our highest political value, this set of broad principles follows consistently. . . .

It is often said by people who receive warnings about declining freedom in America that such a charge is preposterous, that there is no freer society on earth. That is true in one sense, but it is immensely deceptive. There has never been such freedom before in America to speak freely, indeed, to wag one's tongue in the hearing of an entire nation; to publish anything and everything, including the most scurrilous gossip; to take drugs and to prate to children about their alleged pleasures; to propagandize for bizarre sexual practices; to watch bloody and obscene entertainment. Conversely, compulsion rules the world of work. There has never been so little freedom before in America to plan, to save, to invest, to build, to produce, to invent, to hire, to fire, to resist coercive unionization, to exchange goods and services, to risk, to profit, to grow.

The strange fact is that Americans are constitutionally free today to do almost everything that our cultural tradition has previously held to be immoral and ob-

scene, while the police powers of the state are being invoked against almost every aspect of the productive process. Even more precisely, Americans today are left free by the state to engage in activities that could, for the most part, be carried on just as readily in prisons, insane asylums, and zoos. They are not left free by the state to pursue those activities which will give them *independence*.

That is not a coincidence. It is characteristic, in fact, of the contemporary collectivist, in both America and Europe, to clamor that freedom pertains exclusively to the verbal and emotional realms. It allows the egalitarian socialist the illusion that he is not trying to weave a noose for the throats of free men, and it renders him all the more dangerous to the credulous. It is difficult, indeed, to identify as a potential tyrant someone who is raising a righteous uproar over your right to fornicate in the streets. But in this as well, our contemporary "liberators" are not original. I transmit to you a warning by Professor Nisbet, professor of humanities at Columbia University, included in his essay "The New Despotism." He says something I consider vital for the contemporary citizen to know because it is the final reason for the invisibility surrounding the destruction of some of our most crucial liberties:

[M]ore often than not in history, license has been the prelude to exercises of extreme political coercion, which shortly reach all areas of a culture. . . . [V]ery commonly in ages when civil rights of one kind are in evidence—those pertaining to freedom of speech and thought in, say, theater, press and forum, with obscenity and libel laws correspondingly loosened—very real constrictions of individual liberty take place in other, more vital areas; political organization, voluntary association, property and the right to hold jobs, for example. . . .

There are, after all, certain freedoms that are like circuses. Their very existence, so long as they are individual and enjoyed chiefly individually as by spectators, diverts men's minds from the loss of other, more fundamental social and economic and political rights.

A century ago, the liberties that now exist routinely on stage and screen, on printed page and canvas would have been unthinkable in America—and elsewhere in the West, for that matter, save in the most clandestine and limited of settings. But so would the limitations upon economic, professional, education and local liberties, to which we have by now become accustomed, have seemed equally unthinkable half a century ago. We enjoy the feeling of great freedom, of protection of our civil liberties, when we attend the theater, watch television, buy paperbacks. But all the while, we find ourselves living in circumstances of a spread of military, police and bureaucratic power that cannot help but have, that manifestly does have, profoundly erosive effect upon those economic, local and associative liberties that are by far the most vital to any free society.

From the point of view of any contemporary strategist or tactician of political power indulgence in the one kind of liberties must seem a very requisite to dimunition of the other kind. We know it seemed that way to the Caesars and Napoleons of history. Such indulgence is but one more way of softening the impact of political power and of creating the illusion of individual freedom in a society grown steadily more centralized, collectivized and destructive of the diversity of allegiance, the autonomy of enterprise in all spheres and the spirit of spontaneous association that any genuinely free civilization requires.

I cite this for another reason. Like others whom I have quoted at length at several points in this book, Mr. Nisbet stands as a living illustration of what I mean by a counterintellectual. It is only the scholar with a profound understanding of the nature of liberty and the institutions on which it rests who can stand ultimate guard over American cultural life. It is only he who can offer the American citizen the authentic and profound choices that our political system and our press no longer offer him.

I do not mean to imply here that it is only on a lofty, scholarly level that the fight can be conducted, although it unquestionably must begin at that level. At any time and on any social level the individual can and should take action. I have done so in my realm, and you, too, can work for your liberty, immediately and with impact. . . .

Stop asking the government for "free" goods and services, however desirable and necessary they may seem to be. They are not free. They are simply extracted from the hide of your neighbors—and can be extracted only by force. If you would not confront your neighbor and demand his money at the point of a gun to solve every new problem that may appear in your life, you should not allow the government to do it for you. Be prepared to identify any politician who simultaneously demands your "sacrifices" and offers you "free services" for exactly what he is: an egalitarian demagogue. This one insight understood, this one discipline acted upon and taught by millions of Americans to others could do more to further freedom in American life than any other.

There is, of course, a minimum of government intervention needed to protect a society, particularly from all forms of physical aggression and from economic fraud and, more generally, to protect the citizen's liberty and constitutional rights. What that precise minimum is in terms of a percentage of the GNP I am not prepared to say, but I do know this: that a clear cutoff line, beyond which the government may not confiscate our property, must be sought and established if the government is not to invade every nook and cranny of our lives and if we are to be free and productive. It is with *our* money that the state destroys our freedom. It is not too soon to start the process of tightening the leash on the state on the individual level, above all, by refusing to be a parasite. In the lowest-income groups in our nation there are men and women too proud, too independent to accept welfare, even though it is higher than the wages they can earn. Surely such pride can be stimulated on the more affluent levels of our society. . . .

It is with a certain weariness that I anticipate the charge that I am one of those "unrealistic" conservatives who wishes to "turn back the clock." There is a good deal less to this criticism than meets the eye. History is not a determinist carpet rolling inexorably in the direction of collectivism, although an extraordinary number of people believe this to be the case. The truth is that it has unrolled gloriously in the opposite direction many times. Above all, the United States was born. There is nothing "historically inevitable" about the situation we are in. There is also nothing "realistic" in couseling people to adjust to that situation. That is equivalent to counseling them to adjust to financial collapse and the loss of freedom. Realism, in fact, requires the capacity to see beyond the tip of one's nose, to face intolerably unpleasant problems and to take the necessary steps to dominate future trends, not to be crushed passively beneath them.

The time plainly has come to act. And I would advise the socially nervous that if our contemporary "New Despots" prefer to conceive of themselves as "progressive" and denounce those of us who would fight for liberty as "reactionary," let them. Words do not determine reality. Indeed, if language and history are to be taken seriously, coercion is clearly reactionary, and liberty clearly progressive. In a world where 80 percent of all human beings still live under harrowing tyranny, a tyranny always rationalized in terms of the alleged benefits to a collectivist construct called the People, the American who chooses to fight for the sanctity of the individual has nothing for which to apologize.

One of the clearest measures of the disastrous change that has taken place in this country is the fact that today one must intellectually justify a passion for individual liberty and for limited government, as though it were some bizarre new idea. Yet angry as I get when I reflect on this, I know there is a reason for it. Seen in the full context of human history, individual liberty *is* a bizarre new idea. And an even more bizarre new idea is the free market—the discovery that allowing millions upon millions of individuals to pursue their material interests as they choose, with a minimum of interference by the state, will unleash an incredible and orderly outpouring of inventiveness and wealth. These twin ideas appeared, like a dizzying flare of light in the long night of tyranny that has been the history of the human race. That light has begun to fade because the short span of 200 years has not been long enough for most of our citizens to understand the extraordinary nature of freedom. I say this with genuine humility. I came to understand this late in life myself, inspired by a very special perspective: I was flying high over the land of one of the bloodiest tyrants on earth. But having understood it, I cannot let that light die out without a battle. . . .

NO

John Kenneth Galbraith

THE SOCIAL CONSENSUS AND THE CONSERVATIVE ONSLAUGHT

THE ECONOMIC AND SOCIAL CONSENSUS

In economic and social affairs we value controversy and take it for granted; it is both the essence of politics and its principal attraction as a modern spectator sport. This emphasis on controversy regularly keeps us from seeing how substantial, on occasion, can be the agreement on the broad framework of ideas and policies within which the political debate proceeds.

This has been the case with economic and social policy in the industrial countries since the Second World War. There has been a broad consensus which has extended to most Republicans and most Democrats in the United States, to both Christian Democrats and Social Democrats in Germany and Austria, to the Labour and Tory Parties in Britain, and to Liberals and Progressive Conservatives in Canada. In France, Italy, Switzerland and Scandinavia also, policies have generally been based on a consensus. Although the rhetoric in all countries has been diverse, the practical action has been broadly similar.

All governments in all of the industrial countries, although differing in individual emphasis, have agreed on three essential points. First, there must be macroeconomic management of the economy to minimise unemployment and inflation. This, particularly in the English-speaking countries, was the legacy of Keynes. Second, there must be action by governments to provide those services which, by their nature, are not available from the private sector, or on which, like moderate-cost housing, health care and urban transportation, the private economy defaults. Finally, there must be measures—unemployment insurance, old age pensions, medical insurance, environmental protection, job-safety and produce-safety regulation, and special welfare payments—to protect the individual from circumstances with which he or she, as an individual, cannot contend, and which may be seen as a smoothing and softening of the harsh edges of capitalism.

From "The Social Consensus and the Conservative Onslaught," by John Kenneth Galbraith, *Milienlum Journal of International Studies*, Spring 1982. Copyright © 1982 by John Kenneth Galbraith. Reprinted by permission of the author.

There is no accepted term for the consensus which these policies compromise. 'Keynesian' policy refers too narrowly to macroeconomic action; 'liberal' or 'social democratic' policy has too strong a political connotation for what has been embraced in practice by Dwight E. Eisenhower, Gerald Ford, Charles de Gaulle, Konrad Adenauer, Winston Churchill and Edward Heath. I will not try to devise a new term; instead I will refer to the broad macroeconomic, public-service and social welfare commitment as the economic and social consensus, or just 'the consensus.' It is the present attack on this consensus—notably in Mrs. Thatcher's government in Britain and by Ronald Reagan's government in the United States—that I wish to examine.

THE CONSERVATIVE CHALLENGE TO THE CONSENSUS

The ideas supporting the economic and social consensus have never been without challenge. Keynesian macroeconomic management of the economy, the first pillar of the consensus, was powerfully conservative in intent. It sought only to correct the most self-destructive feature of capitalism (the one Marx thought decisive), namely its tendency to produce recurrent and progressively more severe crisis or depression, while leaving the role of the market, the current distribution of income and all property rights unchallenged. Despite this, numerous conservatives, especially in the United States, for a long time equated Keynesian economics with subversion. There was discomfort among conservatives when, thirty years after Keynes's *General Theory*[1] was published and the policy it prescribed was tending visibly towards obsolescence, Richard Nixon, in an aberrant moment, was led to say that all Americans, including Republicans, were Keynesians now. A reference to the welfare policies of the consensus—'the welfare state'—has always encountered a slightly disapproving mood; something expensive or debilitating, it was felt, was being done for George Bernard Shaw's undeserving poor. The need to compensate for the failures of capitalism through the provision of lower-cost housing, lower-income health care and mass transportation has been accepted in all countries; but, in the United States at least, not many have wanted to admit that this is an unavoidable form of socialism. In contrast, in all countries at all times there has been much mention of the cost of government, the level of taxes, the constraints of business regulation and the effect of these on economic incentives.

There has always been a likelihood, moreover, that an attack on the economic and social consensus would be taken to reflect the views of a larger section of the population than was actually the case, because a large share of all public comment comes from people of relatively high income, while the consensus is of greatest importance to those of lowest income. High social business and academic position gives access to television, radio, and the press, and those who are professionally engaged in the media are, themselves, relatively well off. It follows that the voice of economic advantage, being louder, regularly gets mistaken for the voice of the masses. Furthermore, since it is so interpreted by politicians, it has much the same effect on legislatures and legislation as a genuine shift of opinion.

In the last thirty-five years we have had many such shifts of opinion—all drastically to the right. Professor

Friedrich Hayek with his *Road to Serfdom;* [2] Senator Goldwater in 1964; the unpoor, non-black, distinctly unradical Dayton, Ohio housewife, the supposed archetype discovered by two American scholars; Vice President Spiro Agnew; George Wallace; and Enoch Powell in Britain—they were all, in their turn, seen to represent a growing new conservative mood, before being, each in his turn, rejected.

However, even if proper allowance is made for the dismal success, in the past, of conservative revival, it seems certain that there is now not only in the United States but in other industrial countries as well, an attack on the economic and social consensus that has a deeper substance. Mrs. Thatcher and Mr. Reagan have both won elections. Of course, much, if not most, of Mr. Reagan's success in 1980 must be attributed to President Carter's economists—to the macroeconomic management that combined a severe recession with severe inflation with a drastic slump in the housing industry with particular economic distress in the traditional Democratic industrial states, and all these in the year of the election. (Economists do some things with precision.) But *effective* macroeconomic management was one part of the consensus and, obviously, there is nothing wrong with the way it now functions.

THE CONSERVATIVE ONSLAUGHT

There is, indeed, substance to the conservative attack on the economic and social consensus, especially in Britain and the United States. It strikes at genuine points of vulnerability. This, however, is not true of all of the attack; some of it is merely a rejection of reality—or of compassion. The conservative onslaught we now witness needs careful dissection and differentiation. . . .

THE SIMPLISTIC ATTACK

The *simplistic* attack, which is currently powerful in the United States, consists in a generalised assault on all the civilian services of modern government. Education, urban services and other conventional functions of government; government help to the unemployed, unemployable or otherwise economically incapable; public housing and health care; and the regulatory functions of government are all in the line of fire. People, in a now famous phrase, must be left free to choose.

In its elementary form this attack on the consensus holds that the services of government are the peculiar malignity of those who perform them; they are a burden foisted on the unwilling taxpayer by bureaucrats. One eloquent American spokesman for this view, Mr. William Simon, the former Secretary of the Treasury, has said that,

Bureaucrats should be assumed to be noxious, authoritarian parasites on society, with a tendency to augment their own size and power and to cultivate a parasitical clientele in all classes of society.[3]

There must, he has urged, 'be a conscious, philosophical prejudice against any intervention by the state into our lives.'[4] If public services are a foisted malignancy—if they are unrelated to need or function—it follows that they can be reduced more or less without limit and without significant social cost or suffering. This is implicit, even explicit, in the simplistic attack.

Other participants in this line of attack are, superficially at least, more sophisticated. Professor Arthur Laffer of the University of Southern California has supported the case with his now famous curve, which shows that when no taxes are levied, no revenue is raised, and that when taxes absorb all income, their yield, not surprisingly, is also zero. Taxes that are too high, as shown by a curve connecting these two points, have at some point a reduced aggregate yield. The Laffer Curve—which in its operative ranges is of purely freehand origin—has become, in turn, a general case against all taxes. Let there be large horizontal reductions, it is argued, and the resulting expansion of private output and income—for those who will believe anything—can be great enough to sustain public revenues at more or less the previous level. For the less gullible, the Laffer Curve still argues for a large reduction in the cost and role of the government.[5]

Another stronger attack on the public services comes from Professor Milton Friedman and his disciples. It holds that these services are relentlessly in conflict with liberty: the market accords to the individual the sovereignty of choice; the state, as it enlarges its services, curtails or impairs that choice—a cumulative and apocalyptic process. By its acceptance of a large service and protective role for the state, democracy commits itself to an irreversible descent into totalitarianism and to Communism. Professor Friedman is firm as to the prospect. He argues that,

If we continue our present trend, and our free society is replaced by a collectivist society, the intellectuals who have done so much to drive us down this path will not be the ones who run the society; the prison, insane asylum, or the graveyard would be their fate.[6]

Against this trend he asks

shall we have the wisdom and the courage to change our course, to learn from experience, and to benefit from a 're-birth of freedom'?[7]

I have called this attack on the social consensus simplistic: it could also be called rhetorical and, by the untactful, vacuous, because it depends almost wholly on passionate assertion and emotional response. No one, after reflection, can conclude that publicly rendered services are less urgently a part of the living standard than privately purchased ones—that clean water from the public sector is less needed than clean houses from the private sector, that good schools for the young are less important than good television sets. In most countries public services are not rendered with high efficiency, a point worthy of real concern. But no way has ever been found for seriously reducing outlays for either efficiently or inefficiently rendered services without affecting performance. Public bureaucracy has a dynamic of its own, but so does private bureaucracy. As road builders promote public highways and public educators promote public education, so private weapons firms promote weapons and other corporate bureaucracies promote tobacco, alcohol, toothpaste and cosmetics. This is the common tendency of organisation, as we have known since Max Weber. Good education, health care and law enforcement do not impair liberty or foretell authoritarianism. On the contrary, the entire experience of civilised societies is that these services are consistent with liberty and enlarge it. Professor Friedman's belief that liberty is measured, as currently in New York City, by the depth of the uncollected garbage is, as I have previously observed, deeply questionable.

Taxes on the affluent do reduce the freedom of those so taxed to spend their own money. 'An essential part of economic freedom is freedom to choose how to use our income.'[8] But, unemployment compensation, old-age pensions and other welfare payments serve even more specifically to increase the liberty of their recipients. That is because the difference for liberty between considerable income and a little less income can be slight; in contrast, the effect on liberty of the difference between *no* income and *some* income is always very, very great. It is the unfortunate habit of those who speak of the effect of government on freedom that they confine their concern to the loss of freedom for the affluent. All but invariably they omit to consider the way income creates freedom for the indigent.

The differential effect of taxes and public services on people of different income is something we must not disguise. Taxes in industrial countries are intended to be moderately progressive; in any case, they are paid in greatest absolute amount by people of middle income and above. Public services, in contrast, are most used by the poor. The affluent have access to private schools, while the poor must rely on public education. The rich have private golf courses and swimming pools; the poor depend on public parks and public recreation. Public transportation is most important for the least affluent, as are public hospitals, public libraries and public housing, the services of the police and other municipal services. Unemployment and welfare benefits are important for those who have no other income, while they have no similar urgency for those who are otherwise provided.

We sometimes hesitate in these careful days to suggest an apposition of interest between the rich and the poor. One should not, it is felt, stir the embers of the class struggle. To encourage envy is uncouth, possibly even un-American or un-British. However, any general assault on the public services must be understood for what it is; it is an attack on the living standard of the poor. . . .

NOTES

1. John Maynard Keynes, *The General Theory of Employment Interest and Money* (London: Macmillan, 1936).
2. Fredrich von Hayek, *Road to Serfdom* (London: Routledge and Kegan Paul, 1944).
3. William Simon, *A Time for Truth* (New York: McGraw-Hill, 1978), p. 219.
4. *Ibid.*, p. 218.
5. Professor Laffer's inspired use of purely fortuitous hypotheses, it is only fair to note, has been a source of some discomfort to some of his more scrupulous academic colleagues.
6. Professor Friedman's foreword in William Simon, *op. cit.*, p. xiii.
7. Milton and Rose Friedman, *Free to Choose* (New York: Harcourt Brace Jovanovich, 1979), p. 7.
8. *Ibid.*, p. 65.

POSTSCRIPT

Has American Government Become Too Big?

Simon offers a series of conclusions drawn from his analysis of the appropriate size and role of government. First, he contends that individual liberty is the highest political value. Second, he believes "there must be a conscious philosophic prejudice against any intervention by the state into our lives, for by definition such intervention abridges liberty." Simon's third conclusion is the "inexorable interdependence of economic wealth and political liberty." Simon also believes that bureaucracies should be viewed as forces of evil, which reduce liberty, productivity, and jobs; that productivity and its growth must be given the highest priority at all times; that wealth is not theft and poverty is not virtue; and that property rights are an essential part of human rights. Simon stresses the essential conservative position that individual liberty and the free market will continue to "unleash an incredible and orderly outpouring of inventiveness and wealth."

In defending the liberal view of the legitimacy of government and the usefulness of its activities, Galbraith begins by citing a broad consensus regarding social policy in industrial countries. This consensus involves three points: government must take action to minimize unemployment and inflation; government must provide those things "which, by their nature, are not available from the private sector . . . "; and government must act "to protect the individual from circumstances with which he or she cannot contend." He goes on to argue that conservative attacks, like those of Simon, are simplistic because it is clear that the services provided by government contribute as much to society's well-being as do those produced by private business firms and that these government-provided "services are consistent with liberty and enlarge it." Indeed, he admits that taxes may reduce the freedom of those who are taxed but maintains that those who benefit from the tax-financed programs experience an increase in freedom.

For a more complete discussion of these issues, see *A Time for Truth* by William E. Simon (McGraw-Hill, 1978); *Economics and the Public Purpose* by John Kenneth Galbraith (Houghton-Mifflin, 1973); *The Denigration of Capitalism: Six Points of View* edited by Michael Novak (American Enterprise Institute, 1979); "Reflections on Social Democracy" by Alfred S. Eichner in *Challenge* (March/April 1982); and *Capitalism and Freedom* by Milton Friedman (University of Chicago Press, 1962).

ISSUE 11

Can Monetary and Fiscal Policies Still Be Used to Solve Our Macroeconomic Problems?

YES: Walter W. Heller, from "Activist Government: Key to Growth," *Challenge* (March-April 1986)

NO: Marc Levinson, from "Economic Policy: The Old Tools Won't Work," *Dun's Business Month* (January 1987)

ISSUE SUMMARY

YES: Shortly before his death economist Heller argued that history demonstrates that an activist government can improve macroeconomic performance. The 1980s has been a period of "antigovernment" and as a consequence there has been a slowdown in economic growth, an increase in poverty, and wasted potential, while productivity has not increased as rapidly expected. Heller believed that a return to activist government with proper alignment and execution of monetary and fiscal policies would solve these problems.

NO: Journalist Levinson believes that the economic environment has changed; flexible exchange rates and large international capital market have internationalized the U.S. economy. As a result monetary and fiscal policies will not work as they have in the past, and this means that "even the greatest of economic powers can no longer control its own destiny."

Although economists disagree as to causes, they all agree that the history of American capitalism is a history of reoccurring business cycles. This pattern of expansion in production and employment followed by contraction is found throughout the nineteenth and twentieth centuries. Prior to the Great Depression of the 1930s, the contractions were normally of short duration and usually described as "financial panics." Economic history books identify a number of such episodes: 1819, 1837, 1857, 1873, 1903–04, and 1907. Each time a panic occurred there was a call for the government to do something to prevent future episodes of instability. Over time various actions were taken. One example was the creation of the Federal Reserve System in 1914. The Federal Reserves owes its existence directly to the panic of 1907. As envisioned the Federal Reserve had three objectives: (1) to give the country an "elastic currency"; (2) "to provide for the discounting of commercial credits"; and (3) "to improve the supervision of banking." Thus the Federal Reserve was seen as an institution that would eliminate the upper limit of the supply of credit during a business expansion. It would also stand ready to provide needed funds to banks should a run develop and thereby lead to a quick restoration of the public's confidence in the banks.

But things did not work out as planned. There were more financial panics in 1920–21 and in 1929. The last panic is usually considered to be the beginning of the Great Depression, the longest and most severe decline in production and employment in American history. Between 1929 and 1933 production fell by 30 percent, the unemployment rate rose from 3 percent to almost 25 percent, prices fell by close to 25 percent, the stock market declined by 80 percent, and the number of bank failures was counted in the thousands. Furthermore, these conditions were unfortunately not limited to this country; the Great Depression was global in scope.

The Great Depression had a dramatic impact on the thinking of economists. Until then most economists believed that economic contractions were only temporary aberrations; the economy might experience a downturn but would correct its course more or less automatically and return to a pattern of growth in output and employment. The Great Depression seemed to provide evidence that refuted this theory.

In 1936 English economist John Maynard Keynes published his seminal book, *The General Theory of Employment, Interest, and Money*. In it he argued that certain conditions could prevent the economy from achieving an automatic recovery and that government actions would be necessary to reestablish full employment and production. The legacy of Keynes' theories in the period after World War II was the belief that a government could maintain prosperity by conducting stabilization policies, particularly fiscal policy. As the economy turned toward a recession a government, either by increasing its spending or by reducing taxes, could quickly turn the economy around and restore prosperity.

Economists who accepted these ideas were called, appropriately, Keynesians. They wanted government to play an activist role using both monetary and fiscal policies to promote maximum macroeconomic performance. Not all economists, however, agreed. One group of economists, called monetarists and led by Milton Friedman, took the position that activist government could in fact make things worse. In his most important book, *A Monetary History of the United States*, 1867–1960, Friedman and co-author Anna Schwartz argued that the Federal Reserve, both in what it did and what it failed to do, had actually made the Great Depression worse. Friedman and others have gone on to argue that post World War II recessions are due to activist government and that actions to stabilize the economy may be ineffective or counterproductive.

The two readings that follow do not, however, represent a simple debate between liberal Keynesians and conservative monetarists. Heller is a Keynesian who believes that a return to the activist government policies of the 1960s would improve macroeconomic performance. But, according to Levinson, the U.S. economy is now a global economy and, consequently, the actions taken by the monetary and fiscal authorities can be offset by international reactions. Heller believes that the old policies will still work; Levinson believes they won't work now.

YES

Walter W. Heller

ACTIVIST GOVERNMENT: KEY TO GROWTH

In a period when government activism, especially in economic affairs, is under attack—indeed, when President Reagan, charming, disarming, and sometimes alarming, tells the country that the government's impact on the economy is somewhere between baneful and baleful and that the greatest contribution he can make is to get government's clammy hands out of our pockets and government monkeys off our backs—against that background, the Joint Economic Committee's 40th anniversary is an especially appropriate time to take stock of the role government has played and should play in the economy.

Let me begin with a broad-brush comparison of U.S. economic performance in the pre- and post-activist eras, with World War II being a convenient dividing line.

First, with respect to *comparative economic stability*: Excluding the Great Depression of the 1930s—for including it would make all comparisons a statistical cakewalk for postwar economic activism—we find that the prewar economy spent roughly a year in recession for every year of expansion. Postwar, it has been one year in recession for every four years of expansion.

Second, as to *comparative economic growth*: Up-dating some of Arthur Okun's numbers, I find that the era of economic activism wins again. Compared with an average real growth rate of 2.8 percent from 1909 to 1929 (and 2.3 percent from 1929 to 1948), the postwar pace was a hefty 3.8 percent before slowing down after 1973 and lagging even more in the eighties, as I will examine later.

Third, as to the *comparative use of our GNP potential*: The postwar activist economy operated far closer to its potential than the prewar economy. Measuring the "net gap" under the trend lines connecting prosperity years, one finds that the gap averaged 5 percent of GNP, prewar, even leaving out the Great Depression, but less than 1 percent postwar (from 1948 to 1979).

From "Activist Government: Key to Growth," by Walter W. Heller, *Challenge*, March/April 1986. Copyright © 1986. Reprinted with permission of M.E. Sharpe, Inc., publishers, Armonk, NY 10504.

THE IMPACT OF PUBLIC POLICY

Now, where has that progress come from? . . . I would agree with Okun that the improved performance record, especially the greater economic stability, must be credited to public policy. As he put it, "It was made in Washington." The automatic stabilizing effect of a larger public sector—both on the tax and on the spending sixes—undoubtedly played an important role. Coupled with it was an aggressive fiscal-monetary policy that, while not always on time and on target, assured private decision makers that recessions would be relatively short and shallow and depressions a thing of the past.

Paralleling the improved economic performance in the postwar era of economic activism was a dramatic decline in the incidence of poverty. From an estimated 33 percent of the population in 1947, poverty fell by one-third, to 22 percent, by 1960—a decline that must be attributed primarily to economic growth plus some increases in public assistance and transfer programs. Then came the uninterrupted growth of the 1960s, coupled with the War on Poverty and other Great Society programs, which cut the remaining poverty in half.

Contrary to Mr. Reagan's assertion that "in the early sixties we had fewer people living below the poverty line than we had in the later sixties after the Great War on Poverty got under way," the president's 1985 *Economic Report* (page 264) shows us that the percent of the population in poverty dropped steadily from 22 percent in 1960, to 19 percent in 1964, to 12 percent in 1969 and then bottomed out at 11 percent in 1973. From then until 1980, growing transfer payments just managed to offset sluggish economic performance, and poverty stayed in the 11–12 percent range until it shot upward in the 1980s. More of that later.

Perhaps the most gratifying testimonial to the success of the activist socioeconomic policy is the striking advance in the economic status of the elderly. Let me cite only one or two salient facts: 25 years ago, 35 percent of older Americans (65 and above) were in poverty. By 1984, that number had dropped to 12.4 percent, 2 points lower than the poverty rate for Americans overall.

DOWN MEMORY LANE

. . . The early postwar years were really vintage years in our fiscal-policy annals. We ran appropriate surpluses (that alone shows I'm dealing in ancient history) in 1947 and 1948. Then, in mid-1950, the Joint Economic Committee, in one of its finest hours, recognized the inflationary potential of the Korean War and led the charge to reverse gears, i.e., to take a tax cut that was halfway through the congressional mill and help convert it to a tax increase. As has been true so often, it was providing the intellectual leadership in Congress on economic policy. . . .

But the 1953–1960 period, with three recessions in seven years, was hardly activist policy at its best, especially during the 1959–60 period of overly tight fiscal-monetary policy.

THE GOOD TIMES

Then came the Golden Sixties, truly watershed years with a revitalizing of the Employment Act of 1946. President Kennedy asked us to return to the letter and spirit of that Act. He ended equivocation about the intent of the Act by translating its rather mushy mandate into a concrete call for meeting the goals of full employment, price stability, faster growth, and external balance—all within the constraints of preserving economic freedom and choice and promoting greater equality of opportunity. He went on to foster a rather weak-kneed antirecession program in 1961 and a powerful growth-promoting tax-cut program in 1962–64. In that process, I counted six firsts for presidential economics:

• He was the first president to commit himself to numerical targets for full employment, namely, 4 percent unemployment, and growth, namely, 4.5 percent per year.

• He was the first to adopt an incomes policy in the form of wage-price guideposts developed by his Council of Economic Advisers. The guideposts, flanked by sensible supply-side tax measures to stimulate business investment, by training and retraining programs, and the like, helped maintain a remarkable record of price stability in 1961–65, namely, only 1.2 percent inflation per year.

• He was the first president to shift the economic policy focus from moderating the swings of the business cycle to achieving the rising full-employment potential of the economy.

• In that process, he moved from the goal of a balanced budget over the business cycle to a balanced budget at full employment.

• He was the first president to say, as he did in January 1963, that budget deficits could be a positive force to help move a slack or recession-ridden economy toward full employment.

• As a capstone, he was the first president to say that a tax cut was needed, not to cope with recession (there was none), but to make full use of the economy's full-employment potential. . . .

Those were the halcyon days of economic policy. Aided and abetted by the Fed, the 1964 tax cut worked like a charm. In mid-1965, just before the July escalation in Vietnam, we saw the happy combination of an inflation rate of only 1.5 percent; unemployment coming down steadily, to 4.4 percent; defense expenditures continuing their four-year decline from 9 percent of GNP in 1960 to 7 percent of GNP in 1965; and the cash budget running $3 billion in the black.

THE DOWNTURN BEGINS

Then came the dark years of Vietnam, in economics as well as in foreign policy. Unlike 1950–51, we did not reverse gears in spite of the timely warnings of the Joint Economic Committee and of most of the economists, both inside and outside the government, who were advising President Johnson. . . . He did not propose a tax increase until early 1967, and no tax action was completed until 1968, long after the inflation horse was out of the barn. . . .

As I put it in testimony before the JEC in July 1970, "There are no magic formulas, no pat solutions, no easy ways to reconcile full employment and price stability. No modern, free economy has yet found the combination of policies that can deliver sustained high employment and high growth side by side with sustained price stability." That was all well and good, as far as it went, but in light of the experience of the 1970s it did not go nearly far enough.

The policy travails of the seventies are too well known to require lengthy review:

• First, there was the Nixon fiasco of freezes and phases serving as a facade for pumping up the economy with tax cuts, spending increases, and a rapid run-up in the money supply, with sure-fire consequences of an overheated economy.

• Superimposed on that were the supply shocks in 1973–74—oil prices quadrupling, food prices jumping 40 percent in two years, and other world raw-material prices doubling in about the same time—that served to consolidate stagflation.

The shocks, of course, were not just to the price level, but the economics profession, led by Keynesians. We learned the sad lesson that as to wages and prices, what goes up, propelled by overstimulative monetary-fiscal policy and a series of external shocks, does not necessarily come down when the fiscal-monetary stimulus and supply shocks subside. We have since learned a lot about sticky wages and prices that stay in a high orbit even without visible means of fiscal-monetary support. At least, they stayed there until we administered a dose of sadomasochism, better known as the double-dip recession of the eighties, the deepest since the Great Depression.

One should not recite the economic sins of the seventies without acknowledging one bright fiscal episode, namely, the tax rebate and tax cut enacted in the second quarter of 1975. Granted, it was a bit late to blunt the recession, but it provided a welcome boost to an economy that had fallen into what, until topped by the recession of the early eighties, was the deepest postwar recession. The 1975 tax cut was a winner in both size and timing.

Though prices behaved very well in 1976, when inflation averaged 4.8 percent (with the help of good crops and no increase in the real price of oil), the combination of an overly strong expansion (partly resulting from economists' overestimates of GNP potential) and the second oil price shock soon pumped inflation back into the double digits. . . .

As one surveys the whole postwar period, activist economics and New Deal intrusions into the marketplace can surely take credit not only for building in strong defenses against depression but also for 25 years (1948–73) of high-octane operation of the economy and sharply reduced instability. Within that framework, one can criticize antirecession fiscal policy as often too little and too late, monetary policy as sometimes too easy and other times overstaying tightness. The far-too-late and considerably-too-little tax increase to finance the war in Vietnam, coupled with excessive monetary ease in 1967–68, has to go down in the annals as one of the flat failures of postwar fiscal-monetary policy. And the stagflation experience of the 1970s still hangs like a pall over expansionary policy today.

Still, it is worth reminding ourselves that even in the face of high performance of the economy, inflation in the 1949–72 period rose above 6 percent only once (during the Korean War), and averaged only 2.3 percent. If inflation was the price of activism in public economics, it was a long time in coming.

THE HAUNTED PROSPERITY OF THE 1980s

Now we pass through the economic portals into the eighties, the age of anti-government. . . . Exactly what is it that haunts our prosperity in this new era of belittled government? The answer is sobering, not to say alarming.

First, it is *slow growth*. After enjoying 4.2 percent annual real growth in the sixties, and managing to average 3.1 percent even in the seventies, we have slipped to less than 2 percent in the first six years of the eighties. Even if we optimistically assume that there will be no recession in the next four years and an average 3 percent growth rate, the decade would come out with just a 2.4 percent real growth rate. And even if we adjust these numbers for the slowdown in the growth of the labor force, the eighties as a whole seem destined to go into the economic annals as a period of pallid performance.

Second, we are haunted by *resurgent poverty*. The percentage of our population in poverty jumped by nearly a third, from 11.7 percent in 1979 to 15.3 percent in 1983. Recovery brought the poverty rate down to 14.4 percent in 1984, but leaving aside the Reagan years, this is still the highest rate since 1966. It is worth noting that, without cash transfers by the government, the poverty rate would be 25 percent and that, with such noncash transfers as food stamps, the rate comes down to 9 percent. But even that is a jump of roughly two-fifths since the late seventies. The tax and budget cuts of the eighties undercut the incomes of the poor and boosted the incomes of the wealthy. The tax-reform proposal, embodying more generous earned-income credits, standard deductions, and personal exemptions, would be a welcome first step in reversing this doleful story.

Third, we are haunted by *wasted potential*. With the unemployment rate, after five years, still stuck at about 7 percent and utilization of our manufacturing capacity stuck at 80 percent throughout the third year of our expansion, we are wasting a big chunk of our productive capacity, presumably as a means of safeguarding the great and welcome gains that have been made on the inflation front.

Fourth, *productivity* advances have fallen far short of expectations. What was until 1985 a respectable performance in manufacturing has been more than offset by disappointing productivity gains elsewhere in the economy.

Causally correlated with this change for the worse in growth, poverty, and wasted potential are some economic policy shifts that haunt us.

• One has to start with the monstrous *tax cut* of 1981. Look at the grisly progression: (1) the Korean War buildup, more or less fully financed by three tax increases in 1950–51; (2) the Vietnam War buildup, with a too-late, too-little tax increase; and (3) a Reagan defense buildup, the biggest in peacetime history, coupled with the biggest tax cut in all history, a combination guaranteed to produce the biggest deficit in history.

• From 1950 through 1979, the *federal deficit* averaged less than 1 percent of GNP. Now, our deficit is running over 5 percent of GNP, most of it structural rather than cyclical.

• These huge deficits and high interest rates have spawned an overvalued dollar and enormous *trade deficits*. From roughly $25 billion in the late 1970s, readily financed by a flow of earnings from overseas investments, the trade deficit zoomed to nearly $150 billion, with no offset from service earnings because we have become a net debtor nation.

• The dismal record on *savings and investment* is another ominous concomitant of the huge budget deficit. Far from being an investment boom, we have been on a consumer binge financed by liquidating our assets abroad, by gorging on a huge flow of imports, and by depressing national savings and investment to the lowest level since the 1930s. Since this runs counter to popular impression, let me cite chapter and verse. First, net *private* saving—individual plus business saving minus replacement investment—ran close to its long-run level of 8–9 percent of GNP in 1984. Second, half of it had to be used to finance the federal deficit, with the result that the *national* saving rate fell from 8 percent to just over 4 percent. Third, only by sucking in huge amounts of foreign saving was the net investment rate held at about 7 percent of GNP. But saving and investment by Americans have dropped to the lowest levels in fifty years. . . .

WHERE DO WE GO FROM HERE?

Where should activist economics go from here? There are plenty of new ideas floating around—and even a few *good* new ideas—but none will make much difference unless we restore the essential conditions for faster and more sustained economic growth, and stop the consumption binge fostered by the irresponsible fiscal policies we have been following in the name of letting the private economy breathe freely. What a travesty: the monstrous deficits generated in the name of unfettered breathing are depriving the body economic of the oxygen essential to the growth of private saving and investment.

It is worth reminding ourselves, however, that it will take a skilled balancing act to put the economy back on the track of long-term growth while maintaining our expansionary momentum in the near term.

Clearly, the vital first step is to shrink the gigantic deficit that, to change the metaphor, is leeching the lifeblood out of growth by absorbing over half of our private savings. One has to hope that a Gramm-Rudmanized budget process will lead to a "deficit disarmament conference" and an agreement to couple tax increases with bearable budget cuts.

Second, even as we move fiscal policy toward restriction, we must maintain, and even step up, the level of aggregate demand in the economy. That's where the high-wire balancing act comes in, namely, offsetting the reduction in aggregate demand from a more restrictive fiscal policy by running a more stimulative monetary policy. That it turn means keeping one eye on the substitution of investment for consumer spending as the budget deficit shrinks and interest rates fall, and the other on the shift of demand from imported goods to domestically produced goods and services as the trade deficit shrinks. There is nothing in the market economy, left to itself, that will make the necessary adjustments.

Third, in a open-economy world we'll have to keep a third eye on our trading partners. As we shrink our imports and expand our exports, the impact on foreign economies will be damaging unless we find some effective way at last to develop truly constructive international cooperation in economic policy.

Fourth, we will need to adjust our structural policies, applying the classical supply-side precepts designed to beef up our productive capacity and productivity—everything from boosting investment in physical infrastructure, in human brain power, and in research and innovation to stimulating private saving and investment.

Lurking in the background of this

whole process will be the perennial tradeoff question: Is an attempt to improve our growth and expansion performance going to reignite inflation?

THE LESSONS OF HISTORY

What does experience tell us about the need to curb our appetites for expansion and faster growth in order to forestall inflation? Is it possible that we are misapplying experience, that we are like the cat that sat on a hot stove and now won't sit on a cold one? The tradeoff between unemployment and inflation may well have moved in our favor. With the hard core of inflation—namely, wage norms—coming down sharply, with plenty of excess capacity in the economy, and with these tendencies buttressed by falling oil prices and soft world commodity prices, isn't it time to test the waters with a more expansion- and growth-oriented policy as outlined above?

And since there's no guarantee that growth alone will reduce inequality—and worse, that with the incidence of poverty shifting so strongly to single-parent families and their children, there's no guarantee that growth will benefit everyone—isn't it about time that the richest country on earth (as we still are, in terms of both wealth per capita and annual goods and services per capita, according to the Kravis-Summers University of Pennsylvania studies), with the lowest taxes—at about 29 percent of GNP—of any advanced country except Japan (which is just a whisker behind us), and with the least socialized industrial economy on earth (as established by late-seventies IMF data and a recent update by *The Economist*, isn't it about time that we stopped asking the poor and near-poor to take the main brunt of the buildup of our defenses?

And isn't it about time that we came out and said that it is a shameful thing to be gorging ourselves on imports and feasting on resources that ought really to be devoted to investment and growth, all in the name of hands-off economics and in the wake of irresponsible deficits and a White House that sees taxes not as the price we pay for civilization, but as the root of almost all economic evil? And isn't it time to stop shortchanging the future, as we are, by stunting growth and running up huge foreign debts in what Rudy Penner calls a case of "fiscal child abuse"?

. . . So while there is much to be said for a brave new world of innovation in public economics, our first order of business is to clear the fiscal decks for action, promote growth with some fairly orthodox measures, and use a modest portion of our vast wealth and taxable capacity to share more of our affluence with the poor and disadvantaged. That may be a bit old-fashioned, but show me something new-fashioned that would be better. . . .

NO

Marc Levinson

ECONOMIC POLICY:
THE OLD TOOLS WON'T WORK

Since the advent of the New Deal more than half a century ago, the federal government has actively helped shape the course of the economy. Its ability, at least in the short run, to pump up the economy in hard times and slow it down when inflation began to boil up has been unquestioned. As recently as 1981, when a sharp cutback in money supply growth pushed the country into recession, or 1983, when the stimulative effects of a tax cut brought the economy back to health, the old elixirs worked as they had in the past.

But in 1986, things were different. Heady growth in the money supply, repeated cuts in the Federal Reserve Board's discount rate and record federal budget deficits all failed to juice the lackluster economy. The old linkages between the government's actions and the economy's responses have changed in ways economists do not fully understand. As a result, the government's economic tools have been partially blunted. Contends Lawrence Chimerine, chairman of Chase Econometrics, "The ability of policy changes to improve the economy is much smaller than ever."

The reason: the growing internationalization of the U.S. economy. Flexible exchange rates and the resulting mushrooming of international capital markets have made traditional economic polices act in unexpected ways. "No one has a reliable theory of exchange rates," says Paul Krugman, a professor of international economics at the Massachusetts Institute of Technology. "That makes it very difficult to be sure of the effects of macroeconomic policy."

These international connections make it increasingly difficult to aim economic weapons at purely domestic targets. Even thinking of "domestic" in terms of economic problems is misleading. "The problem is global overcapacity and global underconsumption," contents Steve Quick, an economist with the Joint Economic Committee of Congress. "But we have no tools. We have no global fiscal policy. We have no global monetary policy." Adds Harold Rose, chief economist of Britain's Barclays Bank: "It's very hard

From "Economic Policy: The Old Tools Won't Work," by Marc Levinson, *Business Month* magazine, January 1987. Copyright © 1987 by Business Month Corporation, 38 Commercial Wharf, Boston, MA 02110.

to see how we can get out of these problems by macroeconomic policy alone."

Certainly, the assumption that the government can "fine tune" the economy has been in disrepute since the early 1970s, when policymakers were helpless as they faced high unemployment and high inflation at the same time. But faith in the government's ability to deal with one of these problems at a time has remained strong. Now, however, the government's very ability to achieve some domestic goals—3% growth in output, 4% unemployment—appears increasingly limited. The jury is still out on whether these limitations are a temporary phenomenon or a permanent fact of life.

Take monetary policy, the Federal Reserve Board's method of influencing the economy's performance by manipulating the money supply. Financial deregulation, of course, has blurred the meaning of the money supply figures. But international capital flows have also made it much more difficult for the central bank to plot the nation's monetary course.

The amount of capital sloshing from country to country in search of the highest return is far greater now than ever before. In 1985 alone, some $127 billion in foreign-owned assets were moved to the United States, while another $32 billion of U.S.-owned assets were brought home. The total amount of foreign-owned assets in the U.S., most of which are in relatively liquid form, now tops $1.2 trillion—twice the level of only five years ago. "Any effort by the Fed to predict the consequences of its policies is much harder than it used to be, because of the internationalization of the economy," says Brookings Institution economist Ralph Bryant, former director of the Fed's International Finance Division.

Suppose, for example, that the Fed wants to boost the economy's growth rate. When international capital flows were small, the central bank could stimulate borrowing by pumping up the money supply or cutting the discount rate. But now, lower real interest rates will spur investors to move their capital out of dollar-denominated investments. Economists can't even begin to estimate the likely extent of those capital flows. If little capital moves abroad, the lower interest rates will powerfully stimulate the U.S. economy. If, on the other hand, lower rates trigger a massive flight from the dollar, higher import prices will inject a strong dose of inflation into the economy, which would discourage the very business spending the Fed wanted to stimulate. Would faster money growth cut the U.S. trade deficit? Nobody knows.

The direction of the overall change remains undisputed: Increasing the rate of money supply growth will stimulate the economy, and reducing it will retard growth. But the magnitude of the change is now almost unpredictable. "If the Fed wants to weigh the effects of expansion versus inflation, that depends a great deal on whether monetary policy works on interest rates or on the exchange rate," says M.I.T.'s Krugman. "We just don't know. That's a significant inhibition on the Fed right now. We've lost certainty."

If the primary effect is on exchange rates, the major result of money supply changes is on demand for exports and imports around the world, argues John Williamson of the Institute for International Economics. "It doesn't make much sense to think of monetary policy being used for purely domestic purposes," Williamson says.

This exchange rate effect, alongside the traditional interest rate effect, may be shy the Fed's policy initiatives now seem to take far longer to move the economy than the six months or so that has long been the rule of thumb among economists. "Those channels are not well understood," points out former Fed Governor Lyle Gramley, now senior vice president of the Mortgage Bankers Association. "We're working with somewhat longer lags than the old policies we worked with."

This growing uncertainty about the relationship between the money supply and the economy bewilders even economists who believe that international capital flows are not at fault, such as the American Enterprise Institute's Herbert Stein. The top White House economist in the Nixon Administration is not willing to pronounce monetary policy less effective than it once was, but he admits that the lags between Fed action and the economy's response have become erratic. "It's like sitting there with a stock of explosives that haven't gone off, so you don't whether to throw in more," he says.

The international forces undermining monetary policy now hamper the action of fiscal policy as well. Traditionally, more government spending and lower taxes boosted both consumption and investment, at least temporarily, leading to faster U.S. economic growth and lower unemployment. But in an internationalized economy, businesses and consumers may buy more from abroad. Meanwhile, faster economic growth will drive up interest rates and thus the value of the dollar. For most Americans, Lesson One in fiscal policy failure was the tax cut of 1981, whose stimulative impact was greatly undermined by the overvalued dollar it brought about.

These international repercussions were hardly considered when the 1981 tax cut was passed, and economists are still unable to forecast exchange rate shifts with any certainty. As a result, it is almost impossible to predict whether the $108 billion deficit reduction that Congress is required to make this year under the Gramm-Rudman-Hollings Act will slow the economy.

There is no doubt that a $108 billion budget slash will cut domestic demand. It will also lower deficits and reduce the government's borrowing from abroad, driving down the dollar. But whether a more favorable exchange rate for exports will boost the economy more than lower government spending retards it is an open question. "We don't know the responsiveness of the economy to a changed deficit," contends economist Mickey D. Levy of Philadelphia's Fidelity Bank. "We don't know the lags." Concurs Rudolph Penner, director of the Congressional Budget Office, "If we had been analyzing that big a change twenty years ago, there wouldn't have been much debate that it would cause a recession."

In fact, economist now shy away from talking about "fiscal policy," because they believe a given amount of government spending can have vastly different effects on the economy, depending upon its purpose and method of financing. A budget financed by government borrowing will affect U.S. interest rates, and thus exchange rates, far more than the same budget financed by taxes, says University of Wisconsin economist Kenneth Rogoff.

The varying economic impacts of such policy choices can only be guessed at. The venerable Keynesian multiplier, which links changes in government spending to predictably larger changes in economic output, can, for all practical purposes, be tossed out the window. Using fiscal policy to reach some desired target in terms of, say, unemployment or Gross National Product is thus far more difficult than in the past.

The use of both fiscal and monetary policy has become even more treacherous as government officials have come to realize that they are not operating in an isolated economy. Indeed, the reactions of other governments can blunt or reverse Washington's initiatives, making economic policy a strategic game, according to a brand new line of economic research. The U.S. must figure out how other countries will respond to its moves, and determine the degree to which those responses will counteract the effects that American policymakers seek to achieve. "We can't make policy without taking into account what our competitor overseas is doing," contends University of Illinois economist Stephen J. Turnovsky.

Consider the reaction of the German government to the Fed's raising the money supply to push the U.S. economy faster. If a faster-growing U.S. economy buys more imports from Germany, boosting the German economy, the Bundesbank may be able to achieve *its* economic growth targets with less monetary stimulus than it had planned, holding down Germany's inflation rate. But higher German interest rates, in turn, could force the Fed to boost the U.S. money supply even further to rev up our economy, accepting far more inflation in return.

One way to deal with the diminishing effectiveness of monetary and fiscal policies, says the Joint Economic Committee's Quick, is to examine the economic impact of policies long considered unrelated, such as foreign aid or regulation of international lending. Increasing the industrial nations' contributions to the International Monetary Fund, for example, could help stimulate growth in the developing countries, which in turn would step up their purchases of U.S. exports. This viewpoint is catching on in Washington, where Congress has finally come to understand that the debts of developing countries are a major drag on U.S. growth.

The Reagan Administration is attempting to get the major industrial nations to coordinate their economic policies to spur faster growth worldwide. But this effort could falter because of insufficient knowledge about the interrelationship between fiscal and monetary policy and exchange rates.

Even if the governments cooperate, economists disagree about the effects of specific coordinated policies. University of California economist Jeffrey Frankel points out that even as the U.S. is urging Germany to boost its money supply to drive its economy faster, economists debate whether faster German money growth would be a plus for the U.S. trade balance by causing more imports or would be a minus by driving down the deutschemark relative to the dollar. "People disagree about the sign," Frankel confesses.

The argument that internationalization has fundamentally changed the nature of the government's policy tools is by no means universally accepted. "I'm not sure it's any harder to target the real

GNP growth rate or the unemployment rate than it ever was," maintains Harvard University economist Lawrence Summers. "We can reduce the unemployment rate to 6% if we want to."

University of Chicago international economist Michael Mussa, currently a member of the Council of Economic Advisers, rejects the suggestion that monetary policy now works primarily through exchange rates rather than interest rates. Although that may be true for some countries, Mussa points out, "for the U.S. that would be a serious error in thinking about monetary policy." Sooner or later, he contends, the tumultuous effects of financial deregulation will wear off and the relationship between money growth and GNP will become more stable, enabling the Fed's tools to regain their former potency.

Still, a world economy with complex and poorly understood interactions requires a much broader view of "economic policy" than the nation has had in the past. Glib recommendations to cut the deficit or lower the discount rate make little sense by themselves. The two must be considered jointly, along with such nontraditional tools as labor laws, banking regulations, foreign aid outlays and the reactions of the nation's trading partners.

The U.S. has long been less dependent on foreign trade than most other countries, and has had far more economic independence as a result. But from now on, Americans must adjust to a new economic reality. In a global economy, even the greatest of economic powers can no longer control its own destiny.

POSTSCRIPT

Can Monetary and Fiscal Policies Still Be Used to Solve Our Macroeconomic Problems?

Heller states that 1980s represents a period of antigovernment and as a consequence a period in which macroeconomic performance has been less than it could be. To demonstrate the benefits of an activist government, he compares the performance of the economy before World War II (excluding the Great Depression) with the performance of the economy after World War II (ending in 1980). The latter period, one in which an active government utilized its fiscal and monetary powers, yielded greater stability, greater economic growth, and greater utilization of the economy's productive potential. The period since 1980 is much like the period prior to World War II; the return to antigovernment brought a decline in macroeconomic performance. During the 1980s there has been slower economic growth, increased poverty, wasted potential, and a slowdown in the growth of productivity. He goes on to argue that to get the economy in better working order it is necessary to return to activist government. Heller makes four policy recommendations: (1) reduction of federal government deficits by combining tax increases with spending decreases; (2) expansionary monetary policy; (3) an effort to achieve "international cooperation in economic policy"; (4) additional policy efforts to stimulate research and development and to increase physical and human capital.

Levinson admits that conventional stabilization policies worked as expected in the early 1980s, but now efforts to stabilize the economy may be doomed to failure. The reason is that the U.S. economy has become internationalized. Today's economy is one of floating exchange rates where the international value of the U.S. dollar changes almost daily. Today's economy is also one where changes in interest rates cause substantial changes in the international flows of financial capital. According to Levinson monetary and fiscal policies cause changes in exchange rates and trade flows that could offset the desired results of the initial policy actions. Thus expansionary monetary or fiscal policies may be unable to generate anything more than a

temporary increase in production and employment. There is an additional complicating factor; foreign governments may set their own stabilization policies in reaction to changes in U.S. policies, again setting in motion forces that would tend to offset the efforts of the U.S. policy makers. The internationalization of the U.S. economy means that the U.S. may no longer be able to control its own destiny.

There are a number of different perspectives on this issue to be found in contemporary economic literature. The *1982 Economic Report of the President* (pages 3–10) presents the views of President Reagan regarding economic policy, the view that Heller has labeled as antigovernment. Herbert Stein examines stabilization from a conventional perspective in "Should Growth be a Priority of National Policy?" (*Challenge* March–April 1986). There are nay number of articles that reflects on the influence of international events on various sectors of the U.S. economy including "The Farm Sector in the 1980s: Sudden Collapse or Steady Downturn?" by Michael Belongia (*Review*, Federal Reserve Bank of St. Louis, November 1986)' "Coping With Globally Integrated Financial Markets" by E. Gerald Corrigan (*Quarterly Review*, Federal Reserve Bank of New York, Winter 1986–87); "Has the Dollar Fallen Enough?" by Craig S. Hakkio and Richard Roberts (*Economic Review*, Federal Reserve Bank of Kansas City, July/August 1987); "New England Manufacturing and International Trade" by Norman S. Fieleke (*New England Economic Review*, September/October 1986); and "Can Services be a Source of Export-Led Growth? Evidence From the Fourth District" by Erica L. Groshen (*Economic Review*, Federal Reserve Bank of Cleveland, Quarter 3 1987). For an analysis of the relationships between the value of the dollar, trade flows, and the macroeconomy see "Trade Deficits & the Dollar: A Macroeconomic Perspective" by Steven A. Meyer (*Business Review*, Federal Reserve Bank of Philadelphia, September/October 1986).

ISSUE 12

Is Tax Reform an Impossible Dream Come True?

YES: Henry J. Aaron, from "The Impossible Dream Comes True: The New Tax Reform Act," *The Brookings Review* (Winter 1987)

NO: Henning Gutmann, from "The Bad New Tax Law," *New York Review of Books* (February 12, 1987)

ISSUE SUMMARY

Yes: University of Maryland economist Aaron believes that the Tax Reform Act of 1986 represents "a major tax overhaul that deserves to be honored as reform." Although the new tax legislation can be criticized for certain things that were done and not done, Aaron argues that it has made the tax system "more conducive to economic efficiency and growth, fairer, and simpler."

No: Reporter Henning Gutmann sees a number of problems with the Tax Reform Act of 1986. He believes it is "a clear step backward for the progressive idea of taxation"; it raises taxes on declining manufacturing industries while benefiting growing service industries; it may damage education; and it is anything but a simplification. He concludes: "The new tax law does not bode well for either the health of the economy or its people."

In 1981 Congress passed and President Reagan signed into law the Economic Recovery Act. In spite of this legislation most Americans and many legislators, both Democratic and Republican, argued for further changes in the federal tax system, changes designed to make the tax system fairer and simpler. Although there were various opinions as to what constitutes fairness, there was general agreement that the tax burden on low income families should be reduced. Disagreement centered on whether the tax burden of upper income individuals should be reduced and if so by how much. The goal of simplicity had two parts: not only should the tax code be changed to reduce the time, effort, and expense that is needed for taxpayers to complete tax forms and comply with tax laws, but the revision should also reduce the distortion of economic decision making and, thereby, reduce the impact of the tax laws on the allocation of scarce resources. To emphasize that the tax change would be true reform, a third goal was added: the changes should be revenue neutral; that is, the tax revenue of the federal government should be the same after the changes as before.

Of course there were disagreements about the exact nature of the changes as Congress debated a new tax law. One problem was the difficulty in defining fairness. And the legislators found that there were tradeoffs in trying to achieve the three stated goals—fairness, simplicity, and revenue neutrality—simultaneously. For a period of time during 1986 it seemed that these disagreements and problems were insurmountable. It was with some surprise that a compromise was reached and the Tax Reform Act became law.

There is no question that the Tax Reform Act constitutes a major revision of the tax code. But did the Tax Reform Act of 1986 achieve its objectives? There seems to be little disagreement on whether it is revenue neutral. Estimates of the revenue consequences of the changes reveal a $24 billion reduction in personal income taxes that is to be offset by a $24 billion increase in taxes on business. But even while granting this, there are some who remain critical. They note that some may be better off because they pay less to the federal government in taxes, but they will be worse off because businesses will pass on their tax increases in the form of higher prices.

Is the new tax code fairer? Here, even though most believe that low income families will be paying less dollars in taxes, there is intense disagreement. Aaron and Gutmann reach different conclusions on this question, in part because they have different views as to what constitutes fairness. They also disagree because their conclusions depend on *specific* interpretations of the new law and the extent to which they consider other taxes besides those affected by the new tax law.

Is the tax code simpler? Here too there is controversy. Aaron believes the new law modestly advances the goal of simplicity: some individuals and families will no longer be on the tax rolls and there will be less distortion of economic decision making. Gutmann takes the position that the new code is anything but simple and some of the changes in economic decision making may work to the long-run disadvantage of the U.S. economy.

It should also be mentioned that evaluation of the Tax Reform Act can and frequently does involve more than an assessment of the extent to which the legislation achieved the three stated goals. Some commentators will be concerned with the consequences of the new law on international trade; others with its impact on the rate of personal saving; and still others with resulting employment patterns in different areas of the country.

YES

Henry J. Aaron

THE IMPOSSIBLE DREAM COME TRUE: THE NEW TAX REFORM ACT

Like the bewitched princess who watched endless suitors perish in the dragon's fire, advocates of tax equity and efficiency have despaired for decades as the occasional brave politician marched off on a futile quest for tax reform. In 1986, to almost universal surprise, the spell was broken. A bipartisan coalition of members of Congress and the president slew a host of political dragons and enacted a major tax overhaul that deserves to be honored as reform.

Any assessment of this landmark reform must address several broad questions: What was accomplished? What retrograde steps were mistakenly taken? What opportunities were missed? And how will the new tax law influence economic behavior?

To begin with, one should be clear on what the 1986 tax reform law is *not*. It is not a revolution in the American tax system in the sense that the introduction of a value-added tax or integration of the personal and corporate income taxes would be. It does not inaugurate a new era of simplicity. Nor will it launch the American economy into a new era of economic growth. It has not purged the tax system of distortions and illogic.

But the Tax Reform Act of 1986 stands as the most important improvement in the broad-based taxes on individual and corporate income in at least two decades. It deals in a fundamental way with many parts of the tax code that created widespread opportunities to avoid taxation and distorted the flow of investment into wasteful uses. By curtailing these provisions, the act makes possible a major reduction in statutory rates without loss of revenue or any decline in progressivity. Of the three stated goals of tax reform—to make the system more conducive to economic efficiency and growth, fairer, and simpler—the new law achieves major advance on the first and second and, on balance, modestly advances the third.

From "The Impossible Dream Comes True: The New Tax Reform Act," by Henry J. Aaron, *The Brookings Review*, Winter 1987. Copyright © 1987 by The Brookings Institution, Washington, DC. Reprinted by permission.

ELEMENTS OF THE REFORM

The most important elements of the reform follow.

—Personal exemptions are increased from $1,080 in 1986 to $1,900 in 1987, $1,950 in 1988, and $2,000 in 1989, and the standard deduction is raised from $3,670 for couples ($2,480 for single persons) to $5,000 for couples ($3,000 for single persons) in 1988. The earned income tax credit is increased to 14 percent of earnings up to $5,714 (a maximum credit in 1987 of $800) and will be phased out, starting in 1988, on income in excess of $9,000 a year. The ceiling and the starting point for the phaseout will be indexed for inflation. These changes boost the amount of income a family of four can receive before having to pay personal income tax from $9,574 in 1986 to $14,480 in 1988.

—The nominal personal tax rate schedule that ran from 11 percent to 50 percent is replaced by two rates: 15 percent, applicable to taxable incomes of $17,850 or less for single persons and $29,750 or less for joint filers, and 28 percent. . . . The maximum corporate income tax rate drops from 46 percent on profits over $100,000 to 34 percent on profits over $75,000.

—The tax base is broadened, most notably by provisions that reduce incentives for tax shelter investments and by the repeal of numerous special business deductions. The result is that both individual and corporate income tax rates can be cut with no loss of revenue.

—Discrepancies among tax rates on various types of investment are reduced by repeal of the investment tax credit, revision of depreciation deductions, and a variety of other provisions.

—The exclusion from taxation of 60 percent of long-term capital gains has been repealed, thereby reducing incentives to convert fully taxable ordinary income into long-term capital gains.

WHAT WAS ACCOMPLISHED?

The achievements of the Tax Reform Act of 1986 are significant in several important respects. First, the act reduces marginal tax rates for most taxpayers. . . .

Because most people will be able to keep more of each additional dollar that they can earn from work, labor supply is likely to increase. Because not all marginal rates go down and most changes are small, the effect on labor supply will not be dramatic—a 1 percent increase in hours, according to estimates made by Jerry Hausman and James Poterba.[1] But that would be enough to increase productive capacity about $35 billion a year in 1986 prices.

Second, the 1986 act restores to the tax system some of the progressivity lost through inflation and recent legislation. The increases in the personal exemption and the standard deduction and the liberalization of the earned income tax credit directly remove approximately six million low-income taxpayers from the tax rolls. These provisions are responsible for the large percentage reductions in tax liabilities of taxpayers with income of less than $20,000.

Congressional staff estimates indicate that all income classes enjoy cuts in *personal* income taxes, reflecting the shift of approximately $24 billion in taxes each year from individuals to corporations. But the increased corporate income taxes also impose burdens on the people who own capital by reducing their after-tax return on assets. If one takes account of these burdens, not all income brackets gain because the plan is revenue neutral (see table 1). The resulting pattern is clearly progressive, with taxpayers in income brackets below $50,000 a year enjoying reductions and taxpayers in income brackets above $50,000 a year bearing increases.

The third major accomplishment will be an increase in the efficiency of investment. Prereform tax law favored certain kinds of investments over others in two ways. First, it imposed highly unequal rates of tax on different assets and industries, which favored lightly taxed but low productivity investment over heavily taxed investment that might be more productive. This distortion hindered growth in output. Second, the prereform law contained a variety of provisions that made "tax shelters" possible. Shelters worked especially well for investments in assets such as commercial real estate, multifamily housing, airplanes, and railroad cars that are good collateral for loans and that can be traded with low transaction costs.

The tax reform act takes large steps to reduce these distortions. The repeal of the investment tax credit and revisions in depreciation schedules narrow the range of effective corporate income tax rates on various assets and industries (see table 2). And the new law erects formidable roadblocks to tax shelters; in addition to repealing the investment tax credit and stretching out depreciation deductions on structures, the reform law curtails deductibility of investment interest, limits the deductibility of losses on passive investments (defined as all real estate investments and other projects the investor does not actively manage), and strengthens the minimum tax to ensure that most taxpayers will pay tax.

The tax reform law also repeals the exclusion of 60 percent of long-term capital gains. Congress has taxed only a portion of such gains because it feared that realization of large gains could subject individuals to high marginal rates in the year of realization and, in recent years, because part of many capital gains has been the illusory result of inflation. Congress also hoped that low tax rates on long-term capital gains would promote greater entrepreneurial daring.

While congressional intentions were well-meaning, the capital gains exclusion was inefficient and produced serious side effects. Repeal of the exclusion will reduce incentives to invest in assets that have low pretax rates of return but that lend themselves to converting ordinary income into capital gains. A standard ploy, for example, has been to borrow to buy an asset, then use deductions allowed for the interest paid on the borrowed money to offset fully taxable income, and ultimately sell the asset for a gain, 60 percent of which would be untaxed. Under prior law, a taxpayer in the 50 percent bracket who paid $100 in deductible interest and realized $100 in long-term capital gains would enjoy a gain of $30.[2] Furthermore, the new rate structure weakens the case for retaining the exclusion.

Finally, the tax reform law simplifies the personal income tax for most taxpayers. Some of the six million taxpayers removed from the rolls because of lower rates will not even have to file. An additional six million taxpayers will no longer need to itemize deductions. Even more important than the simplification in filling out one's return is the simplification that occurs because numerous provisions discourage tax-motivated investments and because the reduction of marginal tax rates

Table 1

Estimated Change in Tax Burdens in 1988 by Income Brackets

Income Class	Change in Personal Income and Corporate Income Tax Burdens	Change in Total Federal Tax Burdens
Under $10,000	−32.0%	−12.5%
$10,000–20,000	−8.1	−3.1
$20,000–30,000	−4.1	−1.8
$30,000–40,000	−4.1	−2.0
$40,000–50,000	−6.1	−3.1
$50,000–70,000	+0.7	+0.4
$70,000–100,000	+5.3	+3.9
$100,000–200,000	+6.0	+5.0
$200,000 and above	+9.2	+8.2

Source: Author's estimates.

curtails the importance of tax considerations on all transactions. Unfortunately these gains in simplicity are offset to a considerable degree by new provisions that add to the complexity for a minority of taxpayers, as explained below.

WHAT HARM WAS DONE?

The most serious charge brought against the Tax Reform Act of 1986 is that it will increase the effective rate of tax on investment. There is something to this criticism but much less than the average increase of corporate income taxes of $24 billion a year during the period 1987 through 1991 would suggest.

About half of this increase consists of tax changes that will not affect marginal investment decisions in most American industries. Other changes reduce deductions that do not enter into calculations of the profitability of a particular project—for example, limits on deductions for meals and entertainment. Still others increase taxes on investments abroad and may add to investment demand here—for example, some restrictions on the foreign tax credit. Another set of

Table 2

Effective Tax Rates by Asset Type and Industry

	Prereform Law	Tax Reform Act of 1986
Asset Type		
Equipment	11%	38%
Structures	35	39
Inventory	58	48
Industry		
Agriculture	41	42
Mining	30	38
Oil Extraction	23	28
Construction	28	41
Manufacturing	43	43
Transportation	23	37
Communications	24	36
Electric/Gas	28	38
Trade	47	44
Services	32	40
Average	38	41

Source: Jane G. Gravelle, "Effective Corporate Tax Rates in the Major Tax Revision Plans." Congressional Research Service Report 86–854 E, August 26, 1986, table 2.

changes withdraws or reduces extreme advantages to particular industries— taxes, for example, are increased on currently highly favored industries such as defense contractors, petroleum extraction, other mining, finance, and insurance. In addition, relatively few companies will be exposed to the minimum tax. These added tax liabilities will reduce corporate "cash flow" (the sum of after-tax earnings and depreciation reserves), a depressing influence on investment as a whole, but will not change most investment incentives at the margin.

For most companies, the increase in the effective rate of tax on investment from 38 percent to 41 percent, an 8 percent increase in effective rates, will be small.[3] This increase results from the repeal of the investment tax credit and amended depreciation deductions offset by lower corporate income tax rates. The 8 percent increase in *effective tax rates* contrasts with the 23 percent increase in *total collections* from all corporate taxpayers. The difference represents acceleration to 1987-91 of some tax payments that would not have been made until after 1991 under old law and some tax changes that affect cash flow.

However measured, the higher cost of capital to corporations will reduce incentives to invest. But this effect will be offset by the increased efficiency in the use of capital. Furthermore, monetary or fiscal policies that reduced interest rates by 0.8 percentage points would fully offset the increase in the cost of capital caused by revision of the corporate income tax.[4]

A second unfortunate characteristic of the reformed tax system is that it somewhat complicates the task of balancing the budget. Although the measure is revenue neutral over five years, it increases revenues in 1987 and decreases them in 1988 and 1989. Congress is using the 1987 windfall to avoid the nasty task of cutting spending or raising taxes to meet the fiscal 1987 deficit reduction targets of the Gramm-Rudman-Hollings Act. Decreased revenues in the following two years, however, will make continued reduction of the federal deficit even more difficult than it has been so far.

Although the Tax Reform Act of 1986 may hinder deficit cuts in the short run, it could facilitate the eventual elimination of the budget deficit. By improving the fairness and reducing the distortions *without sacrificing revenues*, the tax reform act may make it easier for Congress to raise taxes as part of a deficit reduction package.[5]

A final negative aspect of the new bill is that a minority of taxpayers will face a more complex tax system than they currently do. The expanded minimum tax is a set of provisions of labyrinthine obscurity. Various rules for recapturing at high incomes tax advantages permitted on low incomes add to the complexity for the small fraction of tax payers to which they apply. These include the phaseout procedures that withdraw from high-income taxpayers the advantage of the 15 percent bracket, personal exemptions, deductions for contributions to individual retirement accounts, and deductions for up to $25,000 of losses on passive investments.

Much of this complexity results from the refusal of both the president and Congress to deal with fundamental inconsistencies that remain in the tax code. The phaseout rules permit Congress to maintain the fiction that the top marginal individual income tax rate is 28 percent. In fact, as noted earlier, it rises to 33 percent over the income range in which the phaseouts of the personal exemptions and 15 percent bracket occur.[6] And because Congress permitted some opportunities for tax avoidance to remain in the tax code, it was compelled to retain a minimum tax. The Treasury Department's proposal of November 1984 would have done away with the need for a minimum tax by eliminating the major devices for avoiding taxes that the old and revised minimum taxes are designed to curb.

WHAT OPPORTUNITIES WERE MISSED?

The president and Congress missed three big opportunities for reform.

First, they wasted an ideal chance to enact automatic adjustments to prevent inflation from distorting the measurement of capital income. Congress retained indexation of exemptions, the standard deduction, and tax brackets, first enacted in 1981, but did not adopt the Treasury Department proposal to index depreciation, interest payments and income, capital gains, and inventory costs. . . .

The president and Congress also failed to make any progress in two other areas that would have advanced equitable and efficient income taxation: the taxation of fringe benefits and the integration of the personal and corporate income taxes. The Tax Reform Act of 1986 does little to bring into the tax base fringe benefits that provide current consumption services to employees. Such fringes include employer-financed health insurance, up to $50,000 a year of term life insurance, group legal insurance, and assorted other items. . . .

The final missed opportunity was the failure to reduce the double taxation of dividend income. Under current law, dividend recipients are taxed twice—once indirectly by the corporate income tax, and once directly by the personal income tax. Most developed nations have instituted some relief for this double taxation. [7] The Treasury Department in 1984 proposed to permit corporations to deduct 50 percent of dividends paid. The White House scaled this deduction back to 10 percent phased in over 10 years. The House dropped the deduction altogether, and the Senate did not revive it.

The dividend deduction would have encouraged corporate managers to pay out a larger proportion of earnings in dividends. This incentive may explain its demise. If dividend payments increased, corporate managers would retain a smaller pool of earning for new investment projects. They would have to rely to a greater extent than they now do on new issues of debt and equity to raise funds. Open market competition for investment funds might increase the efficiency with which those funds are allocated, but it would assuredly complicate the fund-raising tasks of corporate managers. The current tax policy of discouraging dividend payment lessens this particular managerial headache. The lack of enthusiasm among corporate managers for a dividend deduction, which made it easy for the White House and Congress to jettison the proposal, probably owes something to this fact of corporate financial life.

WHAT WILL BE THE ECONOMIC EFFECTS?

The effects of the tax bill on overall economic performance are likely to be small. The shift in taxes from individuals to corporations will cause an increase in personal disposable income. Because consumption is closely tied to personal disposable income, consumption outlays may go up in 1987 and beyond. Because deductions for state and local sales taxes will be repealed as of January 1, 1987, the bill may also cause some increase in purchases of costly consumer durable goods during the last quarter of 1986.

The overall effects on investment are difficult to gauge because many offsetting factors are at work. On one hand, the increase in corporate income taxes will reduce corporate cash flow, a development that, as noted, will discourage corporate investment. The increase in the effective tax rate on investment will also tend to reduce investment.

On the other hand, the same increase in effective tax rates will increase the tendency for the value of the U.S. dollar to fall, a development that should make U.S. goods more competitive in international markets. This effect follows because higher taxes will reduce the appeal of U.S. assets relative to foreign assets and thereby reduce the demand for U.S. dollars. Additional decline in the value of the dollar will improve U.S. competitiveness. Whether the dollar's decline will also increase investment depends on what happens to U.S. interest rates.

While the tax reform will have only modest effects on the economy as a whole, it will have important impacts on particular industries and companies. For example, the cost of capital for such "tax shelter" investments as office buildings and multifamily housing will increase. Other industries, such as trade, computers, and some manufacturing, will gain more from lower tax rates and liberalized depreciation on equipment that they will lose from repeal of the investment tax credit and slower depreciation on structures.

Eliminating tax preferences that hampered investment efficiency and the growth of the economic capacity was a primary objective of tax reform. But there is no way to correct past imbalances and achieve these gains in efficiency without shifting tax burdens among industries. And when tax incentives, which have contributed to overinvestment in favored activities, are reduced, the adjustments may be difficult and protracted. For example, the vacancy rates for offices, which exceed 20 percent in many cities and which are attributable in part to tax shelters that encouraged construction even when potential occupants could not be identified, will take many years to decline to economically efficient levels.

A FINAL APPRAISAL

Although these missed opportunities and the harmful elements of the tax reform should not be ignored—if possible they should be corrected in future legislation—they should not obscure the major achievements in the Tax Reform Act of 1986. By removing millions of poor families from the tax rolls and reducing the burdens of millions of other low-income families, by slashing marginal tax rates and thereby reducing the importance of taxes in economic decisions, by ending the distinction between long-term and short-term capital gains, and reducing the incentives to engage in complex tax-avoidance maneuvers, by curbing tax shelters, and by equalizing effective tax rates on various kinds of investment, the tax bill represents a significant improvement in the structure of personal and corporate income taxes. That a good bill contains flaws, some of them important, may make us yearn for what might have been, but it should not prevent us from celebrating a splendid political and economic achievement.

NOTES

1. Jerry A. Hausman and James M. Poterba, "Household Behavior and the Tax Reform Act of 1986," *Journal of Economic Perspectives*, forthcoming.

2. The taxpayer paid $100 in interest but saved $50 in taxes because the interest is deductible, for a net cost of $50. The tax liability would be only $20 on the $100 capital gain because only $40 of the gain would be subject to tax; hence the net gain is $80. The $80 net capital gain less the $50 net interest cost equals $30.

3. Jane G. Gravelle, "Effective Corporate Tax Rates in the Major Tax Revision Plans: A Comparison of the House, Senate, and Conference Committee Versions," Congressional Research Service Report 86–854 E, August 26, 1986, table 2.

4. Estimates reported to the author by Jane G. Gravelle, Congressional Research Service.

5. James M. Buchanan, "Tax Reform and Political Choice," *Journal of Economic Perspectives*, forthcoming.

6. The tax law also contains other phaseouts—of the exclusion of contributions to individual retirement accounts for example—that generate other effective marginal rates.

7. Joseph A. Pechman, "Tax Reform Prospects in Europe and Canada," *The Brookings Review*, vol. 5 (Winter 1987), pp. 11–19.

NO

Henning Gutmann

THE BAD NEW TAX LAW

The U.S. Tax Reform Act of 1986 has been praised by the leaders of both parties, from the intellectual "founder" of the idea, the moderate Democratic senator Bill Bradley, to Ronald Reagan, the most conservative president in recent memory, who made it the chief domestic policy goal for his second term. Proponents of the bill said it would make the tax code both fairer and simpler, by lowering tax rates for the common man and curtailing a wide variety of special deductions, credits, and loopholes that the rich had used to avoid paying their fair share of tax.

The bill was also promoted as a boon to the working poor—six million low-income taxpayers will be taken off the tax rolls entirely—while remaining "revenue-neutral.," i.e., providing neither more not less income to the government. But those who have had high expectations for the bill are in for a shock. Not only does it amount to a substantial tax cut for many of the rich, but it also contains hidden dangers to the idea of equal opportunity in America.

The new bill replaces the current system of fourteen tax brackets ranging from 11 percent to 50 percent with only two tax brackets, 15 percent and 28 percent.[1] This is a clear step backward for the progressive idea of taxation—that the rich should pay a greater share of the tax burden. The current system is only mildly progressive, because many upper-income taxpayers have used deductions and shelters to pay less than their nominal rate of tax.[2] But the new law is a gift to the rich unmatched since Calvin Coolidge pushed through a 24 percent top rate for 1929. In the new law, the top rate also extends far down into the middle class; single taxpayers begin paying a marginal 28 percent on every dollar earned over $17,850. Thus, for example, a science researcher making $22,000 a year pays the same 28 percent marginal tax rate as lee Iacocca, who makes over $1,000,000 a year.

The new low rates create a windfall in tax savings for those taxpayers making over $200,000 a year who didn't take advantage of many deductions or tax shelters; their top tax rate falls from nearly 50 percent to 28 percent. For example, a stockbroker earning $500,000 a year who paid 40 percent, or

From "The Bad New Tax Law," by Henning Gutmann, *The New York Review of Books*, February 12, 1987. Copyright © 1987 Nyrev, Inc. Reprinted by permission.

$200,000, in federal tax in 1986 gets a $60,000 cut to 28 percent, paying $140,000 on the same income in 1988. Such taxpayers make up only 0.3 percent of the total but will, in 1988, save $19.7 billion in taxes, according to the Joint Committee on Taxation—an astonishing 32 percent of the bill's benefits to individuals in that year. For a government facing huge budget deficits, this is a large gift to bestow on an already privileged part of the population. It is only partially balanced by $17.3 billion in increased revenues expected from those in this income class who are giving up shelters and other deductions.

By contrast, the cost to the government of relieving six million poor people from the obligation to pay any federal income tax is only $2 billion. And the effect of the law is only to restore late 1970s' real rates of tax on these poor taxpayers. Not that the government ceases taxing these people altogether—they and their employers are subject to social security tax, currently 7.15 percent and scheduled to increase later in 1987. For many of the working poor, this is a large portion of the taxes they have been paying and, because of the high cost to employers, it is an economic threat to the creation of low income jobs. Finally, the new law actually penalizes 1.7 million taxpayers earning less than $10,000 a year, who see their tax rate rise from 11 percent to 15 percent; the average tax increase for this group will be $214 in 1988, a substantial amount for anyone earning less than $10,000.

To return to the rich, those with incomes over $200,000 who previously managed to keep their tax bill low will have to scramble to avoid sharp tax increases. But we can expect that these taxpayers have the means and the inge-

nuity to do just that. Failure to act would mean an average $55,700 tax increase in 1988 for this 0.2 percent of the taxpaying population, who, for example, exploited tax shelters—investments in which the taxpayer does not participate actively in management, such as a limited partnership for construction of an office building—that yielded losses used to write off actual income. The new bill generally allows deduction of shelter, or passive, losses only against earnings from other passive investments.

The trick for rich investors who can afford it is that passive losses may be carried forward into future years until passive income is found. For example, a taxpayer may have participated as a partner in two tax shelter schemes: one, a complex of rental apartments in Coral Gables, Florida, and another, a cattle deal in Wyoming. In the first several years, the apartment complex, which is still under construction, provides the taxpayer with passive losses; these may total $30,000 in 1988. The cattle ranch is not yet profitable so it also generates $30,000 in losses. Under the new law's transition rules, only 40 percent of these losses can be used to reduce the taxpayer's 1988 taxable income. So he can lower his income by only $24,000, compared to the full $60,000 under the old rules. However, the unused $36,000 in losses can, if the investor has enough capital to meet interest and other costs, be used in later years to offset the income that would result when the apartments get built, the cattle deal becomes profitable, or when the taxpayer disposes of his interest in either.

Some real-estate entrepreneurs who manage properties may be able to claim their income as passive, and thus use it to offset their losses. It is also possible for a well-heeled taxpayer to buy shares in profit-producing passive investments, such as a city parking lot or a block of rental units. If he can keep borrowing to a minimum, our taxpayer may, for example, be able to obtain $36,000 in income from his shares in a new parking lot in 1989 or 1990, and can offset that income with the $36,000 in losses carried over from 1988. Thus, in effect, our taxpayer builds his equity in the apartments and obtains additional income from the parking lot, all of it tax free.

Such benefits are available only to those who can afford to purchase passive income; a middle-income taxpayer with little cash to spare just has to take his losses and hope his investment makes a profit or can be sold soon. For the well-to-do, other choices also exist. They can buy tax-exempt bonds, for example. The well-to-do will also benefit because the new bill broadens the category of investment income. Under the old law, a rich investor with $300,000 in income from investments such as stocks and bonds, royalties, or venture capital stock could deduct up to the amount of investment income—$300,000—in interest costs incurred in borrowing money for these and other investments. The new bill adds long-term capital gains and income and loss from certain working oil and gas interests into the category of investment income. Thus if the well-off investor takes a $200,000 long-term capital gain on sale of stock in 1988, and maintains his income from other investments at 1986 levels, he will be allowed to deduct a full $500,00 of the interest he paid to borrow money for investment that year, enabling him to expand his holdings significantly, while deducting interest costs. This preferential tax treatment won't be available to taxpayers without the capital

to generate substantial investment income. So the rich will stay rich, while much of the middle class will have to struggle to stay afloat.

The elimination of tax shelters provides only a part of the revenue that was required to make the bill revenue-neutral. The lowering of rates is expected to cost $120 billion over the five years to 1991, and as the House-Senate Conference Committee approached its recess deadline of August 16, the revenue estimates by the committee's staff kept coming up short of expectations. Yet the lawmakers never considered raising the rates;[3] instead they continued to seek new sources of revenue. This was accomplished at a price, of course. As Senator John Danforth, the Missouri Republican who voted against the bill after initially supporting it, said:

> The whole nature of the bill, right from the outset, has been that we in the Congress have become—and myself included—intoxicated by the low rates. We have been willing to do anything to accomplish low rates. We were willing to dump more and more taxes on our industrial sector, on research and development, on education in order to placate this god that we had formed of low rates.

The bill's treatment of heavy industry provides an example. The auto, steel, chemicals, and textile industries are already in decline and are struggling to remain competitive with imports. Yet the bill eliminates the investment tax credit, a 6 percent or 10 percent credit for equipment purchases which many of these companies relied on, and makes equipment depreciation schedules less generous. The bill also lowers the corporate tax rate from 46 percent to 34 percent, but this benefits primarily service companies that don't invest heavily in plant and equipment and that currently pay high tax rates, such as retailers, wholesalers, consumer-product companies, and various other service firms. The apparently unintended result could be a sharp blow to American industry. As Danforth noted: "I think we should strive for a balanced economy, and for a country that can make things and for an industrial sector which can compete with the rest of the world. I do not think we should shove them over the cliff. I believe that is what this bill does."

Tax lawyers and economists, three months after passage of the bill, admit that they are confused about the effects of the legislation on the economy. To collect more revenue, the bill eliminates some tax credits, alters depreciation schedules, and changes accounting rules—whose effects only time will make evident. Tax lawyers do agree, however, that the new bill is anything but a simplification. The new law has led to frenetic activity among tax advisers, and many aspects of the bill remain to be interpreted by the Treasury Department and the Internal Revenue Service.

Clearly, however, education in the U.S. could be heavily damaged by the provisions of the new bill that are intended to raise revenue. The bill no longer allows interest costs on most loans, including student loans, to be deducted. It thus effectively increases the cost of borrowing for higher education, just when students are becoming more and more dependent on borrowing large sums of money to attend expensive colleges and universities. The bill also inexplicably taxes scholarships and fellowships. This rule will particularly hurt graduate students, especially if they have families to support, since the remainder of their small stipends not used for tuition or books and equipment will be taxed.

Of course, the main provision of the bill, its lower rates, hurts both education and charities simply because the value of the deduction given to a charitable or educational institution is reduced. At a 50 percent tax rate, a $500 gift to a university yields a $250 benefit. At 28 percent, the same $500 gift will yield only a $140 benefit. John Brademas, president of New York University, has said the new law will reduce charitable contributions to higher education by as much as $1.2 billion annually. It is likely that other nonprofit organizations will also be unable to raise as much money as they had previously done.

The bill also makes fund raising for colleges and universities more difficult by imposing a stiff new minimum tax on gifts of appreciated property, such as stocks, bonds, and valuables. Such property makes up about 40 percent of all charitable contributions made to universities, and some donations will be reduced since they will no longer be fully tax deductible for the donor. The bill also no longer allows charitable contributions to be deducted by those who do not itemize deductions. In addition, the bill imposes a new institutional limit of $150 million on tax-exempt bond issues by private universities. This will hurt especially the leading research universities, many of which are well above that amount and rely heavily on such bond issues to raise money to build new laboratories and other facilities. The limit does not apply to public institutions, however, which retain full rights as governmental entities. The new bill thus strikes a particular blow at private institutions.

Middle- and upper-middle-income parents trying to save money for their children's education will also have their task made more difficult by the new bill. Previously, parents as a means of saving for tuition expenses were able to shift to the child an unrestricted portion of their income every year, to be taxed at the child's lower rate. Under tax revision, shifting income to children, at the child's rate, will be limited to the first $1,000 every year until the child is fourteen, at which time parents can begin setting aside larger amounts of money in a fund for the child's education. So parents making full use of tax-advantaged saving for a child can at most set aside $14,000 in investment income earned in the child's account by the time the child turns fourteen. With costs of a four-year education rising rapidly and nearing $80,000 at the best private schools, and already between $25,000 and 30,000 at many state-supported schools, this provision seriously curtails the ability of a middle- or upper-class family to save for a child's education.

The treatment of other individual deductions draws a sharp line between those who own property and those who do not. The bill no longer allows deductions for any debt interest not tied to a mortgage. It also disallows state and local sales taxes and limits other widely used deductions, including employee business expenses such as professional journals, continuing education courses, union and professional dues, job-hunting expenses, work uniforms, and tax and investment advising services. Medical expenses allowed for deduction are also reduced; in 1987, only those costs over 7.5 percent of gross income may be deducted compared to 5 percent previously. These are deductions taken by many middle-class taxpayers, who will either have to cut back on them or face, in some cases,

sharply higher tax bills. Those who don't own property will be hit hardest, since almost all deductions available to them are curtailed, while the bill preserves full deductibility of mortgage interest on first and second homes, as well as on all property taxes.

Homeowners also will be able to borrow under the new law and deduct their interest costs by refinancing their homes, or taking out a second mortgage. For instance, a couple who bought a house for $50,000 twenty years ago and have added $30,000 in improvements will, under the new law, be able to borrow up to the original value of the house and the improvements, or $80,000, for any purpose, and deduct the interest expense from their taxes. If the house is now valued at $300,000, the couple may borrow up to that value, or an additional $220,000, for educational and medical expenses. Renters, even if they could borrow such sums from a bank or another source, will effectively pay more than their propertied counterparts because they cannot deduct the interest costs on such loans. Here the bill again evidently favors the homeowners who make up much of the middle class, and this is part of its political appeal; but what has been less evident is that the bill once again favors the well-to-do because the government's largest subsidies—in the form of interest deductions—go to homeowners with the biggest and most expensive properties.

For many people without property, the new law may mean they will no longer make purchases that require borrowing. It can be argued that people can do without dishwashers, VCRs, or new cars. But it will be a serious loss when the children of a working couple decide they cannot go to college because expenses, both during their time as students and thereafter—in the form of loan repayments totaling hundreds of dollars a month—are too high. Many will have to forego "elective" medical expenses—everything from psychiatric help to orthodontics—because of the reduced sum of medical bills that are deductible and the inability to write off borrowing costs.

Those without property will also have fewer opportunities to try to start a business. Shelters have been a way to attract venture capital to new businesses since investors, without direct participation, could write off the losses usually accrued at the onset of a business. For example, under the old rules, a man in California could lend his brother in New York $100,000 to open a pizza parlor. The brother in California could then write off the initial losses on the business in New York until the other brother could make the pizza parlor profitable. It will be more difficult to set up such an arrangement after 1986 because the investor won't have immediate use of his loss, and direct management participation is required to take business loss deductions. Someone starting out will either have to have sufficient capital himself or be able to show an immediate profit to an investor, an unlikely event in any business requiring some initial investment. This will certainly stifle business activity and, in effect, close off access to the American Dream.

A closer look at tax reform shows that it supports not the idea of the land of opportunity but instead something like a "landed gentry." Those who start with some ingenuity, some enterprising energy, will have a much harder time establishing themselves in business. Quality education, which traditionally has been the way to rise in this country, will become increasingly inaccessible to all but the very rich. In the meantime, those who have the capital and own the property will consolidate their wealth, and opportunities for the have-nots will dwindle. The result in the end will be the further polarization of society, a widening gap between the rich, on the one hand, and, on the other, the middle class and the poor, and therefore less interplay between people from diverse socioeconomic and ethnic backgrounds. This goes to the very heart of the nation's vitality; without it the country will have an increasingly small inbred elite. The new tax law does not bode well for either the health of the country or its people.

(I would like to acknowledge the assistance of Sheldon S. Cohen, commissioner of the Internal Revenue Service between January 1965 and January 1969, now a partner in the law firm of Morgan, Lewis, and Bockius in Washington, DC, and Michael Schlesinger, partner in Schlesinger and Sussman, New York City.)

NOTES

1. A third, 33 percent marginal rate applies to certain ranges of upper-middle income, i.e., $71,900 to $149,250 for a married couple, to phase out the benefits of the 15 percent bracket. The effect, if the full adjustment applies, is that all taxable income above the threshold level is taxed at an effective top rate of 28 percent.
2. See Joseph Pechman, "The Rich, The Poor, and the Taxes They Pay" (Westview Press, 1986), pp. 23–25.
3. The conferees did agree, at one point, to raise the top individual tax rate to 28 percent from 27 percent and the top corporate rate to 34 percent from 33 percent, but no significant rate increase was considered.

POSTSCRIPT

Is Tax Reform an Impossible Dream Come True?

Economist Aaron believes that the Tax Reform Act (TRA) represents a "splendid political and economic achievement" in spite of the fact that the legislation did not change certain things that should have been changed and that some of the changes have adverse consequences. He argues that the new law represents four major accomplishments. First, TRA reduces tax rates for individuals. This is good not only because its involves a reduction in the tax burdens of individuals, but because it will enhance productive capacity by increasing the supply of labor. Second, TRA enhances the progressivity of the tax system with lower and middle income individuals and families paying less in taxes and higher income taxpayers paying more. Third, TRA alters some of the features of the old tax code that made certain kinds of investment more attractive than others. Repeal of the investment tax credit and changes in depreciation rules will reduce if not eliminate former distortions and thus enhance the efficiency of investment. Fourth, TRA makes it easier for the majority of taxpayers to file taxes and comply with tax law. For some 6 million taxpayers there is no need to file at all and another 6 million will no longer need to itemize deductions.

Reporter Gutmann believes that TRA is bad for it represents not only "a substantial tax cut for many of the rich, but it also contains hidden dangers to the idea of equal opportunity in America." He gives a number of specific examples to support this claim. First, the cost to the federal government to eliminate the taxes on some 6 million low income families is only $2 billion while the loss in tax revenues from persons with incomes in excess of $200,000 and who did not take

advantage of pre-reform deductions and tax shelter is almost $20 billion. Second, those with high incomes will still be able to avail themselves of certain tax advantages; they have both the financial resources and know-how to take advantage of rules regarding passive income and losses. Third, the changes in taxation of business, especially the elimination of the investment tax credit, hurts heavy industries which already suffer from international competition. The repeal of the deductibility of personal interest also applies to student loans. This gives rise to a fourth problem: it raises the cost of higher education. Education is also damaged in several other ways, for the tax reform may reduce charitable contributions to educational institutions. Finally, other changes adversely affect low income taxpayers: persons who do not own property will face higher costs for borrowing to finance other activities besides education, including certain medical treatments and starting their own businesses.

The Reagan administration's support of TRA is presented in the *1987 Economic Report of the President* (pp. 79–96). A number of articles critical of TRA have appeared including "The Tax Reform Legislation: A Step Backward" by William B. Cannon (Fall 1986, *Social Policy*); "A Fair Tax Act That's Bad for Business" by Lawrence H. Summers (March/April 1987, *Harvard Business Review*); and "The Economic Fallout of the Tax Reform Act of 1986" by Norman B. True (April 8, 1987, *Economic Policy Bulletin*). *The Journal of Economic Perspectives* (Summer 1987) offers a symposium on tax reform containing eight papers by both liberal and conservative economists.

ISSUE 13

Is The Welfare System Causing Poverty?

YES: Charles Murray, from the *Wall Street Journal* (May 15, 1985)

NO: Richard D. Coe and Greg J. Duncan, from the *Wall Street Journal* (May 15, 1985)

ISSUE SUMMARY

YES: Researcher Murray believes that the welfare reforms of the 1960s and the changes in the ways government treated the poor caused low income youth to "become decoupled from the mechanism whereby poor people in this country historically have worked their way out of poverty."
NO: College professor Coe and researcher Duncan argue that "typical welfare spells are brief, interspersed with work, do not break up families, and are not passed on from parent to child."

Most of the discussion regarding poverty revolves around two questions: (1) how many people are poor? and (2) what should be done to reduce or eliminate poverty?

The answer to the first question can be approached in different ways. There is the relative approach which considers an economic unit poor if it has substantially less than the typical or average unit. The absolute approach classifies an economic unit as poor if it is unable to provide itself with essentials. Generally the relative approach yields a higher poverty count than the absolute approach.

Government efforts to count the number of poor began in the late 1950s and early 1960s and the absolute approach was chosen. The first step in the counting process is to determine poverty threshholds, the dollar cost of an economic unit's essentials. These threshholds will vary from economic unit to economic unit because of such differences as the size of the unit and its age composition. The second step is to measure the economic unit's ability to cover these costs; this is done by calculating the unit's income. The third step is to compare the two dollar figures: if the economic unit's income is below its poverty threshhold, it is poor.

The government statistics can be disputed on a number of grounds. There is the attack by those who prefer the relative approach over the absolute approach. There is the criticism that the poverty threshholds are too low because they ignore such things as the health status of the economic unit. There is the criticism that the poverty count is too high because the government does not include as income certain programs that benefit the poor such as food stamps and Medicaid.

But the debate between Murray on the one hand and Coe and Duncan on the other is not over the counting question. They basically accept the government's statistics. These statistics reveal that in 1960 there were approximately 40 million poor persons in the U.S., a little more than 20 percent of the population. During the 1960s there was a steady decline in the number of poor: in 1969 the count was 24 million persons or 12 percent of the population. This pattern of progress did not continue during the 1970s. With some increases and decreases over the decade, the number of poor in 1979 was almost exactly the same as it was in 1970, 25 million poor. During the 1980s the poverty count began to rise dramatically. During 1980 the number of poor increased by more than 4 million and by 1983 there were over 35 million poor people.

The second poverty question really is a request to explain these figures. The point is that during the 1960s, a number of social welfare programs were created that were intended to reduce or eliminate poverty and the benefits of preexisting programs increased. The statistics for the 1960s suggest that these programs were working as designed. However, the data for the 1970s indicate that if these programs had indeed helped to reduce the poverty count during the 1960s, they no longer were doing so during the 1970s.

So the issue was again joined: what should be done to reduce poverty? The fundamental conservative position is that people, if given appropriate incentives, will work themselves out of poverty. Appropriate incentives mean that an able-bodied person can become better off by working rather than relying on overly generous government programs. And they argue today's anti-poverty programs are too generous and thereby create poverty. Liberals dispute these claims. They believe that most persons, including the able-bodied, find themselves in poverty because of conditions over which they have no control. These include changing family conditions such as divorce and the loss of jobs because of recessions. These conditions tend to be temporary, so poverty for most people is temporary. Society needs to give all persons adequate support when they encounter poverty.

Murray presents the latest case made by conservatives while Coe and Duncan articulate the liberal position. Again, the disagreement is not over the poverty statistics themselves but rather on the interpretation of the numbers.

YES

Charles Murray

WELFARE DEPENDENCY

I was fascinated by the data in "Years of Poverty, Years of Plenty," (University of Michigan, 1984). But the inferences I draw from them are at complete odds with the picture painted by the authors.

Contradictory results do not mean that anyone is trying to lie with statistics. They do not mean that "statistics can be made to say anything." But they do mean that "findings" have to be distinguished from "interpretations." Here are some of the ways in which Richard D. Coe, Greg J. Duncan and their colleagues (the book summarizes several separate studies) and I can agree on the findings and reach quite different interpretations.

Sometimes the difference is as simple, and as unresolvable, as a choice among perspectives. A classic example involves one of the most furiously debated topics about welfare, whether Aid to Families With Dependent Children leads to long-term dependency. The data base that Mr. Duncan et al. use reveals the 48% of all women who received AFDC during the study were off the rolls within two years. That is a finding. It has also been used as the basis for claiming that welfare dependency is not a major problem. Now, consider exactly the same data, used to calculate another statistic: Of all women who were on AFDC at one time, 50% were in the midst of a spell on it that would last for eight or more years. For a typical year during the study, that translated into roughly 1.6 million families and more than five million people. Which view of the situation do you consider important? Greg Duncan examines such data and sees a situation in which AFDC is providing needed help to people in temporary difficulty. I see an underclass, and worry that the benefits of the short-term help are outweighted by the harm of the long-term dependence. The findings are the same. The interpretations are almost mirror images.

A second source of contradictory results is the straw-man problem, something that has been a constant source of frustration in the debate over "Losing Ground." Everybody knows what conservatives are supposed to think about welfare—they think the system is loaded with cheats who live contentedly off the dole, and that women have babies so they can get a

From "Welfare: Promoting Poverty or Progress?" by Charles Murray, *The Wall Street Journal*, May 15, 1985. Copyright © Dow Jones & Co., Inc., 1985. Reprinted by permission of *The Wall Street Journal*. All rights reserved.

bigger check. "Losing Ground" is against welfare, therefore it must make the same arguments. The data that Mr. Duncan uses refute such stereotypes, and they by extension are said to refute my book. But they don't, because those arguments are not ones that I actually made.

"Losing Ground" contends that the reforms of the 1960s—not just reforms in welfare, but reforms that transformed the ways in which "the poor" were treated by government policy—had the combined effect of encouraging low-income youths to put together a varying package of some work, some income from the underground economy, and some welfare. They were not always "poor" as defined by the government's poverty line, but they had become de-coupled from the mechanism whereby poor people in this country historically have worked their way out of poverty. "The problem with this new form of unemployment," I wrote, "was not that young black males—or young poor males—stopped working altogether, but that they moved in and out of the labor force at precisely that point in their lives when it was most important that they acquire skills, work habits, and a work record." Similarly, poor young women were reaching their mid-20s with children but no husband (because they either had never married or had been abandoned), and were consigned to the margins of U.S. society. If I am right, then the results to be predicted correspond very closely to what was actually found by the data that Messrs. Coe and Duncan describe.

A SOURCE OF CONTRADICTION

Specifically, I would predict that low-income people who are caught in the trap that "Losing Ground" describes will hover near the poverty line, and not escape into the secure working class. The findings of the data in "Years of Poverty, Years of Plenty" track extraordinarily well with this expectation. Messrs. Coe and Duncan interpret these findings as evidence that people are victims of cir-cumstance, and ask us to consider how much worse things would be if we did not have the income-transfer programs to cushion their bad luck. I have no problem with this interpretation as it applies to the elderly and the disabled. But when it comes to healthy working-age people, I ask whether we are wit-nessing protection against "bad luck" or a system for *producing* it.

Definitions are another source of con-tradiction in the argument about both dependency and poverty. The conclusion of "Years of Poverty, Years of Plenty" is that "only two percent of the population could be classified as persistently depen-dent upon welfare income"—a very small number. When one considers how many of those are elderly or disabled, it seems that there must be hardly any welfare dependency at all among the healthy working-age. But a few para-graphs back I pointed out that about five million people were in families in the midst of at least an eight-year spell on AFDC. Aren't all of them dependent?

It all depends on how one defines "persistently dependent." To me, anyone who gets any welfare at all and would be unable to provide for his family without it is dependent on welfare at that mo-ment. For Messrs. Coe and Duncan, a family is not dependent on welfare un-less more than 50% of its income is from welfare. To me, anyone (again, healthy and working-age) who gets used to the idea that welfare assistance is an accept-able supplement to earned income is "persistently dependent." For them, the only people who are persistently dependent on welfare income are those who received more than half of their income from welfare during at least eight out of the 10 years of the study. And if you think that definition makes it extremely difficult to be defined as "persistently dependent," consider that, in computing "half the income," the book "Years of Poverty, Years of Plenty" ignores Medicaid, housing assistance, child nutrition and unemployment payments—meaning for practical purposes that for Mr. Duncan and his colleagues there can be no such thing as a young, healthy, two-parent family that is welfare-dependent. Even for AFDC mothers, the exclusions discount so much of the welfare package that a long-term AFDC mother who periodically holds a job is likely to be counted as "not dependent on welfare."

AN INDISCRIMINATE MIX

In the case of economic mobility, perhaps the most widely publicized topic of "Years of Poverty, Years of Plenty," the problem is not a misleading definition, but the lack of one. Mr. Duncan and his colleagues measured family income in 1971 and again in 1978, and found a high degree of economic mobility in the U.S., both within a single generation and from parents to children. This is, we assume, good news. "Economic mobility" immediately brings to mind youngsters of poor parents moving into the working class, or people moving from the working class to the middle class, all of which is what the American way is supposed to be about.

But the data offered indiscriminately mix several kinds of mobility. One has to do with a normal earnings profile. Almost everyone is at the bottom of the income distribution at some early moment after setting out on one's own. For blue-collar workers who stay in the work force, the entry-level wage is likely to be extremely low, likely to rise rapidly during the early work years, and then tend to level off. For professionals, graduate school is likely to be a time when one is counted as a separate household (thus qualifying for the book's sample) but has very little income—an income that abruptly jumps after graduation. At any given slice of time, these populations of job entrants and the "about-to-be-affluent poor" comprise some millions of people. A second kind of mobility has to do with marriage. Several million of those who were single in 1971 had formed two-income families by 1978 (70% of all married-couple families under the age of 35 were two-income in 1978). For them, it was almost impossible to avoid a dramatic jump up the income-distribution scale.

The limited point here is that the real income of many millions of people rose substantially from 1971 to 1978 for reasons that had nothing to do with Horatio Alger. In light of that, how do we interpret the finding in "Years of Poverty, Years of Plenty" that of the bottom quintile (20%) of the family income distribution in 1971, 4.5% had moved up at least two quintiles by 1978? The interpretation that Greg Duncan and his colleagues reach is that "[t]hese figures suggest a substantial and perhaps surprising degree of income mobility at the bottom end of the income distribution." I read the same numbers. I look up the national household income distribution in 1971 and 1978 and find that I could go from the bottom quintile to the third quintile if my household income increased from roughly $6,000 to $12,000 (in constant 1978 dollars) in the seven intervening years. I make some ballpark estimates of the subpopulations that could be expected to do so as a matter of course. My question is: How could the proportion that moved up be so low? And I am left with another question: Once we subtract the subpopulations moving up because of normal life-cycle trends, how much room is left for the kind of economic mobility we want to see? Unfortunately, their own analysis of the dynamics of income movement within the low-income groups suggests that the answer is very little.

If I were a reader of this and the article by Messrs. Coe and Duncan, I think my reaction by this time would be: Why don't you folks get together and thrash it out? Instead of endlessly giving us conflicting versions of the same data, why not reach some sort of consensus? To which my reaction, and I suspect theirs as well, is: Yes, it is about time we do just that. When we finally get a grip on who the "poor" really are, some major policy disputes will begin to resolve themselves.

NO   Richard D. Coe and Greg Duncan

ON "LOSING GROUND"

In his book "Losing Ground," (Basic, 1984) Charles Murray carries the neoconservative critique of Great Society social policies to its logical extreme. He argues that the programs launched in the 1960s have not only failed to help the disadvantaged, but have actually created dependency by discouraging work, breaking up families, diluting the quality of education and promoting out-of-wedlock births. Mr. Murray thinks the U.S. would be better off eliminating all federal welfare programs. "Cut the knot," he urges, asserting that "the lives of large numbers of poor people would be radically changed for the better."

This is strong stuff and calls for convincing evidence to warrant the attention it has received. However, his argument rests primarily on 30 years of annual Census Bureau statistics on poverty, family instability, crime and employment. Mr. Murray himself notes that such information, obtained from annual cross-sectional surveys, is not well-suited for disentangling causation or even describing the longer-term position of particular population groups. Successive annual counts may show unchanging numbers of welfare recipients or numbers of poor people but cannot reveal whether those numbers are made up of an unchanging group. "What we would really like," he writes, "is a longitudinal sample of the disadvantaged."

In fact, there is such a longitudinal study, and it provides a much clearer view of some of the issues Mr. Murray wishes to address. For the past 18 years, the University of Michigan's Panel Study of Income Dynamics has been tracking the economic fortunes of a large representative sample of U.S. families—both the disadvantaged and the advantaged. The PSID does not reach back into the 1950s, as the Census Bureau's data can, nor cover all the issues addressed (crime, school quality) or ignored (nutrition, infant mortality) by Mr. Murray, but it does provide a wealth of information on patterns of work, on welfare use and on family composition changes ever since the Great Society programs were begun. In 10 volumes of detailed analysis, in articles by numerous independent researchers and in the summary book

From "Welfare: Promoting Poverty or Progress?" by Richard D. Coe and Greg J. Duncan, *The Wall Street Journal*, January 6, 1986. Copyright © Dow Jones & Co., Inc., 1986. Reprinted by permission of *The Wall Street Journal*. All rights reserved.

"Years of Poverty, Years of Plenty," the PSID reveals a picture of economic mobility and of generally benign welfare programs that differs dramatically from "Losing Ground."

NOT A LONG-TERM EXPERIENCE

Mr. Murray's attack on the core social programs—Aid to Families With Dependent Children and food stamps—is based on the premise that they foster dependency by discouraging work and marriage and reduce the stigma formerly attached to a life on the dole. He concludes, with regret, that these programs cannot be regarded as insurance against temporary misfortune, nor are they an acceptable means of providing a minimally adequate diet or home environment for needy children.

The facts, as shown by PSID data, are remarkably inconsistent with his assumptions.

Fact: Welfare use is not typically a long-term experience. The typical spell of welfare receipt is fairly short—half extend for periods of no more than two years and only one in six lasts for more than eight years. While 50 million Americans lived in families that received some welfare income during the 1970s, only five million could be characterized as persistently dependent on it.

Fact: Most welfare recipients mix work and welfare during the years in which welfare is received. Fewer than half of the people who received welfare, whether for a single year or over many years, relied on it as the source of more than half of their total family income over a given period.

Fact: Welfare dependency is not typically transmitted from one generation to the next. The PSID study of the women who grew up in families that depended heavily upon welfare in the late 1960s and early 1970s found that the vast majority—four-fifths—were not themselves heavily dependent upon welfare once they left home and established independent households. For black women, there was no significant link between their welfare status and that of their parents.

Fact: Mr. Murray's assertions notwithstanding, there is no conclusive evidence of strong links between the generosity of existing welfare programs and the incidence of births, divorces, marriages or remarriages. The most comprehensive study of this issue, by Harvard researchers David Ellwood and Mary Jo Bane, completed after "Losing Ground" was written, concluded that "welfare simply does not appear to be the underlying cause of the dramatic changes in family structure of the past few decades."

In short, typical welfare spells are brief, interspersed with work, do not break up families and are not passed on from parent to child.

The temporary nature of most welfare spells is part of the much larger picture of economic mobility painted by the PSID data. Ours is clearly a dynamic society in which individual and family economic fortunes undergo substantial change. It can correctly be inferred from these longitudinal data that the longer-term distribution of income and, quite likely, economic opportunity are indeed more equal that single-year figures would indicate. This evidence is fundamentally inconsistent with Mr. Murray's view that the welfare system invariably produces persistent poverty and dependency.

A SIGNIFICANT NUMBER

A look behind the general mobility shows that these changes are frequently for the better, but some are for the worse and many—favorable and unfavorable—appear to result from events largely beyond the control of the individual. Misfortunes are not limited to the lower end of the income scale; their damaging effects can touch all economic levels. Anyone familiar with the economic circumstances of divorced women and their children, who are nearly three times as likely to fall into poverty as divorced men, or with the consequences of a sudden disability or layoff can corroborate this fact. Given time, however, such setbacks are usually overcome as individuals seize some new opportunity provided by a dynamic society to rebuild their lives. In the meantime, the welfare system provides for the majority of recipients precisely what most Americans, including Charles Murray, believe it should: a temporary safety net to ease the burden of hard times.

The darker side of this picture of mobility is the plight of the individuals left behind in its wake. Even with welfare payments added to family income, more than one-tenth of all children (and nearly half of black children) spent a substantial portion of their childhood in poverty. And while they constituted a small fraction of all those who came into contact with welfare, the number of people spending most of the 1970s in welfare-dependent families was far from insignificant — totaling some five million. Since these long-term recipients tend to accumulate on the rolls, they account for a disproportionate share of total program expenditures.

Why do the parents in these persistently dependent families fail to work their way off welfare? Perhaps, as Charles Murray suggests, the unintended incentives of the welfare system played a role. For many, however, even year-round employment in the jobs typically available to them would fail to lift their families out of poverty. Although we are far from understanding the relative importance of discrimination, unemployment, low skills, child-care availability and welfare disincentives in this process, there is encouraging experimental evidence from the Manpower Development Research Corporation to indicate that job-skills programs offer hope for moving long-term welfare recipients into the labor force.

Where does all this leave the welfare debate? Charles Murray sees welfare as a sinister, debilitating force, creating more poverty than it alleviates. But he and other neoconservative writers have simply failed to digest the emerging facts about the dynamic nature of welfare use. We see the system as an indispensable safety net in a dynamic society, serving largely as insurance against temporary misfortune and providing some small measure of equal opportunity in the home environments of children who, after all, constitute the majority of recipients. Viewed in this light, Mr. Murray's proposal that we eliminate welfare for the good of the poor is a cruel joke at best. Despite the welfare system's flaws, its misdirected initiatives and its potentially perverse incentives, it has in fact provided economic assistance to millions of needy Americans without trapping them into dependency.

POSTSCRIPT

Is the Welfare System Causing Poverty?

Murray begins by declaring that the differences between his position and Coe and Duncan's are matters of interpretation and emphasis, and he goes on to demonstrate how their different interpretations arise. Murray first uses the example of women who use Aid to Families with Dependent Children (AFDC). Coe and Duncan reveal that 48 percent of all women who used AFDC only used it for two years. Murray states that of all the women who used AFDC, 50 percent used it for eight or more years. Focusing on the former statistic suggests a temporary use of welfare, the latter a long-term dependency on welfare. Another reason differences occur, according to Murray, is that Coe and Duncan are not attacking what he says but what they think he is saying. Murray claims that he does not argue that welfare programs mean youths never work. What he does say is that these programs cause young poor males to move in and out of the labor force at precisely the point in their lives when it is most important for them to acquire skills and work habits. And lastly, Murray believes that they differ because of how each side defines terms. For Murray, his definitions of welfare programs, welfare dependency, and economic mobility are more reasonable and thus support his conclusions that welfare programs help to create poverty.

Coe and Duncan make their case by arguing that Murray relies on the wrong kind of data; the behavior of specific groups of people is more appropriate and yields four facts that contradict Murray: (1) welfare is used for short, not long, periods of time; (2) while receiving welfare most people do work; (3) welfare dependency is not passed from generation to generation; and (4) increases in welfare benefits are not related to increases in births, divorces, marriages, or remarriages. Coe and Duncan conclude that welfare programs provide "an indispensable safety net in a dynamic society."

For a more detailed investigation, see: *Losing Ground* (Basic, 1984) and *Years of Poverty, Years of Plenty* (University of Michigan, 1984). The conservative position is presented in "Government and the Rich," by Yale Brozen, in *National Review* (July 1982) and in *Free to Choose* (HBJ, 1980), by Milton and Rose Friedman. For the liberal position, try Robert Greenstein's "Losing Faith in 'Losing Ground,' " *The New Republic* (March 25, 1985). Detailed poverty statistics are published annually by the Department of Commerce and are available through the Government Printing Office.

ISSUE 14

Can Federal Budget Deficits Be Good for the Economy?

YES: Robert Eisner, from "Will the Real Federal Deficit Stand Up?" *Challenge* (May-June 1986)

NO: Paul Wonnacott, from "The Nominal Deficit Really Matters," *Challenge* (September-October 1986)

ISSUE SUMMARY

YES: Economist Eisner believes that to correctly measure the impact of the deficit on the economy, the budget figures must be adjusted for changes in output or employment and inflation. This measure is the adjusted high-employment budget. Using this measure Eisner argues that the recession of 1981–82 was partly the result of "relatively tight fiscal policy" while the subsequent recovery was due to a switch from contractionary to expansionary fiscal policy. His analysis also suggests that an effort to achieve a conventionally measured balanced budget would cause a severe recession.

NO: Economist Paul Wonnacott accepts Eisner's point that to measure correctly the thrust of fiscal policy the budget deficit needs to be adjusted for the level of unemployment. But he rejects the idea that there should be further adjustment for inflation. Adjusting the budget for inflation may give the wrong signals to the policy makers and may be destabilizing. Finally he notes that, although it may not be necessary to eliminate the current deficit completely, if there is not a significant reduction in the deficit, then the long run stability of the economy is endangered.

The Full Employment and Balanced Growth Act of 1978 lists a number of economic goals for the federal government. Besides the familiar objectives of full employment, price stability, and increased real income, the act specifically mentions the goal of a balanced federal budget. This means the federal government is to collect taxes in an amount equal to its expenditures. Despite this legislative call to action, the federal government has failed to balance its budget, and recent deficits have been of record proportions. For example, for the years 1940 through 1975, there were only two instances when the deficit was in excess of $50 billion: 1944 and 1975. For the years 1980 through 1986 the federal government deficit has averaged $146 billion, reaching a record high of more than $200 billion in 1986.

When the federal government runs a deficit it sells securities: treasury bills, notes, and bonds. In this respect the government is just like any business that sells securities to raise funds. The total of outstanding government securities is called the public debt. Thus when the federal government runs a deficit the public debt increases by the amount of the deficit. In this fashion the public debt is a summary of all prior deficits (offset by the retirement of securities if the government chooses to repurchase its securities when it has a surplus). By the end of 1986 the total public debt was approximately $2.3 trillion. This debt is owned by (been purchased by) different groups, including individuals, commercial banks, life insurance companies, pension funds, federal government agencies, state and local governments, and corporations. Some securities are also sold to foreign individuals, businesses, and governments.

There are two major questions to be considered regarding federal government deficits and debt. The first question concerns the causes of the deficit. One possibility is that the government spends more than it collects in revenues because it does not exercise fiscal restraint. That is, it is easy for politicians to spend more money but difficult for them to increase taxes to fund this increased spending. No elected official wants to be attacked in a bid for reelection as someone who increased taxes. But the budget position of the government is also influenced by the state of the economy. The deficit is likely to increase if the economy enters a recession. A downturn in economic activity will decrease tax revenues (lower incomes means less income tax revenues) and will increase government spending (more expenditures for such programs as unemployment compensation). Because a deficit can arise for different reasons, it is important to understand exactly what forces create a deficit.

The second major question about the deficit concerns the economic consequences of deficits and increasing public debt. There are those who perceive deficits as always harmful. With a deficit the government borrows funds that would otherwise have been available to business firms who would have built new factories and purchased new machinery with the borrowed funds. This is referred to as "crowding out" since government deficits crowd out private investment and thereby slow productivity. These same individuals note that public debt is like private debt and must be repaid. This implies that deficits impose a burden on future generations.

In what sense can deficits be beneficial? If the deficit is caused by a recession, the deficit may minimize the fall in output and income; that is, increased government spending is a substitute for decreased spending in some other sector of the economy. And if the deficit involves spending that improves the environment, then future generations will benefit from a current deficit.

In the two readings that follow the basic disagreements regarding the effects of deficits are resurrected. But Eisner and Wonnacott add a new dimension to the debate: how should the deficit and the debt be measured. To get an accurate reading of the causes and effects of the deficits, Eisner believes that the actual deficits need to be corrected for changes in the state of the economy and for inflation. Wonnacott accepts the first correction but believes that to focus on the real deficit (the deficit corrected for inflation) creates significant problems. As for current policy, they reach opposite conclusions. Eisner sees real problems if the budget were to be balanced while Wonnacott foresees a dim economic future if efforts are not made to cut the deficit in half.

YES

Robert Eisner

WILL THE REAL FEDERAL DEFICIT STAND UP?

In some circles, the federal budget deficit has become the hottest political issue since Vietnam. Democrats and Republicans echo each others' proclamations of disaster and largely restrict their differences to proposed remedies and the casting of blame. Scoring political points has replaced almost all efforts at sober economic analysis.

Deficits do matter, but to know how and how much, you have to measure them right. And deficits can be good as well as bad. . . .

DEFICITS AND THE ECONOMY

But how can we measure the effects of deficits on the economy? Do they cause inflation or recession? Do they reduce unemployment or crowd out investment? Do they stifle economic growth or stimulate it? Do they increase our foreign debt and wreck our balance of trade, or do they contribute to world prosperity?

A simple, naive approach would be to relate the federal deficit to some of the broad aggregates in which we are interested. We might check the correlations among deficits and GNP, business investment, or the rates of unemployment or inflation. The difficulty, a common one in economics, is especially serious here: we cannot distinguish between cause and effect.

The problem is that the economy affects the deficit, perhaps as much as or more than the deficit can be expected to affect the economy. When economic conditions are good, incomes, profits, and employment are high. Treasury receipts, tied as they are to individual and business income taxes and payroll taxes on employment, are hence high. Further, government expenditures for unemployment benefits and welfare payments will be less when the economy is prosperous.

The combination of higher tax receipts and lower expenditures means a lower deficit. But it is clearly the high GNP, income, profits and employment that have caused the low deficit, and not the reverse. Since high rates of

From "Will the Real Federal Deficit Stand Up?" by Robert Eisner, *Challenge*, May/June 1986. Copyright © 1986. Reprinted with permission of M.E. Sharpe, Inc., publishers, Armonk, NY 10504.

saving and investment generally accompany high GNP, incomes, and profits, they too would be associated with smaller deficits. The interference that the smaller deficits brought on the higher saving and investment would be similarly unwarranted.

The inverse relation between deficits and inflation is somewhat more complex. At first blush it might appear that inflation would have a neutral effect on the deficit. While higher prices would mean larger nominal incomes and hence greater tax payments to the Treasury, the government would also have to pay more for what it buys. If federal salaries and Social Security benefits are indexed to the cost of living, we might conclude that expenditures and receipts would both be increased by inflation and the deficit therefore not changed.

There are, however, a number of complications. First, income taxes historically have risen more, proportionately, than increase in income brought on by inflation. This has happened because of the notorious "bracket creep"—inflation has pushed more of income into taxable brackets and into higher brackets with higher tax rates. . . .

Inflation also brings about more-than-proportionate increases on the expenditure side. These stem from the higher interest rates and hence greater Treasury interest payments as inflation expectations take hold.

In the past, bracket-creep effects of higher prices were such that inflation tended on balance to reduce deficits. But such an association of higher inflation and lower deficits does *not* imply the inverse relation—that deficits reduce inflation.

Actual budget deficits are therefore not a good measure of fiscal policy. The administration and the Congress might be following a tight fiscal policy, keeping discretionary expenditures down and tax rates up, and yet a recession would create a substantial deficit. Indeed the tight fiscal policy, by depressing aggregate demand, might bring on such a recession.

THE HIGH-EMPLOYMENT BUDGET

To ascertain what deficits do to the economy, we need a measure that is uncontaminated by what the economy does to deficits. Economists have been able to develop one that removes some of the contamination—brought on by cyclical fluctuations in income and employment. It has been variously called the full-employment, high-employment, standardized-employment, cyclical adjusted, and structural budget.

Whatever its name, the important thing about this budget is that it presents estimates of what expenditures and receipts, and hence the deficit, *would be* if the economy were at a level of activity independent of cyclical variations in employment, output, and income. Since the cyclical variations in output and income are closely associated with those of employment and unemployment, the budget has usually been defined for a constant rate of unemployment. . . .

The comparison of actual and high-employment budgets is intriguing. From 1955 to 1965 the actual budget was in deficit five times and in surplus six. The high-employment budget was never in deficit. When the actual budget was in surplus, the high-employment budget was more so. All this reflected the fact that actual unemployment was more than the high-employment rate over this period. Hence, actual tax revenues were

Table 1

High-Employment Surplus as Percentage of GNP, 1955–84

Year	Official	Adjusted for price effects	Adjusted for interest effects	Adjusted for price and interest effects	Percent change in GNP
		Percentage of GNP			
(1)	(2)	(3)	(4)	(5)	(6)
1955	1.30	2.81	2.26	3.77	6.72
1956	1.87	3.83	2.79	4.74	2.14
1957	1.37	2.46	0.11	1.20	1.82
1958	0.00	0.93	1.32	2.24	−0.42
1959	1.11	2.09	1.96	2.94	5.99
1960	2.39	2.83	0.45	0.89	2.15
1061	1.35	1.99	1.81	2.45	2.63
1962	0.53	1.28	0.12	0.87	5.78
1963	1.24	1.79	1.70	2.25	4.02
1964	0.17	0.78	0.12	0.72	5.27
1965	0.13	0.98	0.58	1.43	6.04
1966	−0.74	0.33	−0.97	0.11	5.97
1967	−1.89	−0.89	−1.33	−0.34	2.70
1968	−1.26	0.06	−1.14	0.18	4.62
1969	0.52	1.94	1.32	2.74	2.79
1970	−0.46	0.77	−1.87	−0.64	−0.18
1971	−1.05	0.11	−1.41	−0.25	3.39
1972	−1.02	0.02	−0.66	0.39	5.66
1973	−0.72	0.89	−0.46	1.14	5.77
1974	−0.02	2.15	−0.16	2.01	−0.64
1975	−1.88	−0.38	−2.04	−0.54	−1.18
1976	−1.01	0.22	−1.75	−0.52	5.41
1977	−1.06	0.46	−0.23	1.30	5.51
1978	−0.73	1.26	0.15	2.15	5.03
1979	−0.08	1.72	0.11	1.91	2.84
1980	−0.65	1.45	−0.13	1.97	−0.30
1981	−0.11	1.57	−0.23	1.45	2.52
1982	−1.06	0.02	−3.10	−2.01	−2.13
1983	−1.72	−1.66	−0.44	−0.62	3.70
1984	−2.51	−1.36	−3.07	−1.92	6.78

Sources: Frank de Leeuw and Thomas M. Holloway, "The High Employment Budget: Revised Estimates and Automatic Inflation Effects," *Survey of Current Business,* 62 (April 1982), pp. 21–33, subsequent issues of the *Survey of Current Business, Economic Report of the President, February 1985,* author's adjustments to maintain a 5.1 percent base for "high employment" in 1983 and 1984, and author's calculations explained in *How Real Is the Federal Deficit?* with deficit figures for 1983 and 1984 revised downward from those published there.
Note: Surplus or deficit (-) on national-income-accounts basis.

less while government expenditures were more.

From 1966 to 1969, with the boom aggregate demand produced by the Vietnam War, actual unemployment was less than the 4 percent rate associated with high employment. (That is an interesting commentary on our view of "high employment" even then. Quite ignoring the Humphrey-Hawkins Full Employment and Balanced Growth Act, we now cheerfully project unemployment in the 6 and 7 percent range.) The low unemployment of those years caused the three actual deficits to be *less* than the deficit associated with high employment and the 1969 surplus to be greater.

The 1970s ushered in the era of unrelenting federal deficits. For none of the last sixteen years has the budget been balanced, let alone in surplus. Those who saw deficits as evidence of unbridled government spending contributing to inflation seemed to have some support for their views. Inflation rose through most of the decade of the seventies, peaking in 1981. But then, as deficits soared to unprecedented heights in 1982, inflation rates dropped precipitously.

The deficits were widely interpreted, nevertheless, as evidence of expansionist fiscal policy. Richard Nixon had said in 1972, "We are all Keynesians now." If the Keynesian analysis, which had presumably come to dominate policymaking, were correct, should not unemployment have been low and the economy sizzling? In fact, unemployment was inching up and the economy was sluggish. What was wrong?

One try at an answer was that it was the actual budget that was showing repeated and generally growing deficits. As we have observed, these deficits may have been essentially the product of poor economic conditions, rather than their cause. We may point, for example, to the then-record deficit of $69 billion in 1975. Clearly that was largely the result of the sharp 1974–75 recession. Unemployment, after all, averaged 8.5 percent in 1975. If we had looked at the high-employment budget might we have had a different picture?

But now comes the shocker. The high-employment budget deficit was less than the actual deficit throughout the 1970s and into the 1980s, but it too was never quite balanced, coming close only in 1974. Indeed, in 1975 the high-employment deficits seemed generally to be getting larger, not smaller. . . .

DEFICITS ADJUSTED FOR INFLATION

We come now to our critical departure. We must adjust deficits for inflation. The real surplus or deficit may be viewed as essentially the sum of three components: (1) the nominal surplus or deficit as currently measured; (2) an adjustment for changes in the market value of government financial assets and liabilities due to changes in interest rates; and (3) an adjustment for changes in real value due to changing general price levels incident to inflation. An identical or analogous set of adjustments is appropriate for the high-employment budget surplus or deficit.

We can then calculate the adjusted high-employment budgets, which, by correcting for these inflation effects, come closer to measuring real surpluses or deficits and the consequent thrust of fiscal policy on aggregate demand. Applying our calculations of net revaluations on actual net federal debt, we originally adjusted the official high-employment budget surplus series for the years 1955 through 1981. Maintaining the 5.1 percent unemployment benchmark for high employment in effect in the official series since 1975, we have now extended our calculations to 1984.

The results, shown in Table 1, are dramatic. Inflation and rates of interest were low and relatively steady in the early 1960s prior to escalation of our military involvement in Vietnam. Corrections to the official high-employment budget surplus are hence generally small in those early years.

But in later, more inflationary years, when the official high-employment budget as well as the actual budget moved substantially into deficit, the corrections are striking. In the 1970s, the entire perceived trend in the direction of fiscal ease or expansion is eliminated or reversed. The high-employment budget surplus, fully adjusted for price and interest effects, was higher as a percent of GNP for every year from 1977 through 1981 than the surplus of all but two of the years from 1966 through 1976. The only exceptions were the tax-surcharge year of 1969 and the oil-price-shock year of 1974.

With similar exceptions, the surplus adjusted only for price (and not interest) effects was higher in every year from 1978 to 1981 than in any other year back to 1963. And since we have accepted Bureau of Economic Analysis increases in the "high-employment" bench mark from 4.0 percent to 5.1 percent unemployment over the period of its "official" series, we may well understate the move to fiscal tightness. The high-employment surpluses would have been even greater in later years if calculated at 4.0 percent unemployment.

NEW LIGHT ON ECONOMIC HISTORY

So some significant rewriting of recent economic history is in order. Inflation could hardly be ascribed to excess demand associated with increasing fiscal ease and stimulus if, at least by the appropriately corrected high-employment budget measure, there was no such movement to fiscal ease. Some explanation of sluggishness in the economy, climaxed by the severe 1981-82 recession, might then be found in a relatively tight fiscal policy, as measured by the adjusted high-employment budget surplus, as well as in the widely blamed (or credited) role of monetary policy.

The record of deficits beginning in 1982 is another matter. We shall come to that later. For now we want to show the relation of budget deficits to the economy. And we will find that prevailing views reflect the distortions of improper measures, the most important of which, again, are those tricks played by the effects of inflation.

A few charts can begin to set the record straight and tell a dramatic new story. . . .

What about the relation between budget deficits and the economy? A single picture may be worth a thousand words, or as many statistics. Figure 1 juxtaposes the percentage change in real GNP and the previous year's price-adjusted high-employment deficit as a percentage of real GNP.

The two curves, it must be conceded, show a remarkable fit. The greater the deficit, the greater the next year's increase in GNP. The less the deficit, the less the increase or the greater the decline in the next year's GNP.

Changes in real GNP, as is well

Figure 1

Lagged Price-Adjusted High-Employment Deficit and Change in GNP

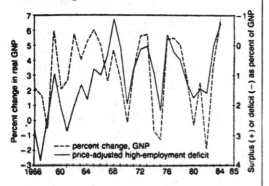

der a substantial amount of more vigorous statistical analysis, reported in my new book, *How Real Is the Federal Deficit?* That analysis indicates that monetary policy, as measured by changes in the monetary base, also affects rates of growth of gross national product and unemployment. The independent effect of budget deficits remains substantial, however, probably greater (when the deficit is adjusted for inflation) than effects of changes in the monetary base.

Budget deficits are found to be positively associated not only with increases in consumption but also with increases in investment. Deficits in the past have generally "crowded in" investment, not crowded it out. There is evidence as well, however, that budget deficits have contributed to the increase in our trade deficit, particularly in their association with substantial increases in imports. It

known, are closely but inversely related to changes in unemployment. Production requires labor, and the more people working the greater the output. When unemployment goes up, real GNP growth slackens or actually becomes negative. When unemployment goes down, GNP goes up. And the faster unemployment goes down, the faster GNP rises.

In view of the relation between the deficit and GNP, we should thus expect a similar close, but inverse, relation between the deficit and changes in unemployment. Figure 2 confirms this. Converting the inverse relation with the deficit into a direct one, it plots the percentage-point change in unemployment and the *previous* year's ratio of the price-adjusted high-employment *surplus* (the negative of the deficit).

The close fit of the two curves is again outstanding. Higher surpluses—or lower deficits—are associated with greater increases or smaller decreases in unemployment.

This relation indicating the stimulative effect of budget deficits has held up un-

Figure 2

Lagged Price-Adjusted High-Employment Surplus and Change in Unemployment

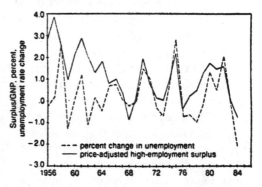

should be added that these increases in our imports have in turn stimulated growth in output in our OECD partners. And it may be added, finally, that, after adjustment for inflation, it turns out that

Japan had the greatest deficits in recent years along with the fastest growth. And the very slow-growing United Kingdom had substantial budget surpluses after inflation adjustment.

THE IMPACT OF THE DEFICIT

Where does all this leave us? The officially reported federal debt has been growing at astronomical rates. Since President Reagan took office in 1981 the gross public debt has more than doubled, from $930 billion to $1.9 trillion. The increase has reflected huge and repeated annual deficits, reaching $212 billion in fiscal 1985.

But this has not all been bad! Indeed, given the economic collapse of 1981–82, smaller deficits would have made the deep recession worse. Unemployment would have risen above the official 10.7 percent figure, which has already the highest since the Great Depression of the 1930s. Total production and business profits would have been less. Without the huge deficits, we would not have had the brisk recovery of 1983 and 1984. And the 1984 election results—for good or for ill—might well have been quite different.

Up to about 1966, when inflation was relatively minor, budget deficits were really budget deficits. In the period from 1966 on, however, when inflation became substantial, the officially balanced budget turned into one of surplus after inflation corrections were made. A balanced, inflation-adjusted, high-employment budget would have been substantially expansionary, producing high rates of growth of GNP and declines in unemployment. As late as 1981, however, we had a roughly balanced *official* high-employment budget, while the budget adjusted for inflation was substantially in surplus.

The Carter administration, which, along with most outside critics, ignored indications of sluggishness in the economy, interpreted the combination of apparent deficits and inflation as indicating excess demand. It initiated moves to combat inflation by encouraging a tight-money policy and, in its final years, striving to reduce budget deficits. This policy continued through the first year of the Reagan administration, as domestic spending was further restrained and more taxes rose than declined.

But in fact, fiscal policy was not stimulative. The high inflation and rising interest rates meant that budgets seemingly in deficit were actually in substantial surplus. Our statistical relations indicate strongly that these inflation-adjusted surpluses contributed significantly to the 1981–83 recession.

This suggests two important correctives to wide-spread views of fiscal and monetary policy. First, the 1981–83 recession cannot properly be interpreted as a triumph of all-powerful monetary constraints over relatively ineffective fiscal ease. Tight monetary policy *and* tight fiscal policy were its proximate causes.

Thus, those who acquiesced in tight money as the only way to slow a presumedly overheated, inflationary economy were wrong on two counts. First, the inflation had come from supply shocks—with critical energy prices up some 500 percent in a decade—rather than excess demand, an inference reinforced by the absence of real increases in fiscal thrust. And second, strong-willed rejection of accommodative monetary policy, rather than balancing budget excesses, offered a near-lethal combination of monetary and fiscal contraction.

But fiscal policy moved in a sharply different direction in 1982. A combination of major tax cuts and increases in military expenditures with a fall in inflation and interest rates converted the adjusted high-employment budget from a very high surplus to a very high deficit. Indeed, the change of 3.46 percentage points, from a surplus of 1.45 percent of GNP in 1981 to a deficit of 2.01 percent in 1982, was one of the greatest such swings to expansion on record. Our estimate of relations between budget deficits and changes in GNP and unemployment predicted a major swing to economic recovery and lower unemployment in 1983 and on into 1984, and that is of course precisely what occurred. . . .

A NEW LOOK AT DEFICITS

Once we get over the notion that deficits are automatically sinful, and once we learn to measure them right, a lot of the easy answers have to be rejected. It is not true that deficits must always be reduced. The current mix of fiscal and monetary policy, with high real interest rates and a huge trade imbalance accountable to an expensive dollar, is far from ideal. Our budget priorities may be all wrong. But it is hard to sustain the knee-jerk reaction that wiping out all the overall official deficit will solve our problems.

The public has feared that budget deficits add to their own debt burden and that of future generations. What we really bequeath to the future, however, is our physical and human capital. A "deficit" that finances the construction and maintenance of our roads, bridges, harbors, and airports is an investment in the future. So are expenditures to preserve and enhance our natural resources or to educate our people and keep them healthy. Federal budgets that are balanced by running down our country's capital or mindlessly selling public assets to private exploiters are real national deficits.

As for that bottom line on what to do about the current federal deficit—it depends. If we were to carry out the projections of the fiscal 1986 Joint Congressional Budget Resolution, and we are seriously committed to a high-employment economy, we would probably have gone far enough in overall budget cutting. The increase in debt for the last five years has been such that even our slower rate of inflation generates a substantial inflation tax. The inflation tax rate is less, but the public debt on which it is paid is more.

Inflation-adjusted budget deficits, on the basis of the budget resolution projections, did not promise to be unduly large. For those who prize economic growth and low unemployment, the risk of insufficient fiscal stimulus must be weighted heavily. One cannot properly counsel budget-balancing in an economy with unemployment still at 7 percent and real economic growth well below its potential. A budget balanced by current federal rules of accounting is an invitation to the worst economic downturn in half a century.

The budget mix is another matter. We may wish to spend more on investment in our public infrastructure and human capital and less on subsidies and support to those with the most political clout. We may also wish to devote more to our nation's welfare and less to warfare. And we may wish to finance our expenditures with a more equitable tax system.

With a sound and balanced fiscal policy, we should look all the more to a monetary policy that permits the economy to move at full speed. No artificial shortage of money should be allowed to drag down private investment or so distort the value of the dollar as to cripple the significant sectors of the American economy that do and should compete in world markets.

A competitive, market-oriented economy is capable of stunning successes. But there remains a major role for government policy to ensure the aggregate demand necessary for full employment and maximum growth. With correct measures, the macroeconomic theory of the past half century can continue to show the way.

NO

Paul Wonnacott

THE NOMINAL DEFICIT REALLY MATTERS

Together with tax reform, the budget deficit is one of the hottest economic topics in Washington. The passage of the Gramm-Rudman-Hollings bill represented a decision by Congress to go beyond the traditional denunciations of deficits, and commit itself (more or less) to a steady reduction in the $200 billion deficit. In a recent article in *Challenge* (May-June 1986), Robert Eisner has forcefully argued that Gramm-Rudman-Hollings not only represents mistaken policy, but is built on a fundamental misunderstanding of what deficits mean.

Specifically, Eisner argues: (1) The government's budgetary calculations are misleading; (2) To get an accurate basis for developing fiscal policy, accounting methods should be changed to adjust for two sources of distortion: (a) the effects of cyclical swings in economic activity on the budget, particularly the effect that recessions have in causing a fall in tax revenues and therefore an increase in deficits; and (b) the effects of inflation on the outstanding debt.

Eisner's complaint about the misleading nature of budgetary calculations is well taken. So is the first proposed solution (a)—one that has already been widely accepted with the use of the cyclically adjusted budget measure. Furthermore, these points are so important—and so often ignored in the current political debate over deficits—that I am reluctant to criticize his article. However, his major innovation (b)—to argue that the budgetary calculations should be adjusted for inflation—represents no improvement. Rather than contributing to stability, it would increase the chances of destabilizing policies.

Eisner correctly points out that inflation reduces the real value of outstanding debt—conspicuously so in a period of double-digit inflation such as 1979–80. He then proposes that the budget be adjusted for inflation, so that deficits would be shown only when the *real* value of the debt is growing. (An increase in the nominal size of the debt is associated with nominal deficits; similarly, an increase in the real size of the debt would be counted as a real deficit.) Thus, if the national debt were to double in nominal terms during a

From "The Nominal Deficit Really Matters," by Paul Wonnacott, *Challenge*, September/October 1986. Copyright © 1986. Reprinted with permission of M.E. Sharpe, Inc., publishers, Armonk, NY 10504.

period when prices doubled, the real size of the debt would be constant; the real budget would be considered in balance.

REAL MAGNITUDES: A TRAP FOR THE POLICYMAKER

Unfortunately, focusing on the real budget would invite destabilizing fiscal policies. Consider what happens during a period of high and rising inflation. The real value of the debt tends to decline—as it did during the Carter years. The budget, according to Eisner's inflation-adjusted measurement, swings into surplus. If the government were to follow the Eisner budget, it would figure that the surpluses were acting as a drag on the economy: the apparent solution would be more spending or a cut in taxes. But additional government spending or tax cuts would add to inflationary pressures.

Similarly, focusing on what is happening to the real debt could lead to trouble during a deflation, such as that of 1929–33. During that period, prices fell almost 25 percent. As a combined result of nominal deficits and falling prices, the real value of the outstanding national debt soared by almost 100 percent. In other words, the real budget moved more sharply into deficit than did the standard budget actually used by the government (unadjusted for inflation). Thus, if the government had used inflation-adjusted budgetary calculations, it might have tried even more vigorously to reduce the deficit. The tax increase of 1932—one of the two major policy blunders of the Great Depression—might have been even larger. More disposable income would have been extracted from the taxpaying public, and the depression would have been even worse.

The major point—that the government may destabilize the economy if it concentrates on real magnitudes—is also true of monetary policy. An attempt to stabilize the real quantity of money could lead to disaster. Consider what happened during the wild German inflation of the early 1920s, caused by the reckless printing of money. The public became eager to spend money quickly, before it lost its value. As a result, prices rose even more rapidly than the quantity of money; that is, the *real* quantity of money fell. If the German government had looked at the declining real quantity of money, it might have come to exactly the wrong conclusion—that there was too little money, when in fact there was much too much. . . .

In brief, the real budget is a poor guide for fiscal policy; the real quantity of money is likewise a poor guide for monetary policy.

REAL AND NOMINAL MAGNITUDES: WHAT'S THE QUESTION?

To show that the real budget is dangerous measure is not, however, to demonstrate that it should never be used. Nor does it demonstrate that the real size of the debt is unimportant. Real magnitudes are important—to answer *some* questions.

At least four issues arise when a proposed budgetary policy is being considered:

1. Will it add to the short-run stability of the economy? That is, will it reduce the severity of business cycles?

2. In the longer run, will it contribute to the desirable trend of aggregate demand?

3. In the longer run, will it contribute to the best composition of output?

4. In the long run, what will be the effects of changes in the government's debt?

In each of these cases, is it better to start with the real or the nominal deficit? The answer to the first has already been given: start with the nominal, cyclically adjusted budget. How about the other three?

The clearest case for using real measures occurs when we look at long-run effects (issue 4). Insofar as we are worried about the burden of the debt to our grandchildren, we should be concerned primarily with the real debt (and therefore, with the size of current real deficits rather than nominal deficits). Furthermore, as Eisner so rightly points out, it is not only the size of the national debt that counts. It is also the fraction of the debt owned by foreign nations—a point worth particular note in light of the recent swing of the United States from a large creditor to a large debtor position.

Nevertheless, even when dealing with the future burden of the debt, we should be careful. Why is a big national debt a problem? One standard answer is that it will create financial strains, and push the central bank into an inflationary monetization of the debt. To the extent that prices are already rising, we are already suffering inflationary consequences; the fact that they are occurring now rather than in the future is cold comfort. Furthermore, even when we are "inflating away" the national debt, this is something that cannot be done without cost. The high current rates of interest may not only be a reflection of the market pressures created by current deficits, but also a delayed reaction of bondholders to the events of the past two decades. They

were devastated by the inflation and negative real interest rates of the 1970s. They are understandably reluctant to buy bonds now, without an interest rate padded to protect them against a repeat.

Although it is still asked with some frequency, the second question is not very sensible. A wide range of fiscal policies—measured either in real or nominal terms—is consistent with a moderate growth trend in aggregate demand, provided that appropriate adjustments are made in monetary policy. Thus, once we have in mind the demand trend we would like to see, the question is not so much what fiscal policy is needed to get there (issue 2), but what mix of monetary and fiscal policies is best (issue 3). The stronger our desire for a high-investment, high-growth path, the more we should lean toward monetary ease and fiscal restraint. Like many of us, Eisner would like to see an adjustment in the current mix, toward more fiscal restraint and monetary ease. But, paradoxically, his proposal for a real deficit measure would make such an adjustment more difficult. Using real rather than nominal accounting would cut the measured deficit, and reduce the pressures for fiscal restraint.

REAL AND NOMINAL MAGNITUDES: WHO'S ASKING?

With the acceleration of inflation during the 1970s, the question of whether accounts should be kept in nominal or real terms became increasingly important. This was true—often in a vague and general way—of households. People wondered if their old life insurance policies were still adequate, and houses became an attractive buy even at interest rates of 10 percent or more. Likewise, businesses began, at least tentatively, to experiment with real bookkeeping. The results often came as a shock. For example, in 1979, AT&T recalculated its profits in real terms, finding them to be less than half the nominal amount. For 1980, Bethlehem Steel found that, when account was taken of inflation, its reported profit of $121 million became a *loss* of approximately $200 million. For a company looking to the future, real losses had to be a source of concern—they raised problems about the firm's long-run viability, unless performance could be substantially improved. For a business concerned with the bottom-line question, "How are we doing?" real accounting represented an important innovation.

But, while it makes a lot of sense for individuals or businesses to engage in real accounting, it makes much less sense for the government. Firms and individuals *respond to* an inflationary environment; their problem is to figure out how they are doing, and how to protect themselves against an erosion of their assets. But the government (including the central bank) is fundamentally different. It does not simply respond to inflation; rather it is *responsible for* inflation. If it keeps its accounts in real terms, it risks making inflation worse during inflationary times, and deflationary worse during periods of depression.

THE STARTING POINT FOR FISCAL POLICY

If Eisner's recommendation for real accounting is so problematic, why is his first point correct? Why are current budgetary calculations misleading? What's wrong with aiming for a balanced budget, using present accounting pro-

cedures? The difficulty is that the balanced-budget target is based implicitly on the assumption of a no-growth economy, and on the assumption that zero inflation is best. In such a world, any large, continuing growth of the national debt would cause it to become larger and larger relative to the economy, with greater and greater distorting effects.

But, of course, we live in an economy with a long-run growth trend of something like 3 percent. Furthermore, zero inflation is not necessarily best. Our understanding of the lower reaches of the long-run Phillips curve is far from complete; there are reasons for believing that a *slow* rate of inflation—of 1 to 2 percent per year—will result in the most stable and prosperous economy. Thus, an increase of something like 5 percent in the nominal quantity of government debt is consistent with long-run stability and the meeting of growth and inflation objectives. The debt can rise by 5 percent indefinitely into the future, without rising as a proportion of GNP and without becoming more and more unmanageable.

With an outstanding debt of roughly $2 trillion, this implies that the first $100 billion of deficit raises no problems of long-run stability and sustainability. Thus, a deficit of $100 billion might be taken as our initial objective in designing policy. (It is appropriate to let the debt grow in line with our long-run inflation *target*, but not—as Eisner would suggest—in line with *actual* inflation. The latter is destabilizing; the former is not. Again, the point may be seen most simply by an analogy with monetary policy. An increase of, say, 5 percent in the appropriately defined nominal quantity of money may result in a continuing, moderate inflation, but it is not dynamically unstable. A target of increasing the real money stock by 5 percent would be destabilizing; it would lead the Federal Reserve to evermore rapid increases in the nominal quantity of money during periods of accelerating inflation.)

Once we reach the $100 billion goal, we may want to go further, and reduce the deficit even more, in order to promote capital formation, growth, and a more balanced international trading position. I, for one, would favor such a move. But we should make any such decision in a calm and reasoned atmosphere, free of fiscal panic. With a deficit of $200 billion, there is cause for concern about the long-run stability of the system. But we do not need to *eliminate* the deficit; we only have to cut it down to size. The second $100 billion represents a big problem. The first $100 billion does not.

Finally, Eisner's work, and the controversy surrounding it, dramatize an important point. One of the problems with inflation is the information problem that it creates: the government may have great difficulty figuring out what is going on, and what policy actions are best.

POSTSCRIPT

Can Federal Government Budget Deficits Be Good for the Economy?

Economist Eisner argues that the state of the economy has a significant impact on the budget position of the government: a recession tends to create a defitict or or increase an existing deficit while inflation tends to eliminate or reduce a deficit. As a consequence it is necessary to use the high-employment budget adjusted for inflation to obtain an accurate measure of fiscal policy—the effects of federal government spending and taxation on the economy. Using his measure of fiscal policy, Eisner concludes that the recession of 1981–1982 was not just the result of contractionary monetary policy, the conventional interpretation, but of contractionary fiscal policy as well. He also states that his measure of fiscal policy indicates that the vigorous recovery of 1983 and 1984 was the result of a significant switch from contractionary to expansionary fiscal policy. His analysis suggests that federal government deficits stimulate consumption and investment, rather than crowding out private expenditures. Government deficits can also benefit future generations as well as present generations by providing future generations with more and better bridges, roads, harbors, and airports. As for current policy Eisner is unequivocal in his opposition to measuring the budget position and the fiscal policy of the government uncorrected for the state of the economy and inflation: "A budget balanced by current rules of accounting is an invitation to the worst economic downturn in half a century."

Wonnacott agrees with Eisner that in order to obtain an accurate measure of the thrust of fiscal policy, the actual budget of the federal government needs to be adjusted for the level of economic activity. But he disagrees with Eisner regarding the necessity of a further adjustment for the rate of inflation. Measuring the budget in real terms rather than nominal terms might lead policy makers into even larger policy mistakes. He uses the Great Depression as an example. During the Great Depression the real deficit, because of deflation or falling prices, increased more than the nominal

deficit. The policy makers who were making a mistake in raising taxes in an effort to balance the budget would have raised taxes even more if they were reacting to the real budget. "The tax increase of 1932—one of the two major policy blunders of the Great Depression—might have been even larger." As for present policy, Wonnacott believes the emphasis on the real deficit may again contribute to improper policy. What is needed is easier monetary policy and tighter fiscal policy. An emphasis on the real deficit (currently less than the nominal deficit) decreases the possibility of achieving the proper policy mix for it "reduces the pressure for fiscal restraint." To avoid the problems of crowding out and inflation, and to create conditions for long run growth, the debt should rise by about 5 percent per year. According to Wonnacott this means that the $200 billion nominal deficit of 1986 needs to be cut in half.

Much of Eisner analysis is based on his book *How Real is the Federal Deficit?* (The Free Press, 1986). Other interesting books include *The Deficit Dilemma* by Gregory B. Mills and John L. Palmer (The Urban Institute Press, 1983) and *Federal Budget Deficits* by Paul N. Courant and Edward M. Gramlich (Prentice-Hall, 1986). An interesting article assessing the consequences of the deficits of the 1980s has been written by John A. Tatom, "Two Views of the Effects of Government Budget Deficits in the 1960s" (*Review,* Federal Reserve Bank of St. Louis, October 1985). For contrasting views on the need for a constitutional amendment to balance the budget, see "Less Red Ink" by Milton Friedman (*The Atlantic,* February 1983) and "You Can't Balance the Budget by Amendment" by Gardner Ackley (*Challenge,* November/December 1982). Interesting articles on the Gramm-Rudman deficit reduction bill include those by Paula Dwyer, "Showdown Time for Gramm-Rudman" (*Business Week,* January 20, 1986); by Howard Gleckman, "The Budget Is Congress' Problem Again" (*Business Week,* July 21, 1986); by Paul Davidson, "Can We Afford to Balance the Budget?" (*New Leader,* January 13, 1986); and by Andy Plattner, Kenneth T. Walsh and Kathryn Johnson, "After Court's Ruling, What Happens to the Budget Now?" (*U.S. News & World Report,* February 17, 1986).

ISSUE 15
Did Monetary Policy Cause the Stock Market Crash of 1987?

YES: Paul Craig Roberts, from " . . . Too Tight Already," *The Wall Street Journal* (October 22, 1987)

NO: James K. Glassman, from "Where Did It All Go?" *The New Republic* (November 9, 1987)

ISSUE SUMMARY

YES: Economist Roberts believes that the stock market crash was caused by the tight monetary policy of the Federal Reserve System. Between December 1986 and October 1987 the Federal Reserve did not allow the money supply to expand. The combination of a constant money supply and a growing economy caused an increase in interest rates. As a consequence investors became pessimistic and sold their stock: "The market understood rising interest rates would wreck the economy and sold off."

NO: Glassman states that in October 1987 the stock market was overvalued: in the year up to the crash, price-to-earnings ratios had risen dramatically and dividend yields were at "one of the lowest levels ever seen in history." Although it's unclear why investors' attitudes changed, the fact remains that the crash represented a return to more realistic, more reasonable stock prices.

In 1929 it was "Black Thursday." In 1987 it was "Black Monday" or, for those who prefer alliteration, "Monstrous Monday." These were days that marked an amazing transformation, when bulls became bears, and economic shock waves raced throughout the world. In the days after October 24, 1929 and October 19, 1987 everyone seemed mesmerized by the stock market. Two questions were asked over and over again. Why did the stock market crash? What would happen next?

As for the stock market crash of 1929, there is the historical record. From its high in September of 1929 to its low in November, the *New York Times* index of 25 leading industrial stocks fell over 200 points, from 452 to 224. A market worth $80 billion in September of 1929 was reduced to a value of $50 billion two months later. By 1932, in the depths of the Great Depression, the market was worth less than $16 billion.

What caused the crash of 1929? Why did the bulls suddenly become bears; that is, why did investor attitudes change from optimistic to pessimistic? Some argue that it was the logical end to a wave of excessive speculation fostered by insufficient government regulation—a block of stock could be purchased with a down payment as low as 10 percent. Still others argued that the market was reacting to an economy already in a recession: the Federal Reserve's index of industrial production had been falling since June and there had been weaknesses in home building and agriculture for several years.

What of the crash of 1987? The bull market, a period of rising stock prices, began in 1982 and peaked in 1987: on August 11, 1982 the Dow Jones Industrial Average was at 777 and reached a peak of 2722 on August 25, 1987. Much of the increase took place during 1987; there was a 44 percent increase in the Dow Jones Industrial Average during the first eight months of 1987. In September the market drifted lower but prices began to rise again late in the month and the increase extended into early October. And then the bulls turned into bears.

Just as the Black Thursday of 1929 was preceded by a sharp decline in stock prices the previous day, there was a sharp decline in stock prices on the last trading day before Black Monday of 1987. On Friday October 18, 1987 the Dow Jones Industrial Average fell a record 108 points to 2247. Almost 340 million shares were traded on the New York Stock Exchange, also a record. For the week it was estimated that the value of stock held by the public had fallen by more than $300 billion. But the records of Friday did not last long. On Black Monday the Dow Jones Industrial Average fell off dramatically, dropping by 508 points and ending the day at 1738. Over 600 million shares were traded on the New York Stock Exchange and an additional $500 billion in market value was lost. From its high of August 1987, the Dow Jones Industrial Average had lost over 25 percent of its value—a financial calamity.

In the four trading days immediately following October 19, 1987, stock, prices began a modest recovery. But on Monday, October 26, there was another meltdown with the Dow Jones Industrial Average falling another 157 points, wiping out the gains that the market had made from October 20 to October 23. As we write in November 1987, the Dow Jones Industrial Average is fluctuating around the 1900 level with no clear sense of direction.

What caused the crash of 1987? Why did the bulls turn into bears this time? Once again there is disagreement; there are almost as many opinions as there are investors. In the following two readings the diversity of opinion is clearly documented. Roberts argues that it is the fault of the Federal Reserve. Investors became convinced that the tight monetary policy conducted by the Federal Reserve would lead to a recession, and they decided to sell their stocks before the recession began. Glassman disagrees, arguing that investors came to realize that the market was overpriced and, therefore, the time was right for them to take their money out of the stock market and place it elsewhere.

Is the crash of 1987 a precursor of another Great Depression? Although the economic environment of 1987 is not the economic environment of 1929, many are concerned that the crash of 1987 will have a severe impact on the economy. Roberts argues that unless the Federal Reserve reverses its policy, a recession seems almost inevitable. Glassman is not quite so worried; he stresses the fact that even with the dramatic events of October the stock market has only returned to its level of 1986.

YES

Paul Craig Roberts

. . . TOO TIGHT ALREADY

The supply-side effort during the 1980s in the U.S., the United Kingdom, and more recently France to restore private-sector economic growth and incentives has been delivered another serious blow by the anti-growth forces that control the world's most important central banks. The unprecedented collapse in global equity markets was caused by the disastrous rise in interest rates the preceded the stock-market crash around the world.

In the U.S., the reserves of the banking system were at the same level this past Oct. 7 as they were Dec. 31 of last year. That is, there has been no money growth in the U.S. in 1987. Since the economy was growing, interest rates had to rise. Prior to the stock-market crash, long-term U.S. interest rates had risen 40%! Last month the Federal Reserve Board actually raised the discount rate, theorizing that a rise in this closely watched rate would reassure financial markets by demonstrating that the Fed was on guard against inflation.

In practice, this theory turned out to be crackpot. The market understood rising interest rates would wreck the economy and sold off. It is difficult to comprehend how the Fed could overlook the accumulated experience that stock markets—especially nervous ones at historic highs—sell off in the face of rising interest rates.

GERMAN POLICY WAS IDIOTIC

If U.S. monetary policy was irresponsible, West German monetary policy was idiotic. Even after the U.S. stock market had turned down, the Germans raised interest rates. The immediate effect was panic in the U.S. market that the Fed would be forced to raise interest rates further in order to "protect the dollar." Treasury Secretary Baker's attempt to forestall panic by ruling out higher interest rates did not succeed, because it caused an equivalent fear that foreigners would sell U.S. stocks to avoid an exchange-rate loss. Anticipating either higher interest rates or a decline in the dollar and foreign selling, Americans sold into a declining market.

From "...Too Tight Already," by Paul Craig Roberts, *The Wall Street Journal*, October 22, 1987. Copyright © 1987 by Paul Craig Roberts. Reprinted by permission.

Other countries, observing the U.S. stock market predict recession, realized the game was up for their export-based economies and sold off their stocks. What we face is a global prediction of a global recession. The prediction's accuracy and the severity of the downturn will depend on the actions of central banks.

It is frightening that the explanations of Monday's stock-market crash do not mention monetary policy and rising interest rates. The *New York Times* blames the U.S. budget deficit, but the week before the crash the government announced that the budget deficit had declined $70 billion, or 32%, surely a reassuring sign. Others blame the U.S. trade deficit, the mainstay of the world economy, predicting a lower dollar and higher inflation. However, if this were the correct explanation, the dollar would have sold off. We should keep in mind that stock markets crashed in countries with large trade surpluses and in countries with near budget balance.

The fact that stocks sold off while U.S. bonds rallied and the dollar remained unchanged is a clear indication that markets believe monetary tightness is leading to recession.

The margin for further monetary error is wide. The Fed staff apparently has convinced the central bank's governors that the rise in interest rates was due to rising inflation expectations rather than to Fed policy. It is extraordinary that the Fed could believe there has been a rise in inflation expectations during a period when there has been no growth in the money supply. A central bank so misguided can compound its error and replay the Great Depression.

The German central bank is even more incredible. It believes that if Americans would raise taxes and reduce consumption, the world economy would be fine.

A stock-market crash of this magnitude brings the left's political agenda out of the closet to which it had been forced by the renewal of prosperity, and it is a gift to the Democratic Party, which previously had no prospect of regaining the White House next year. Now Democrats can blame President Reagan for the stock-market crash and for any recession that might follow. The opportunity to blame Mr. Reagan means the Democrats have no incentive to hold the independent central bank accountable, thereby increasing the likelihood of further errors in monetary policy.

Even more unpromising, some supply-side advocates, including the editorial page of *The Wall Street Journal*, agree with the Fed's self-serving argument that the dollar must be defended to avoid exchange-rate instability even if it means higher interest rates. Facts do not seem able to penetrate this point of view. The day of the stock-market crash, the *Journal's* lead editorial said: "Time to Stand Tight." The day after the crash, the *Journal's* editorial explained the greatest destruction of wealth in history as a mere "warning shot" about "exchange-rate instability" and "a possible collapse of the value of the dollar." The high interest-rate policy of supporting the dollar crashed the market. One can only marvel that influential supply-siders are willing to help engineer their own destruction.

FED MUST SEIZE OPPORTUNITY

There is little doubt that exchange-rate stability is desirable, but so is economic stability. And to sacrifice the latter to the former will bring left-wing governments to power and not a gold standard.

Consistent with the stock market's prediction of recession, a strong rally has started in long-term Treasury bonds (and gold stocks have collapsed). The Federal Reserve must seize this opportunity to cut the discount rate, and it must sustain the drop in long-term interest rates by purchasing bonds if necessary. If the Federal Reserve aborts the recovery of the bond market, stocks will go lower and recession will set in. With it could go the promise of economic renewal that the supply side brought to the world economy.

NO

James K. Glassman

WHERE DID IT ALL GO?

"Financial insanity," wrote John Kenneth Galbraith, "can be a source of pure enjoyment." Sure, it's a kick to watch Carl Icahn and $200,000-a-year punk Wall Street traders flounder. After all, when the Dow goes down 508 points, Galbraith says, "nothing is being lost but money."

In fact, it's not even money. For most of us, it's something else called wealth, or value. When the stock market falls, not a penny comes out of your pocket unless you sell. Six hundred million shares traded on Monday, and while that may sound like a lot, it's only a tiny fraction of the total shares traded on the New York Exchange. The owners of most of those shares didn't really lose money on Monday; instead, the value of their companies declined, on average, by a fifth to a quarter. Nonetheless, a fifth of productive wealth of the world was wiped out in less than two days. Where did it go? To the land of the lost buttons and car keys?

It didn't go anywhere finite because it wasn't finite to begin with. A crash brings us back to earth and reminds us that the value of financial assets is all in the mind. The market decides on the value through means that are mathematical and aesthetic, mechanical and psychological. But mostly value is based on predictions, and telling the future is a tricky business.

Consider a group of friends who start a Cajun restaurant issuing 100,000 shares of Cajurama at $1 apiece, paying for them in cash. The value of each share is easily calculated. If you own one percent of the firm, you own one percent of its total assets of $100,000. The restaurant prospers, and soon the corporation owns a chain of restaurants, making profits of $700,000 a year. What is the value of the company now?

The value is simply what someone is willing to pay for all the stock. How does a purchaser make that valuation? He bases it on how profitable the restaurant is likely to be in the future and the firm's assets, both tangible (cash, fixtures, etc.) and intangible (staff, recipes, good will). He also looks at what investors are willing to pay for other publicly traded restaurant chains. If investors are paying $15 for every dollar of profits or 15 times earnings for restaurant stocks, that would make a share of stock in this burgeoning chain worth $105, or $10.5 million for the 100,000 shares.

From "Where Did it All Go?" by James K. Glassman, *The New Republic*, November 9, 1987. Copyright © 1987 by The New Republic, Inc. Reprinted by permission.

Now, let's say that the potential purchaser tells the stockholders he'll buy them out for $105 a share. The stockholders are pleased but decide not to sell. Suddenly, Cajun food falls out of favor. Cajurama is still doing well, but the owners are worried, so they go to another potential buyer and say they want to sell. This buyer offers them just $70 a share since he knows that in the future the restaurants won't be able to make as much money selling blackened redfish. No other buyer will pay more. So, overnight, the value of the chain has fallen by one-third. Instead of paying $15 for every $1 of earnings, investors are only willing to pay $10, fearing that, in the future, earnings may fall.

That is what happened early last week. Just as one-third the value of the Cajun restaurant evaporated, more than a trillion dollars vanished from the value of the world's largest corporation. What was the cause? Pick one: the rejection of Judge Bork (*The Wall Street Journal's* favorite), the budget deficit, the trade deficit, declining international monetary cooperation, rising interest rates, Jim Baker's big mouth, David Ruder's big mouth. After all, the value of Cajurama can fall because of macroeconomic conditions (fear of a recession, say) as well as micro ones (the declining popularity of blackened redfish). One thing about crashes is that they can become self-fulfilling prophecies. A huge drop in stock prices may be the result of worries about a recession, and there is a good chance that the drop itself will produce a recession.

Many of the big-deal forces played a role in the Monday massacre, but it's more important to understand that markets are existential; they have their own internal logic, or illogic. They go down simply because they are too high.

For the past year or two, in the back of the mind of every investor has been the notion that stocks are too high. But prices kept rising, and who wanted to ruin the fun? Anyway, if prices started to go down, investors figured they could always get out before the real damage. The on Monday, as the market headed down, everyone headed for the exit at once, and investors panicked, screaming to get out at any price.

In a week the Dow had fallen 1,000 points, or about one-third. But, as horrifying as that might sound, it was only getting back to where it started a year ago, and it was still more than twice as high as when the bull market started in August 1982.

Foreign exchanges have risen even more in the past year. The Australian market fell 25 percent on Tuesday, but before the decline it had been up 82 percent for the year. The Hong Kong exchange, which suspended trading until Friday, had been up 87 percent; Singapore, 76 percent; Spain, 57 percent; Japan, 46 percent. So which is crazier—that the total value of the world's public corporations has risen by more than half in a year, or that the value declined by a fifth in a day?

An easier way of seeing how high stocks have been is to look at individual companies. If you had the guts on Tuesday morning, you were looking for bargains. But there weren't too many to be found, even after the Dow had fallen 22 percent. Apple was down nearly 12 points (25 percent) on Monday, but it was still trading at 23 times earnings; that is, you had to pay $23 for every $1 of Apple profits, a return on investment of barely four percent. AT&T was off more than 6 points (20 percent), but it was trading at 17 times earnings. Gannett dropped 10; it was off by nearly one-half from its high for the year, but it was still trading at 18 times earnings.

Before the crash, the price-to-earnings ratio of the Standard & Poor's 500-stock index was 22. The decline brought it to around 16, exactly where it was a year ago—and still high by historic standards. The yield (that is, total dividends as a percentage of total stock prices) on the Dow was 2.61 percent at the market peak two months ago, one of the lowest levels ever seen in history. Richard Russell, publisher of *Dow Theory Letters*, predicted in an article in *Barron's* that appeared two days before Monday's crash that historically bull markets give up one-half of their total gains. If this bull market started running in 1974 when the Dow was 578, and it peaked in August at 2722, then it will fall to around 1650. Not even Russell expected that that would almost happen in a single day.

One of the worst things about a crash is that it makes everyone a moralist. The question is not value, but values—living beyond our means, not cooperating, etc. My own piece of moralizing is that the crash could have a salutary effect. It reminds us that it's only money, and that it can be gone in a flash, for reasons beyond our control, no matter how brilliant we are. Sir Isaac Newton, probably the smartest man who ever lived, lost 13,000 pounds in the South Sea Bubble. Still, in America, money is all we've got. Tocqueville wrote, "When the prestige attached to what is old has vanished . . . there is thus hardly anything left but money which makes very clear distinctions between men."

So maybe financial insanity is not as funny as Galbraith thinks. In a way, panics are pathetic. They say to us that our grip on "prestige" and everything else that matters is based on a phantom that, one bright Monday, can flee for the land of lost buttons and keys, leaving us all alone. No wonder we're scared.

POSTSCRIPT

Did Monetary Policy Cause
the Stock Market Crash of 1987?

Roberts begins by asserting that the supply-side economic policies that have generated the current economic expansion are threatened by anti-growth forces. The anti-growth forces are the "world's most important central banks" including the Federal Reserve System. These groups oppose growth by undertaking contractionary monetary policy in an effort to restrain inflation. Roberts offers three statistics in evidence of the Federal Reserve's tight or contractionary monetary policy: (1) no increase in banking reserves between December 31, 1987 and October 7, 1987; (2) no increase in the money supply during the first nine months of 1987; and (3) an increase in the discount rate in September 1987. The combination of tight monetary policy and an expanding economy led to an increase in interest rates. Investors became convinced that the rising interest rates would choke off the economic expansion and they decided to sell their stocks: "The market understood that rising interest rates would wreck the economy and sold off." Roberts concludes that unless the Federal Reserve reverses its tight monetary policy and supports a decline in interest rates, stock prices will continue to fall and a recession is inevitable.

According to Glassman the stock market was overpriced just before the crash. Whether or not a stock is overpriced depends on two key characteristics; its price-to-earnings ratio (the price of a share of a company's stock divided by its earnings or income per share) and its dividend yield (the dividends paid per share divided by the current price of a share of a company's stock). An examination of the price-to-earnings ratio and the dividend yield for the 500 stocks included in the Standard & Poor's Index reveals the following: (1) in the year preceding the crash the price-to-earnings ratio had risen very rapidly, from 16 to 22 and (2) just before the crash the dividend yield was 2.61 percent—"one of the lowest levels ever

seen in history." The crash simply lowered the price-to-earnings ratio back to 16 and raised the dividend yield to a level more consistent with historical patterns. As to why this correction occurred at this time, Glassman offers no answer; he simply asserts that stock prices "go down simply because they are too high." He even suggests that the crash may be beneficial: "It reminds us that it is only money, and that it can be gone in a flash, for reasons beyond our control, no matter how brilliant we are."

For those interested in the crash of 1929 there are a number of interesting books and articles to read: *The Great Crash of 1929* by John Kenneth Galbraith (Avon, 1979); *The Stock Market Crash—and After* by Irving Fisher (Macmillan, 1930); and "Once upon a Time in October" by Otto Friedrich in *Time* (November 2, 1987). For an alternative view that it was easy monetary policy and not tight monetary policy that caused the crash of 1987 see "Not Tight Enough . . . ," by Victor A. Canto and Arthur B. Laffer in *The Wall Street Journal* (October 22, 1987). For an article supporting Glassman's position see "Why All the Fuss? Maybe Stocks Were Just Too High" by Chris Welles in *Business Week* (November 16, 1987). For an interesting comparison of the economic environments of 1929 and 1987 see "A Look at Array of Data Shows Some Parallels, Many Differences" by Alfred L. Malabre, Jr., in *The Wall Street Journal* (October 26, 1987). "A Shock Felt Round the World" by Ed Magnuson in *Time* (November 1, 1987) presents an hour-by-hour, country-by-country account of financial news for the week of October 19, 1987. For greater details of the events up to, during, and immediately after the crash of 1987, the daily issues of *The Wall Street Journal* and the *New York Times* for October and November 1987 are highly recommended. Also see the November 2, 1987 issue of *Business Week*, the November 16, 1987 issue of *Forbes* and the November 23, 1987 issue of *Fortune*.

General Electric Co.

PART 3

INTERNATIONAL TRADE

For many years America held a position of dominance in international trade. That position has been changed by time, events, an¹ the emergence of other economic powers in the world. Decisions that are made in the international arena will, with increasing frequency, influence our lives. Protectionist measures are being discussed in Congress, and the jobs of many Americans may depend on the outcome of those discussions. The willingness and ability of Third World nations to devote resources to paying their debts will directly affect our domestic banking system. And the impact that multinational corporations have on host countries—South Africa is a case in particular—has ramifications in the United States as well.

Should the United States Protect Domestic Industries from Foreign Competition?

Will the Third World Pay Its Debt?

Is the Pain and Suffering Associated with Disinvestment and Sanctions Worth It for Black South African Workers?

ISSUE 16

Should the United States Protect Domestic Industries from Foreign Competition?

YES: Bob Kuttner, from "The Free Trade Fallacy," *The New Republic* (March 28, 1983)

NO: Michael Kinsley, from "Keep Trade Free," *The New Republic* (April 11, 1983)

ISSUE SUMMARY

YES: Columnist Bob Kuttner alleges that David Ricardo's eighteenth century view of the world doesn't "describe the global economy as it actually works" in the twentieth century. He says today "comparative advantage" is determined by exploitative wage rates and government action; it is not determined by free markets.

NO: Social critic Kinsley replies that we do not decrease American living standards when we import the products made by cheap foreign labor. He claims protectionism today, just as it did in the eighteenth century, weakens our economy and only "helps to put off the day of reckoning."

The basic logic of international trade does not differ from the basic logic of domestic trade. The fundamental questions of "what?" "how?" and "for whom?" must be answered. The difference is that, in this case, the questions are posed in an international arena. This arena is filled with producers and consumers who speak many different languages, use strange currencies, and are often suspicious of the actions and/or reactions of foreigners.

However, if markets work the way they are expected to work, free trade simply increases the extent of the market and, therefore, increases the advantages of specialization. Market participants should be able to buy and consume a greater variety of inexpensive goods and services after the establishment of free trade than they could before free trade. You might ask: Why, then, do some wish to close our borders and deny our citizenry the benefits of free trade? The answer to this question is straightforward: These benefits do not come without a cost.

There are two sets of winners and two sets of losers in this game of free trade. The most obvious winners are the consumers of the "cheap" imported goods. These consumers get to buy the low-priced color TV sets, automobiles, or steel that is made abroad. Another set of winners are the producers of the exported goods. All the factors in the export industry, as well as in those industries that supply the export industry, experience an increase in their market demand. Therefore, their income increases. In the United States, agriculture is one such export industry. As new foreign markets are opened, farmers' incomes increase, as do the incomes of those who supply the farmers with fertilizer, farm equipment, gasoline, and other basic inputs.

On the other side of this coin there are losers. The obvious losers are those who control the factors that are employed in the import-competing industries. These factors include the land, labor, and capital that are devoted to the production of United States-made color TV sets, United States-made automobiles, and United States-made steel. "Cheap" foreign imports displace the demand for these products. The consumers of exported goods are also losers. For example, as United States farmers sell more of their products abroad, less of them are available domestically. As a result, the domestic price of these farm products rises.

The bottom line is that there is nothing "free" in a market system. Competition—whether it is domestic or foreign—creates winners and losers. Historically, we have sympathized with the losers when they suffer at the hands of foreign competitors. However, we have not let our sympathies seriously curtail free trade. Kuttner argues that we can no longer afford this policy. He maintains that United States workers face "unfair foreign competition." He asserts that the international rules of the game have changed. Michael Kinsley replies that this is "pure, unadorned protectionism." He goes on to conclude that "each job 'saved' will cost other American workers far more than it will bring the lucky beneficiary."

YES

Bob Kuttner

THE FREE TRADE FALLACY

In the firmament of American ideological convictions, no star burns brighter than the bipartisan devotion to free trade. The President's 1983 Economic Report, to no one's surprise, sternly admonished would-be protectionists. An editorial in *The New York Times*, midway through an otherwise sensibly Keynesian argument, paused to add ritually, "Protectionism might mean a few jobs for American auto workers, but it would depress the living standards of hundreds of millions of consumers and workers, here and abroad."

The Rising Tide of Protectionism has become an irresistible topic for a light news day. Before me is a thick sheaf of nearly interchangeable clips warning of impending trade war. With rare unanimity, the press has excoriated the United Auto Workers for its local content legislation. *The Wall Street Journal's* editorial ("Loco Content") and the *Times's* ("The Made-in-America Trap") were, if anything, a shade more charitable than Cockburn and Ridgeway in *The Village Voice* ("Jobs and Racism"). And when former Vice President Mondale began telling labor audiences that America should hold Japan to a single standard in trade, it signaled a chorus of shame-on-Fritz stories.

The standard trade war story goes like this: recession has prompted a spate of jingoistic and self-defeating demands to fence out superior foreign goods. These demands typically emanate from overpaid workers, loser industries, and their political toadies. Protectionism will breed stagnation, retaliation, and worldwide depression. Remember Smoot-Hawley!

Perhaps it is just the unnerving experience of seeing *The Wall Street Journal* and *The Village Voice* on the same side, but one is moved to further inquiry. Recall for a moment the classic theory of comparative advantage. As the English economist David Ricardo explained it in 1817, if you are more efficient at making wine and I am better at weaving cloth, then it would be silly for each of us to produce both goods. Far better to do what each does best, and to trade the excess. Obviously then, barriers to trade defeat potential efficiency gains. Add some algebra, and that is how trade theory continues to be taught today.

From "The Free Trade Fallacy," by Bob Kuttner, *The New Republic*, March 28, 1983. Copyright © 1983 by The New Republic, Inc. Reprinted by permission.

To bring Ricardo's homely illustration up to date, the economically sound way to deal with the Japanese menace is simply to buy their entire cornucopia—the cheaper the better. If they are superior at making autos, TVs, tape recorders, cameras, steel, machine tools, baseballs, semiconductors, computers, and other peculiarly Oriental products, it is irrational to shelter our own benighted industries. Far more sensible to buy their goods, let the bracing tonic of competition shake America from its torpor, and wait for the market to reveal our niche in the international division of labor.

But this formulation fails to describe the global economy as it actually works. The classical theory of free trade was based on what economists call "factor endowments"—a nation's natural advantages in climate, minerals, arable land, or plentiful labor. The theory doesn't fit a world of learning curves, economies of scale, and floating exchange rates. And it certainly doesn't deal with the fact that much "comparative advantage" today is created not by markets but by government action. If Boeing got a head start on the 707 from multibillion-dollar military contracts, is that a sin against free trade? Well, sort of. If the European Airbus responds with subsidized loans, is that worse? If only Western Electric (a U.S. supplier) can produce for Bell, is that protection? If Japan uses public capital, research subsidies, and market-sharing cartels to launch a highly competitive semiconductor industry, is *that* protection? Maybe so, maybe not.

Just fifty years ago, Keynes, having dissented from the nineteenth-century theory of free markets, began wondering about free trade as well. In a 1933 essay in the *Yale Review* called "National Self-Sufficiency," he noted that "most modern processes of mass production can be performed in most countries and climates with almost equal efficiency." He wondered whether the putative efficiencies of trade necessarily justified the loss of national autonomy. Today nearly half of world trade is conducted between units of multinational corporations. As Keynes predicted, most basic products (such as steel, plastics, microprocessors, textiles, and machine tools) can be manufactured almost anywhere, but by labor forces with vastly differing prevailing wages.

With dozens of countries trying to emulate Japan, the trend is toward worldwide excess capacity, shortened useful life of capital equipment, and downward pressure on wages. For in a world where technology is highly mobile and interchangeable, there is a real risk that comparative advantage comes to be defined as whose work force will work for the lowest wage.

In such a world, it is possible for industries to grow nominally more productive while the national economy grows poorer. How can that be? The factor left out of the simple Ricardo equation is idle capacity. If America's autos (or steel tubes, or machine tools) are manufactured more productively than a decade ago but less productively than in Japan (or Korea, or Brazil), and if we practice what we preach about open trade, then an immense share of U.S. purchasing power will go to provide jobs overseas. A growing segment of our productive resources will lie idle. American manufacturers, detecting soft markets and falling profits, will decline to invest. Steelmakers will buy oil companies. Consumer access to superior foreign products will not necessarily compensate for the decline in real income and the idle resources. Nor is there any guarantee that the new industrial countries will use their burgeoning income from American sales to buy American capital equipment (or computers, or even coal), for they are all striving to develop their own advanced, diversified economies.

Against this background of tidal change in the global economy, the conventional reverence for "free trade" is just not helpful. As an economic paradigm, it denies us a realistic appraisal of second bests. As a political principle, it leads liberals into a disastrous logic in which the main obstacle to a strong American economy is decent living standards for the American work force. Worst of all, a simple-minded devotion to textbook free trade in a world of mercantilism assures that the form of protection we inevitably get will be purely defensive, and will not lead to constructive change in the protected industry.

The seductive fallacy that pervades the hand-wringing about protectionism is the premise that free trade is the norm and that successful foreign exporters must be playing by the rules. Even so canny a critic of political economy as Michael Kinsley wrote in these pages that "Very few American workers have lost their jobs because of unfair foreign trade practices, and it is demagogic for Mondale and company to suggest otherwise." But what is an unfair trade practice? The Common Market just filed a complaint alleging that the entire Japanese industrial system is one great unfair trade practice!

To the extent that the rules of liberal trade are codified, they repose in the General Agreement on Tariffs and Trade (stay awake, this will be brief). The GATT is one of those multilateral institutions created in the American image just after World War II, a splendid historical moment when we could commend free trade to our allies the way the biggest kid on the block calls for a fair fight.

The basic GATT treaty, ratified in 1947, requires that all member nations get the same tariff treatment (the "most favored nation" doctrine), and that tariffs, in theory at least, are the only permissible form of barrier. Governments are supposed to treat foreign goods exactly the same as domestic ones: no subsidies, tax preferences, cheap loans to home industries, no quotas, preferential procurement, or inspection gimmicks to exclude foreign ones. Nor can producers sell below cost (dumping) in foreign markets. . . .

In classical free trade theory, the only permissible candidate for temporary protection is the "infant industry." But Japan and its imitators, not unreasonably, treat every emerging technology as an infant industry. Japan uses a highly sheltered domestic market as a laboratory, and as a shield behind which to launch one export winner after another. Seemingly, Japan should be paying a heavy price for its protectionism as its industry stagnates. Poor Japan! This is not the place for a detailed recapitulation of Japan, Inc., but keep in mind some essentials.

The Japanese government, in close collaboration with industry, targets sectors for development. It doesn't try to pick winners blindfolded; it creates them. It offers special equity loans, which need be repaid only if the venture turns a profit. It lends public capital through the Japan Development Bank, which signals private bankers to let funds flow. Where our government offers tax deductions to all businesses as an entitlement, Japan taxes ordinary business profits at stiff rates and saves its tax subsidies for targeted ventures. The government sometimes buys back outdated capital equipment to create markets for newer capital.

The famed Ministry of International Trade and Industry has pursued this essential strategy for better than twenty years, keeping foreign borrowers out of cheap Japanese capital markets, letting in foreign investors only on very restricted terms, moving Japan up the product ladder from cheap labor intensive goods in the 1950s to autos and steel in the 1960s, consumer electronics in the early 1970s, and computers, semiconductors, optical fibers, and just about everything else by 1980. The Japanese government also waives antimonopoly laws for development cartels, and organizes recession cartels when overcapacity is a problem. And far from defying the discipline of the market, MITI encourages fierce domestic competition before winnowing the field down to a few export champions. . . .

The Japanese not only sin against the rules of market economics. They convert sin into productive virtue. By our own highest standards, they must be doing something right. The evident success of the Japanese model and the worldwide rush to emulate it create both a diplomatic crisis for American trade negotiators and a deeper ideological crisis for the free trade regime. As Berkeley professors John Zysman and Steven Cohen observed in a careful study for the Congressional Joint Economic Committee last December, America, as the main defender of the GATT philosophy, now faces an acute policy dilemma: "how to sustain the open trade system and promote the competitive position of American industry" at the same time.

Unfortunately, the dilemma is compounded by our ideological blinders. Americans believe so fervently in free markets, especially in trade, that we shun interventionist measures until an industry is in deep trouble. Then we build it half a bridge.

There is no better example of the lethal combination of protectionism plus market-capitalism-as-usual than the steel industry. Steel has enjoyed some import limitation since the late 1950s, initially through informal quotas. The industry is oligopolistic; it was very slow to modernize. By the mid-1970s, world demand for steel was leveling off just as aggressive new producers such as Japan, Korea, and Brazil were flooding world markets with cheap, state-of-the-art steel.

As the Carter Administration took office, the American steel industry was pursuing antidumping suits against foreign producers—an avenue that creates problems for American diplomacy. The new Administration had a better idea, more consistent with open markets and neighborly economic relations. It devised a "trigger price mechanism," a kind of floor price for foreign steel entering American markets. This was supposed to limit import penetration. The steelmakers withdrew their suits. Imports continued to increase.

So the Carter Administration moved with characteristic caution toward a minimalist industrial policy. Officials invented a kind of near-beer called the Steel Tripartite. Together, industry, labor, and government would devise a strategy for a competitive American steel industry. The eventual steel policy accepted the industry's own agenda: more protection, a softening of pollution control requirements, wage restraint, new tax incentives, and a gentlemen's agreement to phase out excess capacity. What the policy did not include was either an enforceable commitment or adequate capital to modernize the industry. By market standards, massive retooling was not a rational course, because the return on steel investment was well below prevailing yields on other investments. Moreover, government officials had neither the ideological mandate nor adequate information to tell the steel industry how to invest. "We would sit around and talk about rods versus plate versus specialty steel, and none of us in government had any knowledge of how the steel industry actually operates," confesses C. Fred Bergsten, who served as Treasury's top trade official under Carter. "There has never been a government study of what size and shape steel industry the country needs. If we're going to go down this road, we should do it right, rather than simply preserving the status quo." . . .

The argument that we should let "the market" ease us out of old-fashioned heavy industry in which newly industrialized countries have a comparative advantage quickly melts away once you realize that precisely the same non-market pressures are squeezing us out of the highest-tech industries as well. And the argument that blames the problem on overpaid American labor collapses when one understands that semiskilled labor overseas in several Asian nations is producing advanced products for the U.S. market at less than a dollar an hour. Who really thinks that we should lower American wages to that level in order to compete?

In theory, other nations' willingness to exploit their work forces in order to provide Americans with good, cheap products offers a deal we shouldn't refuse. But the fallacy in that logic is to measure the costs and benefits of a trade transaction only in terms of that transaction itself. Classical free-trade theory assumes full employment. When foreign, state-led competition drives us out of industry after industry, the costs to the economy as a whole can easily outweigh the benefits. As Wolfgang Hager, a consultant to the Common Market, has written, "The cheap [imported] shirt is paid for several times: once at the counter, then again in unemployment benefits. Secondary losses involve input industries . . . machinery, fibers, chemicals for dyeing and finishing products."

As it happens, Hager's metaphor, the textile industry, is a fairly successful example of managed trade, which combines a dose of protection with a dose of modernization. Essentially, textiles have been removed from the free-trade regime by an international market-sharing agreement. In the late 1950s, the American textile industry began suffering insurmountable competition from cheap imports. The United States first imposed quotas on imports of cotton fibers, then on synthetics, and eventually on most textiles and apparel as well. A so-called Multi-Fiber Arrangement eventually was negotiated with other nations, which shelters the textile industries of Europe and the United States from wholesale import penetration. Under M.F.A., import growth in textiles was limited to an average of 6 percent per year.

The consequences of this, in theory, should have been stagnation. But the result has been exactly the opposite. The degree of protection, and a climate of cooperation with the two major labor unions, encouraged the American textile industry to invest heavily in modernization. During the 1960s and 1970s, the average annual productivity growth in textiles has been about twice the U.S. industrial average, second only to electronics. According to a study done for the

Common Market, productivity in the most efficient American weaving operations is 130,000 stitches per worker per hour—twice as high as France and three times as high as Britain. Textiles, surprisingly enough, have remained an export winner for the United States, with net exports regularly exceeding imports. (In 1982, a depressed year that saw renewed competition from China, Hong Kong, Korea, and Taiwan, exports just about equaled imports.)

But surely the American consumer pays the bill when the domestic market is sheltered from open foreign competition. Wrong again. Textile prices have risen at only about half the average rate of the producer price index, both before and after the introduction of the Multi-Fiber Arrangement.

Now, it is possible to perform some algebraic manipulations and show how much lower textile prices would have been without any protection. One such computation places the cost of each protected textile job at several hundred thousand dollars. But these static calculations are essentially useless as practical policy guides, for they leave out the value over time of maintaining a textile industry in the United States. The benefits include not only jobs, but contributions to G.N.P., to the balance of payments, and the fact that investing in this generation's technology is the ticket of admission to the next.

Why didn't the textile industry stagnate? Why didn't protectionism lead to higher prices? Largely because the textile industry is quite competitive domestically. The top five manufacturers have less than 20 percent of the market. The industry still operates under a 1968 Federal Trade Commission consent order prohibiting any company with sales of more than $100 million from acquiring one with sales exceeding $10 million. If an industry competes vigorously domestically, it can innovate and keep prices low, despite being sheltered from ultra-low-wage foreign competition—or rather, thanks to the shelter. In fact, students of the nature of modern managed capitalism should hardly be surprised that market stability and new investment go hand in hand.

The textile case also suggests that the sunrise industry/sunset industry distinction is so much nonsense. Most of America's major industries can be winners or losers, depending on whether they get sufficient capital investment. And it turns out that many U.S. industries such as textiles and shoes, which conventionally seem destined for lower-wage countries, can survive and modernize given a reasonable degree of, well, protection.

What, then, is to be done? First, we should acknowledge the realities of international trade. Our competitors, increasingly, are not free marketeers in our own mold. It is absurd to let foreign mercantilist enterprise overrun U.S. industry in the name of free trade. The alternative is not jingoist protectionism. It is managed trade, on the model of the Multi-Fiber Arrangement. If domestic industries are assured some limits to import growth, then it becomes rational for them to keep retooling and modernizing.

It is not necessary to protect every industry, nor do we want an American MITI. But surely it is reasonable to fashion plans for particular key sectors like steel, autos, machine tools, and semiconductors. The idea is not to close U.S. markets, but to limit the rate of import growth in key industries. In exchange, the domestic industry must invest heavily in modernization. And as part of the bargain, workers deserve a degree of job security and job retraining opportunities.

Far from being just another euphemism for beggar-thy-neighbor, a more stable trade system generally can be in the interest of producing countries. Universal excess capacity does no country much of a favor. When rapid penetration of the U.S. color TV market by Korean suppliers became intolerable, we slammed shut an open door. Overnight, Korean color TV production shrank to 20 percent of capacity. Predictable, if more gradual, growth in sales would have been preferable for us and for the Koreans.

Second, we should understand the interrelationship of managed trade, industrial policies, and economic recovery. Without a degree of industrial planning, limiting imports leads indeed to stagnation. Without restored world economic growth, managed trade becomes a nasty battle over shares of a shrinking pie, instead of allocation of a growing one. And without some limitation on imports, the Keynesian pump leaks. One reason big deficits fail to ignite recoveries is that so much of the growth in demand goes to purchase imported goods.

Third, we should train more economists to study industries in the particular. Most economists dwell in the best of all possible worlds, where markets equilibrate, firms optimize, the idle resources re-employ themselves. "Microeconomics" is seldom the study of actual industries; it is most often a branch of arcane mathematics. The issue of *whether* governments can sometimes improve on markets is not a fit subject for empirical inquiry, for the paradigm begins with the assumption that they cannot. The highly practical question of *when* a little protection is justified is ruled out *ex ante*, since neoclassical economics assumes that less protection is always better than more.

Because applied industrial economics is not a mainstream concern of the economics profession, the people who study it tend to come from the fields of management, industrial and labor relations, planning, and law. They are not invited to professional gatherings of economists, who thus continue to avoid the most pressing practical questions. One economist whom I otherwise admire told me he found it "seedy" that high-wage autoworkers would ask consumers to subsidize their pay. Surely it is seedier for an $800-a-week tenured economist to lecture a $400-a-week autoworker on job security; if the Japanese have a genuine comparative advantage in anything, it is in applied economics.

Fourth, we should stop viewing high wages as a liability. After World War II, Western Europe and North America evolved a social contract unique in the history of industrial capitalism. Unionism was encouraged, workers got a fair share in the fruits of production, and a measure of job security. The transformation of a crude industrial production machine into something approximating social citizenship is an immense achievement, not to be sacrificed lightly on the altar of "free trade." It took one depression to show that wage cuts are no route to recovery. Will it take another to show they are a poor formula for competitiveness? Well-paid workers, after all, are consumers.

NO

Michael Kinsley

KEEP TRADE FREE

Free trade is not a religion—it has no spiritual value—and Bob Kuttner is right to insist, as he did in TNR two weeks ago, that if it is no longer good for America in practical terms, it is not a sensible policy for liberals anymore. He and I would also agree that a liberal trade policy ought to be good for working people in particular (including people who would like to be working but aren't). The question is whether free trade is just a relic from two happier eras—the period of liberal clarity two centuries ago when Adam Smith and David Ricardo devised the theories of free enterprise and free trade, and the period of American hegemony after World War II when we could dominate world markets—or whether it is still a key to prosperity.

Kuttner argues that Ricardo's theory of "comparative advantage"—that all nations are better off if each produces and exports what it can make most efficiently—no longer applies. Local factors such as climate and natural resources don't matter much anymore. As a result, "most basic products . . . can be manufactured almost anywhere" with equal efficiency. This means, Kuttner says, that the only ways one nation (e.g., Japan) gains comparative advantage over another (e.g., us) these days are through low wages or "government action." Either of these, he says, makes nonsense of Ricardo's theory. In addition, Kuttner says, Ricardo didn't account for the problem of "idle capacity"—expensive factories sitting unused.

"Idle capacity" is an argument against any competition at all, not just from abroad, and has a long history of being carted out whenever established companies (the airlines, for example) want the government to prevent newcomers from horning in on their turf. If you believe in capitalism at all, you have to believe that the temporary waste of capital that can result from the turmoil of competition is more than outweighed by the efficiency of competition in keeping all the competitors on their toes. A capitalist who builds a plant knowing (or even not knowing) that it is less efficient than a rival abroad deserves whatever he gets. As for older plants that are already built—that capital is sunk. If the cost of running those plants is higher than

From "Keep Free Trade Free," by Michael Kinsley, *The New Republic*, April 11, 1983. Copyright © 1983 by The New Republic, Inc. Reprinted by permission.

the cost of buying the same output from abroad, keeping them running is more wasteful than letting them sit idle.

This brings us to the real problem; not sunk capital but sunk lives. The middle-class living standard achieved by much of the United States working class is one of the glories of American civilization. Yet Kuttner says, "semi-skilled labor overseas is producing advanced products for the U.S. market at less than a dollar an hour. Who really thinks that we should lower American wages to that level in order to compete?"

We shouldn't, of course. But importing the products of cheap foreign labor cannot lower American living standards as a whole, and trade barriers cannot raise living standards. This is not a matter of morality: it is a matter of mathematics. If widgets can be imported from Asia for a price reflecting labor costs of $1 an hour, then an hour spent making widgets adds a dollar of value to the economy. This is true no matter what American widget makers are being paid. If foreign widgets are excluded in order to protect the jobs of American widget makers getting $10 an hour, $1 of that $10 reflects their contribution to the economy and $9 is coming out of the pockets of other workers who have to pay more for widgets. Nice for widget makers, but perfectly futile from the perspective of net social welfare.

After all, if this economic alchemy really worked, we could shut our borders to all imports, pay one another $1,000 an hour, and we'd all be rich. It doesn't work that way. In fact, as a society, we're clearly better off taking advantage of the $1 widgets. The "comparative advantage" of cheap Asian labor is an advantage to us too. That's why trade is good. But what about the poor widget

makers? And what about the social cost of unemployment? If former widget makers aren't working at all, they aren't even adding a dollar's worth to the economy. Protectionism is, in effect, a "make work" jobs program—but a ridiculously expensive one, both directly and indirectly. The direct cost, in this example, is $9 an hour. The indirect cost is in reducing the efficiency of the economy by preventing international specialization.

If the disparity between American and foreign wages is really that great, Americans just shouldn't be making widgets. We could pay widget workers at $8 an hour to do nothing, and still be better off. We could put them to work at their current wage doing anything worth more than a dollar an hour. We could spend the equivalent of $9 an hour on retraining. And we owe it to widget workers to try all these things if necessary, because they are the victims of a change that has benefited all the rest of us by bringing us cheaper widgets (and because, as Lester Thurow points out, doing these things will discourage them from blocking the needed change). To protect them while they keep on making widgets, though, is insane.

These suggestions are, of course, overt tax-and-spend government programs, compared to the covert tax-and-spend program of protectionism. In a period of political reaction, the covert approach is tempting. But hypocrisy is not a sensible long-term strategy for liberals, nor is willfully ignoring the importance of economic productivity.

In many basic industries, American wages are not all that far out of line, as Bob Kuttner seems to acknowledge in the case of autos. Modest wage adjustments can save these jobs and these industries for America. It is uncomfortable for a well-paid journalist to be urging pay cuts for blue-collar workers. On the other hand, steelworkers (when they are working) make more than the median American income. Protectionism to preserve wage levels is just a redistribution of national wealth; it creates no new wealth. Nothing is wrong with redistribution, but in any radical socialist redistribution of wealth, the pay of steelworkers would go down, not up. So it's hard to see why the government should intervene to protect steelworkers' wages at the expense of general national prosperity. This is especially true when millions are unemployed who would happily work for much less, and there is no jobs program for them.

But Bob Kuttner believes that protection can be good for general national prosperity even apart from the wage question, in an age when other nations' "comparative advantage" comes from government policies that include protectionism. It is important to separate different strands in the common protectionist argument that we have to do it because Japan does it. Many politicians of various stripes, and William Safire in a recent column, argue (on an implicit analogy between trade war and real war) that only by threatening or building trade barriers of our own can we persuade the Japanese to dismantle theirs and restore free trade. Kuttner, by contrast, thinks that the idea of free trade is outmoded; that the Japanese are *smart* to restrict imports and we would be smart to do the same as part of an "industrial policy."

Both Safire and Kuttner assume incorrectly that free trade needs to be mutual. In fact, the theory of free trade is that nations benefit from their own open borders as well as the other guy's. This may be right or wrong, but the mere fact that

Japan is protectionist does not settle the question of what our policy should be.

Certainly, it's worth looking at Japan for clues about how to succeed in the world economy, and certainly one key to Japan's success seems to be a government-coordinated industrial policy. (The current vogue for "industrial policy" is assessed by my colleague Robert Kaus in the February *Harper's*—forgive the plug.) But why must such a policy include trade barriers? One reason Japan thwarts imports is a conscious decision to reduce workers' living standards in order to concentrate national resources on industrial investment. I presume this isn't what Kuttner and other liberal trade revisionists have in mind. Kuttner and others include protectionism in their "industrial policy" for two other reasons. First, as a sort of bribe to get unions to go along with sterner measures—possibly necessary, but not a case for protection on its own merits. Second, to give promising industries a captive market in which to incubate and gather strength before taking on the world.

The trouble with this "nurture" argument is that there's no end to it. Kuttner himself says that it's "not unreasonable" to "treat every emerging technology" this way, and also says that "most of America's major industries can be winners" with the right treatment. After you add the few hopeless loser industries where we must allegedly create barriers to save American wages, you've got the whole economy locked up, and whether this will actually encourage efficiency or the opposite is, at the very least, an open question. And if every major country protects every major industry, there will be no world market for any of them to conquer.

Kuttner's model for "managed trade"

is the Multi-Fiber Arrangement, an international agreement that restricts imports of textiles. This, according to Kuttner, permitted the American textile industry to modernize and become productive, to the point where exports exceeded imports—a less impressive accomplishment if you recall that the M.F.A. *restricts* imports.

Kuttner concedes that, despite the productivity gains, textile prices are higher than they would be without protection from cheap foreign labor. (Indeed, the current situation in the textile industry, as Bob Kuttner describes it, seems to vindicate Luddites, who got their start in textiles; human beings could do the work more efficiently, but machines are doing it anyway.) So what's the point? According to Kuttner, "The benefits include not only jobs, but contributions to G.N.P., to the balance of payments, and the fact that investing in this generation's technology is the ticket of admission to the next." Yet Kuttner does not challenge the "alegbraic manipulations" he cites that show how each job saved costs the nation "several hundred thousand dollars" in higher textile prices. The only "contribution to G.N.P." from willful inefficiency like this can be the false contribution of inflation. The balance of payments is a measure of economic health, not a cause of it; restricting imports to reduce that deficit is like sticking the thermometer in ice water to bring down a feverish temperature. As for the suggestion that the *next* generation of technology will bring the *real* payoff—well, they were probably promising the same thing two decades ago when the Multi-Fiber Arrangement began.

Kuttner also worries that "without some limitation on imports," Keynesian fiscal policies don't work. This is like the monetarists who worry that financial advances such as money market funds will weaken the connection between inflation and the money supply. Unable to make their theory accord with life, they want the government to make life accord with their theory. There *is* a world economy—which Bob Kuttner seems to recognize as a good thing—and this means Keynesian techniques will increasingly have to be applied internationally. . . .

There can be no pretense that domestic content legislation has anything to do with "industrial policy"—improving the competitive ability of American industry. It is protectionism, pure and unadorned, and each job "saved" will cost other American workers far more than it will bring the lucky beneficiary. Like most protectionist measures, far from aiding America's adjustment to world competition, it just helps put off the day of reckoning.

POSTSCRIPT

Should the United States Protect Domestic Industries from Foreign Competition?

Kuttner argues two basic points in his essay. First, he contends that the world English economist David Ricardo modeled in 1817 is starkly different than the world we know today. He describes our world as "a world of learning curves, economies of scale and of floating exchange rates," as a world where comparative advantage "is created not by markets but by government action." Second, he maintains that although free markets will lead to factor price equalization—that is, wage rates in developing countries will rise and our wage rate will fall as long as there is a differential—we should not, and cannot, allow this to happen. He asks us: Do we want wage levels in the United States to fall to a dollar an hour? Should we allow some nations to exploit their workforce so that we Americans can consume cheap goods and services?

Kinsley does not believe that free trade is a "relic" from the past. He maintains that Kuttner has just forgotten the lessons from his introductory economics course. After looking at the simple mathematics of Kuttner's proposal, Kinsley contends: "Protectionism is, in effect, a 'make work' jobs program . . . a ridiculously expensive one, both directly and indirectly." He believes we can achieve the same end without sacrificing the benefits of "international specialization." Kinsley goes on to argue that when "every major country protects every major industry"—the natural consequences of Kuttner's national industrial policy—"there will be no world market for any of them to conquer." He contends that we will return to the isolationists' world, a world that is poorer than it need be.

The presence of high unemployment levels both here and abroad has resulted in a new interest in protectionism. As in the case of the Kuttner essay, this plea for protection is often coupled with a plea for an "industrial policy." Robert Reich of the Kennedy School at Harvard clearly articulates this view in a two-part article that appeared in *The Atlantic Monthly* in March and April of 1983, and in his book entitled *The Next American Frontier* (Times Books, June 1983). The conservative response is equally well articulated. See, for example, Walter Olson, "Don't Slam the Door," *The National Review* (March 4, 1983); John Hein, "A New Protectionism Rises," *Across the Board* (April 1983); and, Richard W. Wilcke, "The Protection Racket," *Inquiry* (April 1983).

ISSUE 17

Will the Third World Pay Its Debt?

YES: Gary Hector, from "Third World Debt: The Bomb Is Defused," *Fortune* (February 18, 1985)

NO: Alfred J. Watkins, from "Going for Broke," NACLA's *Report on the Americas* (March/April 1985)

ISSUE SUMMARY

YES: Business journalist Hector argues that the danger of an international financial calamity "now appears remote."
NO: Economist Watkins suggests that "a rather simple benefit-cost analysis" indicates that "default may be the most viable and profitable option" for the debtor nations.

Early in 1986, the debt owed by Third World countries will exceed $1 trillion. More than forty percent of that total will be owed by Latin American countries. Indeed, three countries with the largest external debts are all from this region of the world: Mexico and Brazil each owe about $100 billion and Argentina owes nearly $50 billion. Thus, the eyes of the world are upon these countries. If these three large debtors and their neighbors decide to repudiate their debt obligations, they will pull down the house of cards that represent the free world's banking system.

It is interesting to trace historically the development of this banking crisis. It began innocently enough in the 1960s. As in all free market transactions, both sides of the market—the suppliers or lenders and the demanders or borrowers—willingly entered into the financial contracts that form the basis of this crisis. The Third World countries were in desperate need of foreign funds to underwrite capital investments which would sustain the level of economic growth these countries experienced in the post-World War II period. The banks, on the other hand, stood ready to supply these funds.

The system worked reasonably well. The funds which were borrowed were used to build new plants and to purchase new equipment. Investment in primary industries such as steel and oil production leaped forward. Industrial output increased, Gross Domestic Production* tripled from 1960 to 1980, and the sale of exports provided enough foreign currency to pay the interest on their foreign debt. Both the borrowers and the leaders were pleased with the system.

The energy shock of 1973–1974 served to accelerate the borrowing process. Both the number of loans and the size of the loans made to the governments and corporations of Third World countries increased markedly. The international banking community had excess dollars to lend. It must be remembered that as oil prices skyrocketed upwards from $2 a barrel to $20, $30 and

$40 a barrel, the oil producing countries could not spend their export earnings fast enough, so many of the dollars we spent on OPEC oil** were ultimately deposited in the large international banks. On the other hand, corporations and the governments of Third World countries were in serious need of loans. In many cases these countries were affected more directly and more severely than developed countries. They not only had to pay higher prices for the energy they imported but they were faced with escalating fertilizer prices since most fertilizers are petrochemicals. However, even in the face of the 1973–1974 energy shock and the second round of energy price increases in 1978, the system continued to work.

But note, to keep the system viable, the debtor nations had to increase their exports so that they could earn the dollars which were needed to service their ever-expanding debt obligations. When North America and Western Europe sank deeper and deeper into recession in the late 1970s and early 1980s, the demand for the exports produced by Third World countries began to fall dramatically. This reduction in spending was coupled with a growing protectionist mood. As a result of these two forces, total world trade began to decline for the first time in 30 years. Remember now, that the Third World was using its earnings to pay the international banks. Without exports there were no earnings and no way to pay even the interest on their debt.

Unfortunately, this is not the end of this tale of woe. At the very time that their export earnings were falling, the U.S. and the rest of the developed world began to raise their interest rates. In 1979, the prime rate*** in the U.S. was about 11%, by 1981 it had jumped to more than 20%. Since the interest rate Third World debtors were obligated to pay was linked to the prime rate, their interest costs nearly doubled overnight. This happened just as their ability to pay their debt obligations fell because of falling export earnings. The net result was that many, if not all, debtor nations were unable to pay their debt obligations. The debtor nations turned to the International Monetary Fund (IMF) and the international banking community. They asked the banks to "reschedule" their loans—spread the loans out over a longer repayment period—and to loan them new money to pay for the interest owed on their old debts. The banks had no choice. They postponed the repayment of the debt by making only the interest due and then loaned the debtor nations the money to pay that interest.

No one denies that this slight-of-hand works in the short run. But in a like manner, no one believes this ruse can be continued indefinitely. The question for us is: Have export earnings risen sharply enough and interest rates fallen far enough to make it economically and politically possible for Third World countries to repay their international debt? Business writer Hector asserts that the "international debt crisis is over." But economist Watkins remains skeptical. He suggests that this is one time that the banks "may well come away empty-handed."

*Gross Domestic Production (GDP) is comparable to our Gross National Product (GNP)—eds.
**OPEC—Organization of Petroleum Exporting Countries—eds.
***Prime rate—the interest rate charged to the best customers of banks—eds.

YES

Gary Hector

THIRD WORLD DEBT:
THE BOMB IS DEFUSED

Evidence is building that the international debt crisis is over. Gone is the nerve-jangling prospect that the world banking system might suddenly collapse as large Latin American countries proved unable or unwilling to honor their external debts. The largest debtor countries, notably Mexico and Brazil, have made stunning economic progress in the past year, posting strong real (inflation-adjusted) growth and surprisingly large trade surpluses. Obstreperous debtors, such as Argentina, have been muscled into accepting austere financial programs. And with Mexico leading the way, the debtor countries and their lenders are working out realistic long-term schedules for repaying the huge loans. Says Rimmer de Vries, chief international economist at Morgan Guaranty Trust Co., "The progress in the debt crisis is coming about three times as fast as we thought possible."

The improvement shows up most dramatically in the international financial accounts of the borrowers. In 1981, the year before the debt problem swelled to nightmarish proportions, the current account deficit of the 16 largest Third World borrowers totaled $55 billion. Morgan Guaranty estimates that last year the deficit shrank to just $12 billion. And while in 1982 the trade surplus of the six largest Latin American debtors covered just 5% of their interest bill, by 1984 the surplus equaled 87% of total interest payments. That's still not enough for these countries to begin paying down their debts, but it's impressive progress.

A feeling of hard times, to be sure, still pervades the major Latin American countries. Their economic feats, mainly in international trade, haven't brought similar gains throughout their economies. These countries are plagued by excess capacity in industries that produce for domestic markets, as well as high unemployment and declining real wages. The slums of Mexico City and Rio de Janeiro still attract thousands of the agrarian poor each day. Although the middle classes crowd swank shopping avenues in cities like Buenos Aires and São Paulo, in private they complain that their real

From "Third World Debt: The Bomb Is Defused," by Gary Hector, *Fortune*, February 18, 1985. Copyright © 1985 Time Inc. Reprinted by permission. All rights reserved.

incomes have plunged, in some cases to as little as 30% of what they were just five years ago. Clouding all these countries' futures is the still-stupendous task of servicing their foreign debt—a total of some $520 billion for the 16 largest Third World debtors, with interest payments amounting to about $55 billion a year. A spike in interest rates, a drop in commodity prices, or a sudden slowdown in the world economy could bring fresh setbacks on the long journey back to creditworthiness.

But while a year ago it seemed the problems of a single large country might spark an international financial calamity, the danger now appears remote. Officials at banks, international agencies, and government finance ministries are confident they can anticipate and avert new crises. And confidence is growing in the debt-restructuring process, the infuriatingly slow and untidy effort that puts debtor nations on the International Monetary Fund's stringent diet of hard-nosed monetary policy, curtailed government spending, and fewer imports.

At the end of 1983 there was little reason to believe the IMF programs would work. Although Mexico had become the darling of the international financial community by cutting its rate of inflation from 100% in 1982 to 80% in 1983 and posting a $13.7-billion trade surplus, the problems of Brazil, Argentina, and dozens of smaller borrowers appeared insoluble. Bankers doubted whether Brazil could ever live up to its agreements with the IMF and wondered whether Argentina might simply refuse to pay its debt, thereby disrupting the whole international restructuring effort. Long-term solutions—beyond the frenzied short-term debt reschedulings that seemed

necessary almost annually—appeared out of reach.

But 1984 surprised even the most optimistic bankers and financial policymakers. Brazil's economic resurgence probably did the most to bolster confidence that measures prescribed by the IMF would work. Early last year experts inside and outside Brazil were predicting that 1984 would be dismal. The country had bumbled along for two years, missing targets set by the IMF and then signing new letters of understanding—some seven separate agreements in 22 months to date. Economists expected the country to remain in a slump and to generate a trade surplus of $7 billion at most—far short of the IMF's target of $9 billion.

But the Brazilian government set out with a vengeance to boost exports. It kept the cruzeiro undervalued against the dollar, adjusting the currency almost weekly. As the U.S. economic boom roared along, so did Brazilian sales of soybeans, coffee, grain, steel, and a host of manufactured goods. Brazil missed critical IMF targets, most notably on inflation. But it shaved the government deficit by reining in spending, and its program got the economy moving again. Real gross domestic product grew at least 4% in 1984, and Brazil's trade surplus zoomed to a record $13 billion.

Mexico's performance proved nearly as impressive. By tightening expenditures and increasing the prices charged by companies in the public sector, the government whittled its budget deficit from 8.7% of gross domestic product in 1983 to 6.5% or so last year. Despite the tighter fiscal policy, the economy began to expand, with GDP increasing by more than 3% after a decline of 4.7% in 1983.

The government brought the inflation rate down further, to about 60% in 1984, missing the IMF's goal of 40% but pushing this important indicator in the right direction.

To fight inflation, the Mexican central bank, in an approach diametrically opposite to that of Brazil, let the peso rise modestly relative to the dollar during 1984. This took pressure off domestic prices but also brought a slowdown in non-oil exports during the second half of the year. Oil sales, which represent 70% of Mexican exports, remained strong. The country's trade surplus was a healthy $13 billion, down only slightly from 1983. International reserves swelled to $8.5 billion, emboldening Mexico to prepay $250 million of principal early in January and to announce plans to reduce its short-term trade credits by $1 billion.

Argentina, in contrast, suffered through a difficult year. Inflation roared out of control, hitting an annual rate of 1,500% during one week in September. It hardly helped that the government of President Raúl Alfonsín, which had won the election on a promise to keep real wages from falling, spent much of the year trying to honor that promise. But Alfonsin attacked government spending, halving the deficit. And early in the fourth quarter Argentina embraced an IMF austerity program, slamming the brakes on money supply growth and slowing inflation to a triple-digit level.

Argentina's real GDP grew at an annual rate of 3.5% during the first nine months but declined sharply in the last quarter, possibly because of the government's initial zeal in carrying out the IMF measures. Despite raging inflation, exports of agricultural products continued to buoy the trade balance, and the country wound up with a $3.7-billion surplus for the year.

Few developments have done more to dispel bankers' anxieties about Third World debt than those that brought Argentina to swallow the IMF's medicine last year. They showed how much pressure can be brought to keep a country from becoming an outcast of the international financial community. Of all the major debtors caught up in the crisis, Argentina was the most likely to default. It is self-sufficient in food and energy and, as the Falkland Islands war proved, unpredictable. But when Argentina took a tough stance with its bankers early in 1984 and refused to pay interest, it found itself virtually isolated.

Four Latin American countries came to Argentina's aid with portions of a stopgap loan—not because they sympathized but because they wanted to keep Argentina involved in the debt-restructuring process. Latin American finance ministers, economists from the IMF and commercial banks, and officials from major industrialized countries dropped by to remind the government of the consequences of defying the lenders.

The U.S. Treasury came up with another bit of persuasion: a list of items that would become scarce in various major debtor countries if they defaulted and imports came to a virtual standstill. R.T. McNamar, Deputy Treasury Secretary, emphasizes that the list did not single out Argentina. But he says it raised such interesting questions as: "Have you ever contemplated what would happen to the president of a country if the government couldn't get insulin for its diabetics?"

Further persuasion came from the Argentine economy. When the government saw inflation skyrocketing last September, it finally signed an agreement with the IMF. Then Alfonsín resolved to come to terms with the lenders. He requested a meeting with major bankers in New

York, arranged by Henry Kissinger, whose role was confined to host and matchmaker. The bankers had an unambiguous message: Argentina would have to pay past-due interest and stick to the IMF program. "It was the first time Alfonsín had met with the bankers," says a senior executive vice president of a leading bank. "From then on we made extremely rapid progress in our negotiations." Speeding progress was a change in Argentina's negotiating team. Enrique García Vazquez, governor of the central bank, replaced the abrasive economics minister, Bernardo Grinspun, as the principal negotiator.

While Argentina bowed to the international financial community, Mexico wrung concessions. In mid-1984 Mexico and its banks agreed on a 14-year debt restructuring that broke banking industry precedents and established a model that other debtor countries are hastening to follow. Some bankers complain that the package was developed by the U.S. Federal Reserve Board and "shoved down our throats." But the package was actually designed and marketed by the Mexicans. The architect was Angel Gurria, the bearded, 34-year-old director of the country's public credit.

A man of explosive enthusiasm and the stamina to negotiate nonstop for days, Gurria is considered a singular force in Latin American financial circles. "There is no one else like him," says an admiring banker, who also remembers enduring Gurria's wrath for once refusing to join a Mexican loan syndicate. "I've never been yelled at for a half-hour by anyone else," the banker says.

Articulate, and with a sense of the dramatic, Gurria masterminded Mexico's bargaining strategy. During a recent three-hour interview in his spartan, dimly lit office on the first floor of the old Palacio Nacional in Mexico City's central square, Gurria glowingly described his handiwork as "state of the art." By early 1984 he was quietly discussing a restructuring plan with sympathetic U.S. bankers. In early June, Fed Chairman Paul Volcker publicly weighed in behind the concept at a Philadelphia bankers' conference.

Gurria pushed for the longest possible repayment schedule. Previous reschedulings had postponed $23 billion of payments to a four-year period from 1987 through 1990. Those payments came atop $20 billion of principal already due in those years, creating towering annual bills of up to $15 billion, not counting interest. One of those payments would have come in 1988, the year of Mexico's next presidential election. Gurria wanted to level this Everest by pushing most of the principal payments out beyond 1990, to a period when little repayment was originally called for.

Aiding him was a nagging fear among bankers that a debtors' cartel, banding together against the banks, might emerge from a June meeting of Latin American governments at the Colombian resort of Cartagena. Although prospects for a cartel looked remote, bankers were anxious to complete the Mexican agreement before that gathering.

The restructuring allows time for the debt to shrink considerably in relation to Mexico's growing economy. If the economy expands more or less steadily at a reasonably healthy rate, total foreign debt will drop from 52% of GDP in 1984 to 32% in 1990. If everything works, Mexico should be able to tap the capital markets within the next few years. But the assumptions underlying Gurria's projections are critical. "Our bottom line is that this can be done if GDP grows steadily at 5% or 6% a year," he says. "If we can't do that, then all this is useless."

The other debtor countries have been fashioning their own versions of Mexico's solution. Venezuela has already agreed in principle to a long-term restructuring. Brazil is in the midst of negotiations on a similar package. Argentina hopes to start talks on a long-term agreement in mid-1985.

The 5% to 6% growth rates on which the restructurings are based look attainable to many economists. During the 1970s, the largest debtor countries hit growth rates of 7% to 10% a year. A lot depends on what happens in the industrialized countries that make up the Organization for Economic Cooperation and Development. If these countries post an average growth rate of 3% a year for the next five years, if interest rates don't soar, and if commodity prices remain relatively stable, the less developed countries can make their growth targets. "Given the good performance of 1984," says Henry C. Wallich, a governor of the Federal Reserve, "even if OECD growth drops to 2.5%, that should provide enough strength to pull us out of this problem."

It still won't be easy. The debtor countries will have to stick with the tough economic programs imposed by the IMF. And they will have to sustain high levels of real growth without being able to borrow as heavily as they did in the heady days prior to 1982.

No one expects the debtor countries to stop borrowing entirely. Gurria's projections for Mexico assume a gradual increase in total foreign debt through 1990. But this needn't mean an increase in the risks faced by bankers. Economists argue that it is possible for the debtor countries to show economic growth of 5% to 6% a year while increasing bank borrowing by well under 5% a year. If the capital of U.S. banks grows by 12% a year, as it has been doing, these banks can make more loans and still gradually reduce their exposure to the Third World as a percentage of their total portfolios.

In each of the largest Latin American debtor countries, 1985 will be a pivotal year, testing political leaders' determination to follow the IMF regimen. Brazil's most daunting problem is inflation, which topped 200% in both 1983 and 1984. Businessmen are assuming that inflation will exceed 250% this year, well above the IMF target of 150%. . . .

Mexico needs to broaden its export base beyond oil, especially now that prices are falling. Every $1-a-barrel drop in the price of crude reduces the country's export income by $560 million a year. Given Mexico's proximity to the U.S. and its bountiful supply of cheap labor, new sources of foreign exchange shouldn't be all that hard to find.

The administration of President Miguel de la Madrid Hurtado has been saying the right things about attracting private foreign capital, which could boost Mexico's current account surplus. But direct investment in Mexico fell to $29 million in last year's first six months from more than $2.5 billion in all of 1981. And the government has just rejected IBM's proposal to build a wholly owned personal computer plant, dooming the plan unless the computer company accepts Mexican participation. "If IBM finally does not invest," cautions Manuel Zubiria, deputy president of Banco Nacional de Mexico, "that will send an obvious negative signal to other potential investors."

Political analysts worry about middle-class discontent with Mexico's austerity measures. One disturbing sign is a recent surge in capital flight after a slowdown during much of 1983. As much as $20 million a day may be moving out of Mexico again. Another sign of disaffection is the growing support for opposition political parties. Businessmen worry that in order to bolster its political position, the PRI, Mexico's ruling party, will resort to lavish government spending. But most U.S. bankers are confident that de la Madrid's tough-minded financial advisers will prevail, and that he will avoid such excesses.

Despite the chaos in Argentina's economy, Raúl Alfonsín's government appears politically secure. The military has been discredited by the Falklands debacle, and the Peronist party, much like the Democrats in the U.S., is divided and impotent. That gives Alfonsin the freedom to stick closely to the IMF program, at least for now.

His commitment to that program has been almost fanatical. After the government slammed the brakes on money supply growth last fall, real interest rates—the rate paid above Argentina's rate of inflation—soared to an unbelievable 20% a month.

"The country is coming to a standstill," complains Rodolfo C. Clutterbuck, a director of Alpargatas SAIC, a diversified manufacturer of inexpensive canvas shoes and other consumer goods. Companies have stopped paying each other, he says, and instead are sticking all available cash in local savings institutions where they can earn sky-high interest. During the fourth quarter Alpargatas slipped sharply into the red.

Argentina's central bank is aware of the pain such interest rates inflict, but it considers them necessary to get inflation under control. The government has already been forced to shape rescue plans for a few large companies faced with bankruptcy, and it stands ready to pick up the tab for others. "We are developing policies to avoid a wave of bankruptcies, but we can't save everyone," says Leopoldo Portnoy, vice president of the Argentine central bank.

It is too early to predict how Alfonsín will fare in this and other battles. He will have to confront the unions' opposition to any erosion in real wages. Strikes and slowdowns are possible, such as a postal slowdown that left most Christmas cards in Buenos Aires undelivered for weeks. But if Alfonsin's policies succeed, inflation and interest rates should come down and economic growth should resume.

As all three countries show, the economic agony goes on even though the specter of an international financial collapse has receded. The IMF's harsh medicine works, but with painful side effects. The challenge for the industrial countries is to pursue sound economic policies themselves, fostering economic growth both at home and in the hard-pressed debtor countries.

_____

NO

Alfred J. Watkins

GOING FOR BROKE?

As bankers and finance ministers convened in Washington, D.C. last September for the IMF and World Bank's joint 1984 meetings, the mood was one of cautious optimism, in marked contrast to the doom and gloom which pervaded the two previous annual meetings. Gone was the fear that the banking system was on the verge of collapse. Mexico, Brazil, Argentina and Venezuela, the big four Latin American debtors, had all promised to repay the banks at the market rate of interest. Proposals calling on the banks to lower interest rates and provide financial relief to debtor nations had proved unnecessary. Beside feeling more financially secure, bankers also felt personally vindicated. Their business acumen, which had been questioned in the press and at congressional hearings, had proved solid. Their solutions had worked. The financial crisis had been weathered, as many bankers predicted, and the forecast was for smooth sailing.

While bankers were quietly celebrating their self-proclaimed victories, the stock market was signalling its belief that some sort of banking crisis is still a distinct possibility. For more than a year, the market had been pummeling bank stocks, in many cases pushing stock prices far below book value. Since book value is a measure of how much of a company's assets each share represents, the market is saying, in effect, that many bank assets, such as loans to Latin America, are no longer worth 100 cents to the dollar.[1]

As the stock market's evaluation suggests, financial analysts are betting that banks are not going to collect every dollar they are owed. If the analysts are correct, their gloomy prognosis raises serious questions about the soundness of the U.S. banking system as well as the sound judgment of U.S. bankers. Because bankers lent with such abandon during the 1970s, the stability of the U.S. banking system in the 1980s is now in the hands of a few government officials in Rio and Buenos Aires. If only one or two of the largest Latin American debtors—Brazil, perhaps, which owes U.S. banks $21 billion, or Mexico, which owes $27 billion—fail to keep making timely principal and interest payments, all of the largest U.S. banks would be operating in the red for years to come.[2]

From *Report on the Americas*, March/April 1985. Reprinted by permission of the North American Congress on Latin America, New York.

Concerning the judgment of bankers, market analysts point out that the highest management echelons of the largest—and supposedly most sophisticated—banks countenanced a whole host of irresponsible lending policies. In order to launch the "go-go" environment of the 1970s, banks exploited loopholes in federal regulations designed to limit the amount of money they are permitted to lend any one borrower. For example, banks made loans to the Brazilian government and the government-owned oil company, Petrobras, arguing that they were legally distinct entities, each entitled to borrow up to the legally permissible limit. As a result of this self-serving, but ultimately self-defeating, interpretation, banks boosted their Latin American loans far above the limits prescribed by U.S. regulations, not to mention common sense and prudence.[3]

Compounding the problem is the fact that several other banking safeguards were permitted to fall by the wayside. Salaries, bonuses and promotions were awarded on the basis of how many loans were made, not by how many loans were repaid. The name of the game was to make loans and move on, leaving the collection problems to someone else.[4] In the same vein, the loan applications were only cursorily reviewed to see if the project was economically sound and if the borrower could at least pay interest. In the days before the crisis hit the front pages, it seemed as if bankers didn't want to let trivial concerns about repayment stand between them and a customer who wanted money.

The result was a veritable frenzy of lending as credit officers, loan documents in hand, pursued any Latin American official willing to sign on the dotted line. Between 1975 and 1982, bank loans to Latin America more than quadrupled, rising from $23 billion at the beginning of the period to $97 billion when the crisis erupted eight years later. As the current crisis would seem to indicate, anyone can lend billions of dollars. But top bank officials are paid six-figure salaries precisely because they are supposed to be able to get the money back with interest. On this count, the market seems to be suggesting, bankers are singularly ill-suited for the task.

Bankers, of course, disagree vehemently. Yes, they admit, there may be individual cases of bad management or just plain stupidity. Bankers are no more immune from these basic human frailties than anyone else. And, they also admit, critics can always cite examples which "prove" that stupid loans were made and that incompetent managers were promoted. But on the whole, bankers deny that the international financial *system* is rife with stupidity and incompetence. More to the point, they deny that any significant number of imprudent loans were made. And, they assert, given time and some temporary additional assistance, debtor nations will be able to repay completely every dollar they borrowed.[5]

To a certain extent, these rebuttals might be discounted as a last ditch show of bravado. After all, if the critics are correct, bankers have nothing to look forward to but capital punishment. Banks will become insolvent wards of the federal government. Top management will be cashiered. Uninsured depositors face the prospect of large losses. And stockholders will be wiped out.

But perhaps their confidence isn't merely a show of bravado. Perhaps the bankers know something that stock market analysts do not, and this explains why, despite the problems of the past two years and the market's pessimistic forecast, bankers don't experience heart palpitations every time they contemplate their Latin American loan portfolios.

To understand the debt crisis from the perspective of bankers, start with the charge that bankers put all their eggs in one basket. Manufacturers Hanover Trust, which last year was threatened with a run on its deposits in the wake of rumors about its "unsound" international lending activities, has outstanding loans in Latin America equal to nearly three times its stockholders' capital. The other major banks rounding out the top echelon of U.S. international banking all have outstanding loans at least equal to their stockholders' equity, and in many cases, the amount is much greater.[6]

With such high exposures comes the potential for crippling losses. According to figures released by A.G. Becker Paribas, a Wall Street investment house, writing off only 10% of their loans to Argentina, Brazil, Mexico and Venezuela would wipe out more than an entire year's profits at Bank of America and Manufacturers Hanover. Other money-center banks, including Chase Manhattan, Citicorp, Chemical, First Chicago, Bankers Trust and Morgan Guaranty Trust, would all be seriously crippled, although each would still be operating in the black.[7] If ever there was a case of bankers lending too much to too few borrowers, this would appear to be it.

Yet from the bankers' point of view, putting all their eggs in one basket, in effect, overlending and deliberately avoiding steps to diversify risks, is a sterling example of "coercive vulnerability." When so many large banks make so many large loans to the same small group of borrowers, the slightest hint that a borrower is having trouble making payments means that it is not merely the survival of one bank that is at stake, but the survival of the entire Western banking system. The possibility of financial chaos virtually assures that the U.S. and other Western governments will weigh in on behalf of the banks, telling debtor nations to tighten their belts and devote more resources to debt payments. And on the slim chance that countries cannot, or will not, pay, coercive vulnerability increases the probability that banks will get some sort of government bailout.

Claiming that loan officers did not carefully evaluate each project also misses the point and, from a banker's perspective, displays profound ignorance about the type of risks inherent in domestic lending as opposed to international lending. Typically, each domestic loan is secured with collateral and a legal contract dedicating a portion of that project's revenues to interest and principal payments. If the projected revenues are not sufficient, the loan application will be rejected.

In the international lending arena, these financial requirements and legal safeguards are both impossible to enforce and meaningless, for at least two reasons. First, what matters to banks is not the economic feasibility of any individual *project* but the economic prospects of a *country*, that is, whether a nation can earn enough dollars by exporting goods and services to repay its loans. If it can, even loans for unproductive purposes, like luxury condominiums in Miami, are perfectly sound.

The borrower simply goes to the central bank, converting his *pesos* or *cruzeiros* into dollars, and remits those dollars to his banker. On the other hand, loans to build an economically productive, highly profitable steel mill may present severe repayment problems if the country runs out of dollars, perhaps because food imports are draining dollars from the economy faster than steel exports can replace them.

Secondly, even if imports are not excessive, bankers have no way of controlling a country's total indebtedness. This is especially significant because even if each loan passes the most rigorous credit evaluation, each succeeding loan increases the number of claims on a country's limited supply of foreign exchange. Inability to pay interest due to a shortage of foreign exchange—known as transfer risk—can transform "good loans" into virtually worthless IOUs. And this happens even though loans to the government sector were kept within safe and prudent bounds and loans to the most credit-worthy private sector borrowers were invested only in productive, profitable assets. Banks ignore transfer risk only at their own peril.

This is not merely a theoretical possibility. In many instances, banks were making loans to the Latin American subsidiaries of top-rated U.S. multinational corporations.[8] The subsidiaries used the borrowed dollars to purchase new factories and other productive assets. Yet when the time came to pay interest, the subsidiary defaulted. And it defaulted because it was producing for the local Latin American market—generating *pesos* or *cruzeiros*—while its liabilities were denominated in dollars. Normally, private borrowers expect to buy whatever dollars they need from their country's central bank. But if too many subsidiaries try to purchase dollars, their demand will soon outstrip the central bank's limited supply. The country will

appear bankrupt, even though not a single imprudent loan was made and every dollar was invested productively.

In foreign lending, in other words, all loans are good until the country has too many outstanding foreign currency loans, at which point all loans suddenly become worth less, if not worthless. Without some agency to monitor and limit the total foreign currency liability of every public and private entity in a country, one bank's loans will wreak havoc on the loan evaluations and collateral of its competitors. But since there are no controls, why go through the motions of performing loan evaluations? It's all a charade anyway, and the banks know it, even if their critics do not.

If, as the bankers believe, the crucial variable is a country's capacity to earn dollars to pay interest—and not some measure of project feasibility, it is not at all intuitively obvious that Citicorp's Walter Wriston and Chase Manhattan's David Rockefeller are the blunderers their critics make them out to be. A country, just like any other borrower, is bankrupt when its liabilities exceed its assets. But as *The Wall Street Journal* noted in a recent editorial, Mexico "could wipe out its foreign debt overnight by selling 20 billion barrels of oil at $4 a barrel."[9] At $29 a barrel, the current OPEC posted price, Mexico's assets are seven times greater than its liabilities. Banks would be hard-pressed to find many Fortune 500 companies that are so well capitalized and such sound risks.

What is true for Mexico is true for all the other Latin American debtors. In virtually every case, potential export revenues are many times greater than the outstanding debt. It is beside the point that current export revenues are not sufficient to pay principal and interest. As the IMF points out in its *1984 World Economic Outlook*, "What is crucial is not the current foreign exchange-earning ability of a country but its future prospects."[10] Seen from this vantage point, claims that the loans will never be repaid are nothing but the chant of modern day Cassandras. With a little belt tightening, the banks explain, every debtor nation can slash imports and increase exports. All they need is time to make the necessary economic adjustments and the political determination to use the newly generated trade surplus to pay interest.

During debt crises earlier this century, U.S. bankers did not believe that Latin American politicians could be trusted to impose the sort of pain that would be needed if the banks were to be repaid. Rather than relying on moral suasion, the United States dispatched Marines to occupy the customs houses of delinquent debtor nations. Their mission was to confiscate all export revenues and remit the proceeds to the banks. Today, gunboat diplomacy is out of fashion. But that doesn't mean the banks have eschewed outside intervention. Instead of Marines in combat fatigues, the shock troops are international bureaucrats from the International Monetary Fund who arrive with three-piece suits and attaché cases.

But no matter what the uniform, the process is the same. National sovereignty is diminished. The nation's productive capacity and raw materials become the de facto property of the banks. And financial policy is conducted with an eye toward ensuring that banks get repaid, irrespective of what happens to the local economy or domestic standards of living.

Today, banks and the IMF are locked in a symbiotic relationship. IMF "adjustment" policies cannot possibly succeed without cooperation from the banks, but banks are reluctant to offer any assistance unless the IMF first assures them that a debtor country's economic policies are oriented exclusively to repaying outstanding loans.

The IMF needs the banks for the simple reason that a national economy cannot generate the required trade surplus overnight. Redeploying resources on such a massive scale takes time. Products that had previously been imported have to be pressed into service-boosting exports. All this takes time, but for the banks, time is the one resource that is in critically short supply. Unless they receive interest payments every 90 days, banks are required by U.S. government regulations to start posting losses on their delinquent international loans. A delay of even one day can do severe damage to a bank's bottom line, converting an otherwise profitable quarterly earnings report into a financial disaster.

To give the adjustment program time to work, someone needs to provide debtor nations with enough cash to keep paying interest. The IMF provides some assistance, but it does not have nearly enough funds to keep every country up-to-date on its interest payments. In this respect, the IMF is simply incapable of bailing out the banks. Unless the IMF program is going to fail before it even gets off the ground, banks have to chip in with new loans and postpone, or "reschedule," payments coming due on old loans. . . .

For banks, the debt crisis is little more than a simple arithmetic problem. As long as a debtor nation can generate a trade surplus equal to its required principal and interest payments, that country is not bankrupt, no matter how much trouble it is currently having meeting its quarterly bank payments. Thus, calls for lower interest rates and other forms of debt relief are met by bankers with steely eyed hostility. Their attitude toward today's pleas for leniency is reminiscent of Calvin Coolidge's response to European countries petitioning for relief from their World War I debts. "They hired the money, didn't they," was his only comment.

Latin American officials do not deny hiring the money. But from their perspective, whether or not to repay the debt at market interest rates is a political and economic question, not a mathematical problem. The key variable is the willingness to pay rather than the ability to generate the additional export revenues. Latin American officials have never claimed that their economies do not have the resources needed to produce the required trade surplus, only that doing so will be politically intolerable and economically disastrous.

Most Latin American leaders have not stinted in their effort to play by the banking community's rules, despite the economic hardship it has caused. The speed with which they have converted trade deficits into trade surpluses—generating dollars with which to pay interest—is nothing short of remarkable. In 1980, Latin America imported $7.4 billion more than it exported. In 1981, the trade account still showed a deficit of $1.6 billion. But by 1982, in the midst of the worst postwar recession, there was a trade surplus of $9.7 billion and in 1983 of $31.2 billion.[11]

The $33 billion turnaround in the merchandise trade balance between 1981 and 1983 was due entirely to a dramatic fall in imports. The value of Latin American imports was reduced by over 40%, falling from $98.5 billion in 1981 to just over $56 billion in 1983. The drop in imports

was especially sharp in Mexico, where a $17 billion turnaround in the merchandise trade balance was caused by a 62% fall in imports from $24 billion to $9 billion. Over the same two-year period, Argentina cut its imports by 50% and Brazil slashed its by 30%.[12]

Imports are also inputs. Thus it is not surprising that such sharp cuts in imports resulted in equally sharp cuts in the resources available for sustaining economic growth and standards of living. . . .

According to a study by the U.N. Economic Commission for Latin America (ECLA), most of the so-called growth generated by additional exports is merely a statistical chimera. The exports will not be used to purchase needed imports and the resources consumed in the export sector will not be available to produce goods and services for domestic use. Instead, all the additional output will be sold overseas and the proceeds turned over to the banks in the form of interest payments.

Consequently, the production of goods and services available for domestic use is expected to be relatively stagnant, at best, and declining in per capita terms. The result, the ECLA study explains, is that "about 90% of the labor force incorporated in the 1980s would be out of work in 1990. . . . In the production field, the decline in investment, the dismantling of installed capacity, and the discouragement rife in business circles gives grounds for fearing that the production potential likely to be achieved in 1990 will be less than that existing in 1980."[13]

Financing the current account deficit with additional borrowing will do little to alter this gloomy prognosis. Borrowing merely changes the timing—not the volume—of the resource drain. Since . . . the IMF expect[s] that banks will be lending debtor nations only as much as they need to keep paying the market rate of interest, Latin American debtors will not really be receiving any new funds. Every penny they receive will be laundered through the debtor nation's treasury and returned immediately to the banks in the form of interest. This laundering process helps banks maintain the fiction that their previous loans are still worth 100 cents to the dollar. But as far as the debtor nations are concerned, these new loans only increase the volume of raw materials and manufacturing output they must export in order to pay interest.

Even more to the point, borrowing to pay interest has been a chief cause of the debt crisis, so it is difficult to see how even more borrowing offers a way out of the morass. Since at least the mid-1970s, banks and debtor nations have been co-conspirators in a giant Ponzi scheme. Virtually all of the increased indebtedness has been consumed by debt service payments. Between 1977 and 1983, for example, Latin America's total external debt rose from $116 billion to $336 billion. Of this $220 billion increase, $154 billion, or 76%, was consumed in interest payments.[14] . . .

Latin American debtor nations are now in the midst of a profound economic transformation. Their current account deficits are not caused by gluttony or excess spending. In virtually every case, imports are down sharply and exports are rising. In other words, the current account deficit is negative, not because Latin American nations are living too well, but because interest payments are too high. Even the IMF admits this is the case. "A growing proportion of the cur-

rent account deficit of the non-oil developing countries has been . . . primarily the result of higher interest payments on the external debt," the fund stated in a recent report.[15]

With this in mind, a growing chorus of Latin American officials is now demanding some limits on the amount of interest they are required to pay. This past May, in a speech before the New York Society for International Affairs, Aldo Ferrer, former Argentine finance minister and current adviser to President Raúl Alfonsín, stated the issue succinctly. "The question now before Latin America's debtors," he said, "is how much of their domestic resources should be appropriated to meeting their foreign commitments."[16]

For over a year, Latin American debtors have been trying to give Western governments an answer. What they are saying, in a nutshell, is that they are prepared to pay much less than the banks are demanding. In January 1984, Latin American debtors convened their first joint consultation, issuing the Quito Declaration and Plan of Action. Heading its list of suggestions is a call to "harmonize the requirements of debt servicing with the development needs of each country."[17] To accomplish this, the Quito Declaration insists that "export earnings should not be committed beyond reasonable percentages."

Six months later, the Argentine government echoed those sentiments. In a letter to Jacques de Larosière, managing director of the IMF, then Economics Minister Bernardo Grinspun stated that "there is no question of nonpayment," but then went on to explain that the government has "decided to limit the volume of such payments to the resources available to it from exports, without reducing imports below the volume essential to maintain" satisfactory rates of investment and economic growth.[18]

Exactly what the Argentines had in mind was clarified a few pages later. From the beginning of 1984 to the end of 1985, Argentina projects that export earnings will grow by $745 million. Over the same period, imports are projected to increase by $650 million. Although it is never explicitly spelled out in the text, the implication of these statistics is clear: virtually all of the future growth in export earnings will be dedicated to reviving the economy. After Argentina has satisfied its domestic needs, the banks can have whatever is left over, in this case only 13% of the additional export revenues.

The precedent Argentina is trying to establish is quite radical. Creditors, especially the big money-center banks, are used to dictating terms. They are not used to having their clients throw down the gauntlet and issue ultimatums. But while the letter to the IMF is a bold departure from tradition, it still displays a remarkable willingness on the part of the government to play by the banking community's rules. Argentina's export earnings are projected to be $9.4 billion, generating a trade surplus of slightly under $4 billion. The government is willing to use this surplus to pay interest. They will tolerate a $4 billion drain. But required interest payments are projected to be approximately $6 billion. The government is absolutely unwilling to slash imports by another $2 billion, on top of the 50% cut implemented since the crisis began, simply so they can pay every penny the banks are demanding.[19]

Although Argentina is generally viewed as the country that is most eager to probe the limits of the financial system's tolerance, it may soon come to be viewed as one of the hemispheric moderates. The new civilian government has said it will not increase the amount of export earnings devoted to paying interest. However, this is far more generous to the banks than a proposal formulated by the Latin American Economic System (SELA),* calling for step reduction in the volume of export earnings committed to interest payments.[20] . . .

As it becomes increasingly evident that the solutions applied over the past two years by the banks and the IMF cannot possibly alleviate the debt crisis, Latin American governments will be impelled to embrace policies like those recommended by SELA. The precise steps they adopt will be determined by a rather simple cost-benefit calculation. The benefits of radical actions are the payments that would have gone to the banks but which can now be used for domestic consumption and investment. The costs are those associated with becoming an international financial pariah: assets will be seized, trade credits will disappear, the country will be forced to conduct its trade on a cash and carry basis, or, if the banking system refuses to clear its checks, the country may be forced on to a barter system. As a result, imports will become more expensive and the profits from each dollar of export sales will be lower.

*SELA was founded on the initiative of Presidents Carlos Andrés Pérez of Venezuela and Luis Echeverria of Mexico, and was endorsed by 23 Latin American and Caribbean nations—including Cuba—in October 1975. SELA's constitution states it is a "permanent regional agency for joint consultation, co-ordination, co-operation and economic and social promotion." Its main purpose is to promote collective efforts toward economic development, economic independence from the United States and improved terms of trade. SELA's headquarters are at the Latin American Council in Caracas.

As debtor nations see it, the costs will probably be the same if the country adopts a relatively moderate posture and announces that it will not increase the percentage of export earnings devoted to paying interest, or if it takes the extreme step of reducing its payments dramatically. The only thing that will vary are the benefits, which increase as the country adopts more extreme measures. At this point, the chief question for debtor nations is at what point will the benefits exceed the costs.

A recent Brookings Institution study by Thomas Enders, former assistant secretary of state for inter-American affairs, and economist Richard Mattione, tries to answer that question.[21] Their calculations indicate that default may be the most viable and profitable option. If the costs of repudiation are equivalent to a 5% fall in export revenues and a 5% rise in import prices, Enders and Mattione report that Brazil, Argentina, Mexico and Venezuela would face hard times for the first year or two. But by 1987, output and standards of living would have rebounded and they would all be better off than if they had followed the IMF's prescription. Even if the hypothetical penalties are doubled, the general conclusion is the same: repudiation would still be an attractive option for Argentina, Brazil and Venezuela.

The actual cost of default may be much less than Enders and Mattione report. Their analysis is based on the assumption that default will provoke a total credit blockade of the offending countries. To the bankers' chagrin, talk of a financial quarantine may be wishful thinking.

In the first place, it is not entirely clear that, in this instance, punishment is even a meaningful concept. As Aldo Ferrer explained, "As the principal debtors are living on their own means, they cannot be punished with the threat of being cut out of essential supplies."[22] Or put another way, since they are already generating large trade surpluses, debtor nations do not need credit to finance essential consumption and investment. With repudiation, they can take the money they were using for interest payments and spend it instead of boost economic growth and standards of living.

Second, smaller regional banks with limited exposure in defaulting countries will see little advantage in joining their crippled rivals in a hemispheric boycott.[23] As many smaller banks are beginning to understand, debtor nations will be excellent credit risks after they default. If they do not have to pay so much to Chase Manhattan and Citicorp, virtually every heavily indebted country will have enough export earnings to service the new loans extended by the new creditors. And to make matters even more enticing, small banks have come to realize that they would be able to charge much higher interest rates on their debtor nation credits. All they have to do to justify these higher rates is cite the debtor's generally bad credit rating and recent history of default. In the unlikely event that smaller regional banks will not want to get involved, U.S. exporters will probably pick up the ball, providing the short-term credits where bankers fear to tread. As debtor nations know, the good will of suppliers is necessary to keep imports flowing. But as long as suppliers are getting paid, there is only a slim chance that they will boycott a country that has the temerity to anger the bankers. No U.S. exporter is going to relinquish such a large market merely because his customer has chosen to pay him instead of someone else. The chance that they will boycott an entire continent following a generalized debt moratorium is virtually nil. Latin America buys more U.S. exports than Western Europe.[24] . . .

One country probably will not act unilaterally, but as the pressures promise never to relent, and the punishment for declaring a moratorium promises to diminish, the ranks of the restless debtors are certain to grow. Already, Bolivia and Ecuador, relative small fry in the ranks of international debtors, have declared a moratorium on all interest payments, pending negotiations to arrange a more favorable payments schedule.[25]

This defiance, coupled with the recent Mexican and Argentine debt reschedulings, are vivid reminders of how rapidly the banks' bargaining power is eroding. As the press reported it, the Mexican debt rescheduling was a triumphant example of the divide and conquer strategy instigated by Federal Reserve Board Chairman Paul Volcker.[26] Since Mexico had been a compliant debtor, dutifully meeting and exceeding the financial targets of its IMF adjustment program, Volcker urged the banks to give Mexico a more lenient financial package, including more time to pay off old loans and lower interest rates.

This September, the banks complied. They agreed to postpone Mexico's principal payments falling due through 1990 and to repackage those payments into a new loan due in 14 years. The lower interest rates the banks agreed to charge will save Mexico $400 million a year on its $12 billion annual interest bill.

In reality, except for the interest rate concessions—which are too small to make any material difference to the Mexican economy's prospects for recovery— the banks had little choice but to sign an agreement with Mexico. Mexico's old repayment schedule, negotiated with the banks and the IMF after the August 1982 collapse, had merely postponed the crisis. Principal payments coming due in 1983 and 1984, which Mexico had no hope of making on schedule, were rescheduled until 1987. This gave Mexico immediate short-term relief, but only at the expense of a vastly bigger repayment burden in 1987. Unless this "payments bulge" were eliminated with a second rescheduling, Mexico would be forced to default. To prevent this from happening, the banks had to act.

The interesting question now is whether other countries will get similar treatment. They too are facing a similar payments bulge, and without new reschedulings and interest rate relief, will be unable to meet their current payment schedule.[27] But the problem from the banks' perspective is that none of these countries has been as compliant as Mexico. Therefore, if the banks' divide and conquer strategy is not to be exposed as a hollow threat, they will have to argue that the less co-operative debtors neither deserve to have their old loans rescheduled nor to get new loans to finance their continuing current account deficits. Will the banks refuse to play ball with the less compliant big debtors?

The answer became clear last December, when the banks announced that Argentina would be given an additional 12 years to repay its bank debt, $4.2 billion of new loans from a consortium of 320 banks and $1.6 billion from the IMF. In exchange for more time and nearly $6 billion in new money, Argentina promised to comply with the IMF's strict economic adjustment policies, pay immediately most of the $1.2 billion of overdue interest it owes to its bank creditors and not fall behind on future interest payments.

But when push came to shove, precisely because it had been so ornery, Argentina walked away from the bargaining table with a better deal than Mexico which was given more time to pay, but not more money with which to pay. In the Argentine deal, each bank in the lending syndicate promised to increase its loans to Argentina proportionately by 16.75%, a much bigger amount than any other debtor nation received since the crisis first erupted more than two years ago.

Argentina's ability to get so much new money is stark proof of how little leverage the banks really have. Simply put, Argentina was not paying the banks on time and there was very little the banks could do about it. When they signed the agreement with Argentina, for example, that country was already more than $1 billion behind on its required interest payments and $10 billion behind on its principal repayments. In addition, more than two-thirds of its bank debt was coming due by the end of 1985. This unpleasant fact of life left the banks with only two choices: they could give Argentina new loans and extend its repayment schedule or they could refuse, recognizing that, irrespective of their decision, they weren't going to get paid.

Put this way, the banks viewed their so-called choice as really no choice at all. By refusing to give Argentina more time to repay and more money with which to resume paying interest, banks would have had to declare their Argentine loans in default and remove them from their balance sheets. Bank earnings would fall, with several big banks operating in the red. To avoid this prospect, bankers showed that they are willing to go to almost any lengths to maintain the fiction that everything is for the best in the best of all possible worlds.

This Panglossian attitude is not without its costs, however. It requires banks to keep lending more money so that debtor nations will have enough cash on hand to keep paying interest on their old loans. Unfortunately, this increases the vulnerability of the international financial system, for two reasons. First, debtor nations find themselves deeper in debt and no closer to being able to service their loans. New loans today mean higher interest payments tomorrow and a second round of additional lending to pay the rapidly exploding interest bill.

In addition, the banks have to borrow the money they are lending, usually by issuing Certificates of Deposits (CDs) or having their parent holding company issue commercial paper. Then U.S. bank regulators require them to raise fresh capital, usually in the ratio of $1 of capital to support every $16 to $20 of new loans. In other words, banks have to dilute their shareholders' earnings per share for the privilege of allowing the Ponzi scheme to continue for a few more rounds. Beyond that, as is the nature of any Ponzi scheme, banks are going deeper in debt to fund loans which allow Third World borrowers to go deeper in debt. This practice does make it seem as if the financial system is still solvent, but only because one debt pyramid is being constructed for the express purpose of fueling a second debt pyramid.

The banks are now finding themselves hoisted with their own petard. As the economics of the payments burden pushes the financial system closer to a crisis, the banks' earlier strategy of coercive vulnerability will come back to haunt them. Even the sort of minor concessions that will almost certainly be necessary to keep debtor nations playing by the rules for a few more months can wreak havoc on the banks' balance sheets. As a result, banks may have no choice but to hold out for all or nothing. To their chagrin, they may well come away empty-handed.

NOTES

1. For example, see Daniel Hertberg, "Big Bank Stocks Fall as Investors Challenge Worth of Foreign Debt," *The Wall Street Journal*, June 8, 1984; "Concern About Quality of Loan Portfolios of Many Major Banks Is Likely to Increase," *The Wall Street Journal*, October 4, 1984; and "Major Banks Avoid Big Loan Write-Offs But Sharply Boost Their Loss Reserves," *The Wall Street Journal*, October 18, 1984; Robert Bennett, "Burden for Bank Shareholders," *The New York Times*, October 24, 1984; "The Blues at Manufacturers Hanover," *The New York Times*, October 14, 1984; C. Edward McConnell, "Argentina—Throwing Good Money After Bad," *Keefe Bank Review* (New York), October 4, 1984.

2. The effect of bank earnings is discussed in Suzanne Andrews, "Accounting for LDC Debt," *Institutional Investor*, International Edition (August 1984), p. 61–66.

3. See "How It All Went Wrong," *The Economist*, April 30, 1983, p. 11–14; Michael Moffitt, *The World's Money* (New York: Simon and Schuster, 1983), chapters 2 and 4.

4. See Lawrence Rout, "Bank Responsibility for Mexico's Woes," *The Wall Street Journal*, October 22, 1982, which quotes one banker: "We don't get promoted for not making loans. I wouldn't be getting raises if I'm warning my home office to slow down while everybody else is charging ahead."

5. For some of the clearest and most forceful statements of this view see the testimony of William S. Ogden, vice chairman, Chase Manhattan Bank, William H. Bolin, vice chairman, Bank of America and George J. Clark, executive vice president, Citibank, all in U.S. House of Representatives, *International Financial Markets and Related Problems, Hearings before the Committee on Banking, Finance and Urban Affairs, 98th Congress, First Session*, February 8, 1983.

6. See for example, prepared statement by Paul A. Volcker in the February 8, 1983 banking committee hearings. Also see "The War of Nerves Over Latin Debt," *Business Week*, June 18, 1984, pp. 20–21; and Henry S. Terrell, "Bank Lending to Developing Countries: Recent Developments and Some Considerations for the Future," *Federal Reserve Bulletin*, Vol. LXX, No. 10 (October 1984), pp. 755–63.

7. As reported in "How Can American Banks Account for Those Latin Loans," *The Economist*, June 2, 1984, p. 87.

8. Robert Cohen, "Bank Financing of the Subsidiaries of Transnational Corporations in Latin America," unpublished mss. (1984).

9. "The Creditors' Club," *The Wall Street Journal*, June 20, 1984.

10. International Monetary Fund, *World Economic Outlook 1984*, Occasional Paper 27 (Washington, D.C.: IMF, 1984), p. 63.

11. Economic Commission for Latin America, *Adjustment Policies and Renegotiation of the External Debt* (New York: ECLA, 1984), p. 4.

12. Ibid, p. 21 and Table 5.

13. Economic Commission for Latin America, *The Crisis in Latin America: Present Situation and Future Outlook* (New York: ECLA, 1984), p. 75.

14. All statistics are computed from IDB, *External Debt*, Statistical Appendix 1 and 2.

15. IMF, *Outlook 1984*, p. 61.

16. Aldo Ferrer, *Debt, Sovereignty and Democracy in Latin America*, Speech presented at the New York Society for International Affairs, May 10, 1984.

17. The text of the Quito Declaration and Plan of Action is printed as an annex in "Letter dated 9 February 1984 from the Permanent Representative of Ecuador to the United Nations addressed to the Secretary-General," General Assembly, Economic and Social Council, Document A/39/118 E/1984/45, February 29, 1984.

18. "Letter from Economy Minister Bernardo Grinspun to M. Jacques de Larosière, Managing Director of the International Monetary Fund," June 9, 1984.

19. All statistics are from Ibid.

20. Latin American Economic System, *Renegotiation of Latin America's External Debt: Proposals for the Implementation of the Quito Declaration and Plan of Action*, (Caracas: SELA), March 1984.

21. Thomas O. Enders and Richard P. Mattione, *Latin America: The Crisis of Debt and Growth*, Brookings Discussion Papers in International Economics, no. 9 (December 1983).

22. Ferrer, *Sovereignty and Democracy*, p. 11.

23. Conclusions about the possible behavior of smaller, regional banks are drawn from private conversations with officers of several banks.

24. U.S. exporters are already beginning to chafe at the lost sales which they attribute to high interest rates charged by U.S. banks. As the exporters see it, every dollar a developing country spends to pay interest is one less dollar which it has to buy goods and services. On this point, see for example, Everett G. Martin, "Latin Debt Crunch Hurting U.S. Firms," *The Wall Street Journal*, May 8, 1984. Also "Export Bust," *The Economist*, March 31, 1984, p. 84.

25. See "Ecuador Says It Wants to Restructure Debts Owed to Governments," *The Wall Street*

Journal, June 5, 1984; "Bolivia Suspends Payments to Foreign Private Banks," *The Washington Post*, May 31, 1984. Also see, S. Karene Witcher, "Bankers Worry That Smaller Latin Debtors Could Be the Next to Face a Payments Crisis," *The Wall Street Journal*, October 17, 1984; Alan Riding, "Pact on Peru's Debt Not Expected Soon," *The New York Times*, December 25, 1984; and "Bolivia: Government and Creditors at Impasse," Inter-Press Service, July 20, 1984.

26. See for example, S. Karene Witcher, "Mexico, Volcker Allied on Debt Strategy," *The Wall Street Journal*, May 29, 1984, which reports, "Sources familiar with the Fed's strategy say it wants to reward countries with generous repayment terms if they follow strict economic austerity plans and stay current on their bank payments." For Argentina's attempts to counter the Fed's divide and conquer strategy, see S. Karene Witcher, "Argentina Spoils 'Reward' Strategy," *The Wall Street Journal*, June 15, 1984.

27. Harold Lever et al., *The Debt Crisis and the World Economy* (London: Commonwealth Secretariat, 1984), chapter 2.

POSTSCRIPT

Will the Third World Pay Its Debt?

Business journalist Hector argues that since Argentina has agreed to "swallow the IMF's medicine," the evidence suggests that the "international debt crisis is over." He rests his case on the following facts. Argentina was the least cooperative debtor nation. But this non-compliant nation yielded to the "pressure" of the international community. Thus if the strong-willed Argentines will yield, other less strident countries will yield.

Economist Watkins is far less optimistic about the future of the international debt situation. He argues that the debtor nations may have the ability to repay their loans, but they may not have the willingness to repay these loans. He indicates that a benefit-cost analysis suggests that the benefits associated with defaulting are greater than the costs associated with defaulting.

If the debtor nations do default, the costs to the international banking community would be immense. Many suggest that without immediate and massive public aid, many large banks would be forced into bankruptcy. Even the suggestion that these loans will not be repaid sent shock waves through the financial networks. Thus, many large banks try to comfort their shareholders in their *Annual Reports*. Therefore, for the best defense of Hector's position, turn to these reports. Much has also been written in support of Watkins' position. Indeed, much of the March/April 1985 edition of *NACLA's Report on the Americas* is devoted to this issue. For an excellent review of the events leading up to the current crisis, you may want to read Jeff Frieden's article in this magazine.

ISSUE 18

Is the Pain and Suffering Associated with Disinvestment and Sanctions Worth It for Black South African Workers?

YES: David T. Beaty and Oren Harari, from "South Africa: White Manager, Black Voices," *Harvard Business Review* (July-August 1987)

NO: Helen Suzman, from "The Folly of Economic Sanctions," *Business and Society Review* (Spring 1986)

ISSUE SUMMARY

YES: Management experts Beaty and Harari argue that whether or not disinvestment will hurt black workers must be examined in light of the fact that many blacks believe that "investment hasn't helped them in the first place."

NO: A long-time member of the Progressive Federal Party in the South African Parliament, Helen Suzman argues that economic sanctions will ruin the South African economy and destroy the "inheritance that blacks inevitably will one day share."

In a democratic country such as ours, it is hard to imagine the reality of a constitutional government which explicitly excludes 73 percent of its population from its protections. Yet this is what exists in the Republic of South Africa. Daily we are reminded of the evils that are associated with South African apartheid that includes the enforcement of more than 300 racially motivated laws that systematically deny blacks their right to vote, to live where they choose, to seek employment where they want, to attend schools that are reserved for white children, and to live in decent housing.

Perhaps because of its economic success—its ability to raise living standards for all members of the South African population, its regional importance for the economies of its neighbors and its significance as an export market for many in the developed world—the Western world has taken great care in responding to the obvious and intolerable practices of the South African government. That is, no one wants to kill the goose that lays the golden egg, but at the same time no one wants to be blamed for standing idly by while that goose pecks to death the offspring of the eggs that do hatch.

Although condemnation of the system can be traced to the turn of the century, an activist economic strategy was not devised by its U.S. opponents until the late 1960s and early 1970s. In these years, church leaders joined college students and civil rights groups to pressure the banking community to withhold loans to the Republic of South Africa. These early tactics had relatively little effect on the loans made to South Africa, but they did prepare the way for the widespread use of stockholders' resolutions which have appeared in the last ten years and have called for disinvestment in South African operations.

The prospect of the devastating economic impact of these resolutions if they became fully implemented have prompted a more moderate response from the business community. One hundred and twenty-seven of the 200 U.S. firms with operations in South Africa have endorsed a code of business conduct that is popularly known as the Sullivan Principles. (The Reverend Leon H. Sullivan is a black Philadelphian minister and a member of the General Motors Corporation's Board of Directors. In consultation with twelve other U.S. firms, he drafted these guidelines in 1977.) These principles required firms operating in South Africa to: 1) provide color-blind eating, comfort and work facilities; 2) follow equal and fair employment practices for all; 3) provide equal pay to all employees doing equal or comparable work for the same time period; 4) initiate and develop training programs to prepare blacks, coloureds and Asians (the official minority classes in South Africa) for management and skilled positions; 5) increase the number of blacks, coloureds and Asians in management and supervisory positions; 6) improve the standard of living of employees, such as improving their housing, transportation, schooling, recreation and health facilities; and 7) "support the ending of all apartheid laws." (This guideline was added in 1985.)

For ten years the Sullivan principles provided the middle ground between those who would disinvest and those who would not meddle in the affairs of this African state. However, after ten years the Reverend Sullivan withdrew his endorsement from the code of ethics which carries his name. In a June 3, 1987 news conference, he stated that although his principles have been "a tremendous force for change," in the end they have "failed to undermine apartheid." Thus he called on all U.S. firms to disinvest in South Africa by March 1988 and for the U.S. to initiate an economic embargo of that state.

What are the consequences for the non-white community, which is the majority population? Beaty and Harari tell us that this can only be judged in light of what investment means for this majority population. Many in this community feel that they have little to lose. M.P. Helen Suzman disagrees. She argues that the costs of disinvestment and sanctions will fall "more heavily on those it is meant to help than on those it is meant to punish."

YES   David T. Beaty and Oren Harari

SOUTH AFRICA: WHITE MANAGERS, BLACK VOICES

James R. is a black South African production worker, married, middle-aged, the father of four children. He has worked in his current job for almost three years. Before this, while he was unemployed, he heard from relatives about a company in the Western Cape that was hiring. He traveled there with his family from the eastern part of the country, a distance of about 800 miles.

As he tells it, James was plagued by anxiety during the trip west because he had no permit to settle in the vicinity of Cape Town. On arrival, he and his family stayed with friends in a new black "township" 30 miles from the city. (Townships are segregated, slapdash communities, usually near white urban centers.) His friends had been ordered to move there from their old home on one month's notice.

The morning after his arrival, James and his friend walked two miles to catch a 3:30 A.M. bus. It was crowded and the two had to stand the whole way, for about an hour. After changing buses downtown James reached the company at 6:30 A.M. He recounts his visit: "The white recruitment officer asked questions about my background, where I lived, and whether I had the necessary documents to prove I was allowed to live and work in the Western Cape. When I told him I didn't have any documents, but that I had moved to the area temporarily while I looked for a job, he told me I had to go and get my documents sorted out before I could be hired. I went to the authorities to get a permit but I was told that there was no housing available for me in Guguletu [one of several townships set aside for blacks who work in the Western Cape] and that I would have to go back to the eastern area where I came from. When I went back to the company, and told them what the authorities had said, I was told: 'No documents, no work. Go away.' "

James concludes his story with an exasperated laugh. "This is free enterprise? Free enterprise for who? Not for us. I see how I live, and I see how my friends live." He leans forward. "Do whites really think that we will accept their free enterprise system when we are not free?"

From "South Africa: White Manager, Black Voices," by David T. Beaty and Oren Harari, *Harvard Business Review*, July/August 1987. Copyright © 1987 by the President and Fellows of Harvard College. Reprinted by permission. All rights reserved.

PRODUCTIVITY & MORALE

We have conducted intensive research over 2½ years into the attitudes of managers and workers in five large South African plants—three owned by South African companies, one by a European multinational, and one by an American multinational. We spoke with 361 black employees and 60 white supervisors and managers. Our intention, at first, was to restrict ourselves to a survey of attitudes toward work, to find the answers to some basic questions: Why is the productivity of black workers in South Africa among the lowest in the world? What do black workers want from their jobs? What do white managers think blacks want? After analyzing the comments of our respondents, however, we abandoned the notion that our original restriction was useful, or even possible.

Instead, we began to listen more patiently to James R. and dozens of other men and women, and we found their stories illuminating in a way we hadn't expected. Of course, we understood that there were political inequalities in South Africa. What we hadn't fully realized was how much these impinged on worker productivity and satisfaction. To understand labor relations in South Africa, one must appreciate how the workplace can seem an extension of apartheid, and how apartheid can seem to have originated precisely in the efforts of former generations of whites to put blacks to work.

To be sure, many blacks—James R. included—will tell you that the modern industrial factory or office can make black workers feel more nearly equal than ever before, what with job training programs, opportunities for skilled work, or even something as basic as an integrated (and tiled) washroom. Yet proximity to white South African co-workers may exact an emotional price of its own. A job does not necessarily bring with it the sense of a promising future. For most of the blacks we interviewed, new privileges at work only heightened their expectations and thus intensified the despair they felt during the long bus ride back to the township.

Indeed, we found that many of the terms that American management specialists and scholars commonly use when speaking about labor relations and productivity—"job security," "effective communication," "production incentives," and the like—can, in South Africa, mean something quite different to blacks than they do to whites. American management textbooks, which abound in South African business courses, hardly prepare novice managers for the resentment and skepticism that black workers will direct toward them.

Although the workplace provides a key to understanding the current social crisis, it is folly to think that reform of the workplace alone will prevent further upheaval.

Unexpected Finding

A white South African, like an American, tends to separate the rigors of a job from the privileges of citizenship. When whites go home, they are no longer subject to somebody else's direction, they can participate in national life. Hence most white managers assume that they can solve productivity and employee morale problems by looking for flaws in the organization's system, structure, policies, or leaders.

Black South Africans look at things differently. They cannot separate their lives inside the corporation from the domination they perceive on the outside.

Even when, superficially, blacks and whites are in accord on the purposes of work, they are actually speaking from two different worlds.

Consider the one striking result produced by our initial survey. We began our research by asking black employees to rank in order of importance the things that would motivate them to work hard: good pay, interesting work, appreciation, and so forth. We then asked their white supervisors and managers to predict the order of black responses. The findings are presented in the *Exhibit*.

Note that, for the most part, blacks emphasized bread-and-butter factors (pay, job security, working conditions, promotion) and that white managers seem fairly accurate in their perceptions of what motivates black workers. Yet the question of "interesting work" seriously confounded white expectations. Blacks ranked it second, right after "good pay." Whites expected it to come sixth, after "being in on things." Behind this difference we found a vast gulf of misunderstanding.

White managers generally defined interesting work in terms of work redesign, autonomous work groups, quality circles, and participative management. Most were surprised that black employees rate this factor as high as they did, and conceded that some of their productivity problems may have resulted from their failure to implement enough enrichment programs. Others expressed concern that blacks had not been much involved in planning such programs.

But one white manager seemed to grasp a deeper problem: "We've instituted participative management systems and quality circles to try and get our workers more involved in the company. In some parts of the company we've had some success, but overall we've not achieved the gains we'd expected. Frankly, workers seem resistant to talking freely either to their white supervisors or to each other. They don't seem to trust the company, us, or, surprisingly, even each other."

Black workers we spoke with admitted that often they do not trust one another—because some blacks are secretly collaborating with police and security forces. "We have informers among us," one of them told us. And unlike white managers, they saw the performance of challenging tasks as a special opportunity to prove their human dignity. As one young worker put it, "We are expected by whites to behave as though we can only perform simple tasks. We are not encouraged to take initiative or make changes in the jobs we've been told to do." According to another, "Every time white managers want to make our jobs more meaningful, they don't involve us in their plans. They make changes in our jobs, but we are not consulted about what we need. If they were interested in really improving our work, they would ask our opinions." Still another worker commented, "They hold all the power anyway. They are not really interested in sharing it."

Inadvertently, it seems, we hit on one of the fundamental tensions of apartheid. For whites, interesting work seemed a remote problem for black employees. That so many South African blacks could be seen doing tedious work—hauling, pitching, digging—only reinforced this prejudice. For blacks, interesting work represented a chance to exert their faculties for planning, reasoning, building, and taking responsibility. Skeptical as blacks were about the political context in which their companies operated, they cherished the opportunity to be more nearly autonomous.

Still, the political facts remained uppermost in their minds: "Whites think they can be nice and helpful in the workplace and everything is fine," said one black worker. "But when we leave this factory, we have to get on a train or a bus that has separate white and black coaches; we have to be careful about not going into a toilet reserved for whites only; we are told that we can't drink in a bar reserved for whites; we must eat in separate restaurants. These things make us angry and suspicious about what whites say and do. When these apartheid laws are torn down so that we can mix freely outside our factory, only then will we mix freely inside the factory."

DIFFERENT LANGUAGES

Once we began to think of whites and blacks as talking different languages, other parts of the survey fell into place. The management texts that had seemed so authoritative during our business training proved especially misleading here. They assumed that while managers would be divided by status and salary, they would at least share a common perspective on the workplace. In South Africa, however, the division ran much deeper. White managers tended to see the organization, and the problems that affected it, as separate from outside life. To the blacks, this was a meaningless distinction.

Pay Equity?

Although whites were largely accurate in predicting the order of black workers' responses, it could hardly be said that they were onto the same principles, even when it came to something as apparently

Exhibit
What Motivates Black Workers in South Africa

Incentives	How black workers ranked incentives	How white managers expected them to respond
Good pay	1	1
Interesting work	2	6
Job security	3	2
Good working conditions	4	3
Promotion	5	4
Being in on things	6	5
Help with personal problems	7	10
Loyalty to fellow employees	8	8
Appreciation of work done	9	7
Tactful discipline	10	9

straightforward as "good pay," which both groups ranked first. While most white managers saw good pay purely as a corporate matter, black workers could not dissociate it from the larger issue of economic freedom. Moreover, the two groups disagreed strongly over whether pay equity existed.

Many, not all, white managers agreed that whites and blacks employed in the same job should receive the same pay. Most whites thought that while pay discrimination toward blacks had occurred in the past, the system was not being reformed. They pointed to the Sullivan

Principles and other guidelines for progressive management that helped initiate, as one manager put it, the "positive changes that are now occurring."

Others saw that increased pay alone did not solve many organizational problems, but thought the solution was to do away with reform. One white production manager (who had worked in both the United States and Europe) expressed a common view: "I can't understand these blacks. They're not like workers overseas. They don't respond to incentive schemes. They complain about low wages. But when you increase their wages, they don't work any harder. I don't care what they say, I don't believe they deserve any more wage increases."

While black workers generally approved of reformist measures like those advocated by the Sullivan Principles, they denounced the notion that a trend toward pay equity was taking shape. One trade union leader referred us to a recent study that showed that South African blacks earned only 60% of what whites in the same job classification got. Another worker angrily pointed his finger, saying: "How do you expect us to believe what white managers say? They claim pay scales are equal. We haven't seen it and don't believe it. Until our leaders are represented in white management ranks so that we know the real facts, we won't believe what whites tell us." Another added, "Whites are taking the profits of the company to line their pockets while we struggle to make enough money to keep bread on the table for our families."

An even more important and emotionally charged issue came up in the discussions on pay: blacks felt that pay equity was meaningless unless accompanied by the eradication of racial laws that restricted ordinary market transactions. Their bitterness can only be partially summarized in the following typical stories.

• A 50-year-old man, married, with six children: "Even though I get pay increases, I have less money to live on. I'm forced to live in a township that is far from where I work. There are houses close to the factory where I would like to live with my family, but they're reserved for whites or for coloureds [a 'mixed race' classification]. I have to leave around 4 A.M. in order to catch two buses and one train so that I can arrive at work by 7:30. Bus and train fares have gone up so much that almost one-third of my paycheck goes into paying for transposition to work. What difference does it make if the company increases my pay when the increase is taken by this oppressive government to pay for ferrying us blacks in and out of white areas? Why can't these managers understand that until we are allowed to live where we choose, pay increases will benefit them, not us?"

• A middle-aged man: "I have to take the pay they offer because they know I can't move to another part of the country to look for more money. I do not like this, It's not fair."

• A young single man: "It makes no sense for a company to pay us more money while outside these factory gates we can't spend it the way we want. We are told where to live, where to spend our leisure time, and who we can mix with. We don't want money handouts to make up for the way we and our families are oppressed. We want apartheid done away with so that we can spend our money how we want. Can't you whites understand that?"

Job 'Security'

Another point of contention came from the difference between white and black perceptions of the idea of job security. Whites generally viewed it strictly in terms of tenure within the company. One forceful white manager summed up the prevailing attitude as follows: "We can't guarantee job security for our employees. We're living in tough times. That's an economic fact of life. We have to tighten up on hiring, and retrenchment means some people have to go. They [blacks] should understand that."

Black workers see things differently. One black trade unionist had this to say: "Whites make unilateral decisions to hire and fire, and then blame us when we go on strike to protest their mass retrenchments. What they don't realize is that workers are prepared to reduce their wages and work 'short time' if it means that nobody will lose jobs. But they never consult us. They act like apartheid oppressors: we are pawns to be picked up and dropped at will."

More alarming was the agreement that job security per se means little for blacks when the society as a whole seems oppressive. One 24-year-old said, "How can managers say that job security means we are secure, when our lives are always threatened by arrests and detention?" Another young man described how one of his friends was arrested and detained for six months after attending a rally held by the United Democratic Front, a political party that opposes the government. His family was given no word of his whereabouts. When he was released, he was nervous and withdrawn—and without a job, as his former supervisor told him that his position had been filled and his services were no longer required. When he finished the story, the young man added cynically,

The Sullivan Principles

These were devised in 1977 by the Reverend Leon Sullivan of Philadelphia as a code of conduct for American multinationals in South Africa. They are:

Principle 1
Nonsegregation of the races in all eating, comfort, locker room, and work facilities.

Principle 2
Equal and fair employment practices for all employees.

Principle 3
Equal pay for all employees doing equal or comparable work for the same period of time.

Principle 4
Initiation and development of training programs that will prepare blacks, coloureds, and Asians in substantial numbers for supervisory, administrative, clerical, and technical jobs.

Principle 5
Increasing the number of blacks, coloureds, and Asians in management and supervisory positions.

Principle 6
Improving the quality of employees' lives outside the work environment in such areas as housing, transportation, schooling, recreation, and health facilities.

Principle 7
Working to eliminate laws and customs that impede social and political justice.

On June 3, 1987, Reverend Sullivan stated in a press conference that adherence to his code by 127 of some 200 American companies in South Africa had "failed to undermine apartheid." He called for both disinvestment and a trade embargo.

"Now I understand what it means when business and government work together."

"Job security is different for blacks," another worker observed. "Even if the company *says* I have job security, I do not believe I *have* job security because if I lose my job, I cannot move to another area to find work, even if I am qualified."

An older black employee argued that security should not end at the company gates: "My life and my home inside the townships are not secure," he said. "The 'comrades' [mostly young blacks opposed to any cooperation with white authorities] tell me not to pay rent, and the white housing authorities tell me to pay rent. They both threaten me. Many people are afraid and insecure in the townships. Until my company puts pressure on the authorities to let us live where we want, we will always be faced with these problems."

Another worker, describing why job security within the company means little to him: "I came from the Transkei [one of the black 'homelands' recognized only by the South African government] with my family to look for work in Cape Town. Since all the townships were overcrowded, I could find no place to live. So I built my own house in Crossroads [a large, quasi-legal settlement outside Cape Town], using scrap metal, wood, and plastic. It was hard work, but eventually I had a place where my family and I had some shelter. I looked for work and found a job as a construction worker. For a few months, we felt safe and secure.

"Then one evening when I came home from work, my wife told me that some white and black policemen had come to tell us that we would have to move to another area called Khayelitsha. I didn't know where it was. I asked my neighbors and they said it was a place far away. I wanted to take my family and run away but I didn't know where. When the soldiers came the next day they began tearing down and burning our homes. They put us into trucks to go to Khayelitsha. I couldn't go to work that day. We were taken to a place where we had to stay in tents. I couldn't find transportation to get to my work because we had been moved far away.

"After a few days, I walked several kilometers to a bus station and went to my work. When I arrived, my boss told me that I didn't have a job because I had

stayed away from work. When I tried to explain to him about what had happened he refused to listen to me and told me to go away."

WORKER APPRECIATION

Given the apparent sincerity of many white managers, it is ironic that some of the angriest responses from black workers pertained to "appreciation for work done." Whites defined appreciation in terms of giving workers praise, recognition, and positive reinforcement for good work.

Many of the white executives we spoke to seemed genuinely frustrated by the failure of their efforts to achieve results. "We've trained our managers and supervisors in the principles of *The One Minute Manager*," said one. "You know, set joint goals, praise employees for good work, and reprimand them when they're not productive. We found in practice that these principles don't work with blacks. Blacks seem to be hostile and resistant to any form of praise or recognition."

An older white manager also expressed discouragement: "We've tried to run competitions for workers who achieve production targets and promised them bonus incentives, recognition in the form of prizes, or even feature articles in our in-house journal. We've had some success, but the amount of money and time we've put into these schemes has just not given us the returns we expected. We've actually had to drop most of them. They've created more antagonism from blacks than cooperation."

Blacks responded to this notion of appreciation with barely suppressed fury. As one older black worker said, "Appreciation? They don't appreciate us as human beings. They show us that every day, at work and outside. Until they open their eyes and listen to what we've been saying, I will reject their insincere attempts to show me 'appreciation.' " A younger worker was equally cynical: "When my white supervisor tells me that he likes the work I do, I wonder to myself, 'what does he want this time?' "

This, finally, from another young black: "Whites must stop talking about 'appreciating' us. They must start helping us do something about the system that makes our lives unbearable outside these gates, or we will continue to be bitter and more violence will result."

BUSINESS AGAINST APARTHEID

What *can* be done about the system? Do our findings suggest a strategy for the American executive who is grappling with the disinvestment dilemma?

For one thing, the question of whether disinvestment will hurt blacks should be understood in the context of black perceptions that investment hasn't helped them in the first place. Just as blacks define the job differently from whites, they also define "help" differently.

Blacks repeatedly stressed that help means action aimed directly toward dismantling — not reforming — apartheid. For South African blacks, corporate actions that simply emphasize internal issues like pay equity, job training, and integrated facilities all miss the point.

Well-meaning white managers may not realize that improvements inside the company only accentuate the bleakness of black life outside. The blacks we talked to agreed that they want foreign multinationals to stay in South Africa only if they are actively involved in the struggle against apartheid itself. As one black employee said, "Making things better at work is not enough. They must help destroy apartheid or they can go home."

Blacks affirmed that they were prepared to suffer short-term economic losses if the multinationals left. . . .

'A BLACK-RUN COUNTRY'

These suggestions undoubtedly present a painful dilemma for American executives and investors. American multinationals want to do the right thing, morally as well as financially, but strategic planning does not ordinarily include highly political acts or attacks on the institutions and laws of the host country. For blacks, however, that is precisely what is required in South Africa.

We conclude with two more voices— the first, a progressive white South African manager, the second, a black trade unionist just released from detention. They plainly differ in tone, but it is folly to ignore what they agree about.

The white manager: "Whites in South Africa are not anticipating the future. They see the future in terms of what they're used to and base their decisions and business strategies on accepted Western principles. But they don't seem to accept that by the 1990s, South Africa is going to be a black-run country. They pay lip service to human upliftment by writing out a check for a few thousand rands, sending it to some university, and going home and having a smug drink. But that's the wrong road to take. Whites must be in the vanguard in promoting a system where everyone, regardless of race or color, will have a stake in running the country and its economy."

The black worker: "For us blacks, nothing has changed from the oppression we've always had to bear. Whites don't know us and haven't bothered to find out about us. We don't believe they're interested in tearing down apartheid, now or gradually. Until white managers do something about liberating us, we will not participate in their schemes to make us work harder. If they won't help us remove our chains, we'll go it alone. You tell your white friends that we mean this. When we are liberated, we will remember the people who helped us. If these American and European companies do not help us in dismantling apartheid, they are not welcome here. They must leave this country; otherwise, we will view them as our enemies."

NO

Helen Suzman

THE FOLLY OF ECONOMIC SANCTIONS

Recently at the Students Union at Oxford University, Dr. Chester Crocker and I opposed the motion "that economic sanctions are necessary for the abolition of apartheid." Not surprisingly, the vote on the motion went against us. But the important point is that the students at Oxford were prepared to listen to the argument. It is doubtful whether this would be the case on any campus in the United States, for there the issue has been reduced to a simple equation—if you are against sanctions you must be for apartheid—you must be a racist.

It should be made clear that the ultimate aim of the motion—the abolition of apartheid—was not at issue. There was consensus that there is no valid argument against the abolition of a system that has so much inherent cruelty and oppression. It was on the means to that end, on the strategy to be employed, that there was a difference of opinion.

Whether criticism of Pretoria constitutes outside interference with domestic affairs, whether there are double standards, or whether expediency is implicit in the strong sentiments presently evident in U.S. public opinion is irrelevant. It would be a sad day if countries like the United States, which cherish human rights as their basic philosophy, allowed apartheid to go unprotested. As for double standards, while it is true that many countries that practice oppression worse than that of the apartheid regime escape the wrath of the world, South Africa claims to belong to the community of Western democracies and therefore must expect to be judged by those standards and not by those observed behind the Iron Curtain or in some Third World countries.

Certainly, there is expediency in the opposition to apartheid in the United States and elsewhere. No doubt, Citibank and Chase Manhattan pulled the financial plug on South Africa at the beginning of August 1985 because of threats of withdrawal by depositors rather than because of moral strictures against apartheid. And no doubt, too, the presence of black voters in their constituencies encouraged many U.S. congressmen to leap onto the anti-

From "The Folly of Economic Sanctions," by Helen Suzman, *Business and Society Review*, Spring 1986. Copyright © 1986, Business and Society Review, 870 Seventh Avenue, New York, NY 10019. Reprinted by permission.

apartheid bandwagon. Why not? Here was one of those rare occasions in politics when expediency and morality coincide.

Nevertheless, the two main factors that motivate people to support the imposition of sanctions are the moral factor and the punitive factor. Both are understandable. The moral aspect is a healthy impulse that makes one want to have nothing to do with the country that implements the repulsive system of apartheid—the "clean hands" syndrome. And that is fine, until it is realized that by divesting or disinvesting, which are two forms of sanctions, any influence that might have been exercised inside South Africa, such as setting an example to others regarding adherence to fair employment practices and exercising their social responsibilities, also disappears. The desire to punish South Africa, to use punitive measures like sanctions against the apartheid regime, is certainly understandable.

But retribution, when it comes, is not selective. Indeed, it falls more heavily on those it is meant to help than on those it is meant to punish. True, white South Africans would certainly feel the impact of sanctions, as indeed they are feeling the impact of the bank freeze and the drastic decline in the value of the rand. Businessmen in particular are now much more vocal than ever before in their opposition to apartheid. But business lobbies have far less influence, far less clout, with the government in South Africa than do their counterparts in the United States. It is not the businessmen who put the National Party regime in power. Most of them support the official opposition, the progressive Federal Party. The government is kept in power by civil servants, programmed over forty years to implement apartheid. About 40 percent of gainfully occupied whites are directly, or indirectly, in government employ in South Africa. Many of them are likely to turn their backs on the government and veer right if it deviates too far from existing policy. The regime is also kept in power by the white artisan class, such as the mine workers and other skilled workers in industry, who are hardly to the forefront of the struggle for black advancement, and by the rural white electorate which is notoriously reactionary.

The brunt of such measures would be felt by blacks at home and in the heavily dependent neighboring countries in South Africa. Whatever harm is done to South Africa's economy will certainly harm the economies of the neighboring black states, all of which are dependent to a greater or lesser degree on South Africa for jobs, markets, and transportation. The former High Commission Territories of Botswana, Lesotho, and Swaziland are part of a Customs Union with South Africa and belong to the rand monetary area. South Africa's Escom is an important source of power for these countries.

They depend entirely on routes through South Africa for trade. Malawi, Zaire, Zambia, and Zimbabwe are also heavily dependent on South African transport and ports for their imports and exports. Trade between South Africa and the rest of Africa is substantial. Alternative sources of supply could only be found at greater cost.

Over a quarter of a million foreign blacks work in South African mines alone, earning $1.1 billion per annum, half of which is repatriated. A further 70,000 blacks are employed in other occupations in South Africa, plus an estimated 1 million "illegals."

At home, blacks are always the first to

get fired during economic recession. Unemployment is no light matter in a country like South Africa, which has no social security safety net. A visit to Port Elizabeth, once a thriving industrial town in the Eastern Cape, would be instructive. Today, Port Elizabeth is dying, in the most painful manner. Ford and other assembly plants have closed down. Unemployment among black workers is up to 60 percent. The townships are in ferment; they are occupied by police and the army. Daily there are reports of shootings and tear gassing. Black-on-black violence is horrific, with kangaroo courts meting out rough justice. Eight murders in a week are not unusual. Transfer this scene throughout the country and anarchy results, with blacks the main victims of the strategy of making the country ungovernable.

To all this the response is usually, "But blacks say they don't care. They say they are suffering so much already, that more suffering, more unemployment, will not matter." Well, generally blacks who say they don't care either have nothing to lose, or they are already unemployed. The second category—those who will lose nothing—are in sheltered employed: their jobs are not in jeopardy. And those in the third category—those who want everyone to have nothing—hope that unemployment will spur on the revolution and will lead to a swift transfer of power to the black majority.

COLLAPSE FEASIBLE?

There is little point in entering into arguments about the first two categories, but the third category deserves some attention. If it were feasible that sanctions would do the trick, the sanctions would bring down the Pretoria regime instantly, or, at worst, within weeks rather than months, to borrow Harold Wilson's famous prediction regarding the demise of Ian Smith's government in Rhodesia (a demise, incidentally, that took a further fifteen years to be accomplished, and with it the death of some 30,000 people), if sanctions would swiftly rid South Africa of the system of apartheid and replace it with a nonracial democracy, no reasonable person could fail to back such action to the hilt.

But this proposition is, in fact, not feasible. The euphoric idea that the Pretoria regime would collapse within a short time following the imposition of sanctions shows a woeful ignorance of the intransigence of the nationalist Afrikaaner character, and indeed one might say also of many English-speaking South Africans and their determination to retain, as long as possible, the status quo of white domination. They will agree to, and indeed already have accepted, incremental change, some of it more than cosmetic. But the total dismantling of apartheid and removal of its foundation stones, such as the Group Areas Act, the Race Classification Act, and the Land Acts, are simply not on the cards in the foreseeable future. Nor is transfer of political power to the black majority.

The Pretoria regime will not fall because of sanctions. It will make the changes it intended to make, which will fall far short of what it believes is demanded of it by the undefined expression "dismantling apartheid and sharing power." Thereafter, if continued pressure is put on it, the Pretoria regime will retreat into the *laager*, bringing with it an even more oppressive system than has been experienced up to now in South Africa.

This is not just a gesture of defiance; it is to the Afrikaaner nationalist the essential for survival. He has no motherland to return to; he represents 75 percent of the white electorate that put him in power to implement the policy of apartheid, and he has formidable military and police forces to back him up. Indeed, part of the 75 percent has already been eroded by the white political parties to the right of the National Party, which oppose any deviation from the old Verwoerdian, pure apartheid dicta.

There is no swift capitulation in sight. There is no possibility that the South African saga will have a rapid and happy end, if only sanctions are imposed. Nor is there any guarantee that a total transfer of power to a black majority will result in the replacement of the existing regime by a democratic nonracial government that will respect the rule of law and ensure a free press, free association, and free elections. The basic premise, that sanctions are necessary for the abolition of apartheid, implies that nothing else will do the trick. This is not true.

INTERNAL FACTORS

Although external factors have played an important role in promoting change, internal factors are likely to be more effective in the future. It is not only defections to the right that are eroding the National Party's power structure. There are also an increasing number of white South Africans, among them Nationalist M.P.s, who realize that apartheid is the disaster that has caused turmoil at home and isolation abroad. In South Africa, it is fashionable these days to say that white politics are irrelevant. On the contrary, white politics are very relevant, because whites are in power. Parliament remains an important forum from which to hold the government accountable for its actions and from which to propagate alternative policies through the press gallery.

South Africa does not consist of only radical blacks on the one hand and pro-apartheid whites on the other. There are hundreds of thousands of white South Africans who abhor apartheid. At the last general election, 20 percent of the white electorate voted for the Official Opposition, which advocates universal adult franchise, the repeal of all racially discriminatory laws, and a bill of rights within a geographic federation.

In addition, within South Africa there are extraparliamentary organizations whose actions could be very effective through black trade union action and black consumer boycotts. Both weapons will be much more effective when blacks dominate the skilled labor market and have increased their consumer power. Blacks will acquire this enhanced economic muscle only in an expanding economy, not in a shrinking market for black manpower induced by sanctions or disinvestment. It never seems to occur to the advocates of such punitive measures that success in their implementation would undermine the most significant power base that blacks could acquire.

The question may well be asked, "Why disapprove of disinvestment and sanctions and not of strike action and consumer boycotts, which are also a form of sanctions?" The reply is that strikes can be settled and called off, and consumer boycotts can be discontinued. They do not destroy the economy permanently. Repeal of mandatory sanctions can be vetoed by one vote at the U.N. Security Council. And once investors have withdrawn, they do not come back, as the experience in black African states has demonstrated.

SELF-DEFEATING SANCTIONS

Sanctions and other punitive measures

are, in fact, self-defeating, for they blunt the cutting edge of the real weapons that blacks ultimately will be able to use against apartheid with which to make demands that will have to be accommodated. All this is long term, and it is manifestly true that blacks, especially young blacks, are demanding liberation *now.* "Liberation before the next school term" was one slogan heard toward the end of last year. Indeed, among the worst of the side effects created by outside pressures for sanctions is the delusion among young blacks that the transfer of power is imminent. Nothing is further from the truth, yet that sort of false impression has kept the unrest at fever point, has kept hundreds of thousands of black pupils out of school for months on end, and has led to the death of more than 1,000 black people over the last sixteen months, some through vicious vigilante gang wars, some through gruesome "necklace" murders, and most by police action.

People living 6,000 miles away from the scene who think they can judge the situation accurately have no idea whatsoever of the strength and ferocity of the police and military inside South Africa.

Indeed, not only is victory not around the corner, it is not even within sight. Not only is the transfer of power not imminent, it isn't even under consideration. Change, however, is. And that is what should be encouraged—attainable objectives—as a forerunner to creating a climate for negotiation about the total dismantling of apartheid and black participation in the political power structure.

The Western democracies should keep up condemnation of apartheid; they should keep up pressure against apartheid, by all means, but not pressure that will lead to chaos and the wrecking of the economy. That is the strategy of despair—destroying the inheritance that blacks inevitably will one day share.

The system of apartheid—legally sanctioned racial discrimination—is an affront to people concerned with civilized values throughout the world. The eradication of apartheid would be an important gain for the civil rights movement and would increase the sum of human freedom, worldwide, but it should not be at the cost of more deaths, more poverty, more misery, more starvation, and more oppression.

———————

POSTSCRIPT

Is the Pain and Suffering
Associated with Disinvestment and Sanctions Worth
It for Black South African Workers?

Professors Beaty and Harari have recently collaborated on a book for Ballinger Press entitled *Management and Public Policy: Lesson from South Africa.* They argue that the more than 300 laws used to enforce apartheid (the African word for separate development) impacts so negatively worker productivity and undermines morale, that blacks are now calling on Western firms to participate actively in the process of dismantling apartheid. If these firms don't take an active role, they will no longer be welcome. The black leadership recognizes that workers will "suffer short-term losses if the multinationals left," but they are willing to pay that price.

M.P. Helen Suzman argues that the black community underestimates the cost of disinvestment and sanctions: 1) Western firms will lose the ability to influence policies such as pay equity, job security, and worker appreciation—the direct concerns of Beaty and Harari, 2) neighboring black states such as Botswana, Lesotho, Swaziland, Malawi, Zaire, Zambia and Zimbabwe would all suffer if the economy of the strongest country in the region was damaged, and 3) most importantly, the white Pretoria regime will fight on for control of the government no matter how many firms leave or how many sanctions are

imposed and in the process they bring into being "an even more oppressive system than has been experienced up to now in South Africa."

And so the debate rages on. Now that multinationals no longer have the Reverend Sullivan's endorsement for their agreed-upon code of ethics, they must draft a new code of ethics and remain in South Africa or they must leave. Where do they turn for guidance? Perhaps the same places that you could turn. One place to start is the Spring 1986 issue of the *Business and Society Review*. Besides the Helen Suzman essays, there are more than two dozen other articles on this crisis. Next look at the Congressional Hearings held before the Subcommittee on Africa-Committee on Foreign Affairs, House of Representatives on December 4, 1984. Lastly, check through your old issues of the *Wall Street Journal*. Here you will find many stories that chronicle the struggle of firms to come to grips with this reality. For example, in early 1987 you will find stories of Union Carbide staying in South Africa; and Dow Chemical, Kentucky Fried Chicken, Black and Decker and Exxon making plans to sell out. No doubt when you look, you will find another half dozen firms announcing their decisions.

PART 4

PROBLEMS FOR THE FUTURE

As we look ahead, what are some of the key economic issues that will shape life in the United States? Two issues that have recently received close attention from economists are the size of the middle class and the state of the manufacturing base of the United States—both thought to be driving forces in economic growth.

Is the Middle Class Shrinking?

Is Manufacturing Alive and Well and Living in the United States?

ISSUE 19
Is the Middle Class Shrinking?

YES: Katharine L. Bradbury, from "The Shrinking Middle Class," *New England Economic Review* (September/October 1986)

NO: Frank Levy, from "The Middle Class: Is It Really Vanishing?" *The Brookings Review* (Summer 1987)

ISSUE SUMMARY

YES: Federal Reserve Bank of Boston economist Bradbury believes that the middle class is shrinking; that is, there was a decline in the percentage of families with middle class incomes between 1973 and 1984. In looking for the causes of this decline, she concludes that demographic changes do not fully account for the shrinking and, therefore, the shrinking of the middle class was not "illusory or temporary."

NO: University of Maryland economist Levy sees substantial stability in the distribution of income over time: "The middle three-fifths of families has received between 52 and 54 percent of all family income in every postwar year." Although there was little income growth between 1973 and 1974, the U.S. has been "able to maintain 'the middle-class dream' through demographic adjustments."

What is the American dream? When asked this question people respond in different ways, but part of the American dream involves economic considerations. One dimension to the economic component of the American dream is an equitable distribution of income. This means that the economic rewards, or the income that individuals receive, depend on their economic contributions, their efforts in the workplace, and not on such factors as age, sex, race, or religion. A second dimension is the expectation of a steady reduction in the number of poor persons. A third dimension is that each succeeding generation should enjoy a higher standard of living—that there be an increasingly larger middle class enjoying an increasingly higher standard of living.

Is the economic component of the American dream a reality? Consider first the question of equity. Government statistics indicate that certain racial groups receive only a fraction of the income enjoyed by the typical individual or family. In 1985 the median income of white families was $29,152 while the median income of black families was $16,786. Racial minorities also experience higher unemployment rates: in 1986 the white unemployment rate was 6 percent while the black unemployment rate was 14.5 percent. Similar statistics indicate substantial differences in the incomes of male and female workers: the median income of year-round full-time male workers 14 years and older in 1985 was $24,999 while the corresponding figure for females was $16,252. Although there is agreement on the existence of these disparities, there is disagreement as to why they exist. Different racial and sexual groups differ in a number of ways including age composition, geographic distribution, occupational distribution, and levels of job experience. The income and unemployment data need to be adjusted for these differences before any conclusions regarding discrimination can be made.

As for the ability of individuals and families to obtain the necessities of life, the usual measuring rod is the government's poverty count. In 1960 there approximately 40 million poor persons. By 1969 the number of poor was significantly lower; because of economic growth and the creation of a number of programs to aid the poor, the number of poor persons was estimated at a little more than 24 million. However, 1979 there were more poor people than in 1969, about 2 million more. During the early part of the 1980s the poverty count continued to increase, reaching a high of more than 35 million in 1983. Again there are disagreements regarding the lack of progress in reducing poverty, but this aspect of the economic portion of the American dream is not being realized.

But this issue is not about income differentials or the poverty count; rather it focuses on the third component of the American economic dream: the status of the middle class. Is the size of the middle class increasing? Is the standard of living enjoyed by the middle class increasing? These questions are addressed in the following readings. To answer these questions certain problems must be resolved. One problem is an appropriate definition of the middle class. Clearly the reference is to those persons and families who are neither rich nor poor, but where exactly should the lines be drawn to separate the various groups? Another problem arises when it is recognized that even if the size of the middle class remains unchanged, the standard of living or real income enjoyed by the middle class may have changed. A third problem involves explanations of changes in either the size or the standard of living of the middle class. Suppose the size of the middle class remained unchanged, what forces were at work to prevent the size of the middle class from expanding? Or worse yet, suppose the size of the middle class was decreasing while the size of the poverty class was increasing, how should one explain the failure of the economy to realize this part of the American dream?

In the debate that follows, Bradbury and Levy try to determine what is happening to the size of the middle class and its standard of living, and they try to ascertain the forces at work that generate the reported results. Bradbury and Levy use different definitions of middle class and this, in part, explains why they reach different conclusions about its size. They *both* suggest, however, that between the years 1973 and 1984 the middle class became worse off. As for the causes of the patterns they identify, both concentrate on demographic changes—changes in the characteristics of the population and of families and their behavior.

YES

Katharine L. Bradbury

THE SHRINKING MIDDLE CLASS

The perception is widespread that the American middle class is shrinking. Reports of more families in poverty and increased media attention to the relatively high-income "yuppies" are cited as evidence. Hypotheses about the causes of the decline abound. Some blame demographic changes: shifts in the age distribution caused by the baby boom, more families headed by women, and the rising proportion of two-earner families. Others point to changes in the national economy. Increases in employment in services and high technology manufacturing, for example, have reportedly replaced the high-wage blue-collar jobs of traditional manufacturing with a two-tier mix consisting of many low-skill, low-paying jobs and a few highly paid professional and technical experts.

The general perception of a shrinking middle is correct. Over the last decade or so, real family income has declined, and its distribution has become more unequal. This study examines changes in the distribution of family incomes in the United States from 1973 to 1984, and relates these changes to shifts in family types and sizes, the labor force status of wives, the age distribution of family heads, the regions in which families live. The analysis thus focuses on demographic changes affecting families rather than on changes in the economy. It finds that demographic changes were not the major reason for the decline in the percentage of families with middle-class incomes from 1973 to 1984.

I. RECENT INCOME PATTERNS AND TRENDS

The incomes of American families rose fairly steadily in real terms from at least 1949 to 1973, pausing only briefly during recessions and reaching new heights during each expansion.[1] Since 1973, however, the ground lost in recessions has not been recovered in the ensuing expansions. Median family income in constant dollars was slightly lower in 1979 (before the 1980 recession) than in 1973 (the year before the 1974–75 recession). It was lower still in 1984, the latest year for which data are available. While family incomes

From "The Shrinking Middle Class," by Katharine L. Bradbury, Federal Reserve Bank of Boston, *New England Economic Review*, September/October 1986. Reprinted by permission.

probably rose in 1985, the general stagna-tion of median income in the 1970s and 1980s to date stands in marked contrast to the experience of the 1950s and 1960s.

The distribution of family income has also changed in the past 10 or so years. Both the fraction of families with in-comes below the poverty level and the fraction with incomes over $50,000 (in 1984 dollars) were higher in 1984 than in 1973. Recent increases in poverty stand in sharp contrast to steep declines during the 1960s and early 1970s and moderately stable poverty incidence during the sec-ond half of the 1970s.[2] At the other end of the distribution, the proportion of fami-lies with incomes over $50,000 (in con-stant 1984 dollars) continued rising more than enough during expansions to offset recession declines. High-income families were apparently less affected by rising unemployment and other adverse eco-nomic trends than those with low incomes. . . .

II. WHAT IS THE MIDDLE CLASS? AND IS IT SHRINKING?

. . . The middle class obviously com-prises the "middle" of the income distri-bution and excludes the very richest and poorest members of society, but any more quantitative definition must be ar-bitrary. The family income range from $20,000 to $49,999 in 1984 dollars is used to define the middle class in this study. This choice implies that about one-half of families are in the middle class, about one-third have lower incomes, and the remainder (roughly 15 percent) have higher incomes. Changes over time in these fractions are the major focus of the study.

The use of simple money income cut-offs to define the middle class has several limitations. For example, families of dif-ferent sizes have different income re-quirements for the same standard of living. Also, costs of living differ across regions. No good data exist to develop measures of family income that reflect cost variations associated with either family size or regional location. Dividing family income by the number of family members would fail to capture econ-omies of scale in consumption—the fact that "two can live as cheaply as one."[3] Although variations in family size and regional living costs cannot be incorpo-rated into the definition of the middle class, this study does consider how shifts in size and family locations have affected the measured size of the middle class.

The use of constant dollar cutoffs as a definition disregards cultural aspects of being middle class. Young couples raised in middle-class homes may well consider themselves members of the middle class before their current incomes are high enough to support a middle-class life-style. Similarly, formerly middle-class families who have raised their incomes to upper-class levels may continue thinking of themselves as part of the middle class. More broadly, the apparent focus of American culture (especially television programming and advertising) on the middle class makes people prone to de-fine the middle class in such a way that they are included. The dollar definitions used here cannot reflect these special circumstances; rather they attempt to embrace the bulk of families that most people would consider to be enjoying a middle-class living standard.

Another complication in defining the middle class is the sizable and growing fraction of the American population that does not live in families (defined as two or more related people sharing living quarters). People living alone or with nonrelatives comprise 27 percent of all households in 1984 (and about 12 percent of the population), up from 20 percent of households in 1973. Partly because economies of scale in consumption reduce the comparability between incomes of single people and those of families, and partly because the cultural view of the middle class seems to focus on families, this analysis includes only family units. . . .

The income measure used by the Bureau of the Census to report family incomes introduces a final complication in defining the middle class. Census money income estimates reflect all cash income before taxes and other deductions. They include wages and salaries, self-employment income, government and private cash transfer payments (including welfare and pensions), and other "unearned" income such as dividends and interest, but not capital gains and other one-time payments. The primary difficulty is that the estimates reflect the addition to incomes of governmental cash transfer payments but not the re-

duction in incomes resulting from taxes or the additions due to noncash income such as Medicare and employer-provided health benefits. Thus the measured distribution of income differs from the distribution of income after taxes and transfers. . . .

Defining the middle class as all those families with Census money incomes between $20,000 and $50,000 yields the patterns shown in Table 1. Using this definition, the fraction of families with middle-class incomes did indeed decline between 1973 and 1984, from 53 percent to less than 48 percent. Most of the decline in the middle-class share was picked up by the lower income class which increased from 32 percent of families to 36 percent; the upper income class grew slightly, from 15 percent to 16 percent of families. (The "middle-class" share also declined over the period according to other definitions of the middle class. For example, the fraction of all families with incomes between $15,000 and $40,000 declined from 52 percent in 1973 to 48 percent in 1984, with virtually

Table 1
Distribution of Families by Income

Income Class[a]	Number of Families (thousands)		Percent of Families			Percent of Families		
	1973	1984	1973	1984		1973	1984	Change
Below $10,000	6,356	9,332	11.5	14.8	Below	32.1	36.4	+4.3
$10,000–20,000	11,319	13,704	20.6	21.7				
$20,000–30,000	12,458	13,224	22.6	20.9				
$30,000–40,000	10,366	10,246	18.8	16.2	Middle	53.0	47.9	−5.1
$40,000–50,000	6,354	6,837	11.5	10.8				
$50,000–75,000	6,006	6,961	10.9	11.0	Above	14.9	15.6	+0.8
$75,000 and above	2,186	2,928	4.0	4.6				
Total	55,045	63,232	100.0	100.0		100.0	100.0	
Median Income	$28,048	$26,000						

[a]Income in 1984 dollars
Source: U.S. Bureau of the Census, Current Population Survey. March 1974 and March 1985, machine-readable data files.

all of the loss picked up by the lower income group.)

The total number of families increased by about 8 million (15 percent) between 1973 and 1984, so the number of middle-class families actually increased about 1.1 million, even as the middle-class fraction of families declined. But if the fraction of families with middle-class incomes had been the same in 1984 as it was in 1973, 3.2 million more families would have been middle class—2.7 million from below the middle and another one-half million families from above.

The fact that American society has become less "middle-class" would not be a source of concern if the families were generally becoming richer. The long history of rising real incomes in the United States has undoubtedly been accompanied by gradual upward revisions in the definition of the middle class. But increasing affluence was not the general case between 1973 and 1984. Thus many families may have been unable to achieve the living standards they had expected to attain at their current stage in life.

Whether anything should be done about the decline of the middle class, and what, depends on what has caused the shrinkage. If demographic changes are to blame, the problem may be transitory. For example, shifts in the income distribution caused by a skewed age distribution may correct themselves as members of the baby boom generation reach middle age and earn the middle-level incomes typical of those years. The problem may even be illusory—families may not be worse off if the decline in median family income simply reflects a decline in average family size or relocations to areas with lower living costs. On the other hand, if rising unemployment underlies the decline, the economy may grow out

of the problem on its own or changes in macroeconomic policies may be called for. If inequality of educational preparation has played a critical role, the remedy might require changes in education and training institutions or individuals' career decisions. Alternatively, if shifts in the mix of occupations and industries are responsible, then the merits of training programs of "industrial policies" to protect or augment middle-class jobs warrant consideration.

III. THE IMPACT OF RECENT DEMOGRAPHIC CHANGE ON THE DISTRIBUTION OF INCOME

Some researchers have hypothesized that changes in family size, the age distribution of family heads, and the mix of family types have been major sources of the recent decline in the size of the middle class and average family income levels. The increasing labor force participation of wives is also thought to have reduced the size of the middle class by lifting a sizable number of middle-class families to higher income levels.

Many of these demographic changes are not exogenous—that is, they may have occurred in response to other demographic or economic changes. For example, a decline in men's average earnings is likely to cause an increase in the labor force participation of wives, which may, in turn, contribute to declines in average family size. Whether exogenous or not, however, demographic shifts are likely to be associated with changes in income. The analysis that follows quantifies the effects of these shifts on the distribution of family incomes between 1973 and 1984 and finds these effects small. The fraction of families with middle-class incomes declined within virtually all demographic groups, however defined. Thus the ultimate sources of the decline in the middle class apparently are not demographic changes. Nevertheless, demographic shifts have altered the characteristics of the middle class in important ways.

The method used to quantify the effects of demographic change is a shift-share analysis that divides the total change (in median income or the fraction of families with middle-class incomes) into two parts: that attributable to changes in the mix of families across demographic groups and that attributable to changes in income patterns within each demographic group. . . .

Interregional Differences in Income

Although income levels differ noticeably among the regions, the extensive movement of population to the West and South has had very minor consequences for the nation's overall distribution of income. Family incomes are below the national average in the South and the Mountain states of the West. Thus one might be tempted to attribute some of the decline in the national median family income to the rapid population growth in these areas. Since living costs are also lower in most of these areas—certainly in the South—a decline in well-being might not be implied.

In fact, median family income declined in all regions, as did the fraction of families with middle-class incomes. If the interregional population shifts had not occurred, the nationwide changes in the distribution of family income would have been only slightly smaller than they actually were, other things equal. Thus, although the purchasing power of $20,000 to $50,000 differs across the regions, interregional population shifts do not mask any underlying increase in the fraction of families with middle-class purchasing power. . . .

Smaller Families

The size of the average family in the United States fell from about 3½ persons in 1973 to 3¼ in 1984, continuing a decline that began a decade earlier. The decline was largely attributable to a decrease in the number of children.

Since large families have higher average incomes than small families one might expect a decline in average family size to be accompanied by a decline in average family income (and vice versa). But small families need less income than large families to attain any given living standard, so a decline in average income combined with smaller family sizes might not imply a decline in living standards. The question is whether actual levels of well-being and the fraction of families enjoying middle-class living standards were rising even as the median family income and measured size of the middle class were declining.

It seems not; average living standards did decline between 1973 and 1984, although they declined somewhat less than median family income declined. First, the shift-share analysis implies that the decline in average family size accounted for only one-fifth of the decline in median family income that occurred between 1973 and 1984, assuming the average (real) incomes of families of each size were unchanged between the two years. (Declining family sizes account for a negligible fraction of the decrease in the size of the middle class.) Second, for each family size group both the median income and the fraction in the middle class declined between 1973 and 1984. . . .

Third, income per family member did

not show an improvement—the median family's income per family member was about the same in 1973 and 1984. Small families have above-average income per family member. If this higher income per member meant that small families had a higher level of economic well-being than large ones, on average, then the shift toward smaller families might raise the average standard of living even as well-being declined for each family size. But because of economies of scale, the same income per family member implies a lower living standard for a small family than for a large one. Hence the observed decline in average family size accompanied by very little change in average income per family member implies a decline in average well-being.

The Baby Boom Generation

The incomes tend to be highest for those families with heads age 35 to 54. Consequently, some observers have hypothesized that the slippage of the median and the decline in the middle class are attributable to shifts in the age distribution. In particular, the baby boom generation is thought to have swelled the ranks of younger families whose incomes are relatively low. It turns out, however, that changes in the age distribution of family heads between 1973 and 1984 had an effect opposite to that hypothesized, raising the median income slightly and augmenting the middle-class fraction of families. A sizable decrease in the number of family heads under age 25 (whose families have very low incomes) coupled with rapid growth in families with heads age 35 to 44 more than offset the income decline associated with increases in the elderly (who have the lowest median income) and decreases in the number of families with heads age 45 to 54, the

group with the highest median income.

The explanation for such contrary results is that, by 1984, the baby boom generation was no longer dominated by the very young. Most definitions of the baby boom say it began in 1946 and ended around 1964. By 1984 baby boomers ranged in age from 20 to 38, and many had therefore reached the age when family incomes are relatively high. Moreover, the age groups most heavily influenced by the baby boom generation—families with heads age 25 to 34 and 35 to 44—have the highest proportions in the middle class. The young and the elderly have much larger proportions of lower income families while those 45 to 54 and 55 to 64 have larger proportions of high-income families. . . .

The Growing Importance of "Nontraditional" Families

Many believe that the decline of the "traditional" middle-class family, consisting of a husband, wife, and perhaps some children, is responsible for the shrinkage of the middle class. Married-couple families accounted for 85 percent of all families in 1973 and fewer than 80 percent by 1984, continuing a pattern of decline that began about a decade earlier. Single-parent families, especially those headed by women, expanded rapidly, their numbers increasing by over 50 percent between 1973 and 1984.

Husband-wife families are concentrated in the middle class, while almost two-thirds of single-parent families have incomes below middle-class levels. Thus one might expect the decline in the number of husband-wife families to have a powerful effect on the size of the middle class. But it did not. If the only change occurring over the 1973-84 period had been the decline in the husband-wife fraction of all families, the middle-class share of all families would have fallen less than 1½ percentage points, not the actual 5 percentage points. Thus the decreasing proportion of husband-wife families contributed more to the decline in the middle class than the shifts in family size, age, and region just discussed, but the effect was still only a small part of the overall change. The key change was not the decline in husband-wife families but rather the decline in the fraction of husband-wife families with middle-class incomes—from 57 percent to 52 percent. In addition to its effect on the middle class, the decrease in married-couple families contributed to the decline in median family income, accounting for more than one-third of the total change.

The proportion of husband-wife families with middle-class incomes would have fallen even more if the labor force participation of wives had not increased. Spouses were working or looking for work in 42 percent of husband-wife families in 1974 and 54 percent in 1985; families with wives in the labor force were much more likely than single-earner husband-wife families to attain middle-class incomes, even though they were younger, on average. Thus the increasing labor force participation of wives actually served to increase the size of the middle class, contrary to the popular perception that the increasing labor force participation of women has increased inequality. . . .[4]

The Changing Status of "Ozzie and Harriet" Families

As supportive evidence that the overall decline in the middle class is not solely attributable to shifts in the composition of American families, the preceding discussion noted that the fraction of families with middle-class incomes declined within most demographic subgroups. But interaction effects may complicate this argument; for example, shifts in family size could underlie the decline in the middle-class fraction of families with heads aged 35 to 44, or shifts in the age mix of family heads might be responsible for some of the decline in the fraction of husband-wife families with middle-class incomes. These concerns can be set aside when examining how the situation changed for more narrowly defined demographic subgroups. How did the stereotypical middle-class family—headed by someone age 35 to 44 with nonworking spouse and two children—fare?

The fortunes of these "Ozzie and Harriet" families shifted in parallel with those of families in general between 1973 and 1984. The median income of 35- to 44-year old husband-wife families with two children declined by 7.4 percent in real terms over the period, from $34,200 to $31,600. And the fraction of these families with middle-class incomes, while higher than for other types of families (65 percent in 1973), declined by a greater amount—almost 8 percentage points compared to a 5 point decline for all families. Just as for all families, the bulk of the middle-class decline for this group translated into increased numbers of families with incomes below middle-class levels; the fraction with above middle-class incomes rose by 1 percentage point. Thus, Ozzie, Harriet, David, Ricky and their peers were particularly hard hit by whatever (nondemographic) changes assailed the middle class in the 1973-84 period. More generally, insufficient disaggregation does not appear to be masking a demographic explanation for the decline in the size of the middle class.

Summing Up the Effects
of Demographic Change

Of the demographic shifts just examined, only the increase in single-parent families contributed measurably to the decline in the fraction of families with middle-class incomes between 1973 and 1984, an effect offset by the increasing labor force participation of wives. Decreases in both average family size and the fraction of families headed by married couples accounted for a sizable part of the observed decline in median family income, but again, these contributions were offset by increases in family income attributable to the increasing labor force participation of wives.[5]

If the labor force participation of wives had not increased, the fraction of families with middle-class incomes and median family income would have declined even more. As it was, with these increases offsetting the effects of other demographic shifts, the income changes to be explained by other factors are almost as large as the total changes that occurred.

The Changing Character
of Middle-Class Families

The decreased presence of nonworking wives is one of the most important changes in the composition of the middle class. By 1984, husband-wife families with wives not in the labor force accounted for only one-third of middle-class families, down from one-half in 1973. Changes in the working patterns of women are probably also part of the reason that smaller families with fewer children comprised a greater fraction of the middle-class and upper-income group in 1984 than in 1973: families with three or more children declined as a fraction of all families, but declined dis-

proportionately as a fraction of families with middle class and higher incomes.

The importance of wives' incomes to the middle class can be interpreted in another light: for an increasing number of families, attainment of middle-class living standards required both spouses to work.[6] The income of wives accounted for 26 percent of the incomes of middle-class families in 1984, a sizable increase from 16 percent in 1973. While increases in work thus prevented more precipitous declines in the standard of living attained by many families, the observed income declines may understate the decline in living standards since they do not take account of the costs of increased labor force participation, including out-of-pocket work expenses and reduced time available for "home production" and leisure. A recent study released by the Joint Economic Committee summarized, "We have gone from a nation where virtually all families could expect increased purchasing power to one in which few can maintain purchasing power even with increased participation in the labor force."[7]

IV. CONCLUSION

The proportion of American families with middle-class income levels declined between 1973 and 1984, while the fractions with higher and lower incomes increased. Over the same period, the real income of the median family in the United States fell. These changes have raised concern that real economic well-being in the nation is on the decline, and even that the fabric of society, dependent on a strong middle-class core, is threatened.[8] In the past, new government policies to redistribute income have been undertaken after each spurt in inequality.[9] But the choice of a policy remedy, if any, depends on the causes of the problem. In particular, if demographic changes, such as shifts in family size, composition, and age, were to blame the difficulty might be illusory (not implying any actual decline in well-being) or temporary.

The analysis of this paper, however, indicates that demographic changes are not responsible for the bulk of the 1973-84 decline in the size of the middle class or in median family income. An increase in single-parent families played some role, but was offset by increases in the labor force participation of wives. Thus it seems that the dwindling of the middle class is real and probably not transitory.

A number of alternative explanations for the decline in the middle class have been advanced. Some commentators have argued that the middle class has become smaller because of shifts in the occupational and industrial mix of jobs in the U.S. economy, specifically the decline of traditional smokestack industries such as autos and steel combined with secular growth in employment in services and the expansion of high technology manufacturing.[10] Others have found that inequality is growing within industry and occupation groups,[11] implying that shifts among these groups cannot be the full explanation for increased inequality in the economy as a whole and that something broader is occurring. Macroeconomic changes occurring during the 1973-84 period have also been cited,[12] including a slowdown in productivity growth, rising unemployment, swings in inflation, several recessions, and alterations in government income maintenance policies.

This study eliminates demographic change from the list of major causes of the decline of the middle class. Further research is needed to understand the importance of competing explanations and to identify appropriate remedies.

NOTES

1. Following methods used by the Bureau of the Census, this study uses the consumer price index to convert all data to 1984 dollars. If the GNP price deflator were used instead, "real" median family income would appear to have been about the same in 1984 as in 1973, after several decades of steady increase. Use of the GNP price deflator would not, of course, change the relative shapes of the income distribution in the two years.

2. The poverty level varies with family size and other family characteristics, and is adjusted from year to year using the consumer price index.

3. One approach sometimes used to adjust incomes for family size and economies of scale divides family income by the poverty line, which reflects how subsistence food costs vary with family size. However, variations in food costs across family size groups for the very poor may bear little relation to how living costs vary across family sizes for those with much higher incomes. Interregional variations in living costs were measured by the Bureau of Labor Statistics "Urban Family Budgets," but this series was discontinued after 1981.

4. Sheldon Danziger and Peter Gottschalk also find that wives' increased labor force participation has reduced inequality. See "How Have Families With Children Been Faring?" Institute for Research on Poverty Discussion Paper 801-86, January 1986.

5. These estimates are not strictly additive since the calculations of the effect of each shift do not control for simultaneous changes in the other factors, but the relative magnitudes are comparable.

6. Richard A. Easterlin argues that increased labor force participation and decreased child-bearing among young adults "reflect chiefly the grim struggle of the baby boom generation to maintain their relative economic status" in "The Struggle for Relative Economic Status," December 1985, paper presented at the Conference on Non-Replacement Fertility, Hoover Institution, Stanford University, November 7-9, 1985, revised December 1985, mimeo, University of Southern California, p. 1.

7. "Family Income in America," prepared for

the Joint Economic Committee, 99 Cong. 1 Sess., November 28, 1985, p. 8.

8. See Lester Thurow, "The Disappearance of the Middle Class," *New York Times*, February 2, 1984; and Robert Kuttner, "A Shrinking Middle Class Is a Call for Action," *Business Week*, September 16, 1985.

9. See Lester Thurow, "New Punishment for the Middle Class: The Hidden Sting of the Trade Deficit," *The New York Times*, January 19, 1986, and "A General Tendency Toward Inequality," paper prepared for annual meetings of the American Economic Association, December 1985, mimeo, Massachusetts Institute of Technology.

10. See, among others, Barry Bluestone and Bennett Harrison, *The Deindustrialization of America* (New York: Basic Books, Inc., 1982); Bob Kuttner, "The Declining Middle," *The Atlantic Monthly*, vol. 252, no. 1 (July 1983), pp. 60–72; Bruce Steinberg, "The Mass Market is Splitting Apart," *Fortune*, November 28, 1983, pp. 76–82; Lester Thurow, "The Disappearance of the Middle Class," *New York Times*, February 5, 1984, and "A General Tendency Toward Inequality," paper prepared for annual meetings of the American Economic Association, December 1985, mimeo, Massachusetts Institute of Technology.

11. Analyses of earnings by occupation and industry generally focus on individual workers rather than on family incomes. Peter Henle and Paul Ryscavage found increasing inequality in the distribution of earnings among men in most industry and occupation categories from 1958 to 1977; see "The Distribution of Earned Income Among Men and Women, 1958-77," *Monthly Labor Review*, April 1980, pp. 3–10. Robert Z. Lawrence provides evidence that the distributions of earnings in high technology and services do not differ much from that for manufacturing as a whole; the basic change stems from a decline in the percentage of workers with middle-class earnings *in all sectors* rather than from shifts among sectors ("Sectoral Shifts and the Size of the Middle Class," *The Brookings Review*, Fall 1984, pp 3–11). Martin Dooley and Peter Gottschalk found increases in earnings inequality between 1968 and 1979 for men within labor force cohorts even after controlling for education, experience, and unemployment in "Earnings Inequality among Males in the United States: Trends and the Effect of Labor Force Growth," *Journal of Political Economy* (1984), vol. 92, no. 1.

12. Frank S. Levy and Richard C. Michel argue that economic stagnation is largely responsible for the increasing "inequality of prospects for achieving the American dream;" see "The Economic Future of the Baby Boom," Urban Institute Research Paper, December 1985.

NO

Frank Levy

THE MIDDLE CLASS:
IS IT REALLY VANISHING?

Inequality, a word used in conjunction with the poor during most of the postwar period, has taken on a broader meaning. Several analysts now argue that not only the poor but the middle class itself is in trouble.[1] There is no shortage of casual observation for this conclusion. Since 1980 perhaps 7 percent of all workers have been displaced, their plants closed or their jobs abolished. The majority are blue-collar workers, most of whom had to take substantial pay cuts. At the same time few days go by without another story about a young investment banker who is making $100,000 or more well before his or her 30th birthday.

When one moves from the individual example to economy-wide statistics, the evidence for a declining middle class is weaker. The U.S. Census Bureau has published annual estimates of the distribution of family income since 1947. They show a highly unequal distribution, but over almost 40 years this inequality has remained fairly stable. In 1984, for example, the richest one-fifth of families received $9.15 of income for every $1.00 received by the poorest one-fifth. But . . . this ratio never fell below $7.20 to $1.00, even in the boom of the late 1960s.[2] And the middle of the distribution has been more stable than the extremes: The middle three-fifths of families have received between 52 and 54 percent of all family income in every postwar year. How is this stability to be reconciled with fears of a vanishing middle class?

An answer begins with a point of perspective. It is easy to imagine the richest one-fifth of families—the group that received 42.9 percent of all family income in 1984—as a group of real estate moguls and arbitrageurs, all with at least six-figure incomes. The image is misleading. In 1984 the richest one-fifth included all families with incomes of $45,300 or more, a standard that counts income from husbands, wives, and all other family members.

If this number seems low, it says something about reference groups. The United States today contains 64 million families headed by a wide variety of people: lawyers, computer repairmen, single 19-year old women, 68-year old retirees in Oregon, and so on. When we judge our own incomes, we often

From "The Middle Class: Is It Really Vanishing?" by Frank Levy, *The Bookings Review*, Summer 1987. Copyright © 1987 by The Brookings Institution, Washington, DC. Reprinted by permission.

think in terms of our immediate peers—for example, young-to-middle-aged professionals; the top quintile of this group today begins at something closer to $65,000.

BEHIND THE STATISTICS: STAGNANT INCOMES . . .

The surprisingly low starting point for the richest quintile also provides the first clue in discovering whether the middle class is really shrinking: In recent years the incomes of U.S. workers and families have stagnated badly. Viewed in terms of income growth, the post-World War II years can be divided into two periods. From 1945 through 1973 real wages and salaries grew 2.5–3.0 percent a year. In 1953 the average 40-year-old man made $15,500 (all income figures are in 1984 dollars). In 1973 the average 40-year-old man made $28,120. Then the steady wage growth stopped.

At the end of 1973 the Organization of Petroleum Exporting Countries substantially raised oil prices. The effect was to transfer a large piece of U.S. purchasing power abroad, and by 1975 real U.S. wages had fallen by about 5 percent. More important, the oil price increase marked the beginning of a dramatic slowdown in the growth of U.S. productivity—output per worker. Rising productivity is the ultimate source of rising wages. For most of the postwar period, worker productivity grew 2.5–3.5 percent a year. But in the decade after 1973 productivity grew at only 0.9 percent a year, a development that even now is not completely understood.

The income loss from the 1973–74 oil shock followed by slow-growing productivity meant that real wages did not regain their 1973 levels until 1979. Then the

Iranian revolution and the second OPEC price increase began the cycle again. The result was more than a decade of declining wages. Had incomes continued to grow moderately after 1973, the average 40-year-old man in 1984 would have earned about $35,000. In fact, he earned $24,600—$3,620 less in real terms than the average 40-year-old man in 1973. Other age groups experienced similar income losses.[3]

Family incomes did not suffer as much as the incomes of individual workers. Between 1973 and 1984 the median income of a 40-year-old men fell by 13 percent, but median family income—the income at the "center point" of the family distribution—fell by only 6 percent, from $28,200 to $26,400. This more moderate decline reflected two demographic trends. One was the big increase in the number of working wives and in families that depended on two incomes rather than one. The second trend was the rapid rise in age at first marriage, which kept many young people from forming what would have been moderate-income families.[4]

A third trend (of which young singles were a part) was the continuing decline in the birthrate, which began in the mid-1960s. Fewer children did not affect family incomes directly, but they increased income per capita within families by lowering the number of capitas that had to be fed. (The issue of birthrates is discussed below).

Nonetheless, the decline in median family income over a sustained period was something new—and unexpected—in post-World War II America. In 1947 median family income stood at $14,100 (in 1984 dollars). It grew fairly smoothly for the next 26 years, doubling to $28,200 in 1973, before it began its slow drop.

This decline helps explain why the middle class appears to be shrinking. Being "middle class" has always had several meanings. One meaning involves being in the middle of the income distribution. A second meaning involves being able to afford a middle-class standard of living as the term is defined and redefined. Between 1945 and 1973 the two meanings were almost interchangeable. The middle of the income distribution got a slightly larger share of the pie but, more important, the pie itself grew rapidly. The whole distribution moved to higher incomes, and families in every quintile experienced substantial economic progress.

Since 1973 the middle share has deteriorated to the level of the late 1940s, *and* average incomes have declined. As a result the bottom five-sixths of the income distribution have lost ground absolutely as well as relatively. Being in the middle of the income distribution no longer guarantees a middle-class lifestyle as it has come to be defined. The middle of the income distribution is not getting much smaller, but it is growing a little poorer—despite more two-earner families.

. . . AND CHANGING DEMOGRAPHICS

Declining incomes are one explanation for fears of a vanishing middle class. A second explanation involves shifting demographics in the income distribution's lower half. Over the past 15 years the average position of elderly families has improved, moving significant numbers of them from the bottom of the income distribution to the lower middle. Younger families took their vacated places.

The improved position of the elderly reflects, in large degree, the effect of Social Security. In 1972 Congress tied Social Security benefits to the Consumer Price Index to guarantee protection against inflation. At that time workers' wages had increased faster than inflation for almost three decades. Giving the elderly an indexed benefit seemed an equitable and inexpensive proposition. Congress could not know that one year later, inflation-adjusted wages would begin more than a decade of decline. In the context of this decline, indexed Social Security benefits (and greater private pension coverage among more recent retirees) meant that successive waves of the elderly had modestly increasing incomes.

At the same time the position of many younger families worsened. Part of the deterioration reflected changes in family structure. The proportion of families under age 65 headed by a woman rose from 12 percent to 16 percent. Among families with children under age 18, the proportion headed by a woman rose from 15 percent to 21 percent. As husband-wife families increasingly relied on two earners, these single-parent families were at a big economic disadvantage. Today fully one-half of them are in the distribution's bottom quintile. Since 1980 significant numbers of two-parent families who were hurt by the 1980–82 recession and its aftermath have also fallen to the bottom of the income distribution (see table 3).

These movements compounded by two other trends, later marriages and lower birthrates, had a profound effect on children. Throughout the 1950s and 1960s the poorest one-fifth of families included 15–17 percent of the nation's children. In 1984 those families contained

24 percent of the children. Children's downward slide in the distribution reflected both the numbers of moderate-income young people who did not have children and the economic troubles of the families who did.[5]

In one sense, these rearrangements of groups within the income distribution affected our perceptions of inequality more than the level of inequity itself. Poor children are more visible in day-to-day life (and in the media) than recent retirees who are doing all right. We see more of what is going wrong than of what is going right, and we draw too pessimistic a conclusion.

In a different sense, these rearrangements do work to increase inequality, not in any one year but on a "life cycle" basis. Imagine, for example, a young husband and wife who begin married life with income in the lower middle of the distribution. As they reach their peak earning years, their family income increases relative to other families, and they move toward the higher end of the distribution. When they retire, they move toward the bottom of the distribution. If all families followed this pattern, income inequality in any one year would have less meaning.

Mobility within the income distribution was never this perfect, but the rearrangements at the bottom of the income distribution have diminished it further. When a middle-class family retires, private pensions and indexed Social Security now keep it from falling as far down in the distribution as it once might have. Conversely, in today's economy, families at the bottom of the distribution—particularly families headed by single women—have weak prospects for income growth that would move them up in the distribution. For both groups, future income is more closely tied to current income. Long-run inequality has increased correspondingly.

In sum, census estimates of a relatively stable income distribution obscure the way in which the middle-class is changing. Family income equality has never been a strong point of the American economy.[6] Nonetheless, rapidly rising incomes and, to a lesser extent, mobility within the income distribution enabled large numbers of families to enjoy a middle-class living standard for at least part of their lives and served as a substitute for greater economic equality. But since the 1973–74 oil price increase, income growth has stagnated while mobility within the income distribution has diminished. To this point, we have been able to maintain "the middle-class dream" through demographic adjustments—more two-earner couples, postponed marriages, and low birthrates. These adjustments can take us only so far. If we do not return to a healthy economy with rising real wages, the middle class, and with it, the nation's social fabric, will come under increasing strain.

NOTES

1. See, for example, Bob Kuttner, "The Declining Middle," *Atlantic*, July 1983, pp. 60–72, and Katherine L. Bradbury, "The Shrinking Middle Class," *New England Economic Review*, September/October 1986, pp. 41–45.

2. Income equality reached its post-World War II high point in 1968–69 when the unemployment rate for adult men stood at a little over 2 percent. Since 1973 the unemployment rate for adult men has averaged slightly over 6 percent.

3. This 13 percent drop (from $28,120 to $24,600) may be slightly overstated in two ways. The calculation is based on inflation adjustments using the Consumer Price Index, a widely used measure that until recently put too much weight on the cost of new housing and so overstated inflation in the post-1973 period. In addition, over the 1970s workers received an increasing portion of their compensation in fringe benefits

(including increasingly expensive health insurance), and so the money-only figures in the text understate total economic gains. These factors together might reduce the 13 percent drop to perhaps a 5–6 percent drop over 11 years. Before 1973, a 25–30 percent rise would have been expected over a similar period.

4. The incomes of single persons (unrelated individuals in census parlance) are tabulated in a separate income distribution. The rapid rise in the age of first marriage helped give a false impression of young people's affluence. Many young people had high discretionary income (despite low incomes) because they had no mortgage to pay or children to feed.

5. This relative decline in children's positions within the income distribution coupled with absolute decline in median family incomes explains the rapidly increasing child poverty rates mentioned by Gary Burtless.

6. Such estimates as exist for the pre-1947 period suggest that the top quintile of families received over 50 percent of all income in the 1920s and that current patterns reflect a leveling that took place during the Great Depression and World War II.

POSTSCRIPT

Is the Middle Class Shrinking?

Economist Bradbury believes that the middle class shrank between 1973 and 1984. Defining the middle class as those families with incomes between $20,000 and $50,000 (measured in 1984 dollars), the percent of middle class families declined from 53 percent of all families in 1973 to less than 48 percent in 1984. To make matters worse, there was a decline in real family income. Bradbury examines five different demographic changes to determine if they can account for the decline in the relative size of the middle class: interregional differences in income, smaller families, the baby boom generation, growing importance of "nontraditional" families, and the changing status of "Ozzie and Harriet" families (families with two children with nonworking spouse and headed by someone aged 35 to 44). Here she concludes that these demographic factors "are not responsible for the bulk of the 1973–84 decline in the size of the middle class or in median family income."

Levy believes that the middle class is not disappearing. Defining the middle class as the middle three-fifths of families in the distribution of income (so that 20 percent of all families have less income and 20 percent of all families have more income than the middle class), the middle class receives about the same percent of income as it did in the past. "The middle three-fifths of families have received between 52 and 54 percent of all family income in every postwar year." Levy admits that while the distribution of income has remained constant, real median family income fell between 1973 and 1984; measured in 1984 dollars, median family income fell from $28,200 to $26,400. Levy also examines the characteristics of the population and families to achieve a better understanding of why the economy produced these results. He concludes that the American economy has been "able to maintain 'the middle class dream' through demographic adjustments—more two-earner couples, postponed marriages, and low birthrates."

The two selections presented here have been shortened considerably, especially the article by Bradbury; the original articles present much more detail in support of their arguments. In addition the Levy article is drawn from his book *Dollars and Dreams: The Changing American Income Distribution* (New York: Russel Sage/Basic Books, 1987). Other articles that support the notion of a declining middle class include those by Robert Kuttner "A Shrinking Middle Class is a Call for Action" in the September 16, 1985 issue of *Business Week* and "The Disappearance of the Middle Class" by Lester Thurow in the February 2, 1984 issue of the *New York Times*. For an interesting article regarding the controversy over wealth distribution see "Scandal at the Fed?" in the April 1987 issue of *Dollars and Sense*. For government statistics on income and income distribution see *Money Income of Households, Families, and Persons in the United States* (U.S. Bureau of the Census, Current Population Reports, Series P-60).

ISSUE 20

Is Manufacturing Alive and Well and Living in the U.S.?

YES: **Molly McUsic**, from "U.S. Manufacturing: Any Cause for Alarm?" *New England Economic Review* (January/February 1987)

NO: **Nicholas S. Perna**, from "The Shift from Manufacturing to Services: A Concerned View," *New England Economic Review* (January/February 1987)

ISSUE SUMMARY

YES: Former Federal Reserve Bank of Boston researcher McUsic examines the behavior of output, employment, and productivity in U.S. manufacturing. She finds that manufacturing has maintained its relative share in U.S. total production and argues that the decline in the number of manufacturing jobs reflects the growth of manufacturing productivity. She concludes that the recent changes in the structure of the U.S. economy do not signal the demise of manufacturing, nor have they brought about a reduction in living standards.
NO: General Electric economist Perna is pessimistic about recent changes in the structure of the economy. He identifies several symptoms of ill health in manufacturing: (1) imports of durable goods have been rising rapidly; (2) the rate at which manufacturing's share of employment has been declining has accelerated; (3) productivity growth in U.S. export industries has lagged behind that of similar industries in other countries; and (4) "industry analysis shows that the U.S. employment mix has shifted towards lower paying jobs, particularly since the 1960s."

The idea that the American economy is undergoing a fundamental transformation is not new, and it has been examined from a number of different perspectives. For example, in his book *The Third Wave*, sociologist Alvin Toffler argues that American society is in the midst of a major restructuring: the first wave was the agriculture phase, the second wave was the industry phase, and the third wave is a future where the principles of industrial society (standardization, specialization, synchronization, concentration, maximization, and centralization) are no longer dominant.

Economists have also addressed this idea of a transformation. Some speak of the deindustrialization of the American economy, of the demise of manufacturing. They are concerned about U.S. manufacturing because they believe that the high standard of living enjoyed by most Americans is the direct result of a growing and prosperous manufacturing base; therefore, if manufacturing is dying, then Americans may face an erosion of their living standards.

How important is manufacturing to the U.S. economy? If importance is measured by size, then for some time now manufacturing has not been the most important sector of the economy. Even back in 1946 manufacturing generated fewer jobs than service activities (e.g., transportation and public utilities, wholesale trade, retail trade, real estate)—14.7 million as opposed to 24.4 million. In 1986 manufacturing employed 19.2 million; service employment totaled 75.2 million. As McUsic indicates, the percent of total production accounted for by manufacturing has been very stable, ranging between 20 and 22 percent since 1947. Although this might suggest that manufacturing is relatively unimportant compared to services, many still believe that a healthy manufacturing sector is the key to the overall health of the economy.

Assessing the health of a particular sector of the economy is no easy task. A major problem is that the economy is always in a state of change. Some of these changes may be temporary as the economy responds to a variety of impulses. One example is the changes the economy undergoes each year as the seasons change: agricultural output expands in the harvest season; there is an influx of students into the labor market as summer vacations begin. Because these seasonal patterns are well known, many economic statistics are adjusted accordingly and carry the note: "seasonally adjusted."

Another type of change reflects the business cycle: the repeated pattern of business expansion followed by business contraction that is a part of the history of capitalist economies. The U.S. economy experienced cyclical contractions in 1980 when total production fell by $5 billion from the previous year and in 1982 when the fall in production was much greater, some $80 billion. If an assessment of the health of the manufacturing sector were restricted to contractionary periods only, the diagnosis would be that the patient was indeed ill.

In addition to seasonal and cyclical changes there are structural changes. The best example here, and one that is referred to in the following readings, is the transformation of the American economy from an agricultural society to an industrial or manufacturing-based society. Farm employment in 1947 exceeded 10 million workers, but by 1986 farm employment had fallen to just slightly more than 3 million. If you contrast farm employment with total employment you find that in 1947 about one out of every five jobs was a farm job while in 1986 only one of every forty jobs was a farm job. Even as farm employment fell, however, because of productivity advances, farm production doubled.

The difficulty for economists is to separate these various kinds of change. If the changes are temporary, there is no cause for concern. A seasonal problem is like a winter cold: both create mild discomfort that will pass. A cyclical downturn is more serious and can be likened to a broken arm—this is certainly more of a problem than a cold, but with time the patient will heal and resume normal activity. A structural change might be considered a major illness like lung cancer. You may or may not survive.

So is U.S. manufacturing alive and well? McUsic sees only minor symptoms of ill health. All things considered, she believes that manufacturing has been performing quite well in the 1980s. Perna thinks that the kind of evidence that McUsic uses is too simplistic and that a more detailed analysis reveals significant problems.

YES

Molly McUsic

U.S. MANUFACTURING:
ANY CAUSE FOR ALARM?

To the laid-off GM employees in Flint, Michigan, who were not called back to work after the recession, the laborers in Gary, Indiana, who can no longer find work in the steel industry, and the patriotic consumer in Boston who cannot find an American-made VCR, U.S. industry appears somehow to be failing. This perception has been amplified by published reports that the United States is not manufacturing enough, that productivity is low, and that jobs are being lost to firms in other countries. The prospect of our manufacturing industries losing their competitive edge suggests a concomitant lowering of living standards to those who fear that this country is losing its capacity to produce tradeable goods.

This article examines the output, employment and productivity of U.S. industry. The study concludes that the recent course of industrial development in the United States corresponds closely with long-standing historical trends here and in other industrialized countries. In many respects our goods-producing industries appear to be faring remarkably well, in view of the rapid development of industrial capacity in other industrialized countries and in newly developing countries. Since at least 1960 manufacturing output has consistently accounted for about one-fifth of GNP in the United States. Although U.S. industrial growth slowed during the 1970s, every indicator of industrial strength recovered during the 1980s. The slump—frequently attributed to high energy prices, high inflation, and a growing proportion of younger, less experienced workers in the labor force—appears to have been only temporary.

In the 1980s the United States has performed as well as other developed nations in every category of industrial growth, and by most measures its level of productivity and standard of living remain the highest in the world. The trend toward services employment, which is consistent with many theories of economic development, appears to be no more rapid here than in other developed nations, and it does not appear to have accelerated significantly during the last decade.

From "U.S. Manufacturing: Any Cause for Alarm?" by Molly McUsic, Federal Reserve Bank of Boston, *New England Economic Review*, January/February 1987. Reprinted by permission.

In general, U.S. goods and manufacturing industries are performing as expected, given global and historical trends.[1] The structural shifts that are occurring—such as the decline in manufacturing's share of employment or the decline in our share of world output—are influenced greatly by worldwide patterns of economic development as well as by changing incomes in the United States. These shifts do not appear to be caused by any intrinsic problem with the U.S. industrial base.

I. OUTPUT

The alleged shift from goods to services has dominated recent discussions about the course of economic development in the United States.[2] Many fear that our economy is producing fewer goods and that a society that survives on services will inevitably slip into decline. Output data provide no clear evidence that the United States is shifting to a service economy; perhaps more importantly, it is not evident that such a shift would be a sign of economic decline. . . .

The breakdown of output by industry shows that it is not manufacturing but the agriculture, mining and construction industries whose relative share of output has declined since 1960, as services' share has risen. Manufacturing industry output has remained a remarkably constant share of GNP, not fluctuating much beyond 20 to 22 percent of total output since 1947.

The recent growth in manufacturing's share of output also follows long-standing historical patterns. Although manufacturing output has expanded at about the same rate as GNP when measured over long intervals, during business cycles its growth has been more volatile. . . . From 1960 to 1985 manufacturing output grew at an average annual rate of 4 percent. It grew 5.3 percent from 1960 to 1973 and then slowed to 2 percent from 1973 to 1980.[3] In the most recent recovery, the expansion of manufacturing output has been particularly robust, faster than GNP growth alone would suggest.

Other industrialized nations have experienced many of the same economic trends as the United States. All the developed countries had lower growth in industrial production during the 1970s than in the 1960s. . . . Only Japan has had greater growth than the United States during the 1980s, due primarily to U.S. recession from 1980 to 1982. Since its economic recovery, the United States has had the highest growth in industrial production.

As a share of world industrial output, U.S. production has declined steadily since the end of World War II. In the late 1940s, the United States produced more than 60 percent of world manufacturing output. By 1983 it produced about 31 percent of developed nations' output.[4] As Germany rebuilt in the early postwar period, as Italy and Japan developed in the 1960s, and as other Third World nations have recently emerged as competitors, it was inevitable that the United States' *share* of output would decline even as its *level* grew. Once the European and Japanese economies were rebuilt, manufacturing accounted for a constant or even declining share of their economic activity also. Only in the newly industrializing countries is manufacturing output's share of GDP growing.

As countries develop, their economies shift from agriculture to manufacturing and then from manufacturing to services.[5] As more developing nations move from agrarian economies to manufacturing, many U.S. industries will have to cope with stiffer competition and will continue to lose market share. Unless economic growth in the United States exceeds that of the rest of the world, our share of world output will continue to decline as other nations catch up with our technology, skills, and living standards. However, this does not imply that the U.S. standard of living will stop rising. Since World War II our share of world output has declined, yet our standard of living has risen. As long as the world economy is growing sufficiently rapidly, U.S. output and living standards will continue to expand.

While goods have accounted for a constant share of GNP in the United States until now, services' share ultimately may increase as the economy continues to develop. Such a shift toward service output would occur not because our manufacturing industries can no longer compete but because society wants more services.

As countries develop, their residents acquire an increasing stock of machines, factories, consumer durables, schools and roads. A given stock of goods, in and of itself, creates a need for services. For example, the purchase of one car requires years of repair service. The demand for services, therefore, will tend to grow along with an expanding stock of goods. The production of new goods also depends on the stock of existing goods. New production supplies enough goods to replace those that have worn out, to meet the needs of an increasing population, and to satisfy each person's demand for additional belongings. With slower population growth and with increasing affluence, the rate of growth of the stock of goods may decline in the

United States. As a result, the demand for newly produced goods would fall relative to the demand for services.[6] . . .

The increasing number of two-earner families will also continue to contribute to the rising demand for services. The larger income attained by two-earner families generates an increase in demand for both goods and services. Initially the demand for housing, consumer durables and clothing increases with income, but at higher levels of income families increasingly value services. Families with growing incomes can afford to increase their quality of life through leisure, education and health services. With rising affluence, the demand for services will eventually increase faster than that for goods. The growth of services also increases as work previously performed by a stay-at home spouse and not included in the GNP accounts becomes purchased services—restaurant meals, laundry service, housekeeping—and is valued as national output. If the trend toward more two-earner families continues, the demand for services may tend to increase relative to goods.

A greater share of services in national output would be a rational market response to continuing economic development. In a maturing economy factors such as rising incomes, changing composition of the labor force, and a mounting stock of goods per person foster a greater need for services relative to goods.

II. EMPLOYMENT

While goods production still accounts for a constant share of GNP, employment in goods-producing industries has long been a declining share of total employment. In 1960, 45 percent of private nonagricultural workers were in goods-producing industries; by 1985 that number had fallen below 31 percent. The share of total nonagricultural private employment in manufacturing has dropped from 37 percent in 1960 to 24 percent in 1985. This shift is not a recent phenomenon. Since at least 1900, service industries have employed more people than manufacturing, which achieved its largest share of total employment around 1920. Moreover, this shift toward service employment is likely to continue. Employment in manufacturing is not expected to grow more than 0.6 percent annually from 1984 to 1995, and because overall employment is expected to grow more quickly, manufacturing's share will decline to an estimated 21 percent by 1995.[7]

Much the same pattern can be found in other industrialized countries. Furthermore, this decline in the share of manufacturing employment is expected to continue abroad as well. In Japan forecasts project an additional 10 million jobs in services during the next 15 years accompanied by a loss of 2.6 million jobs in manufacturing.[8] Only in the newly industrializing nations, where manufacturing is of rising consequence in GNP, is its share of total employment increasing.

It is not just manufacturing's relative share of employment that is declining in the United States, but the absolute number of people employed in manufacturing as well. In 1969 employment in manufacturing reached 20.2 million persons, a level not surpassed until almost 10 years later. In 1979 employment peaked at 21 million persons, after which it declined until 1983 and then recovered slightly to its 1985 level of 19.4 million.[9]

These figures probably underestimate the number of people who work for manufacturing industries, however. Employment in business services has soared from 871,000 in 1960 to 4,612,000 in 1984, and this rapid growth is expected to continue.[10] Formerly many of these business service jobs were done within the manufacturing industries and categorized as manufacturing. Now the jobs are done by outside consultants and classified as services. When a textile company hires an outside security force, or an electronics manufacturer brings in engineering consultants, employment in manufacturing is lower than if the same work had been done by the manufacturer's employees. If even one-third of the business service jobs were done by manufacturers, there would have been no drop in "manufacturing employment."

Even a decrease in manufacturing employment is not a sign of U.S. deindustrialization. Manufacturing employment is an inadequate measure of the health of either manufacturing industries or the total economy. Due to the complex relationships between output, employment and productivity, one measure cannot suggest the whole story.

The error in overemphasizing employment figures is most easily illustrated by agriculture. Between 1929 and 1985 the agricultural sector suffered an absolute decline in employment of 70 percent. According to the employment figures alone, farming was distressed. In fact, over that period farming was a success story. Technological advances enabled fewer farmers to produce more, thereby increasing the non-agricultural work force and helping to advance U.S. living standards to the highest in the world. . . .

The relationships among output, employment and productivity in manufacturing are similar. In the past five years output in manufacturing has grown 3.3 percent per year but productivity grew more quickly, so employment dropped by 0.9 percent annually. As the U.S. economy matures, demand for manufactured goods is not expected to grow as rapidly as it once did. With limited growth in demand and increasing productivity, manufacturing employment will not rise as it did in the 1960s.

The recent decline in manufacturing employment has not meant a decline in total employment or the standard of living. Overall, the United States has been successful in providing jobs for its population. The civilian labor force has risen from 59 percent of the population in 1960 to 65 percent in 1985. Civilian employment, a measure dependent on the business cycle, has also risen, from 56 percent of the population in 1960 to 60 percent in 1985. During the 1970s, despite the slower average growth in output, the economy was able to absorb a large number of new workers. Civilian employment actually grew more quickly in the 1970s than in the 1960s or 1980s. Employment has not grown so rapidly in Europe and Japan, and employment as a proportion of population has declined there as well.

The U.S. standard of living, measured as gross domestic product per capita, has risen throughout the past four decades, although its rate of growth slowed in the 1970s as it did in other countries. Between 1960 and 1984 average GDP per capita in Europe and Japan increased more rapidly than in the United States. Because living standards here still appear to exceed those prevailing in other countries, the growth of GDP per capita abroad will tend to exceed that in the United States as living standards converge across all nations.[11]

III. PRODUCTIVITY

Throughout U.S. history, high productivity has enabled domestic industries to pay high real wages while remaining competitive in world markets. Since 1973 the growth of productivity in the United States has slowed considerably, and many now fear that our products will no longer be competitive and our standard of living will decline. With the considerable public attention paid to productivity measures has come misunderstanding. Productivity measures have valid uses to both engineers and economists, but used alone they are not a clear indicator of the health of industry.

From 1960 to 1973 productivity in nonfarm business, measured as output per hour, grew at an annual rate of 2.4 percent. From 1973 to 1985 it grew only 0.6 percent per year. Growth in manufacturing productivity declined from 3.2 percent between 1960 and 1973 to only 2.2 percent between 1973 and 1985. These broad intervals obscure important variations, however. Productivity growth depends on economic growth. In early stages of recovery, real output expands faster than employment, increasing labor productivity. As the recovery continues, firms begin hiring new workers and the rate of growth in labor productivity declines. Late in the business cycle, productivity begins to fall as output declines but employers are reluctant to lay off workers immediately. The nature of the recovery also is important. If capacity utilization remains low during the expansion, productivity does not increase as rapidly.

The influence of recessions and recoveries may be minimized by comparing productivity growth during periods between cycle peaks.[12] From 1973 to 1980 nonfarm business productivity grew only 0.3 percent, while from 1980 to 1985 it grew 1.0 percent per year and after 1982 growth accelerated to 1.6 percent annually. Manufacturing productivity grew 1.2 percent from 1973 to 1980, while between 1980 and 1985 it increased 3.7 percent per year. After 1982 manufacturing productivity increased at a rate of 4.7 percent annually. Another way to reduce cyclical effects in the comparisons is to consider productivity growth over the last five recoveries. The results show that manufacturing productivity growth has been higher in the current recovery than in any recent recovery period.

Productivity growth in the United States since 1980 compares favorably with the expansion of productivity elsewhere in the world. From 1960 to 1973 and again from 1973 to 1980 this country had the lowest rate of productivity growth of the seven largest OECD countries, measured both by output per hour in manufacturing and by GDP per employed person. This reflected to some extent the high level of productivity already enjoyed by the United States. As U.S. technology dispersed, it was inevitable that productivity would grow more quickly abroad than in the United States. Since the last recession, however, U.S. productivity growth has been higher than almost any OECD country and the overall level of manufacturing productivity remains the highest in the world.[13]

This slowdown in productivity growth in the 1970s was not a structural problem caused by the shift of employment from goods to services. If service industries had a lower productivity level or slower productivity growth than the goods-producing industries, an increase in service employment relative to goods might be expected to decrease overall productivity growth. However, in the last 25 years

service productivity has not depressed total productivity.[14]

Not all service industries are labor-intensive, low-productivity industries. On average, services tend to be more capital-intensive than goods industries, and historically the range of their productivity growth rates has not been significantly narrower than that of the goods-producing industries.[15] During the period of greatest productivity slowdown, from 1973 to 1980, productivity grew more in services than in the goods-producing industries, and the increasing share of employment in services apparently has had a negligible effect on the economy's overall productivity growth.[16]

Whatever the productivity trends, it is not clear whether productivity data should be seriously considered as an indicator of U.S. industrial decline or growth, since there are serious problems both in measuring and in interpreting productivity data. Declining productivity is not synonymous with a loss of efficiency or an erosion of competitiveness. For example, as a result of rising energy prices in the 1970s, many industries used less capital and more labor. This adjustment tended to lower labor productivity as these firms adopted the most economical mix of more labor-intensive inputs to produce their output most efficiently. In the medical service industry the rise in the number of employees and the accompanying drop in productivity was at least partly the result of highly skilled professionals conserving their time by transferring some of their responsibilities to less skilled employees or to laboratories. Such an increase in efficiency would tend to be accompanied by a drop in measured labor productivity.[17]

Improvements in quality of output,

unless reflected in a price change, also are not shown in productivity measurements. In the past 10 years electronic products such as computers and calculators have undergone vast technological improvements. Since their relative prices and therefore their value in the GNP accounts have decreased, the measured productivity of the industries making these products has declined despite the improvements in quality.

Comparisons of measures of productivity for different nations can be especially misleading. Different methods of national accounting, different measures of hours (hours worked vs. hours paid) and various levels of sophistication in collecting and reporting the data, increase the degree of unreliability. The Bureau of Labor Statistics, which publishes the most dependable series, adjusts foreign data for greater consistency with U.S. measures but differences in statistical concepts and methods remain. . . .

IV. INDUSTRY SPECIFICS

The data for individual U.S. industries provide a more detailed view of the relationships between output, employment, and productivity in the U.S. economy. . . .

Output in most manufacturing industries grew from 1973 to 1980 and again from 1980 to 1984, with two-thirds enjoying a higher rate of growth in the 1980s. As in the aggregate, employment growth slowed for most manufacturing industries in both periods. Since 1980 employment has increased only in a few manufacturing industries—furniture and fixtures, electric and electronic equipment, motor vehicles and other trans-

portation equipment, rubber and miscellaneous plastic products, and publishing and printing—and even in these industries, except for printing and publishing, employment declined until 1983. The motor vehicle industry had especially robust employment growth recently, 8 percent from 1982 to 1983 and 14 percent from 1983 to 1984. Productivity grew for most manufacturing industries in both periods and accelerated between 1980 and 1984. Only in petroleum and coal refining, which had to adjust to volatile pricing of inputs and changing demand, did productivity actually decline. . . .

Service industries in general experienced greater growth in employment and output than manufacturing industries, but lower productivity growth. Output in nearly half of the service industries grew more slowly during the 1980s than in the 1970s, but output actually decreased from 1980 to 1984 only in transportation, where rising output in air transportation was offset by large declines in intercity trucking and bus and railroad transportation.

Employment has risen in every service industry since 1973 except for the telephone and telegraph industry, where productivity grew more rapidly than output. The two industries were output grew most, credit agencies and financial brokers, and business services, also had the largest growth in employment. The brokerage industry combined employment growth with productivity growth, while business services experienced a productivity decline.[18] . . .

V. CONCLUSION

In 1938 Alvin Hansen told the American Economic Association that "The economic order of the western world is undergoing in this generation a structural change no less basic and profound in character than . . . the Industrial Revolution. We are passing . . . over a divide which separates the great era of growth and expansion of the nineteenth century from an era which no man . . . can as yet characterize with clarity or precision."[19] In 1961 Robert Theobald wrote, "Despite the continuing increase in manufacturing, the number of people employed in this field appears to have reached a peak, at least in the United States."[20] In 1983 Representative Stan Lundine wrote, "In the last three and a half years, the United States has lost over three million jobs in manufacturing alone. Old factories sit like tombstones in the graveyard of industrial America. . . . There are people who will never return to their old jobs, factories that will never reopen."[21] The current publicity is not the first alarmed report about the prospects for U.S. manufacturing.

During the 1970s, U.S. industrial output, employment, and productivity grew more slowly than in the 1960s, but it is not obvious that the 1970s were a blueprint for the future. Since the recovery in 1982, U.S. manufacturing output has risen faster than its historical trends, overall employment has reached new peaks, and manufacturing productivity has been increasing more quickly than in the 1960s.

The fears of a rising service economy, with barber shops and laundromats replacing steel mills and auto plants, are greatly exaggerated. Since the 1940s both manufacturing and goods have accounted for a constant share of output. Employment declined in most manufacturing industries but the cause was growth, not deindustrialization: produc-

tivity grew so quickly that falling employment accompanied increasing output. Eventually services may account for a larger share of output in the United States, but this alone would not be an omen of decay or loss of competitiveness. Instead, it may be a natural adjustment of our maturing economy to the accumulating affluence of its residents and the inevitable development of our trading partners.

While that data reviewed in this article do not show that all U.S. industries are flourishing, they also reveal no evidence of profound economic ills. The courses of output, employment, and productivity today are consistent with long-standing historical trends that have prevailed both in the United States and in other industrialized nations.

NOTES

1. One area, of course, in which U.S. manufacturing has been faring badly is international tread. While it is beyond the scope of this article to examine the possible causes behind the deterioration in the U.S. merchandise trade balance, the data discussed here reveal no support for the theory that the U.S. trade deficit is either causing or caused by a "deindustrialization" of America. For a detailed survey of the causes and composition of the U.S. trade deficit, analyzed by geographic source and major commodity category, see Norman S. Fieleke, "The Foreign Trade Deficit and American Industry," *New England Economic Review,* July/August 1985. Fieleke concludes that the causes of the trade deficit are not to be found in an analysis of industry-by-industry competitiveness and that rising import competition is not an accurate indicator of industrial health. He reached similar conclusions in a more recent article that focused on New England: "New England Manufacturing and International Trade," *New England Economic Review,* September/October 1986.

2. Goods-producing industries include agriculture, mining, construction, and manufacturing. Service-producing industries include transportation, public utilities; wholesale and retail trade; finance, insurance and real estate; and other services.

3. The equation $\%\triangle IP = -2.98 + 2.28\triangle\%$ GNP was estimated using annual data from 1960 to 1985. IP is the Federal Reserve Board's industrial production index for manufacturing. GNP is measured in constant 1982 dollars. Robert Z. Lawrence estimated the same equation for 1960 to 1973 and found that the percent change in industrial production was 2.24 times the percent change in GNP. See *Can America Compete?* The Brookings Institution, 1984, p. 21.

The periods—generally running from a business cycle peak to the subsequent peak—have been selected to reduce the influence of the business cycle on reported growth rates. The growth rates for manufacturing output are calculated using the Federal Reserve Board's industrial production index for manufacturing. For a description of this series see "A Revision of the Index of Industrial Production," *Federal Reserve Bulletin,* July 1985, pp. 487–501. The deflated manufacturing output series from Table 6.2 of the *Survey of Current Business,* produced by the Bureau of Economic Analysis, usually shows lower growth rates: 3.4 percent for 1960 to 1984; 4.8 percent for 1960 to 1973; and 1.0 percent for 1973 to 1980.

4. The estimate of U.S. share of world manufacturing output in the late 1940s is from William H. Branson, "Trends in United States International Trade and Investment since World War II," in Martin Feldstein, ed., *The American Economy in Transition,* 1980, p. 183.

The 1983 share estimate was calculated by adding together the manufacturing output in Canada, the United States, Japan, Australia, Austria, Belgium, Denmark, Finland, France, Germany, Greece, Italy, Netherlands, Norway, Sweden, Turkey and the United Kingdom using constant 1980 prices and 1980 exchange rates. The output figures were published in the OECD *National Accounts, Vol. II, 1971–1983.* The U.S. output share figure in 1983 would have been smaller if the newly industrializing countries' manufacturing output had been included.

5. See Colin Clark, *The Conditions of Economic Progress,* Macmillan & Co., 1951, and Victor R. Fuchs, *The Service Economy,* NBER #87 General Series, 1968.

6. Suppose goods decay at the rate d, that the population grows at the rate n, and that the stock of goods per capita grows at the rate g. Then the production of goods equals $(d + n + g)G$, where G is the stock of goods. Suppose that the demand for services per unit of accumulated goods is s, then the ratio of service production to GNP is $s/(d + n + g + s)$. This ratio will rise if s should rise or if d, n, or g should fall. The level of s could be increasing because a set amount of goods requires more servicing (people own their cars longer, for example, so more service is re-

quired) or because services themselves create a need for more services. See Lynn E. Browne, "Taking in Each Other's Laundry—The Service Economy," *New England Economic Review,* July/August 1986.

7. Valerie A. Personick, "A Second Look at Industry Output and Employment Trends through 1995," *Monthly Labor Review,* November 1985, p. 34.

8. Leslie Helm, "Will Japan Really Change?" *Business Week,* May 12, 1986, p. 58.

9. These figures are from the U.S. Bureau of Labor Statistics Current Employment Statistics Program (survey of business establishments). According to the Current Population Survey, also one by the BLS, manufacturing employment was 20,746,000 in 1970, 22,459,000 in 1979 and 20,879,00 in 1985. All U.S. employment figures are taken from the Establishment Survey because of its more detailed breakdown by industry. For international comparisons the U.S. data were taken from the Current Population Survey because these data are most comparable to those of other nations. Roughly speaking, the Establishment Survey uses data from payroll records and is a count of jobs and workers. The Current Population Survey is a household survey and is a count of persons including the self-employed, unpaid family workers and private household workers. For a more detailed description see *Handbook of Labor Statistics,* March 1984, p. 174. Although the two survey results differ quantitatively, they show the same trends in manufacturing and goods employment.

10. Valerie A. Personick, "A Second Look," p. 278.

11. Other published figures show that GDP per capita in other nations exceeds that of the United States. These alternative figures are calculated using market exchange rates rather than purchasing power parity exchange rates, which are the number of currency units required to buy goods and services equivalent to what can be bought with one unit of United States currency. The measures using purchasing power parity exchange rates are more accurate, because market exchange rates seldom reflect only the relative purchasing power of currencies. See R. D. Norton, "Industrial Policy and American Renewal," *The Journal of Economic Literature,* March 1986, p. 28.

12. The years 1960, 1973 and 1980 were peaks in the business cycle. In 1960, 1980 and 1985 manufacturing capacity utilization was about 80 percent but in 1973 capacity utilization was 87 percent. Although some differences in the selected years do exist, examining growth rates over these periods should tend to reveal underlying trends.

13. GDP per employed person is unpublished

data from the Bureau of Labor Statistics. The figures are based on purchasing power parity exchange rates in U.S. 1984 dollars and OECD price weights. Manufacturing productivity growth rates were calculated from the productivity indexes published by the BLS. Relative manufacturing productivity levels are a series constructed by the author. The measure of productivity in various countries is crude but can provide a rough comparison. Manufacturing output is for 1983, taken from the OECD *National Accounts Vol. II 1971–1983* deflated to 1980 dollars using purchasing power parity exchange rates from the Bureau of Labor Statistics. Hours are calculated using number of employees multiplied by average hours. Numbers of employees and average hours data are also from the Bureau of Labor Statistics.

Other authors have differing estimates of productivity levels, although most agree that the United States still maintains a lead. A. D. Roy in "Labor Productivity in 1980: An International Comparison," *National Institute Economic Review*, no. 101, August 1982, p. 29, quoted in Robert Z. Lawrence, *Can America Compete?* p. 33, estimated that in 1980 U.S. output per employed worker-year was 16 percent higher than Japan, 21.7 percent higher than Germany, and 31.3 percent higher than France.

Robert Z. Lawrence in *Can America Compete?* p. 33, reported that the Japanese Ministry of International Trade and Industry estimated the value-added labor productivity in Japanese manufacturing to be about 17 percent below that of the United States in 190.

William J. Baumol and Kenneth McLennan got different results by extrapolating the Japan Productivity Center's 1977 productivity level estimates. They estimated that in 1981 the level of manufacturing productivity in the U.S. and Japan was virtually identical. See their chapter "U.S. Productivity Performance and Its Implications, in Baumol and McLennan, eds., *Productivity and U.S. Competitiveness*, 1985, p. 15. Martin Bronfenbrenner in "Japanese Productivity Experience" in the same volume, p. 70, calculated that in the late 1970s American productivity remained well above the Japanese in most major industries.

14. See Ronald E. Kutscher and Jerome A. Mark, "The Service Producing Sector: Some Common Perceptions Reviewed," *Monthly Labor Review*, April 1983, pp. 21–24; also Edward F. Denison, "The Shift to Services and the Rate of Productivity Change," *Survey of Current Business*, October 1973, pp. 20–35.

For a complete review of sources on both sides of the issue see Edward N. Wolff, "The Magnitude and Causes of the Recent Productivity Slowdown in the United States: A survey of Recent Studies," in Baumol and McLennan, eds., *Productivity and U.S. Competitiveness*.

15. The average capital intensity (capital stock in billions of dollars divided by hours paid) of goods is .029 compared to .039 for services. From 1973 to 1980 productivity growth rates in goods industries ranged from -8.87 to 3.67. In services the range was -3.2 to 6.6. The average growth rate was .15 for goods and .28 for services.

From 1980 to 1984 the range for goods was -3.3 to 13.9 and -4.5 to 4.8 for services. The average growth rate for goods was 3.3 and services 0.6.

16. This analysis is similar to that used by Kutscher and Mark, "The Service Producing Sector," pp. 21–24.

Productivity was measured as the gross product originating in goods and services divided by hours worked with each sector weighted by its share of total hours. Productivity growth was separated into three components: (i) productivity growth within goods industries and within service industries; (ii) productivity growth due to the change in service share of total hours; (iii) an interactive effect. The interactive effect was divided evenly between (i) and (ii).

Hours worked (U.S. Bureau of Economic Analysis) was used rather than hours paid because it is a more accurate measure of productive time. Productivity growth measured as output per hour paid also showed little effect from the increased importance of services. See Krent Kunze, "New BLS Survey Measures Ratio of Hours Worked to Hours Paid," *Monthly Labor Review*, June 1984, p. 3 for an explanation of the differences between hours paid and hours worked.

17. The medical service industry example is from Denison, "The Shift to Services," pp. 20–35.

18. Although productivity growth has fallen for business services it is unlikely that this has depressed overall productivity growth. Presumably companies hire business services because management believes that those who provide business services are no less efficient than the company's own employees.

19. Alvin H. Hansen, "Economic Progress and Declining Population Growth," *American Economic Review*, March 1939, quoted in R. D. Norton, "Industrial Policy and American Renewal," p. 5.

20. Quoted in James Fallow, "America's Changing Landscape," *The Atlantic*, March 1985.

21. Stan N. Lundine, "Industrial Strategy Yes," *Challenge*, July/August 1983, p. 17.

NO

Nicholas S. Perna

THE SHIFT FROM MANUFACTURING TO SERVICES: A CONCERNED VIEW

I. SUMMARY AND CONCLUSIONS

The benign view of the changing U.S. industrial structure tells us "not to worry." Manufacturing has been doing just fine and has performed well during the current recovery. Its share of GNP has been stable for years, and the declining proportion of jobs in manufacturing is simply the continuation of a long-term trend that reflects superior productivity. The shift to services is just normal economic evolution, very similar to the earlier move out of agriculture that raised U.S. living standards. Furthermore, plenty of high-paying service jobs are available. The United States is not in danger of becoming a nation of fast-food franchises.

An alternative view says that things may not be so rosy and certainly are not so simple. During the current recovery, manufacturing has not climbed nearly as far above its previous peak as it did in earlier cycles. Moreover, it is important to recognize the special difficulties of measuring long-term economic trends. Each time the U.S. Department of Commerce changes the base year used in calculating real GNP it alters the manufacturing share of the U.S. economy. Recasting the historical data gives the impression of long-term stability. However, because of these measurement problems, we cannot be sure whether manufacturing's share of GNP has remained stable. The alternative view holds that in reality the manufacturing share of GNP has declined sharply during the postwar period. A large part of this decline can be found in the compression of profit margins in the wake of slowing economic growth and intensifying international competition. Interestingly, U.S. *consumption* of durable goods has risen as a share of GNP while the *production* share has fallen due to rising imports. This is not consistent with the view that the shift away from goods is a simple matter of maturity, affluence, or income elasticities.

Manufacturing's share of jobs has been decreasing at an accelerating rate since the late 1960s and early 1970s. This decline reflects *nonmanufacturing's*

From "The Shift from Manufacturing to Services: A Concerned View," by Nicholas S. Perna, Federal Reserve Bank of Boston, *New England Economic Review*, January/February 1987. Reprinted by permission.

inferior productivity combined with its faster output growth more than it reflects the superior efficiency of U.S. manufacturing, however. Labor productivity growth has stagnated in nonmanufacturing for more than a decade, requiring that extra output be obtained entirely through more labor input. This also helps explain the slowdown in overall productivity growth in the United States and the virtual disappearance of real wage gains. Multifactor productivity data, which take the contributions of both capital and labor into account, tell the same tale.

International comparisons of overall manufacturing levels can also be misleading, especially with respect to the industrialized nations. Data for Japan indicate that productivity in some major export industries is probably well ahead of that in the United States even if Japanese overall manufacturing efficiency is not. As for the newly industrializing countries, their productivity *growth* rates are so far above those in the United States that it will not be long before their productivity levels equal or surpass ours. Meanwhile, their shortcomings in productivity are offset by lower wages. Lack of overall productivity growth will make the adverse shift in the terms of trade that is currently underway all the more difficult for the United States to digest.

While there are many high-paying nonmanufacturing jobs and numerous low-paying manufacturing jobs, industry analysis shows that the U.S. employment mix has shifted towards the lower-paying jobs, particularly since the late 1960s. Also, the historic drift from farm to factory may not be the relevant analogy, since that movement was from low-productivity farming to higher-productivity industrial work. The current movement may well be in the opposite direction.

Finally, manufacturing plays a very important role in U.S. international trade. Much of our rather small potential for services exports is in areas where other countries may have (or soon acquire) significant advantages: that is, services that benefit from highly skilled labor and low capital costs.

The issue is not whether eventually we will all cook each other's hamburgers, do each other's washing, manage each other's financial portfolios, or nurse each other's illnesses. Rather, will productivity in hamburgers, laundries, financial and medical services rise fast enough to keep overall real incomes growing at an acceptable pace? Is productivity growing fast enough in manufacturing and in services to enable the United States to export more of both and to redress our growing balance of payments disequilibrium without sizable reductions in living standards? Again, recent record gives cause for continuing concern.

II. THE BENIGN VIEW OF U.S. MANUFACTURING

The position of those supporting the benign view of the changing U.S. industrial structure[1] generally takes the following form: 1) *Share of GNP:* The manufacturing share of real GNP has not declined, nor has the goods share. Factory output in the current recovery has been strong relative to past cycles. 2) *Share of Jobs:* The manufacturing share of jobs has been falling, but this trend is decades old. It reflects manufacturing's superior productivity as well as the mature stage of economic development in an affluent society. This development is quite similar to the earlier decline in agriculture's share of the U.S. economy, which was accompanied by sharply higher U.S. living standards. 3) *Further Issues and Implications:* The effects of these changes in interindustry mix are probably positive or at least neutral. The shift to services has not retarded the overall rate of productivity gain, nor has it reduced average wage levels. Just as there are ample domestic opportunities for the growth of services, there must be plenty of opportunities for exporting them.

III. U.S. MANUFACTURING: A COUNTERVIEW

Manufacturing has grown less than in previous expansions but about in line with real GNP when quarterly data are used to capture cyclical movements.[2] However, it is important to keep in mind that manufacturing previously underwent a long and steep slide that dated back to 1979 and by mid-1986 the amount by which manufacturing exceeded its past peak was still much less than in previous cycles. GNP did a somewhat better job relative to past cycles.

Measuring Manufacturing's Relative Share of the U.S. Economy
Defining manufacturing's real share of the U.S. economy poses some major measurement problems. For one thing, value added by manufacturing is calculated by subtracting deflated purchases of materials and services from deflated sales, yielding a residual with a potentially wide error margin.

The second difficulty is a more fundamental index number problem: the size of manufacturing's share is very sensitive to the particular base year used in calculating real GNP.[3] The more recent the base year, the smaller the manufac-

turing share of real GNP. For 1969, moving the base from 1958 to 1982 reduced the manufacturing share from 31 percent to 22 percent. The same thing happens to the goods share of GNP when the base years are shifted. Very much the same issues arise in connection with the Consumer Price Index. When the market basket becomes obsolete, the Bureau of Labor Statistics updates it. However, in contrast to the GNP, the historic data are not recast to reflect the new weights. That is because the 1980s proportion of consumer spending is no more relevant for the 1950s than the 1950s basket is for the 1980s. The problem exists whether one looks at GNP from an industry vantage point (for example, manufacturing) or from a product point of view (for example, goods). The further one gets from the base period, the less representative it is of the economy's actual structure.

Current-dollar value added may well be a better measure of manufacturing's share of GNP, or at least an important additional gauge. It avoids both measurement problems described above, while indicating changes in the major components of value added. The compensation share has declined by one-fourth between 1968 and 1985. The profits share plunged by two-thirds during the same period while profits plus depreciation have dropped by more than one-third. One explanation may be the combination of slow growth and intense international competition.

There is a third measurement problem. Some observers claim that a sizable amount of manufacturing employment and output has really been transferred to the service sector as, for example, business consultants take over for corporate staffs and factories hire workers from service sector firms specializing in temporary help.[4] There does not appear to be more than anecdotal support for this claim. McKenzie and Smith cite the decline in value added as a percentage of manufacturing shipments, as evidence of such contracting out. They recognize, however, that this could also reflect the shift towards increased use of imported components. Recent analysis of occupational patterns within various industries does not provide evidence of large volume of contracting out.[5] Rather, one must look elsewhere for explanations of the rapid growth of business services employment.

Production versus Consumption

U.S. consumption of manufactured goods has risen much faster than U.S. production. Consumption of durables of all types (consumer goods, capital goods, defense hardware) has been rising rapidly as a percentage of GNP since World War II and particularly after 1978. This does not support the view that a declining "goods" share of GNP is a virtually inevitable by-product of rising affluence and the higher income elasticities for services than for goods. The production share has fallen since 1978, as a growing fraction of domestic consumption is being met through imports.

Manufacturing's Declining Share of Jobs

Manufacturing's declining share of jobs is not simply the continuation of a long-term trend. The "rate of decay" has accelerated: -0.9 percent annual average decline between 1948 and 1968; -2.1 percent between 1968 and 1978; and -2.5 percent between 1978 and 1985. Thus the annual rate of decline between 1978 and 1985 was nearly triple that of the 1948–68 period.

Relationship to productivity.

Arithmetically, most of manufacturing's falling job share reflects the faster growth in labor productivity in the manufacturing sector than in nonmanufacturing. However, this does not indicate a superior record in manufacturing so much as it reflects the lower productivity in nonmanufacturing. Productivity gains in nonmanufacturing were almost on a par with those in manufacturing between 1948 and 1968, but they have since turned negative. Manhours growth has accelerated in nonmanufacturing despite the slowing growth in real output, because productivity has become so poor. Although services productivity poses measurement problems, it is not clear that the net result is an understatement of gains. For example, one reason for the rapid rise of gasoline station productivity is the spread of self-service pumps. Here, customer labor has been substituted for employee labor, or equivalently, quality has deteriorated.

The most important comparisons for U.S. manufacturing are not with U.S. nonmanufacturing, but with foreign competitors. U.S. manufacturing productivity growth is below that of our most important global competitors, particularly the newly industrializing countries. While the level of productivity is important for competitive comparisons, it is not the level of overall manufacturing productivity that is relevant. This is affected by the mix of industry output as well as by goods that are not traded internationally. Much more critical is the productivity level of those industries that sell in global markets. Here the available data go back to 1982, but are illuminating, nonetheless. Japanese manufacturing productivity was below the overall

U.S. average but with considerable dispersion around the average. The Japanese were considerably below the United States in domestically oriented industries such as food processing and publishing but above it in important export industries such as motor vehicles and electrical machinery.

Productivity is growing so much faster in the developing countries than in the United States that it will not take long to erase any existing U.S. advantage. In the meantime, the productivity level disadvantages of the developing countries are more than offset by significantly lower levels of labor compensation.

Comparison with agriculture.
The current shift in the U.S. industrial structure and employment mix is very different from the decline in the farm share of U.S. jobs from about 50 percent in the 1880s to 3 percent in 1980s. That shift raised living standards as workers moved from lower productivity farming jobs to higher productivity manufacturing jobs, pulling up the average. The current movement appears to be in the opposite direction, from high productivity manufacturing to lower productivity non-manufacturing, thereby lowering the average.[6]

IV. FURTHER ISSUES AN IMPLICATIONS

Impact of Nonmanufacturing on Productivity Growth
Some statistical studies conclude that the current shift towards services is not reducing the productivity growth of the economy.[7] The index number problem discussed above may affect these calculations. Since the decline in the manufacturing share is understated, the effect of the changing mix on productivity may also be understated.

. . . [T]he slowdown of productivity growth in nonmanufacturing must have lowered the overall average, as manufacturing productivity continued to grow at about the same rate as before. The picture for nonmanufacturing productivity has gotten progressively worse, from a slowdown between 1968 and 1978 to an outright decline from 1978 to 1985.

The U.S. Bureau of Labor Statistics series on multifactor productivity, which attempts to capture the contributions of both capital and labor, tells the same tale: that multifactor productivity in the overall private nonfarm sector and in manufacturing rose at about the same rate from the late 1940s to the early 1970s. Since then, private nonfarm productivity has been essentially flat; this, again, reflects declining productivity in nonmanufacturing.

The consequences of this overall slowdown are also straightforward: real wage gains have shrunk in the wake of dwindling labor productivity improvements.[8] The decline in the rate of real wage growth provides independent corroboration that the United States has, in fact, been experiencing a productivity slowdown and not simply a productivity measurement problem.

Effect of Changing Industry Mix on Average Incomes
Average annual employee compensation ranges widely within manufacturing and across other industries (Table 1). But overall, manufacturing pay is one-fourth higher than nonmanufacturing pay and almost double the pay in retail trade.

Table 1

**Average Annual
Employee Compensation in 1985[a]**

All Industries	$25,294
Manufacturing	29,992
High: Petroleum and Coal Products	56,665
Low: Apparel and Other Textile Products	15,559
Nonmanufacturing	24,108
Transportation and Public Utilities	34,725
Railroads	46,052
Air Transportation	39,663
Electric, Gas and Sanitary Services	39,542
Communication	40,270
Telephone and Telegraph	42,125
Radio and TV Broadcasting	31,784
Wholesale Trade	28,874
Retail Trade	15,516
Finance, Insurance, Real Estate	27,658
Banks	25,559
Security and Commodity Brokers	55,711
Services	21,401
Auto Repair	18,377
Health Services	24,296
Legal Services	34,488
Educational Services	17,496
Private Households	11,924
Government	28,075

[a]Per full-time equivalent employee
Source: U.S. Bureau of Economic Analysis.

Some of the highest nonmanufacturing pay is to be found among the more "industrial" services: railroads, electric and other utilities. In many ways, these are a lot more like manufacturing than services. For example, producing electricity and running a refinery are both highly capital-intensive, continuous-flow operations. Yet electricity is counted as a service, while oil refining is included in nondurable manufacturing. The compensation data shown in Table 1 have advantages over some of the more familiar series. They include forms of pay that have become increasingly important but are not included in the average hourly or weekly earnings series: fringe benefits as well as lump-sum and profit-sharing payments.

Has the changing industrial composition of the U.S. economy raised or lowered average incomes? Neil Rosenthal of the U.S. Bureau of Labor Statistics has found that the occupational mix of the work force has been moving towards higher-paid jobs.[9] However, this movement has been even more pronounced within manufacturing than in nonmanufacturing. Rosenthal's article really does not attempt to assess the impact of changes in the industrial mix of the U.S. economy. Marvin Kosters found that the changing mix of U.S. industry accounts for some of the real wage slowdown, but that the preponderance is due to the productivity problem.[10]

My analysis, using data from the U.S. Bureau of Economic Analysis on compensation and the number of full-time equivalent workers, shows that industry mix has had a negative effect on average compensation since the late 1960s.[11] The shift in the industrial composition of jobs has reduced average compensation by about 1 percent relative to 1978 and 3 percent compared with 1968. The methodology is straightforward: 1985 compensation per worker for each of the roughly 70 industry classifications was weighted by the job mix of earlier years, to show what 1985 average compensation would have been if the earlier industry mix had prevailed. The job share of other high-pay sectors (mining, transportation and public utilities) has also declined, but manufacturing has had the largest negative impact on average pay. Furthermore, some of the decline in those other sectors is linked to manufacturing; for example, there is less need for U.S. electricity when imports of manufactured goods replace domestic production.

In an important sense this approach may understate the impact of the shift in the industrial composition of jobs, since it examines only the movement from high-wage to low-wage employment to no-wage unemployment. On the other hand, this analysis does not take into account the extent to which faster growth of compensation outside of manufacturing may have offset the effects of the declining weight of manufacturing on average pay levels. In any event, more research is needed in this area.

Services and the Balance of Payments

There is a reason to worry about how and when U.S. international payments will be brought into equilibrium.[12] How will the United States service its huge foreign debt? Manufacturing now accounts for roughly two-thirds of merchandise exports.

The potential for stepping up exports of services is surprisingly limited relative to the magnitude of current trade deficits. Over 60 percent of services exports is investment income; that is, interest, dividends, and corporate retained earnings. While this percentage is likely to grow in the future, so will the comparable outflows, reflecting earnings on increased foreign investment in the United States. Travel and transportation, which amount to about 20 percent of services exports, are running a sizable deficit. There is likely to be only modest improvement in this deficit over the next few years, mainly because the real dollar exchange rate has declined very little when weighted to reflect travel rather than trade patterns.[13] Exports of telecommunications, business consulting, and the like are relatively small. Even very rapid growth won't make much overall difference for the trade deficit five years

from now. Moreover, there is every reason to expect increased imports of services, particularly those that are labor-intensive and those provided by countries with lower capital costs than the United States.

NOTES

1. See Molly McUsic, "U.S. Manufacturing: Any Cause for Alarm? *New England Economic Review* January/February 1987), and, for example, Michael F. Bryan, "Is Manufacturing Disappearing?" Federal Reserve Bank of Cleveland, *Economic Commentary*, July 15, 1985); J. Baxter, "Please, No More Myths About the Decline of U.S. Manufacturing," *Iron Age* (Oct. 18, 1985); and Ronald E. Kutscher and Valerie A. Personick, "Deindustrialization and the Shift to Services," *Monthly Labor Review* (June 1986) pp. 3–13.
2. This statement is at odds with John A. Tatom's findings in "Domestic vs. International Explanations of Recent U.S.Manufacturing Developments," Federal Reserve Bank of St. Louis *Review* (April 1986), pp. 5–18. His equation relating real manufacturing output growth to real GNP growth underpredicted actual growth by 2 percentage points from 1980:4 to 1985:4.
3. A succinct but nontheoretical discussion of how shifting the base period affects the growth rates of real GNP and the GNP deflator as well as the relative shares is given in "A Note on the Effect of Shifting the Base Period," in "Revised Estimates of the National Income and Product Accounts of the United States, 1929–85: An Introduction," *Survey of Current Business* (December 1985), p. 14. In general, when an item's relative price falls (when its price rises less than other prices), then its relative share of the total GNP will fall as the base year is moved forward in time. The issues are covered quite thoroughly by Robin Marris in his *Economic Arithmetic* (London: Macmillan & Co., 1958), Chapter 9, in the context of measuring real income.
4. Molly McUsic, "U.S. Manufacturing," and, for example, Richard B. McKenzie and Stephen D. Smith, *The Good News About U.S. Production*, Publication No. 72 (St. Louis, MO: Washington University Center for the Study of American Business, 1986).
5. Bobbie H. McCrackin, "Why Are Business and Professional Services Growing So Rapidly?" Federal Reserve Bank of Atlanta *Economic Review* (August 1985), pp. 14–28.
6. In making these interindustry productivity

comparisons, it is important to exclude the effects of the imputation for owner-occupied housing in the GNP. In 1985 this amounted to $106 billion and was allocated to the GNP originating in the real estate sector. Since there is no employment associated with this imputation, the net result is to overstate productivity in real estate and, thus, productivity in services.

7. See Ronald E. Kutscher and Jerome A. Mark, "The Service-Producing Sector: Some Common Perceptions Reviewed," *Monthly Labor Review* (April 1983), pp. 21–24.

8. The relationship between productivity and real wages is defined by Allen M. Cartter in *Theory of Wages and Employment*, (New York: Irwin, 1958).

9. Neil H. Rosenthal, "The Shrinking Middle Class: Myth or Reality?" *Monthly Labor Review* (March 1985), pp. 3–10.

10. Marvin H. Kosters, "Free Markets Bring Change and Growth," prepared for the 40th Anniversary Symposium of the Joint Economic Committee of Congress and reprinted in *Challenge* (March/April 1986), pp. 55–64.

11. *Survey of Current Business*, July 1986, Tables 6.4B to 6.7B.

12. See Paul R. Krugman and George N. Hatsopoulos, "The Problem of U.S. Competitiveness in Manufacturing," *New England Economic Review* (January/February 1987).

13. Bruce Kasman, "Prospects for the U.S. International Travel Deficit," Federal Reserve Bank of New York *Quarterly Review* Summer 1986), pp. 44–46.

POSTSCRIPT

Is Manufacturing Alive and Well and Living in the U.S.?

McUsic assesses the status of U.S.manufacturing by examining patterns of change in output, employment, and productivity. With respect to output she finds that since 1947 manufacturing's share of Gross National Product has been quite constant, between 20 and 22 percent. She also finds that during the 1980s U.S. industrial output has grown more rapidly than that of other industrialized countries with the exception of Japan. She goes on to note that although the U.S. share of world output has declined, this decline was to be expected and the U.S. standard of living has increased in spite of this decline. Employment data reveal a decline in manufacturing jobs, both in terms of absolute numbers and in terms of the percentage of total jobs. But this result should not be alarming. It is a pattern found in other industrialized countries and it indicates that manufacturing productivity has been increasing. Turning specifically to productivity, McUsic is optimistic. She finds that productivity growth as been higher since the 1982–83 recession than it has been in recent recoveries. She also finds that U.S. productivity patterns for the 1970s were due to special circumstances that have subsequently disappeared. She concludes: "While the data reviewed in this article do not show that all U.S. industries are flourishing, they also reveal no evidence of profound economic ills."

Perna's examination of the data regarding U.S. manufacturing suggests that "things may not be so rosy." He lists several reasons to be worried about U.S. manufacturing. First, the U.S. has satisfied an increasing demand for durable goods by expanding imports rather than expanding domestic production. Second, the number of jobs in manufacturing, expressed as a percent of the total number of jobs, has been falling much more rapidly in the 1978–85 period than in the 1948–68 period. Third, the belief that the shift from manufacturing to service jobs is like the shift from agricultural to manufacturing jobs is fundamentally incorrect. The agriculture to manufacturing shift was from lower productivity jobs to higher productivity jobs

while the manufacturing to service shift is from higher productivity jobs to lower productivity and lower paying jobs. Fourth, when productivity patterns are compared across countries, other countries have been outperforming the U.S. in the production of those commodities in which there is international competition. Fifth, the lack of performance in the manufacturing sector combined with the prospect of increasing international competition in service exports suggests that the U.S. will be unable to achieve a balance in its international payments.

For readings that are consistent with the position taken by McUsic, see "Is Manufacturing Disappearing?" by Michael F. Bryan (*Economic Commentary*, Federal Reserve Bank of Cleveland, July 15, 1985); "Please, Please No More Myths About the Decline of U.S. Manufacturing," by J. Baxter (*Iron Age*, October 18, 1985); "Deindustrialization and the Shift to Services," by Ronald E. Kutscher and Valerie A. Personick (*Monthly Labor Review*, June 1986); "Why Has Manufacturing Employment Declined?" by John A. Tatom (*Review*, Federal Reserve Bank of St. Louis, December 1986); "Is Manufacturing Dead?" by David L. Birch (*Inc.*, June 1987); and "The Growing Share of Services in the U.S. Economy—Degeneration or Evolution?" by Mack Ott (*Review*, Federal Reserve Bank of St. Louis, June/July 1987). For readings that are more consistent with the position taken by Perna, see "The Problem of U.S. Competitiveness in Manufacturing," by Paul R. Krugman and George N. Hatsopoulos (*New England Economic Review*, January/February 1987); "The Service Sector's Productivity Problem," by Alan Murray (*Wall Street Journal*, February 2, 1987); and *Why Manufacturing Matters: The Myth of the Post-Industrial Economy* by Stephen S. Cohen and John Zysman (Basic Books, 1987). Other interesting readings include "Taking in Each Other's Laundry—The Service Economy," by Lynn E. Brown (*New England Economic Review*, July/August 1986) and *Can America Compete?* by Robert Z. Lawrence (Brookings Institution, 1984).

CONTRIBUTORS
TO THIS VOLUME

EDITORS

THOMAS R. SWARTZ was born in Philadelphia in 1937. He received his B.A. from LaSalle College in 1960, his M.A. degree from Ohio University in 1962, and his Ph.D. from Indiana University in 1965. He is currently a professor of economics/college fellow at the University of Notre Dame and the director of the Notre Dame Center for Economic Education. He writes in the areas of urban studies and economic education. He and Frank J. Bonello are often co-authors. They co-edited *Alternative Decisions in Economic Policy* (Notre Dame Press, 1978) and *The Supply Side: Debating Current Economic Policies* (Dushkin Publishing Group, 1983).

FRANK J. BONELLO was born in Detroit in 1939. He received his B.S. from the University of Detroit in 1961, his M.A. degree from the University of Detroit in 1963, and his Ph.D. from Michigan State University in 1968. He is currently associate professor of economics at the University of Notre Dame. He writes in the areas of monetary economics and economic education. This represents the seventh book that he has either authored or edited.

AUTHORS

HENRY J. AARON is a senior fellow in the Economic Studies Program at Brookings and a professor of economics at the University of Maryland.

ROBERT ALMEDER is a professor of philosophy at Georgia State University. He is a highly regarded philosopher who has published widely.

DAVID T. BEATY had been senior lecturer at the Graduate School of Business of the University of Cape Town and is currently assistant professor of management at Loyola Marymount University in Los Angeles.

BARRY BLUESTONE teaches at Boston College and focuses his work on public policy and regional labor markets. He also serves as the director of the Social Welfare Research Institute.

JOSEPH R. BOVE is professor of laboratory medicine at Yale University Medical School, where he has taught since 1959. He is the director of Blood Transfusion Services at the Yale-New Haven Hospital.

STEPHAN CHAPMAN served as the associate editor of the *New Republic* and is currently a columnist with the *Chicago Tribune*.

RICHARD D. COE is associate professor of economics at the New College of the University of South Florida.

BYRON DORGAN is a representative from North Dakota.

GREG J. DUNCAN is senior study director in the Survey Research Center of the University of Michigan.

ROSS D. ECKERT is professor of economics at Claremont McKenna College and Claremont Graduate School.

ROBERT EISNER has been the William R. Kenan Professor of Economics at Northwestern University since 1974. He is president-elect for 1987 of the American Economic Association.

MILTON FRIEDMAN is currently senior research fellow at the Hoover Institute at Stanford University, where he has been since 1977. He was awarded the Nobel Prize for Economics in 1977. He is widely read professionally and by a lay audience, and he is probably the best known spokesperson for conservative economics.

JOHN KENNETH GALBRAITH is an internationally renowned economist who has written widely. He is a professor of economics at Harvard University.

ROBERT S. GAY is vice president for economic development, Economics Department, at Morgan Stanley & Co., Inc.

TERESA GHILARDUCCI is assistant professor of economics at the University of Notre Dame.

JAMES K. GLASSMAN is a contributing editor at *The New Republic*.

HENNING GUTMANN has been a reporter on international economics for AP-Dow Jones Service and is now on the staff of the *New York Review of Books*.

CLIFFORD HACKETT served in the Foreign Service and on the staffs of congressional committees involved in foreign affairs.

OREN HARARI is associate professor of management at the McLaren College of Business of the University of San Francisco, where he specializes in management and organizational behavior.

BENNETT HARRISON is a professor of economics and urban studies at M.I.T. He has also taught at the University of Maryland and the University of Pennsylvania.

GARY HECTOR writes on financial affairs for *Fortune* magazine.

WALTER W. HELLER, before his death in 1987, was Regents' Professor of Economics at the University of Minnesota and was chairman of the Council of Economic Advisors under Presidents Kennedy and Johnson.

GERALD L. HOUSEMAN is professor of political science at Indiana University at Fort Wayne.

MICHAEL KINSLEY is an author, editor and social critic.

BOB KUTTNER is a columnist for the *New Republic* who writes on social and political subjects.

MARC LEVINSON is a senior editor of *Dun's Business Month*.

FRANK LEVY is on the faculty of the University of Maryland's School of Public Affairs. In 1987 he was a Guggenheim fellow on leave at Brookings as a visiting fellow in economic studies.

RICHARD B. McKENZIE is a professor of economics at Clemson University. He is a journalist and author who is known for his many contributions to the area of public choice.

MOLLY McUSIC is a former senior research assistant at the Federal Reserve Bank of Boston.

CHARLES MURRAY is a senior research fellow at the Manhattan Institute.

RUTH NEEDLEMAN is an assistant professor and coordinator of labor studies at Indiana University, Northwest.

JOHN D. PAULUS is managing director of the Economics Department at Morgan Stanley & Co., Inc.

NICHOLAS S. PERNA is manager of economic analysis at General Electric Company.

PAUL CRAIG ROBERTS, who was assistant treasury secretary for economic policy during 1981–82, holds the Simon Chair in Political Economy at the Center for Strategic and International Studies.

HELEN SUZMAN has been a member of the South African Parliament since 1953. For thirteen years, 1961–74, she was the sole member of the opposition Progressive Federal Party in Parliament.

WILLIAM SIMON is a former treasury secretary who has written widely on economic issues and public policies.

ALFRED E. WATKINS is a Washington, DC-based economist whose work has appeared in *The Nation, The New Republic*, and *Dissent*.

MURRAY L. WEIDENBAUM writes widely in the area of government regulation. He is the director of the Center for the Study of American Business at Washington University and was the assistant secretary for economic policy of the U.S. Treasury.

PAUL WONNACOTT is professor of economics at the University of Maryland.

STAFF

Marguerite L. Egan   Program Manager
Brenda S. Filley   Production Manager
Whit Vye   Designer
Libra Ann Cusack   Typesetting Coordinator
Lynn Shannon   Graphics Coordinator
Diane Barker   Editorial Assistant
Richard Tietjen   Editorial Systems Analyst

INDEX

Aaron, Henry J., in defense of Tax Reform Act of 1986, 196–205, 212, 213
activist government: and comparative advantage, 257, 263, 265, 267; effect of, on macroeconomic performance, 180–194
Acquired Immune Deficiency Syndrome, *see* AIDS
adjusted high-employment budget: and impact of deficit on economy-fiscal policy, 224, 227–229; and inflation, 229, 230
age distribution, and size of middle class, 312, 317, 323
aggregate demand, 187, 229, 236, 237
Agricultural Adjustment Act of 1933, 21, 27
agriculture: against government regulation of, 20, 21, 32–38; in defense of government price supports for, 20–31
agrifactory, vs. family farm, 20–39
AIDS, threat of, to blood banking industry, 40–59
AIDS-Related Complex, *see* ARC
Aid to Families with Dependent Children, and issue of welfare dependency, 216–218, 221, 223
Alfonsin, Raul, and payment of debt by Argentina, 272, 275, 282
Almeder, Robert, on social responsibility of business, 2, 3, 10–19
American Agricultural Movement, 36
American Association of Blood Banks (AABB), 41, 42
American Blood Commission (ABC), 44
American dream, 310
American Red Cross, 41, 43
Amish community, economic system of, 3
antibody to AIDS virus, blood test for, 42, 43, 47, 48, 55
antidumping, 259
antitrust legislation, 78, 79
apartheid, 290–307
Apple Computer, 248
ARC, incidence of, in U.S., 40
Argentina, payment of debt by, 268, 270–273, 276, 278, 282, 283, 285, 286, 289
Arvin Case, 79
asset liquidation, 84
AT&T: 238, 249; example of sex discrimination by, 70–71
Auchter, Thorne, 104, 107

baby boom generation, and question of shrinking middle class, 312, 315, 317
balanced budget: 224–241; effect of Tax Reform Act on, 202

bankers, and debt crisis of Third World countries, 268, 270, 276, 277
bank failure, 180
banking system: effect of default by Third World countries on world, 268, 270, 276, 277; and Federal Reserve, 180
bankruptcies, farm, 20, 22
Bartlett, Steve, 150, 151
Bass Brothers, 79, 83
Bates Manufacturing Company (Maine), as example of closing of profitable plant, 114, 115
Beaty, David T., on effect of disinvestment and sanctions on black South African workers, 290–300; 306, 307
Bergsten, C. Fred, 260
birth rate, and size of middle class, 323, 234
Black Monday, 242
blacks: effect of disinvestment on, in South Africa, 290–307; and equity pay statistics, 310, 311; and welfare, 217, 220, 221
Black Thursday, 242
blood: cash, 41, 44, 48, 49, 51; delivery system for, 41; designated, 50, 54–59; FDA requirement labeling cash vs. noncash, 44, 51; and origin of blood bank monopolies, 43–45; quality of, from national blood system, 40–59; storage, 41, 57; *see also,* blood banking industry; blood bank system; blood clubs; blood test
blood banking industry: need for competition in, 40–53; deregulation of, 40–59; use of donor screening and antibody testing by, 42, 43, 47, 48, 55; and labeling required for cash and noncash blood, 44, 51; and liability exemptions, 46; lack of safety incentives of, 45–46
blood bank system, history of, 40–41, 43
"blood clubs," 42
blood test: for AIDS virus antibody (HTLV-III), 42, 43, 47, 48, 55; for hepatitis, 49, 50, 51
Bluestone, Barry, on community impact of closing of profitable plants, 110–121
Boesky, Ivan, 79, 80
Bolivia, as international debtor, 285
Bove, Joseph R., on hazards of deregulating blood banking industry, 40, 41, 54–59
bracket creep, 227
Bradbury, Katherine L., and debate over the shrinking of middle class, 310–326
Bradley, Bill, 206
Brazil: payment of debt by, 268, 270, 271; restructuring of debt for, 274, 276, 278
Brookings Institute, 284
brown lung, *see* byssinosis

budget deficit: 186, 187, 224, 225; causes of, 225; and full employment, 184; and high-employment budget, 227–229; and inflation, 229–232; inflation adjusted-, 235–241

Bureau of Census, 314

Bureau of Economic Analysis, 230

business: qualities of successful, 29; social responsibility of, 2–19; requirement of, to provide unpaid parental leave, 132–145; *see also,* business cycles; business mobility

business cycles, and American capitalism, 180

business mobility, pros and cons of restricting, 110–130

buy-outs: and antitrust, 81; consequences of, 82–83; leveraged, 83–84

Byron Dorgan, on importance of federal policy favoring family-size farms, 20–31

byssinosis, as occupational illness, 104

capital gains, and Tax Reform Act of 1986, 199, 200

capitalism: 180; impact of corporate social responsibility on, 2–19

Carter administration: grain embargo under, 25; and relationship of inflation to budget deficit, 232; and protectionism for steel industry, 259, 260

cash blood: labeling of noncash vs., as required, 44, 51; quality of, 41, 48, 59; vs. volunteer donor blood, 44

cash-cow, profitable subsidiary as, 115

cash plasma and blood products market, 45

Catalyst Survey, on parental leave policies of U.S. companies, 138–140

central bank: and money supply, 190; and stock market crash of 1987, 245, 250; and Third World debt repayment, 275, 278

Certificates of Deposit, 286

Chapman, Stephen, against government regulation to preserve family-size farms, 20, 21, 32–38

charitable deductions, and Tax Reform Act of 1986, 209

Chase Manhattan Bank, disinvestment in South Africa by, 301, 302

Chemical Bank, Third World loans by, 278

children: shifting income to, and new tax law, 210; and welfare, 214–222

Christensen v. Iowa, 68

cigarette advertising, and social responsibility of business, 10, 14

Citibank, disinvestment in South Africa by, 301, 302

Citicorp, and Third World countries, 278

Civil Rights Act of 1964, Title VII, 63, 74, 133

Clayton Antitrust Act of 1914, 79

Coe, Richard D., and debate over low income families and welfare dependency, 214–216, 220–221

coercive vulnerability, 278

Cohen, Steven, 259

collectivism: 169; social responsibility of business as, 2–9, 17

commercial credits, and Federal Reserve System, 180

commodity loan, 27

Common Market: and protectionism, 258, 261; vs. U.S. food export prices, 25

community, impact of plant closings on, 111

comparable worth: as valuable, 62, 63, 70–76; as worthless, 60–69

comparative advantage: and idle capacity, 257, 258, 263; and protectionism, 254, 256, 263–265, 267

competition: need for, in blood banking industry, 40–53; comparable worth as destructive of, 66; need for corporate restructuring to strengthen U.S., 87–93; and idle capacity, 263; effect of minimum wage increase on international, 153; and debate over protectionism, 254–267

conglomerate mergers: 79; *see also,* mergers

Congress: criticism of, for farm assistance to larger farms, 24; views of, on parental leave legislation, 132–145; and debate over Tax Reform Act of 1986, 196–213

Congressional Budget Office, 191

conservatives, view of role of government by, 167

Constitution, 310

consumer debt, and Tax Reform Act, 196

Consumer Price Index, 324

corporate executive, responsibility of, 2–19

corporate farms, vs. family farms, 20–39

corporate income tax, and Tax Reform Act of 1986, 199, 201, 208

corporate raiders: 79; greenmail payment to, 82–83

corporate responsibility, 2–19

corporate restructuring, role of mergers in, 87–93

corporations, closing of profitable plants by, 110–130

cost-benefit analysis: pros and cons of, for government regulations, 96–108

cotton dust standards, 104–108

Cotton-Oil Trust, 78

Council of Community Blood Centers (CCBC), 41

Council of Economic Advisors, 184

credentialism, 66

criminal prosecution, of corporate management, 16–17

crowding in, 231

crowding out, and budget deficits, 225

cruzeiro, 271, 279

interest rates, impact of high, on farming community, 21, 24, 25
international capital flow, 190
International Harvester, 23
internationalization, and United States economy, 180, 189–194
International Monetary Fund (IMF): 192; and Third World debt, 269, 271–276, 280, 282, 285, 289
International Telephone and Telegraph Corporation, alleged unethical behavior of, 10
international specialization, 264, 267
international trade, and United States use of protectionism, 254–267
investment(s), and Tax Reform Act of 1986, 200, 201, 202
investment tax credit, and Tax Reform Act, 197, 200, 208
invisible hand (Smith), 11, 26
itemized deductions, and new tax law, 209

Japan: 333, 341; and comparative advantage, 257; and protectionism, 257–259
Japan Development Bank, 258
Jefferson, Thomas, on American agriculture, 32
job classifications, 65, 70, 74
job security, and black workers in South Africa, 297, 298
Joint Committee on Taxation, 207
Joint Congressional Budget Resolution, 233
Joint Economic Committee: and free trade, 259; and role of government in economy, 182–192
junk bonds, 83–85

Kennedy, Edward M., 149
Kennedy, John F., and economic policy in Sixties, 183, 184
Kennedy-Hawkins bill: 48; as beneficial to working women, 148, 149, 155–161; as detrimental, 148–154
Keynes, John Maynard: and activist government to solve macroeconomic problems, 181; and free trade, 257, 262
Keynesian economics, 174, 175, 181–189
killing innocent people for profit, justification of, 13–16
Kinsley, Michael, and criticism of protectionism by United States, 254, 255, 263–266
K mart, 116
Kosters, Marvin, 345
Kuttner, Bob, and defense of protectionism by United States, 254–267

labor relations, and worker satisfaction in South Africa, 293–295
Laffer, Arthur, 177
land, decrease in price of farm- , 21

landed gentry, 211
Langer, William "Wild Bill," 22
Latin America, and debt of, 268–289
Latin American Economic System (SELA), 283
legislation: antitrust, 78, 79; criticism of, restricting hostile takeovers, 79; of workers' rights to parental leave, 132–145
leveraged buy-outs, 83–84
Levinson, Marc, on internationalization of United States economy, 180, 181, 189–194
Levy, Frank, on shrinking middle class, 310, 311, 322–327
Levy, Mickey D., 191
liability exemptions, of blood banking industry, 46, 50–51
liberals, view of role of government by, 167
loans: agricultural, 35; average amount of farmers', 24
"Losing Ground," and welfare dependency, 216, 217, 220, 223
low income families, and Tax Reform Act of 1986, 196, 206
low income youth, and welfare, 214–219
Lundine, Stan, 337

managed trade, as alternative to protectionism, 261, 262, 265, 266
manufacturing, debate over health of, in United States, 328–349
market oriented economy, 233
marriage, 218, 324, 325
McKenzie, Richard B., on hazards of restricting business mobility, 110, 111, 122–130
McUsic, Molly, on manufacturing in United States as not declining, 328, 329–339, 349, 350
medical leave, existing policies of businesses regarding, 137–140
men: comparable worth for, 65, 75; and legislation for guaranteed parental leave, 132–145
mergers: as beneficial to productivity, 87–93; waves of, in American economic history, 78–79
Mexico, and debt repayment problem, 268, 270–273, 276–279, 285
middle class: problem of defining, 311–314, 324; and mobility, 218; debate over shrinking, 310–327; and Tax Reform Act of 1986, 209, 210; decline of traditional family in, 317–318
minimum wage: as beneficial to working women, 148, 149; as detrimental, 148–154; history of origin of, 148–149
Minimum Wage Coalition to Save Jobs, 151
Minimum Wage Restoration Act of 1987, see Kennedy-Hawkins bill

WHITMAN COLLEGE LIBRARY